# Commitment and Cooperation on High Courts

# Commitment and Cooperation on High Courts

## *A Cross-Country Examination of Institutional Constraints on Judges*

Benjamin Alarie

Andrew J. Green

OXFORD
UNIVERSITY PRESS

OXFORD
UNIVERSITY PRESS

Oxford University Press is a department of the University of Oxford. It furthers the University's objective of excellence in research, scholarship, and education by publishing worldwide. Oxford is a registered trademark of Oxford University Press in the UK and certain other countries.

Published in the United States of America by Oxford University Press
198 Madison Avenue, New York, NY 10016, United States of America.



Library of Congress Cataloging-in-Publication Data

Names: Alarie, Benjamin, author. | Green, Andrew James, author.
Title: Commitment and cooperation on high courts : a cross-country examination of institutional constraints on judges / Benjamin Alarie, Andrew J. Green.
Description: Oxford [UK] ; New York : Oxford University Press, [2017] | Includes bibliographical references and index.
Identifiers: LCCN 2017012927 | ISBN 9780199397594 ((hardback) : alk. paper)
Subjects: LCSH: Judges—United States. | Judges—Selection and appointment—United States. | Judicial process—United States. | Political questions and judicial power—United States. | Courts—United States.
Classification: LCC KF8775 .A94 2017 | DDC 347/.035—dc23
LC record available at https://lccn.loc.gov/2017012927

9 8 7 6 5 4 3 2 1

Printed by Edwards Brothers Malloy, United States of America

**Note to Readers**

This publication is designed to provide accurate and authoritative information in regard to the subject matter covered. It is based upon sources believed to be accurate and reliable and is intended to be current as of the time it was written. It is sold with the understanding that the publisher is not engaged in rendering legal, accounting, or other professional services. If legal advice or other expert assistance is required, the services of a competent professional person should be sought. Also, to confirm that the information has not been affected or changed by recent developments, traditional legal research techniques should be used, including checking primary sources where appropriate.

*(Based on the Declaration of Principles jointly adopted by a Committee of the American Bar Association and a Committee of Publishers and Associations.)*

*For my Dad, for unwavering support.—AG*

# CONTENTS

# ACKNOWLEDGMENTS

This manuscript represents the culmination of thousands of hours of work by ourselves, friends and colleagues, and numerous research assistants. Over the past several years we are grateful to have worked with an unreasonably strong collection of research assistants at the University of Toronto, including Nicholas Arrigo, Jesse Boretsky, Jacob Brown, Taylor Cao, Maeve Chandler, John Chapman, Elizabeth Creelman, Adrienne Ho, Aaron Hunt, Ila Mada, Kathryn McGoldrick, Paul Pereira, Graeme Rotrand, Kevin Siu, and Ramin Wright.

Special thanks are owed also to our friends and colleagues who reviewed and commented on earlier versions of this manuscript, saving us from potential mistakes and pointing out ways to sharpen and improve our analysis and its presentation. Among those we would like to thank for reviewing and commenting on the draft manuscript are Professors David A. Green, Michael J. Trebilcock, Emily A. Satterthwaite, Albert H. Yoon, Edward Iacobucci, Anita Anand, and Michael Bailey. We are grateful to the Faculty of Law at the University of Toronto for its consistent support of this project, to the Social Sciences and Humanities Research Council for providing research funding, and to the Canadian and American Law and Economic Associations for providing the venues in which several parts of the manuscript were presented, debated, and refined.

Final thanks to Oxford University Press for believing in this project from the outset, for their patience in awaiting the delivery of the manuscript, and for their expert guidance in the production process. Any errors or omissions are of course our own.

# INTRODUCTION

This book is about how the design of a high court influences how judges decide appeals. It is comforting and convenient to believe the "Rule of Law" dictates how a judge on a high court will decide crucial issues ranging from the death penalty and national security to regulation of banks or railways. However, we argue that how a court is designed can make a fundamental difference in who wins a particular case and how the law develops.

One element of the design of high courts has been front and center in the news in many countries recently—how judges are appointed. With the death of Justice Antonin Scalia in the United States, the appointments process for justices of the US Supreme Court was thrown in disarray with Republican members of the Senate refusing to even consider President Obama's nominee. In Canada, the retirement of Justice Thomas Cromwell provided an opening for newly elected prime minister Justin Trudeau to make good on his promises to make the appointments process more transparent. At the same time he has to determine how to fulfill his promise of ensuring any nominee is fully bilingual. In India, the Supreme Court recently ruled that an attempt to wrest control of the appointment process from the judges themselves is unconstitutional. The Indian Supreme Court then embarked on its own review of its processes to make the system more transparent, yet allow the judges to retain control of who sits on the Court.

The appointment process is obviously central to how a court decides as that process determines the expertise and values that are brought to bear on appeals. Each of these countries has chosen a different design for appointing judges to their high courts. In the United States, the president appoints judges with the "advice and consent" of the Senate in a highly public and political process. The prime minister of Canada appoints justices to the Supreme Court of Canada after consulting a range of parties in what has tended to be a highly secretive, closed process. In India, the chief justice and the four most senior judges on the Court select new judges. These distinctive processes have the potential to yield profoundly different courts.

However, although the appointment process is important, it is not the only design feature of high courts that matters or way in which high courts differ in design. For example, the US Supreme Court has nine justices hearing recently about 80 cases per year with all nine justices hearing almost all appeals. The UK Supreme Court, on the other hand, has 12 members who tend to sit in panels of five judges to hear about 90 appeals per year, and the Supreme Court of Canada has nine members sitting in panels of five, seven, or nine judges to hear about 80 cases. At the far extreme, the Indian Supreme Court has up to 31 members hearing most of its over 7,000 appeals in panels of two or three judges.

We argue that such differences in design—in how judges are appointed, whether they sit in panels, in how many cases the court hears—matter to how a court functions and how its judges make decisions. In particular, we think of these different design elements as wedges that push courts in different directions on two key dimensions by constraining or shaping the choices made by judges and other actors such as litigants and legislators. First, they influence the extent to which judges follow their own personal views of the appropriate outcome of an appeal—that is, how committed they are to following their personal views in deciding cases rather than in some narrower sense applying the "law." Second, they affect how willing the judges are on a court to be collegial—how cooperative they are in reaching decisions. We argue that these two factors—commitment and cooperation—are fundamental bases for differentiating high courts and that the design of the court influences courts in both these dimensions.

The design of a court, and the level of commitment and cooperation it engenders, is central to a just legal system. It creates the basis for the rule of law—most obviously by influencing the extent to which outcomes are determined by personal preferences of judges—but in other ways such as through framing the influence of democratic principles. It fosters access to justice such as through rules about standing and appeals to high courts. It guides the development, consistency, and coherence of the common law through, for example, affecting the availability and strength of precedent.

Ours is principally a positive exercise: how does design matter? Answering this question is key for understanding a particular court and seeking to improve its operation. Part of our argument is that there are trade-offs across the main design elements that reinforce or mitigate the influence of each element. Moreover, each court is embedded in a web of other institutions that have different strengths and weaknesses. As a result, we do not view this as an exercise in determining what the optimal design of a high court would look like but of evaluating ways to make high courts more just. Amartya Sen has argued that it is better not to seek an ideal set of just institutions but to examine and compare feasible, actual institutions to ascertain how to make society more just.[1] In this spirit, we seek to compare how courts are actually designed and how these design features affect outcomes to aid in identifying high court reforms that make particular courts more just.

We begin in Chapter 1 by setting out and justifying the building blocks of commitment and cooperation. We see these two dimensions as allowing us to situate high courts relative to each other. We use them to focus on the five main high courts in our study—the US Supreme Court, the UK Supreme Court (and its predecessor House of Lords), the Supreme Court of Canada, the High Court of Australia, and the Indian Supreme Court. Chapter 1 provides both a preliminary assessment of how these courts sit relative to each other along these two dimensions and a brief overview of the key design choices made by each of these courts.

We argue that high court design influences how judges decide. Chapter 2 provides the basic theoretical structure for this argument. We primarily build on Epstein, Landes, and Posner's labor market model of how judges decide.[2] We argue that a judge makes decisions like any other individual, influenced by a range of factors such as his own view of the law and the preferred outcome of the appeal, his reputation, his workload, and even in some cases financial or material concerns. How he balances these various factors depends on the design of the court. We set out a preliminary framework for thinking about the relationship between the institutional design and how individual judges reach decisions.

The balance of the book looks at particular design choices made for different courts. Chapter 3 examines one of the most central—the appointment process. As described above, appointment processes vary considerably across countries—from very open, political procedures to secretive, closed processes and even self-selection by judges. Chapter 3 finds that there is some broad correlation between these design elements and whether judges on a court are polarized, are consistent in their decisions across areas of law, and tend to dissent in appeals.

It is not only who is appointed to a court that matters but also who hears particular appeals. Does it make a difference whether all judges hear each appeal or whether certain subsets of judges hear particular appeals? We argue that it matters a great deal. In Chapter 4 we look at whether the identity of the judges on

1. Amartya Sen, *The Idea of Justice* (Cambridge, MA: Harvard University Press, 2009) [Sen, *Idea*].

2. Lee Epstein, William M. Landes & Richard A. Posner, *Behavior of Federal Judges: A Theoretical and Empirical Study of Rational Choice* (Cambridge, MA: Harvard University Press, 2013) [Epstein, Landes & Posner, *Behavior*].

the panel matters, holding for Chapter 5 the relationships between the judges on a given panel. The US Supreme Court has largely taken the identity issue out of play by having all nine judges hear all appeals. However, for the other countries, a chief justice has the power to set the size and composition of the panel hearing an appeal. She may use this power to make the court operate more efficiently, such as by ensuring the court is able to hear more cases than if all judges sit together. Alternatively, the chief justice may set panels that increase the probability of a particular result. We find evidence that chief justices use panels for both these purposes in some countries.

A judge is rooted in various relationships including with the other judges on a panel or on the court as a whole, and with other institutions such as the legislature. In Chapter 5 we look at whether these relationships influence how judges vote. We find that a judge does tend to respond differently depending on who else is with him on the panel deciding the appeal. However, we find at best mixed evidence that a judge is influenced by his position on the bench (either as a new judge hearing his first few terms of cases or, at the other extreme, as the chief justice) or by other branches of government.

Judges on high courts in general do not just have a set of appeals given to them and make a decision. To a greater or lesser extent the judges also choose the cases they hear. In Chapter 6 we discuss how the rules about how courts are designed influences the set of cases the court hears. Judges take in account various factors such as their overall workload and signals of the importance of the case. In addition, however, they also at times consider the potential outcome of the appeal, choosing cases to get a particular result by either overturning or affirming the decision below. Judges may also avoid hearing a case if there is a risk that a hearing will result in an outcome they do not want.

High courts then differ in the process for choosing who sits on the court, the size and composition of panels, and the cases the court hears. Once the case is before the court, a judge may also be influenced by the particular parties that appear in the appeal. Chapter 7 examines this influence. The government, for example, tends to be more successful in many cases than other parties. This success may be due, for example, to the government having more resources than other parties or being a repeat player in front of the court. Further, judges seem to at least be modestly influenced by interveners, who are not actually the parties to the appeal but seek to provide additional information to the judges about the implications of their decision. Judges appear to take into account to at least a limited extent the information provided by the interveners in some contexts, though the presence of interveners also appears connected to an increase in the probability of a judge dissenting.

Finally, in terms of design, we look at how judges are influenced not just by formal rules of how the court is to arrive at decisions but at norms of decision-making. In particular, in Chapter 8 we discuss the existence and strength of norms of consensus on different courts. Courts vary to a surprising extent in the magnitude and causes of disagreement amongst judges. The two most extreme cases in our sample are the US Supreme Court with over half of the cases having at least one dissent and the Indian Supreme Court where only about 5 percent of cases involve a dissent. We find evidence that, depending on the country, a judge is influenced in whether she dissents by policy differences with other judges and her own workload. However, a judge's decision to dissent also appears related to the background norms of whether it is acceptable to dissent and the leadership of the chief justice and president of the court.

Chapter 9 provides our conclusion. As we have said, we do not attempt to define an optimal court. However, we argue that high court design influences how judges decide and therefore we need a better theory of institutional design and improved ability to tease out how and when design matters. The differences across courts are both important and interesting in terms of where they come from and their implications. They help us understand what may be necessary to improve high courts in particular countries. We cannot move toward better institutions without understanding how design features relate to each other and to the factors that underlie how judges decide. To date, considerable academic work has focused on studying courts in isolation without understanding the broader suite of design options and their implications.

With this book, we aim to begin the process of synthesizing, generalizing, and expanding upon the existing work so that our highest appellate courts can be increasingly appreciated and improved using insights from a comparative institutional perspective.

# 1

# Commitment and Cooperation on High Courts

In July 2009 two young men, one with a distinctive silver handgun, robbed a jeweler. The police soon arrested Kevin Fearon on suspicion of the robbery. During the arrest, the police searched Fearon and found a cell phone. The phone was not password protected and the police accessed a text message about the robbery with the words "We did it" as well as pictures of a handgun. Only later did the police obtain a warrant to search the phone. At trial Fearon argued that the judge should not admit the text message and photos as evidence as the police violated his right against unreasonable search and seizure by examining the phone without a warrant. The trial judge admitted the cell phone evidence and convicted Fearon of armed robbery and possession of a loaded restricted firearm.[1]

After losing an appeal to the Ontario Court of Appeal, Fearon asked the Supreme Court of Canada to hear his appeal. A panel of three justices of the Supreme Court agreed that the Court should hear the appeal. The Court allowed the attorney generals of Quebec and Alberta, the British Columbia Civil Liberties Association, the Canadian Civil Liberties Association, the Canadian Association of Chiefs of Police, the Criminal Lawyers' Association, and other groups to take part in what was seen as an important conflict between privacy rights and law enforcement. At the time of the hearing eight justices sat on the Court. Chief Justice McLachlin chose seven of those eight justices (including herself) to hear and decide the appeal.

Immediately following the hearing, the seven justices would have retired to a special conference room to discuss the appeal. Typically the most senior justice speaks first, followed by each justice in order of seniority. The chief justice would then have chosen the justice or justices who would draft opinions in the appeal. In this case, four justices agreed that the appeal should be dismissed, allowing the conviction to stand. The other three justices joined in a dissenting

1. These facts are drawn from *R v Fearon,* 2014 SCC 77, [2014] 3 SCR 621.

opinion, arguing that a person's privacy interest in his personal phone outweighed the state's interest in performing a warrantless search except in urgent circumstances.

Kevin Fearon lost his appeal to the highest court in Canada. What should Fearon make of this result? Should he be concerned that Conservative prime ministers appointed all four justices who decided against his appeal whereas two of the three who would have decided in his favor were appointed by Liberal prime ministers? Would the result have been different if members of all parties in the legislature had the chance to question nominees to the Court and had to agree to the nomination, similar to how judges are appointed in the United States? Or if the current chief justice and the four most senior justices selected new members to the Court, as in India?

Should Fearon be concerned that the chief justice had the opportunity to select the justices who would hear the appeal, in this case leaving off one justice? In the United States, the entire court hears almost all appeals. In Israel, on the other hand, appeals are generally heard by panels of three of the nine to fifteen members of the Court, although the president can decide to make the panel larger. Does it make a difference to how these judges decided Fearon's appeal that the Court decided to hear this particular appeal and not others? Or that the Court allowed groups focused on civil liberties, criminal lawyers, or police chiefs to present arguments in the appeal?

Countries have adopted different answers to all these questions about how to set up their highest courts. They have chosen various combinations of features such as how to choose judges for the high court, whether the judges hear all appeals together or in smaller panels, whether the court gets to choose for itself which appeals it hears, and who gets to present arguments before the court. Our question is—do these choices affect how judges on high courts decide appeals? We argue that they do. These design choices across features of a high court influence two core aspects of how judges decide appeals: whether or not they decide appeals in accordance with their own personal views of the correct policy, and whether they decide together collegially or act as separate, independent decision-makers.

## COMMITMENT: JUDGES AND THEIR PERSONAL VIEWS

Given that a judge may decide anything from who spends time in jail and who has custody of children to which companies can merge, there is surprisingly little consensus about how he decides the case in front of him.[2] Most simply,

2. Lee Epstein, William M. Landes & Richard A. Posner, *Behavior of Federal Judges: A Theoretical and Empirical Study of Rational Choice* (Cambridge, MA: Harvard University Press, 2013) [Epstein, Landes & Posner, *Behavior*]. The authors attempt to bring together a number of

he could be deciding based on the "law," constrained in his choice by the facts in the particular case along with any relevant statutes, regulations, or prior decisions. On this understanding (which has been termed the "legal" model), he mixes these legal ingredients along with background legal norms or principles to prepare an answer for even novel issues or questions about ambiguous statutes. Suppose, for example, a judge must decide whether a skateboard falls under a ban under the *Parks Act* stating "no vehicles are allowed in the park." On this view of how he decides, the judge would determine whether a skateboard was a "vehicle" under the Act by combining the purpose of the *Parks Act*, how the Act deals with other issues, how skateboards are used, and what other judges have decided is a vehicle under the Act. He would then produce an opinion on whether skateboarders can use the park and, in fact, must follow this recipe for reaching an opinion and live with the results, whether or not he personally thinks skateboards should be allowed in the park.

However, there is another commonly held view of judges: that they decide based not on the law but on their own personal attitudes and intuitions about the right answer. These attitudes may be shaped by ties to a political party, prior experience such as working as defense counsel, or growing up poor or rich. Our judge may view skateboarders as troublemakers or he may think that restrictions in parks result from an overly active government. These attitudes about skateboarders or the government then shape his interpretation. This view of judges founding their decisions in their own preferred outcomes (which is called the "Attitudinal" model[3]) is most strongly associated with the sharply divided judges on the US Supreme Court, grouping together most famously in *Bush v Gore* on whether to allow a statewide manual recount of ballots in the presidential election.[4]

To compare the highest courts of different countries, we can sort courts by whether the judges on the court tend to decide in accordance with one of these two views. Imagine a horizontal line with these two views of how judges decide cases as extremes at either end, as in Figure 1-1. The line shows the level of commitment of the judges to following their own views of the best outcome as opposed to following the law.[5] At the farthest left on the line, all judges on

theories under a single labor-market theory, but this approach has not yet been widely adopted. See Chapter 2 for a more detailed discussion of theories of judicial decision-making.

3. Jeffrey A. Segal & Harold J. Spaeth, *The Supreme Court and the Attitudinal Model Revisited* (Cambridge: Cambridge University Press, 2002) at 86, setting out the principal models of judicial decision-making [Segal & Spaeth, *Attitudinal Model*].

4. *Bush v. Gore*, 531 U.S. 98 (2000).

5. This figure is derived from Benjamin Alarie & Andrew Green, "Should They All Just Get Along? Judicial Ideology, Collegiality, and Appointments to the Supreme Court of Canada"

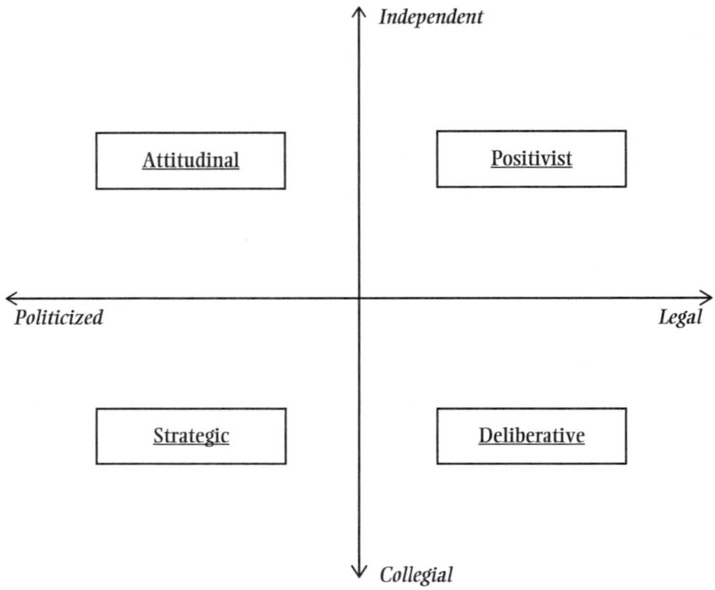


**Figure 1-1** Commitment and Cooperation on High Courts—the CC Space. High courts may be arrayed across four quadrants created by two key divisions. The first (vertical) division differentiates courts where the judges act independently from those with more collegial judges. The second (horizontal) division distinguishes courts with judges who act more "politically" from courts whose judges are more likely to decide according to legal factors. The quadrants allow identification of four types of courts: attitudinal, positivist, strategic, and deliberative.

a particular court decide cases according to what they each believe best meets their preferred outcome, regardless of the underlying law or norms. We call this type of court "politicized." At the opposite extreme, the judges on the court decide based on the law or legal norm, regardless of their own preferred policy choice. We call this type of court "legal."

The high court of a particular country, however, likely does not lie at either extreme and may even shift along the line in either direction as the judges, the area of law, or the norms of the court change. A court is a mix of individual judges, each of whom may be more or less committed to following his or her personal views. This mix may change over time if, for example, a judge who

(2008) 58 *University of New Brunswick LJ* 73 [Alarie & Green, "Should They All"]. As we discuss in Chapter 2, it can be difficult to separate out attitudes from different approaches to law. See Joshua Fischman & Tonja Jacobi, "The Second Dimension of the Supreme Court" (2016) 57 *Wm. & Mary Law Review* 1671.

decides based on her personal views leaves the court and is replaced by a judge who decides based on the law. Further, even if the judges on a court are all equally willing to follow their own personal views, they may have more space to do so when there is greater ambiguity in the law—when deciding when a search is "unreasonable" as opposed to whether a very specific tax form has been filed. Similarly, judges facing novel situations such as police using new investigative technology have greater room to pursue their vision.[6] Conversely, of course, detailed laws or common situations make it easier for a judge to follow the law.

Judges on a court face an additional constraint: social norms that either encourage or discourage judges from following their personal views. Norms signal appropriate behavior and can be very powerful. Consider cities where there is no norm against littering. People may feel free to throw their garbage on the ground rather than in a bin, and a city can quickly slip beneath a sea of refuse. Similarly, if the judges on a court do not follow a norm against deciding according to their personal views, the court may gravitate toward the politicized end of the scale. We will spend some time in Chapter 8 discussing the influence of norms and how they arise. It is enough for now to see that courts may vary in levels of ideological commitment across time and between countries depending on the composition and norms of the particular court.

## COOPERATION: JUDGES AND THEIR COLLEAGUES

A judge may not only follow her own personal views to a greater or lesser extent but may be more or less cooperative with her fellow judges. She may be averse to conflict, working and agreeing with others because she does not want them to think she is difficult or contrarian. She may wish to work toward a common agreement on the court as she believes agreement fosters trust or belief in the court. Or she may believe that working in a deliberative fashion leads to better decisions.

More negatively, the judge may merely wish to avoid the work of having to develop a dissenting opinion if she does not go along with the majority. Thomas Jefferson, criticizing Chief Justice John Marshall's policy of having the US Supreme Court issue a single unanimous decision rather than seriatim decisions (that is, each judge presenting his own decision), commented that "The practice is certainly convenient for the lazy, the modest, & the incompetent. It saves them the trouble of developing their opinion methodically and even of making up an opinion at all."[7] Alternatively, a judge could also agree with other

6. Epstein, Landes & Posner, *Behavior, supra* note 2.

7. Rebecca Wood, *Why Do High Court Judges Join? Joining Behaviour and Australia's Seriatim Tradition* (PhD Dissertation, Michigan State University, 2008) [unpublished] at 37.

judges on some appeals in order to obtain their agreement in other appeals about which she cares more, just as politicians regularly trade votes (or logroll) on legislation to further their overall policy goals. If judges are avoiding work or trading votes to best meet their policy views, a court could appear to be very cooperative. The underlying reason for the agreement therefore can be important.

If we turn again to our comparison across high courts in Figure 1-1, we see that courts may be more or less cooperative depending on how the judges interact. The most cooperative or collegial courts lie at the bottom of the vertical line. In its simplest sense, one can think of collegiality as judges agreeing on the final result, though it may involve also agreeing on a common reason for the result.

At the top of the vertical line sit courts where judges are more independent. Judges may not cooperate. A judge may simply not agree or be unwilling to find common ground with judges with different personal views. She may then dissent if she disagrees with the majority of other judges. She may view her role as providing an independently thought-out answer to whatever question is raised on the appeal. She could see such independence as fostering coherence and consistency in her reasoning and providing the greatest scope for diversity of views and values, which deepens the understanding of the law. Judges on courts toward the top of the line in Figure 1-1 dissent more frequently than on collegial courts and may also write a greater number of reasons for the results, at the extreme with each judge writing a separate opinion.

## COMBINING COMMITMENT AND COOPERATION

One may then be able to situate the high courts of different countries relative to each other on Figure 1-1 based on the commitment and cooperation of the judges on each court. We call this the "CC Space." Further, the CC Space in Figure 1-1 can be divided into four types of courts by identifying how committed and cooperative they are: the attitudinal court, the positivist court, the strategic court, and the deliberative court.

An *attitudinal court* consists of judges that are both politicized and independent. Judges on an attitudinal court look to their personal views on the outcome when deciding the appeal. Each justice places little or no value on cooperating with other justices and does not sign onto judgments by another judge unless there is a high level of ideological alignment or agreement with that judge. They do not even seek to cooperate or align with other judges to fulfill their personal preferences about the outcome. In the event of a disagreement between judges, each writes his or her own opinion rather than attempt to persuade or compromise with colleagues. These courts are therefore likely to have multiple opinions on each appeal, either through concurrences (separate opinions agreeing in the result but for different reasons) or dissents.[8]

On a *positivist court*, judges are independent and ground their decisions in legal considerations. As on an attitudinal court, judges on a positivist court place little value on attempting to reach agreement with their colleagues. However, unlike the attitudinal court, judges decide independently based on the legal merits of the appeal rather than on their own personal views of the best outcome. They may view cooperation with other judges as compromise, raising the risk of not deciding on the "true" legal merits. Judges on a positivist court may disagree less than judges on an attitudinal court if the judges differ more in personal views than in independent assessments of the law.

A *strategic court* is composed of judges who are politicized but also collegial. The judges are strategic in that they seek to advance their personal views and preferences, which may require them to cooperate with other judges.[9] They may deliberate together in an attempt to understand and use each other's personal views to produce either an agreed result or well-reasoned, sharply divided opinions. Alternatively, the judges may trade votes on cases they care less about to achieve their own preferred results in other cases, reflecting a decision-making process that resembles that of a legislature. The judges on a strategic court agree more (have lower rates of concurrences and dissents) than those on an attitudinal court. However, there may still be dissents and concurrences if the judges are unwilling to trade-off outcomes because they have very strong differences of opinions about outcomes of appeals.

Finally, on a *deliberative court*, judges try to find the best answer based on the law and are collegial in the search. They focus on the legal merits of the case and yet are open to discussing and working with their colleagues on the outcome and reasoning. These judges dissent less than positivist courts and produce fewer independent opinions. At best, then, deliberative courts have a high level of agreement and produce decisions with a high quality of legal reasoning resulting from a deliberative and inclusive process. The risk is that the drive to cooperation and agreement may be so strong that it undermines the

8. The increase in the number of opinions would in this case occur despite such factors as workload or leisure preference of the judges, which may increase the opportunity cost of writing a separate judgment. See Lee Epstein & Jack Knight, *The Choices Justices Make* (Washington, DC: CQ Press, 1998) [Epstein & Knight, *Choices*]; and Tracey George & Albert Yoon, "Chief Justices: The Limits of Attitudinal Theory and the Possible Paradox of Managerial Judging" (2008) 61 *Vanderbilt Law Review* 1.

9. For discussions of the strategic model of judicial decision-making, see e.g. Melinda Gann Hall & Paul Brace, "Order in the Courts: A Neo-institutional Approach to Judicial Consensus" (1989) 42 *Western Political Quarterly* 391; Epstein & Knight, *Choices, supra* note 8.

benefits of disagreement, such as where dissents point toward future directions in the development of the law.

## ARE COMMITMENT AND COOPERATION RELATED?

One question that immediately arises is whether commitment and cooperation are separate, independent qualities of judges and courts or whether they pull each other in predictable directions. If they are separate, adding a judge who decides in accordance with her personal views to a court may shift the court to the left in CC Space in Figure 1-1—changing it, for example, from a deliberative to a strategic court. The addition of the judge would not, however, affect the level of cooperation.

Commitment and cooperation may, on the other hand, be linked such that changing one affects the other. Adding a judge who decides based on his personal views may diminish the level of cooperation—the judges on the court may be less willing to seek common, objective ground. The court in our example may then move from a deliberative court to an attitudinal court with the breakdown of cooperation. Yet any change likely depends on the starting point. Adding a judge who decides based on his personal views to a court already well stocked with such judges could shift an attitudinal court to a strategic court if the judges can more readily find judges who will trade votes with them. More judges deciding in accordance with their personal views could then be associated with more or less cooperation.

We therefore view commitment and cooperation as linked but not in a way that eliminates the possibility of certain types of courts. Altering the way the court operates or who sits on a court may change the type of court by influencing either or both the level of commitment or cooperation. Understanding such change requires an appreciation of how the various choices about the design of a high court relate to each other and to how judges decide cases. We seek to deepen this appreciation by examining the wide array of choices made by and for past and current high courts in different countries.

## WHY COMMITMENT AND COOPERATION?

Before we talk about differences in high courts across countries, one other natural question arises: Why should we compare courts based on commitment and cooperation? High courts differ along other dimensions such as how "active" they are in deciding policy issues, how consistent they are in their decisions over time, or even how many cases the judges hear. Courts can be compared in a myriad of ways. We address commitment and cooperation as they help frame many of these other ways to compare courts and the important debates about the role of high courts.

Take, for example, how willing a court is to decide policy issues. Debates continually arise about how "activist" a court is in making decisions. Does the court strike down legislation as unconstitutional too often? The answer, and even what "activist" means, depends in part on how the court makes decisions. One may be less happy with a highly political court that engages in political trade-offs striking down laws as unconstitutional than with a court composed of judges who try to decide more closely on the law. Or maybe not. It may be that one's view of the law and the role of the courts provides scope for and even depends on judges following their own political views. In any case, how one feels about a court's role, and even how one classifies a court, will depend on its level of commitment and cooperation.

Similarly, consider how consistent a court's decisions are over time. Does the court change its view regularly on important issues? Does it unswervingly apply a conservative or liberal approach to all areas of law from tax to criminal to human rights? Consistency in and of itself has benefits. Individuals can know how to plan their lives better if they have a greater sense of how the law is developing. Litigants can make better decisions about their cases, whether to continue to fight or to settle or drop a case. Lower courts can more faithfully follow the higher court's position. However, one's view of consistency may depend on how the decisions are made. A court continually stocked with individuals from similar backgrounds and who decide in line with their personal views may give consistent and predictable decisions. Those decisions may not, however, be fair or just. Moreover, dissents may provide a less clear or consistent view of a court's opinion on an issue but may be valuable in signaling future paths the court may follow. Again commitment and cooperation tend to at least influence our views of the value of consistency.

We view commitment and cooperation as fundamental dimensions for comparing across courts and addressing larger questions about the role of courts. They are intimately connected with other possible distinctions across courts such as how many cases different high courts hear. Courts hear very different numbers of cases—the US Supreme Court hears about 80 cases per year while the Indian Supreme Court holds about 7,500 regular hearings annually. The number of cases a court hears may reflect its view of its role. Does it see itself as correcting errors in the lower courts, or just as dealing with cases raising issues of national importance? Yet it may also have profound effects on how judges make decisions. A judge may hear so many cases that she is unable to adequately consider each case, leading to poorer quality decisions and perhaps less cooperation with her colleagues.

As we noted earlier, we are engaged here in a positive exercise—looking at how the design of high courts influences how judges decide. There is of course a normative question about what type of court and what sort of design is best. Is it possible to design an "optimal" court? We do not seek to answer this question. Instead we view the CC Space as providing a framework to discuss how altering the design of a court affects how it decides. By comparing across existing design choices, we may be able to find a range we should be working toward, where a particular court's location inside or outside the range and the path toward a more just court may depend on other factors such as the strength of other institutions.[10] We may be able to point to examples of courts outside the range—possibly because they are too political or too overwhelmed by the caseload to decide effectively and fairly. However, the road to any discussion of different designs must first lie through establishing what affects court decisions. Once we have a better idea if and to what extent decisions vary with things such as the use of panels or the appointments process, we can start asking what we may want to change.

## COMPARING HIGH COURTS

Commitment and cooperation then provide a map for locating different high courts. It is probably impossible to locate any particular high court precisely in CC Space in Figure 1-1. However, we can get a sense of where courts lie at a particular point in time. Courts where judges more often decide according to their personal views will lie toward the left of the space, with attitudinal and strategic courts having higher rates of such decisions than positivist or deliberative courts. Attitudinal courts should have lower rates of agreement than deliberative courts, all other things being equal, which should show itself in more dissents and concurrences. Situating the courts is not, however, straightforward. It can, for example, be hard to determine whether a court with judges who are less likely to decide based on their personal views is positivist or deliberative if there are few concurring opinions. A deliberative court may look positivist if the judges have very different legal backgrounds and therefore have difficulty reaching agreement, though they strive for it.

Beyond the United States there has been limited empirical work in many countries on how national high courts decide appeals. Analysis of other high courts such as in Canada, Israel, or the UK trails behind. There is even less work that compares across high courts. Moreover data on decisions of high courts in countries other than Canada and the United States is relatively sparse and of variable quality. For much of the analysis in this book, we expand on the existing empirical literature through use of the High Courts Judicial Database

10. Amartya Sen, *The Idea of Justice* (Cambridge, MA: Harvard University Press, 2009) (arguing for a comparative theory of justice that seeks to compare across feasible, existing institutions to move toward more justice, rather than to identify ideally just institutions).

(HCJD). The HCJD covers decisions of high courts from a range of countries from about 1970 to the early 2000s.[11] Although there naturally are limitations in this data given its broad scope, it allows us to examine using a consistent set of data the relationship between high court design and how judges decide cases across countries.[12]

Given the limited nature of the data and prior work, the best we can hope for at this stage is some general sense of where courts lie relative to each other. Such relative positioning, however, is sufficient to orient the question of how differences in the set-up of courts influence their decisions. We chose to examine only certain common law courts in order to keep at least some of the context the same in our comparison. Our primary focus will be on the US Supreme Court, the Supreme Court of Canada, the UK Supreme Court (and former House of Lords), the Indian Supreme Court, and the Australian High Court, though we will also look at other courts in less depth such as the Israeli Supreme Court. Although not a large sample of courts, as we will see in the following brief overview of each court, these courts still differ widely in many ways.[13] The United States, Canada, Australia, and the UK in particular work from a similar structure but with some interesting design differences that let us ask interesting questions about the potential influence of altering the design of the court. We chose to also include the Indian Supreme Court as it has ties to the same legal traditions but has made such divergent design choices that it makes a good counterpoint to the similarities across the other countries.

## United States

We start with an overview of the Supreme Court of the United States, because it is the most studied court and for that reason the most easily located in CC Space. It provides a relatively clear point from which to situate other courts. There is no objective location for the origin in CC Space as there is no clear measurable counterpart to either dimension. We will therefore use the US Supreme Court as a base point and define all other countries relative to it.

11. See Appendix 1 for a more detailed description of Stacia L. Haynie et al. (2007) High Courts Judicial Database. Accessed at the University of South Carolina Judicial Research Initiative, online: www.cas.sc.edu/poli/juri [HCJD].

12. See Chapter 9 and Appendix 1 for a discussion of some of the limitations of the data for our purposes.

13. The courts are discussed in greater detail in the following chapters.

The Supreme Court of the United States has nine justices who hear appeals *en banc*—that is, all nine judges sit on all appeals.[14] The president appoints the justices "by and with the Advice and Consent of the Senate."[15] The executive branch (the president) and the legislative branch (through the Senate) therefore share the appointment power. The president nominates a candidate generally after consulting with Senate party leaders, members of the Senate Judiciary Committee, and other party leaders or interest groups.[16] The Senate Judiciary Committee then holds a public hearing after a pre-hearing investigation and makes a recommendation to the full Senate, which holds a debate on the candidate. If the Senate votes in favor of the candidate, the president appoints him or her to the bench.

The US court system has both a federal court system with District Courts and Courts of Appeals as well as a system of state courts. Unlike some other high courts, the US Supreme Court has almost complete control over the cases it hears (its "docket").[17] It hears appeals from lower courts in the federal court system as well as appeals from state supreme courts relating to federal law. The justices have clerks who prepare memos including recommendations on each petition to be heard by the Court. The chief justice creates a list of all petitions he believes should be considered. The justices of the Court then vote on the petitions on the list according to the Rule of Four—at least four justices must vote for the petition to be heard by the Court. The Court typically hears about 1 percent of the appeals that apply to be heard (in 2009–2010, for example, the Court granted 82 of the approximately 8,000 applications to be heard).[18]

The US Supreme Court seems clearly to be an attitudinal court (see Figure 1-5). We can measure how politicized a court is in many ways such as by whether judges vote in cases according to the politics of who appointed them, by how conservative or liberal they appear at the time they are appointed, or by how conservatively or liberally they vote relative to other judges over the course of

14. The Court does sit with fewer than nine judges when there is a vacancy on the Court or if one of the judges has a conflict of interest in hearing the particular appeal.

15. U.S. Const. art. I, § 2, cl. 2.

16. See Denis Steven Rutkus ed, *Supreme Court Appointment Process: Roles of the President, Judiciary Committee, and Senate* (New York: Nova Science, 2005) (Congressional Research Service) (an overview of the appointment process).

17. There are some appeals that the Court must hear such as certain death penalty issues. See e.g. Ryan C. Black & Christina L. Boyd, "Selecting the Select Few: The Discuss List and the U.S. Supreme Court's Agenda-Setting Process" (2012) 94:4 *Social Science Quarterly* 1124 [Black & Boyd, "Selecting"] (an overview of the US certiorari process).

18. Black & Boyd, "Selecting," *supra* note 17 at 1124.

their careers. The US Supreme Court can be considered politicized on all these measures. For example, US Supreme Court justices appointed by Republican presidents predictably tend to vote in a more conservative fashion than those appointed by Democratic presidents.[19]

One way to picture this is to see whether judges on a court tend to vote in a predictable fashion. We will discuss more of this in Chapter 3 but the US empirical literature has made an industry out of dividing votes in various areas of law into "liberal" and "conservative." Liberal votes are, for example, a decision by a judge in favor of a criminal in criminal cases, a claimant in a civil rights case, or a union in a labor case. If we sum up all the cases in which a judge votes in a liberal direction and divide by the total number of decisions made by that judge over the whole period we are studying, we can obtain that judge's long-term liberal voting rate.[20] To see how similar judges on a court are in terms of voting liberally versus conservatively, we can look at the range of these long-term liberal voting rates on the court in any year (that is, the difference between the judge with the highest and the lowest long-term liberal voting rate on the court in any given year). Figure 1-2 shows how these ranges varied across courts over the period 1970 to the early 2000s. The US Supreme Court had the greatest range in its justices over the five courts in the figure, with the bulk of years having about a 40 percent difference between the justice with the highest long-term liberal voting rate and the justice with the lowest (the median of the ranges was 43 percent). The size of the range does not provide direct evidence of politicization but it gives one (partial) indicator of the degree of polarization on a court. We will discuss other measures in more depth in Chapter 3.

Further, in terms of cooperation, justices on the US Supreme Court dissent at a much higher rate than judges in other countries. For the term beginning in October 2014 it decided 30 cases unanimously out of 74 total cases, (a unanimity rate of 41 percent) while 19 cases (26 percent of the total) were decided by a bare majority of five of the nine justices.[21] As can be seen from Figure 1-3, if we look over the period from 1970 to the early 2000s, countries varied widely in the percent of cases per year with at least one dissent. The US Supreme Court's

19. See e.g. Segal & Spaeth, *Attitudinal Model, supra* note 3; Alarie & Green, "Should They All," *supra* note 5 at 74.

20. These results are based on the HCJD, *supra* note 11, which sorts cases into "pro" and "con" directions that for present purposes, we will take as "liberal" and "conservative." For a description of the categorization of cases and outcomes that we used based on the HCJD, *supra* note 11, see Appendices 1 and 2.

21. Kedar Bhatia, "Final Stat Pack for October Term 2014: Merits Cases by Vote Split" (June 30, 2015) *SCOTUSblog* (blog), online: http://sblog.s3.amazonaws.com/wp-content/uploads/2015/07/SB_votesplit_OT14.pdf at 5.

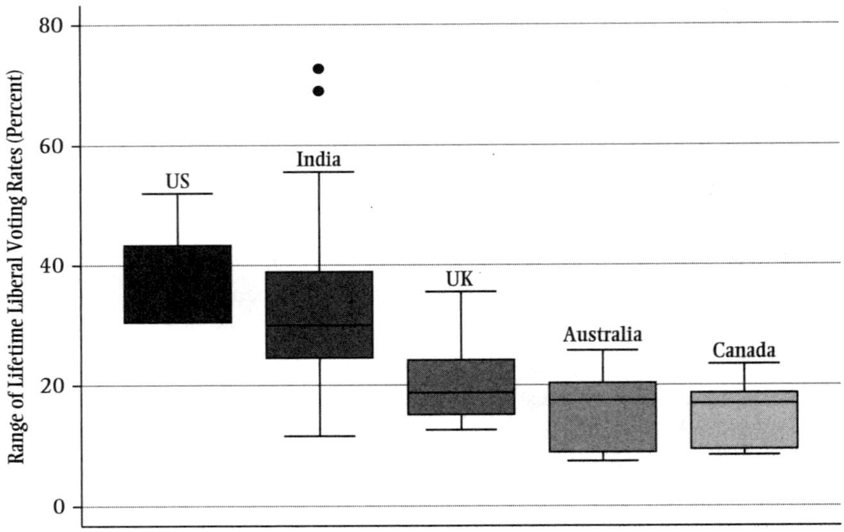


**Figure 1-2** Range of long-term liberal voting rates of judges on the court in a given year (the difference between the judge with the highest long-term liberal voting rate and the lowest long-term liberal voting rate on the court in that year) over the period 1970 to the early 2000s. The box shows the middle 50 percent of the values taken by the range, and the line within the box is the median range over the period. The lines above and below the box are the maximum and minimum ranges in the period. The United States had the highest median range in long-term liberal voting rates over the period, whereas the UK, Australia, and Canada had median ranges that were less than half that of the United States.
SOURCE: HCJD and Spaeth database.

decisions more often than not tended to involve at least one dissent over this period whereas the judges of the Indian Supreme Court only rarely dissented.

Another measure of the extent of non-cooperation is how many judges dissent (as opposed to just whether a decision has at least one dissenting opinion). To get at this measure, we can look at what Epstein, Landes, and Posner call the "fraction of dissenting opinions," which they define as the number of dissenting opinions in a term divided by the number of decisions in the term.[22] Figure 1-4 shows the fraction of dissenting opinions for various countries from 1970 to the early 2000s.[23] The US Supreme Court clearly has a much higher rate of non-cooperation than the other countries on this measure, with a median of about 1.5 dissenting opinions for every decision.

22. Epstein, Landes & Posner, *Behavior, supra* note 2 at 281–282.

23. See Appendix 1 for a description of the data and Appendix 3 for a discussion of fraction dissenting.

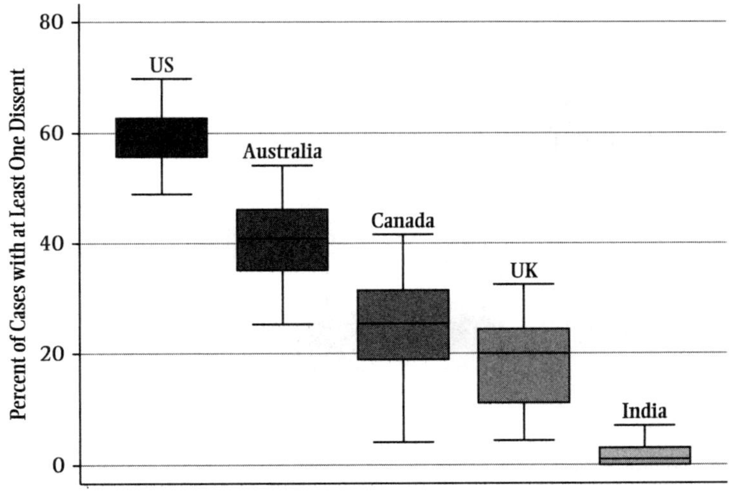


**Figure 1-3** Percent of cases per year that have at least one dissent over the period from 1970 to the early 2000s. The box shows the middle 50 percent of the data for each country, and the line in the box shows the median percentage for cases with at least one dissent over the period. The lines above and below each box provide the maximum and minimum annual percentages of opinions with at least one dissent for each country in the period. The United States had by far the highest rate of dissenting with over 50 percent of opinions having a dissent in most years. At the other extreme, most years India had less than 5 percent of opinions with at least one dissent. Canada and the UK had similar rates of opinions with dissents. Australia had the second highest level of dissent with in general over 40 percent of opinions having a dissent.
SOURCE: HCJD and Spaeth database.

We have placed the courts we are looking at in CC Space in Figure 1-5. It provides a sense of how we view these courts relative to each other, but of necessity is quite general based on our review of the literature and the data for each court. As a point of reference for other high courts, therefore, the US Supreme Court is quite politicized and not very collegial.

## Australia

The High Court of Australia consists of seven justices.[24] Although technically the governor general in council (cabinet) appoints the justices, in practice the

24. *Commonwealth of Australia Constitution Act 1900* (Cth), s 72 [*Australia Constitution*]. The bench has consisted of seven justices since 1946. See Paresh Kumar Narayan & Russell Smyth, "The Consensual Norm on the High Court of Australia: 1904–2001" (2005) 26:2 *International Political Science Review*) 147 at 151 [Narayan & Smyth, "Consensual Norm"].

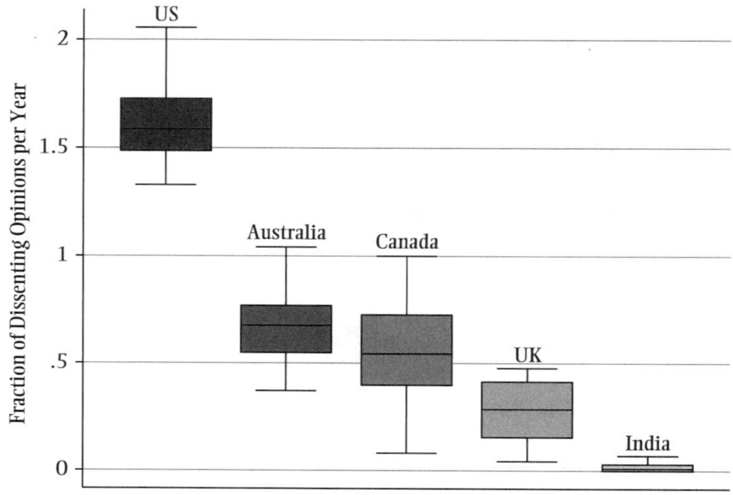


**Figure 1-4** Fraction of dissenting opinions per year (number of dissenting opinions in the year divided by the total number of decisions in the year) over the period from 1970 to the early 2000s. The box shows the middle 50 percent of the data for each country, and the line in the box shows the median value of the fraction of dissenting opinions over the period. The lines above and below each box provide the maximum and minimum fraction of dissenting opinions for each country in the period. As with Figure 1-2, the United States had by far the highest rate of dissenting opinions over the period and India by far the lowest. Australia and Canada had similar levels of fraction of dissenting opinions with the UK slightly less.
SOURCE: HCJD and Spaeth database.

cabinet appoints justices on the recommendation of the attorney general in consultation with state attorneys generals.[25] According to Narayan and Smyth, the actual appointment process is not clear.[26] There is no senate hearing, no legislative review, and no legislative requirement that the government engage in consultation with the judiciary or the profession.[27] The prime minister works

25. Mita Bhattacharya & Russell Smyth, "The Determinants of Judicial Prestige and Influence: Some Empirical Evidence from the High Court of Australia" (2001) 30:1 *Journal of Legal Studies* 223–252 at 229 [Bhattacharya & Smyth].

26. Narayan & Smyth, "Consensual Norm," *supra* note 24 at 151. See also Bhattacharya & Smyth, *supra* note 25 at 229–330.

27. Narayan & Smyth, "Consensual Norm," *supra* note 26 at 151; Jason Pierce, "Institutional Cohesion in the High Court of Australia: Do American Theories Travel Well Down Under?" (2008) 46:3 *Commonwealth & Comparative Politics* 318 at 320 [Pierce].

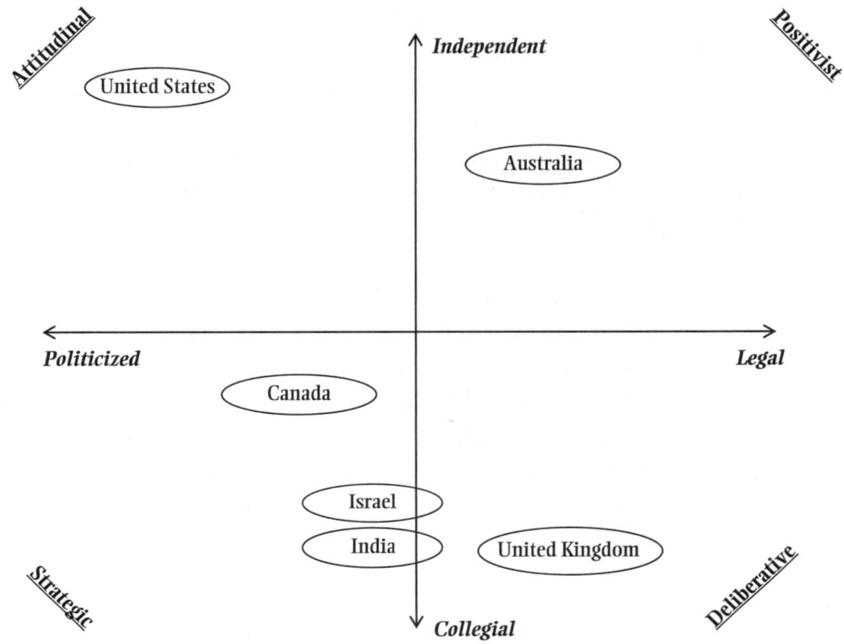


**Figure 1-5** Relative commitment and cooperation of various high courts. High courts of different countries may be provisionally arrayed on the quadrants from Figure 1-1 based on the existing literature and initial data relating to both how political and how cooperative are the judges on the courts. The US Supreme Court appears to be an outlier in terms of both its politicization and level of disagreement. However, there is also some differentiation amongst the other high courts.

with the attorney general in the appointment of the chief justice.[28] Unlike the United States, then, the executive holds the primary power of appointment.

The High Court is the final court of appeal for the federal courts and state and territorial supreme courts, but also is the first court to hear certain matters including constitutional issues.[29] Almost all appeals require leave to appeal

28. George Winterton, "Appointment of Federal Judges in Australia" (1987) 16 *Melbourne University Law Review* 185 at 186–187.

29. *Australia Constitution, supra* note 24, s 75 gives original jurisdiction to the High Court in a number of listed matters such as matters arising under treaty whereas *Australia Constitution, supra* note 24, s 76 empowers the parliament to pass legislation conferring original jurisdiction on the High Court in other matters including those arising under the Constitution. The *Judiciary Act* 1903 (Cth) [*Judiciary Act*] gives original jurisdiction over constitutional matters to the High Court. See also Bhattacharya & Smyth, *supra* note 25 at 229. The High Court became the final court of appeal in 1986 with some appeals from the High Court going to the Judicial

from the Court.[30] To get heard, an appeal must involve either a sufficiently important legal principle or a significant irregularity in how the matter was dealt with by the lower court.[31] When leave is refused, a single justice speaks for the court, but may confer briefly with colleagues.[32] Unlike some of the other countries studied, Australia does not have a Bill of Rights or equivalent set of constitutional rights. However, the High Court does hear a significant number of appeals relating to federalism issues.[33]

Most appeals are heard by panels of five, with sessions *en banc* (or "full court" as they are known in Australia) held for constitutional and unusually complex cases.[34] The chief justice chooses the panel that hears the appeal. According to Pierce, the chief justice, with the deputy registrar, chooses the justices "basing assignments on the type of case and the judges" workload, planned leaves, and other official responsibilities.[35] The justices tend to write seriatim decisions—that is, their own opinions—although at times there is a single unanimous decision or justices joining in on others' judgments.[36]

Committee of the Privy Council before that time. See Paresh Kumar Narayan & Russell Smyth, "What Explains Dissent on the High Court of Australia? An Empirical Assessment Using a Cointegration and Error Correction Approach" (2007) 4:2 *Journal of Empirical Legal Studies* 401 at 404 [Narayan & Smyth, "What Explains Dissent"].

30. The Court obtained docket control through the leave-to-appeal process in 1984, prior to which there was a right to appeal from many courts and tribunals. See Russell Smyth, "The 'Haves' and the 'Have Nots': An Empirical Study of the Rational Actor and Party Capability Hypothesis in the High Court 1948–99" (2000) 35:2 *Australian Journal of Political Science* 255 at 270 [Smyth, "The 'Haves' and the 'Have Nots'"]. There are certain exceptions for some family law matters. See Matthew Groves & Russell Smyth, "A Century of Judicial Style: Changing Patterns in Judgment Writing on the High Court 1903–2001" (2004) 32 *Federal Law Review* 255 at 259 [Groves & Smyth].

31. Narayan & Smyth, "What Explains Dissent," *supra* note 29 at 405.

32. Groves & Smyth, *supra* note 30 at 260. Generally the judge provides only limited reasons.

33. Bhattacharya & Smyth, *supra* note 25 at 232–233; Smyth, "The 'Haves' and the 'Have Nots,'" *supra* note 30 at 268–269.

34. Russell Smyth, "'Some Are More Equal than Others'—An Empirical Investigation into the Voting Behaviour of the Mason Court" (1999) 6:1–2 *Canberra Law* Review 193 at 200 [Smyth, "Some Are More Equal"]; Pierce, *supra* note 27 at 323.

35. Pierce, *supra* note 27 at 323. See also Russell Smyth, "Judicial Interaction on the Latham Court: A Quantitative Study of Voting Patterns on the High Court 1935–1950" (2001) 47:3 *Australian Journal of Politics and History* 330 at 336 (stating that in 1935–1950 the Court sat in panels of three or four judges for over 50 percent of the cases, and never sat on panels of seven judges).

36. Russell Smyth & Paresh Kumar Narayan, "Hail to the Chief! Leadership and Structural Change in the Level of Consensus on the High Court of Australia" (2004) 1:2 *Journal of Empirical Legal Studies* 399 at 404 [Smyth & Narayan, "Hail to the Chief"].

The reputation of the Australian High Court suggests that it is a positivist court. The High Court is not considered to be highly politicized, particularly relative to the US Supreme Court.[37] It is seen as having a strong tradition of legalism (Sir Owen Dixon, who was chief justice of the High Court from 1952 to 1964, famously espoused "strict and complete legalism" in judicial decision-making[38]), but personal and ideological beliefs do play some role in decision-making.[39] The spread of judges in terms of their lifetime liberal voting rates seen in Figure 1-2 is at the low end, signaling at least that the High Court has not been as polarized as, for example, the US Supreme Court. In terms of cooperation, the tradition of seriatim judgment writing means that the decision-making of the court tends toward individualized judgments.[40] Perhaps relatedly, returning to Figures 1-3 and 1-4 we see that Australia had the second highest rate both of judgments with at least one dissent and of fraction of dissenting opinions in the past, though in terms of the fraction of dissenting opinions it was closer on this measure to Canada and the UK than to the US Supreme Court.

## Canada

The Supreme Court of Canada has nine justices. The prime minister appoints the justices, although the *Supreme Court Act* formally grants the appointment power to the governor in council.[41] Three places are reserved for justices from Quebec[42] and by convention three justices are typically from Ontario, one from the Atlantic Provinces, and two from the western provinces.[43] In the past, the minister of justice identified potential candidates through a process that involved consultations with the chief justice of the Court along with the attorney general and senior members of the bar from the relevant region.[44] The process more recently involved a limited parliamentary review of the nominated

37. Bhattacharya & Smyth, *supra* note 25 at 229.

38. Bhattacharya & Smyth, *supra* note 25 at 231

39. Bhattacharya & Smyth, *supra* note 25 at 232. See also Michael Coper, "Concern about Judicial Method" (2006) 30 *Melbourne University Law Review* 554.

40. Narayan & Smyth, "What Explains Dissent," *supra* note 29 at 405.

41. *Supreme Court Act* RSC 1985, c S-26, s 4(2) [*Supreme Court Act* Canada].

42. *Supreme Court Act* Canada, *supra* note 41, s 6.

43. Peter McCormick, "Selecting the Supremes: The Appointment of Judges to the Supreme Court of Canada" (2005) 7:1 *Journal of Appellate Practice and Process* 1 at 13 [McCormick, "Selecting the Supremes"].

44. McCormick, "Selecting the Supremes," *supra* note 43 at 14.

justices but even that has been bypassed for recent appointments.[45] However, the process is currently in flux with Prime Minister Justin Trudeau seeking to alter the process to make it more transparent.[46] The prime minister also appoints the chief justice, typically from justices on the Court, with a weak (possibly extinct) convention of appointing the most senior justice on the Court but also alternating between French and English-speaking justices.[47]

The Supreme Court is the final court of appeal in all civil and criminal matters in Canada, hearing appeals from the federal court system as well as the provincial and territorial courts. The Court must hear certain criminal appeals (these are termed "appeals as of right") where there is a dissent on the court of appeal or the court of appeal overturns an acquittal.[48] However, the Court has control over most of its docket as all other cases require the Court to grant leave to appeal before it hears the case.[49] Three justices hear each leave-to-appeal application, with the test being whether the appeal raises an issue of "public importance." In addition, the federal and provincial governments can refer issues for the Court to decide.[50] For example, the federal government referred to the Court the question of whether its plan to create a national securities regulator was constitutional.[51] This practice stands in contrast to the US Supreme Court, which cannot decide a legal question unless there is an actual "case or controversy" being disputed by directly affected parties.[52]

The Supreme Court of Canada hears appeals *en banc* or in panels of five or seven justices.[53] The chief justice determines both the size of the panel for a

45. Benjamin Alarie & Andrew Green, "Policy Preference Change and Appointments to the Supreme Court of Canada" (2009) 47 *Osgoode Hall LJ* 1 at 7–8 [Alarie & Green "Policy Preference"]; Adam M. Dodek, "Reforming the Supreme Court Appointment Process, 2004–2014: A 10-Year Democratic Audit" (2014) 67 *The Supreme Court Law Review: Osgoode's Annual Constitutional Cases Conference* 111. In 2014, Prime Minister Harper dispensed with the parliamentary review altogether to appoint Justice Gascon, following a decision from the Supreme Court that a nominated candidate was ineligible to sit on the Court.

46. See Chapter 3 for a more detailed discussion of appointments in Canada.

47. Peter McCormick, "Choosing the Chief: Duality, Seniority, and Beyond" (2013) 47:1 *Journal of Canadian Studies* 5 at 6.

48. *Criminal Code*, RS C 1985, c C-46, s 691.

49. *Supreme Court Act* Canada, *supra* note 41, s 40(1).

50. *Supreme Court Act* Canada, *supra* note 41, ss 36, 53.

51. *Reference Re Securities Act*, 2011 SCC 66, [2011] SCR 837.

52. U.S. Const. art, III, § 2, cl, 1.

53. *Supreme Court Act* Canada, *supra* note 41 ("[a]ny five of the judges of the Court shall constitute a quorum and may lawfully hold the Court," s 25).

particular appeal and which justices will hear the appeal. Before 1975, when the docket was composed largely of appeals as of right, the Court mainly used panels of five. However, after the Supreme Court gained control over most of its docket through the leave-to-appeal process, the average panel size has increased.[54]

The Canadian Supreme Court appears to be more of a strategic or possibly almost a deliberative court relative to the United States. Unlike earlier justices of the Supreme Court of Canada (prior to the 1990s)[55], justices of the Court in recent years have not voted as clearly in line with their personal policy preferences as US Supreme Court justices.[56] However, justices do appear to vote in line with their personal views to a greater extent in certain areas of law such as search and seizure and some Charter cases.[57] If we look at the range of lifetime liberal voting rates over the 30-year period starting in 1970 shown in Figure 1-2, the Supreme Court of Canada was much less polarized than the US Supreme Court and on par with the UK and Australia. Canadian justices then appear only mildly ideologically committed in most areas of law relative to US justices.[58]

Further, Supreme Court of Canada judges very often agree unanimously on decisions. Recently, for example, Chief Justice McLachlin has made a conscious

54. McCormick, "Selecting the Supremes," *supra* note 43 at 11.

55. Donald E. Fouts, "Policy-Making in the Supreme Court of Canada, 1950–1960" in Glendon Schubert & David Danelski, eds, *Comparative Judicial Behavior: Cross-Cultural Studies of Political Decision-Making in the East and West* (New York: Oxford University Press, 1969) 257 ("[o]ur analysis has shown that the Supreme Court of Canada resembles its U.S. counterpart in significant respects [...] its decisional philosophy is strikingly similar to that espoused in the U.S. Court a generation earlier. The behavioral analysis [...] serves to challenge the orthodox positivist view that the judges merely discover and apply the law" at 284); Peter McCormick, "Birds of a Feather: Alliances and Influences on the Lamer Court 1990–1997" (1998) 36 *Osgoode Hall Law Journal* 339 [McCormick, "Birds of a Feather"]; Peter McCormick, "Blocs, Swarms, and Outliers: Conceptualizing Disagreement on the Modern Supreme Court of Canada" (2004) 42:1 *Osgoode Hall Law Journal* 42 99 at 137.

56. Alarie & Green "Policy Preference," *supra* note 45 at 42; C.L. Ostberg & Matthew E. Wetstein, *Attitudinal Decision Making in the Supreme Court of Canada* (Vancouver: University of British Columbia Press, 2007) at 191–192 [Ostberg & Wetstein, *Attitudinal Decision Making*].

57. C.L. Ostberg & Matthew E. Wetstein, "Search and Seizure Cases in the Supreme Court of Canada: Extending an American Model of Judicial Decision Making across Countries" (1999) 80:4 *Social Science Quarterly* 757; Benjamin Alarie & Andrew Green, "Charter Decisions in the McLachlin Era: Consensus and Ideology at the Supreme Court of Canada" (2009) 47 *Supreme Court Law Review* 475 at 500–501.

58. Matthew E. Wetstein et al., "Ideological Consistency and the Attitudinal Conflict: A Comparative Analysis of the U.S. and Canadian Supreme Courts" (2009) 42:6 *Comparative Political Studies* 763.

effort to reduce disagreement where possible, leading the recent Court to be reputed to be more cooperative than the Court in the 1970s.[59] Figures 1-3 and 1-4 show that even in the 1970s through the 2000s, the Supreme Court of Canada had a much lower percentage of judgments with at least one dissent and fraction of dissenting opinions than the US Supreme Court and was between the United States and Australia on the high side and the UK and India on the low side on both these measures. Voting alliances on the Court in recent years appear quite fluid with the Court becoming more consensus-oriented in recent years.[60] The Court therefore may have shifted over time from a more attitudinal court toward its current strategic or deliberative form relative to the US Supreme Court.

## India

The Indian Supreme Court began in 1950 with eight judges faced with about 1,000 petitions per year and holding 225 regular hearings in 1951. By 2010, the Court consisted of up to 31 judges receiving almost 70,000 applications and holding over 7,500 regular hearings.[61] The number of judges on the Court increased in increments over time,[62] and this growth was closely related to the growth in the number of cases. The increase in the Court's workload was in part due to the Court expanding public interest litigation, through which citizens can seek direct access to the Court without going through the lower court system.[63] The Indian Supreme Court plays a key role in India (and potentially the world, in view of the size of the Indian population and economy) given a perception that other institutions are weak, such as the lower courts.[64]

The chief justice and the four most senior members of the Court select the new judges, although the president of India formally makes the appointments.[65] The

59. Emmett Macfarlane, "Consensus and Unanimity at the Supreme Court of Canada" (2010) 52 *Supreme Court Law Review* 379 at 385.

60. McCormick, "Birds of a Feather," *supra* note 55 at 1.

61. See Nick Robinson, "Structure Matters: The Impact of Court Structure on the Indian and U.S. Supreme Courts" (2013) 61:1 *American Journal of Comparative Law* 173 at 180–181 [Robinson, "Structure Matters"].

62. The number of justices rose from eight in 1950 to 11 in 1956, 14 in 1960, 17 in 1977, 26 in 1986, and 31 in 2008. See Robinson, "Structure Matters," *supra* note 61 at 182.

63. Robinson, "Structure Matters," *supra* note 61 at 181.

64. Robinson, "Structure Matters," *supra* note 61.

65. Robinson, "Structure Matters," *supra* note 61 at 187.

chief justice is traditionally the most senior member of the Court.[66] Two new laws create a Judicial Appointments Commission that would include the chief justice, the two next most senior justices, the Minister in Charge of Laws and Justice and two others appointed by the prime minister, the chief justice, and the leader of the opposition.[67] The Supreme Court recently found these laws to be unconstitutional and embarked on its own review of the appointment process.[68]

The Indian Supreme Court sits on top of a court structure, followed by the High Courts and then District Courts of the states and union territories. The Court both hears appeals and is the first court to hear some cases (including certain fundamental rights cases and disputes between states or the federal government and states).[69] The vast majority of its caseload is made up of appeals that are heard as a result of special leave petitions.[70] The Court hears these petitions in panels of two judges and has accepted between 15 percent and 26 percent of petitions for hearing in recent years.[71] The number of petitions increased between 2005 and 2011 (up 44 percent) but significantly, the number of acceptances of such petitions increased even more (74.5 percent) over the period.[72]

The Court hears cases in panels. Most panels are composed of two to three justices though some panels have five or more justices.[73] The number of panels of five or more justices has decreased over time from about 100 per year in the 1960s to about 9 per year in recent years.[74] The chief justice has discretion to set the size and composition of the panels, although if panel members decide that the matter should be heard by a larger panel than was originally set they can request that the chief justice set a larger panel.[75] Robinson speaks of an "automated" system that the chief justice can override.[76] With such a high caseload, it would seem logical that the chief justice does not personally assign a

66. Robinson, "Structure Matters," *supra* note 61 at 186.

67. *Constitution (One Hundred and Twentieth Amendment) Bill, 2013; Judicial Appointments Bill, 2013.*

68. See Chapter 3 for a more detailed discussion of the appointment process.

69. *The Constitution of India 1950*, arts 132–136.

70. Nick Robinson, "A Quantitative Analysis of the Indian Supreme Court's Workload" (2013) 10:3 *Journal of Empirical Legal Studies* 570 at 571–572 [Robinson, "Quantitative Analysis"].

71. Robinson, "Quantitative Analysis," *supra* note 70 at 581, 588.

72. Robinson, "Quantitative Analysis," *supra* note 70 at 581.

73. Robinson, "Structure Matters," *supra* note 61 at 176, 183.

74. Robinson, "Structure Matters," *supra* note 61 at 183.

75. *Supreme Court Rules 1966*, Order VI, Rules 1, 2.

76. Robinson, "Structure Matters," *supra* note 61 at 187.

panel for every case. However, it is not clear just how often chief justices do, in practice, handpick panels for particular cases. In recent years some specialist panels have been set up for issues such as the environment and tax.[77] The system of precedent attempts to take account of the size of the Court and the size of panels by requiring that panels follow decisions of panels of the same size or larger.[78] Combining this system of precedent with the power of the chief justice to set panel size and composition potentially gives the chief justice considerable power to influence change.

The Indian Supreme Court is therefore set up in a starkly different fashion than courts in other countries. In the face of increasing demand for the Court to hear appeals, the number of judges was increased and the panel size was kept small rather than making it harder for cases to be heard by the Court. Perhaps because of these institutional choices, the Court appears to be a strategic court. According to Robinson, judges on the Court "are viewed as less politicized than in the United States."[79] However, other studies have found that at least in cases involving the government and private parties, judges may vote in line with their personal views.[80] For instance, Justice Pasayat was frequently willing to uphold a death sentence for serious crimes such as rape and murder, but when Justice Sinha decided death penalty cases he interpreted the jurisprudence so that the death penalty "would almost never be imposed."[81] Figure 1-2 points toward this intermediate level of politicization at least on the measure of polarization of lifetime liberal voting rates. India has the second highest range in lifetime liberal voting rates based on a sample of 100 cases per year over the period 1970 to 2000, lower than the United States but considerably higher than the UK, Canada, or Australia.

There is at the same time a very high rate of unanimity (consistently over 90 percent of the cases are unanimous[82] or, put another way, a very low rate of decisions with at least one dissent (see Figure 1-3)) and an extremely low fraction of dissenting opinions (Figure 1-4). There are many possible reasons for this unanimity including that there is a culture of "dissent aversion" (with junior judges deferring

77. Robinson, "Structure Matters," *supra* note 61 at 191.

78. Robinson, "Structure Matters," *supra* note 61 at 187; Robinson, "Quantitative Analysis," *supra* note 70 at 582 notes that the growth in the applications for leave (relative to a lower growth in lower court decisions) may indicate that litigants view the supreme court panels as inconsistent despite the precedent system.

79. Robinson, "Structure Matters," *supra* note 61 at 187, 190.

80. George H. Gadbois, Jr., "Indian Judicial Behaviour" (1970) 5:3 *Economic and Political Weekly* 149 [Gadbois, "Indian Judicial Behaviour"].

81. Robinson, "Structure Matters," *supra* note 61 at 185.

82. Gadbois, "Indian Judicial Behaviour," *supra* note 80 at 187.

to senior),[83] a sense of "brotherhood" because judges already on the court select the new judges,[84] and a very heavy workload. The Court therefore appears to be more collegial than the US Supreme Court, and likely on the strategic side rather than the deliberative.

## United Kingdom

The United Kingdom high court underwent a significant change in 2005. Prior to 2005, the Appellate Committee of the House of Lords was the highest court. The lord chancellor and the prime minister selected its members, almost always from the Court of Appeal. Although the lord chancellor consulted with the judiciary and the legal profession, there were "no appointment hearings, no merit-based appointments, and no published selection criteria."[85] The Court of Appeal sat on civil and criminal appeals from English, Northern Irish, and Scottish courts (other than criminal appeals from Scottish courts).[86] In general, parties needed leave to appeal from the House of Lords, with three law lords deciding that the issue raises "a point of law of general importance."[87]

Reforms in 2005 replaced the Appellate Committee of the House of Lords with the Supreme Court of the United Kingdom (UKSC).[88] The UKSC has 12 members who are nominated by the lord chancellor and confirmed by the prime minister.[89] A judicial selection commission chooses candidates for nomination.[90] The commission must include the president of the Supreme Court,

83. Robinson, "Structure Matters," *supra* note 61 at 186.

84. Robinson, "Structure Matters," *supra* note 61 at 187.

85. Chris Hanretty, "Political Preferment in English Judicial Appointment, 1880–2005" (2012) American Political Science Association 2012 Annual Meeting Paper 1 at 2 [Hanretty, "Political Preferment"].

86. Hanretty, "Political Preferment," *supra* note 85 at 4. Each of England and Wales, Northern Ireland, and Scotland has a court system, which for the most part the UK House of Lords and now the UK Supreme Court sits above.

87. Sangeeta Shah & Thomas M. Poole, "The Impact of the Human Rights Act on the House of Lords" (2009) LSE Law, Society and Economy Working Paper No 8/2009 [Shah & Poole]. Leave to appeal can also be granted in some cases by lower courts.

88. *Constitutional Reform Act* 2005 (UK), c 4 [*CRA*]. The Supreme Court actually came into being in 2009.

89. *CRA*, *supra* note 88, ss 23(2), 26–29. Her Majesty may increase the number of judges upon Parliamentary approval: *CRA*, *supra* note 88, ss 23(3), (4).

90. Chris Hanretty, "Lumpers and Splitters on the United Kingdom Supreme Court" (2013) American Political Science Association 2013 Annual Meeting Paper, 4 [Hanretty, "Lumpers and Splitters"].

a senior UK justice nominated by the president, and a member of the judicial appointments commissions of England and Wales, Scotland, and Northern Ireland.[91] Both the lord chancellor and the commission are required to undertake consultations. The commission submits a selection to the lord chancellor who in effect has the power to reject one candidate, but then must submit the commission's subsequent selection to the prime minister.[92]

The UKSC continues as the court of appeal for England, Wales, Northern Ireland, and, for the most part, Scotland.[93] It also reviews exercises of statutory power granted by the UK parliament to the legislative and executive bodies in England, Wales, Scotland, and Northern Ireland ("devolution" matters).[94] In addition, UKSC may hear direct appeals from the High Court or the Divisional Court in England or Wales or the High Court in Northern Ireland where the matter involves a point of law of general importance that is related to the construction of a statute.[95] It heard about 60 cases per year in its first three full years, which is similar to the number of cases heard in the mid-2000s by the House of Lords, but higher than the 40 to 50 cases heard per year in the 1990s.[96] The caseload has gradually increased; in the period from April 1, 2013, to March 31, 2014, it heard 120 appeals.[97]

The Supreme Court does not have complete control over its docket. From April 1, 2013, to March 31, 2014, 37 of the 120 appeals heard by the Supreme Court were as of right, that is, appeals that the Supreme Court was required to hear.[98] Appeals from decisions of the Courts of Appeal in England and Wales or Northern Ireland

91. *CRA, supra* note 88, schedule 8, ss. 1–3; updated requirements in *The Supreme Court (Judicial Appointments) Regulations 2013*, SI 2013/2193, part 3.

92. *CRA, supra* note 88, ss 28–31.

93. Hanretty, "Lumpers and Splitters," *supra* note 90 at 4, the exception being certain criminal appeals from Scotland.

94. These issues, and the procedure to refer questions about them to the Supreme Court, are defined by the *Government of Wales Act 2006* (UK), c 32; *Scotland Act 1998* (UK), c 46; *Northern Ireland Act 1998,* (UK), c 47.

95. *Administration of Justice Act 1969* (UK), c 58, s. 12. There are also direct appeals where the matter involves a point of law of general importance that was previously considered by the Court of Appeal or House of Lords, by whose precedent the trial judge is bound.

96. Lorne Neudorf, "Intervention at the UK Supreme Court" (2013) 2:1 *Cambridge Journal of International and Comparative Law* 16, at 25–27. The UKSC heard between 58 and 63 cases in its first three full years and the UK House of Lords heard between 56 and 74 cases between 2005 and 2008. See also Shah & Poole, *supra* note 87 at 15. The House of Lords heard about 40–50 cases per year in the later 1990s with an increase to between about 50 and 74 in 2001–2007.

97. UK, HC, *The Supreme Court Annual Report and Accounts 2013–2014*, at 24 (June 9, 2014) [*SC Annual Report*].

98. *SC Annual Report, supra* note 97 at 26.

require permission from either the Court of Appeal or the Supreme Court (with application to the Supreme Court only where the Court of Appeal has rejected the petition). Appeals from decisions of the High Courts in England and Wales or Northern Ireland, on the other hand, require both certification by the High Court and permission of the Supreme Court. Finally, no permission is generally required to appeal from decisions of the Court of Session in Scotland, only certification by two counsel that the appeal is reasonable.[99] Leave to appeal applications are heard by a "permission to appeal" (PTA) committee of three justices with the composition determined by the staff of the Judicial Office.[100] The appeal must raise an arguable point of law of general public importance.[101]

The UKSC typically hears appeals in panels of five, seven, or nine justices, with panels of five being the most common.[102] The president of the Court can decide the panel size and composition.[103] Although the House of Lords generally decided cases with seriatim opinions, this practice has changed with the UKSC, which has tended to have more opinions entered into by a number of justices (including many where all the justices join together in a single opinion).[104]

Of all the courts, the UK Supreme Court seems most likely characterized as a deliberative court (see Figure 1-5). Few studies have found much of a connection between judicial voting and markers of personal views or ideology.[105] Arvind and Stirton argue that the courts in the UK are less likely to exhibit a liberal/conservative divide than the United States because of differences in the cases they hear.[106] The UKSC hears more private law cases than the US Supreme Court and fewer challenges to statutes. Arvind and Stirton argue that the former cases are less likely to lead to a left/right split whereas the latter are

99. One exception is that leave to appeal is required where the lower court (Court of Session) was unanimous or dismissed the claim on a preliminary point without hearing the merits.

100. The Supreme Court of the United Kingdom, Practice Direction 3.1.1; Alan Paterson, *Final Judgment: The Last Law Lords and the Supreme Court* (Oxford: Hart, 2013) at 67–69 [Paterson].

101. The Supreme Court of the United Kingdom, Practice Direction 3.3.3.

102. Hanretty, "Lumpers and Splitters," *supra* note 90 at 4. Panels must consist of an uneven number of justices (at least three), and more than half the panel must be permanent justices (*CRA, supra* note 88, s 42).

103. *CRA, supra* note 88, s 42.

104. Hanretty, "Lumpers and Splitters," *supra* note 90 at 3–4.

105. See e.g. Brice Dickson, "The Processing of Appeals in the House of Lords" (2007) 123:4 *Law Quarterly Review* 571; Hanretty, "Lumpers and Splitters," *supra* note 90.

106. T.T. Arvind & Lindsay Stirton, "Lawyers and the Legal Model: Judicial Ideology, Judicial Professionalism and Institutional Strategy among the Law Lords" (2012) at 21, online: https://extranet.sioe.org/uploads/isnie2012/arvind_stirton.pdf [Arvind & Stirton].

more likely to result in such a split. Further, Hanretty has found that there was only a weak connection between the background of justices in the House of Lords between 1969 and 2009 and how they voted in cases. He argued that the differences across justices may be more reflective of their relative willingness to dissent than their willingness to vote in line with their personal views.[107] In terms of polarization (Figure 1-2), the UK House of Lords was at the low end with Canada and Australia in terms of the median range of lifetime liberal voting rates on the court between 1970 and the early 2000s, although it did have some years of a greater spread in voting rates.

In terms of cooperation, the UK had the second lowest rate of opinions with at least one dissent among the countries we examined (behind India, which has a higher caseload) when its highest court was the House of Lords (Figure 1-3).[108] Further, as can be seen from Figure 1-4, the UK House of Lords had a significantly lower fraction of dissenting opinions than the other high courts except for the Indian Supreme Court. It is too soon to say whether the UKSC will exhibit a higher or lower rate of dissent in the long term: Hanretty observed that the average unanimity rate from 2009 to 2012 was 75 percent (down from 82 percent during the preceding House of Lords period),[109] but when Lord Neuberger took over as Supreme Court president in 2012 the dissent rate dropped again.[110] Along with a high unanimity rate, there is an increasing rate of single judgment decisions although there are still a considerable number of multiple concurring opinions.[111] A norm of "professionalism" (in the form of an unwillingness to dissent) may have kept the agreement rate high in the past.[112] Although the greater number of nine-judge panels and an increase in the number of human rights case may threaten the norm of consensus, the UKSC is currently maintaining a high rate of cooperation.[113]

107. Chris Hanretty, "The Decisions and Ideal Points of British Law Lords" (2012) 43 *British Journal of Political Science* 703 at 703–704 [Hanretty, "Ideal Points"].

108. Hanretty, "Ideal Points," *supra* note 107 at 706. The unanimity rate is approximately 80 percent.

109. Chris Hanretty, "Dissent on the UKSC, update" (August 28, 2012), *Odd Bits of Quantitative Political Science* (blog), online: Chrishanretty.co.uk/blog/index.php/2012/08/28/dissent-on-the-uksc-update.

110. Kate Dowell, "Judicial Dissent Wanes under Neuberger Regime at UK Supreme Court," *The Lawyer* (April 23. 2014), online: www.thelawyer.com/news/practice-areas/litigation-news/judicial-dissent-wanes-under-neuberger-regime-at-uk-supreme-court/3019664.article.

111. Paterson, *supra* note 100 at 107, 113–114.

112. Arvind & Stirton, *supra* note 106 at 5, 35–39.

113. Hanretty, "Ideal Points," *supra* note 107 at 716.

## CONCLUSION

High courts both are designed and decide in very different ways in different countries. Figure 1-5 suggests that justices on the high courts of the various countries behave differently in terms of ideological commitment and cooperation. Some of these courts hear decisions in panels, some do not; some have greater discretion than others in the cases they hear; some have greater involvement of political decision-makers in the appointment process than others. In this book, we look at the relationship between the design of courts and how they behave. We argue that design matters to how judges decide. Where a court sits in CC Space depends in part on how the court is set up.

A large number of studies examine how high court judges make decisions, such as the influence of policy preferences as opposed to the "law." However, it is difficult, if not impossible, to draw conclusions about judicial decision-making or make policy prescriptions for improving high courts without an understanding of how the institutional context impacts decision-making. Our interest is in examining the influence of institutional choices made by a particular country or court on how ideologically committed and cooperative are its judges.

The combination of design elements and the attendant location in CC Space has significant implications. First, certain combinations of design elements and location may offend notions of the rule of law. For example, a highly political court that hears appeals in small panels may mean that the outcome at the highest level of court will depend on the panel that hears the particular case. Although some variance across time and across panels is inevitable, adherence to the rule of law would seem to militate against such inconsistency or arbitrariness in outcomes. Second, the design choices and level of cooperation and commitment will also affect outcomes. Norms are a good example. If a court is cooperative but logrolling (vote trading) is the norm, or if a court has a norm of political appointments and deciding solely in accordance with individual political preferences, outcomes may be less likely to foster social welfare than norms that discourage such logrolling or political decision-making. Third, access to justice may be dampened in certain cases. For example, if the appointments system yields judges on a high court who are highly politicized and homogeneous, these judges may limit the ability of certain groups or classes of cases to get on the docket. Finally, the public's perception of the justice or fairness of a court's decisions may depend on both how cooperative and committed are its judges. High levels of disagreement, for example, may undermine both the legitimacy of and trust in a court.

We will spend the bulk of the book discussing the influence of different design features, including the appointments process (Chapter 3), the use of panels (Chapter 4), the relationship between judges and others such as their colleagues or the government (Chapter 5), the ability to choose the cases to hear (Chapter 6), the parties that appear before the court (Chapter 7), and the norms of the court (Chapter 8). However, before we embark upon that discussion, we first set out in Chapter 2 our understanding of the potential theoretical role of institutional factors on judicial decision-making.

# 2

# How Do Judges Decide?

Differences in how courts are designed—the numbers of judges, how the judges are selected, whether they decide cases in panels—create different incentives and options for how judges can decide cases. They can, for example, raise or lower the costs of a judge dissenting on an appeal. If a judge has to hear hundreds of appeals each year, she may not be as willing to take the time to write a dissenting opinion.[1] If she is on a panel of three judges, would she be more or less likely to dissent than if she were on a panel of nine judges? The answer may lie in how the other judges view dissent and whether they would hold the disagreement against a dissenting judge.

To compare across high courts, then, we need to understand two things. First, we need to understand what judges consider when they decide appeals. They likely consider many things—the law, their reputation, their preferred outcome, and the other personal and professional demands on their time. Each may be important at different times. Second, we need to think about how these factors interact with how courts are set up. Our hypothesis is that the design of the particular court is central to what judges consider in deciding appeals. Given the role of judges in making their own rules, however, it is not a simple causal story about court structures dictating outcomes. A court's design includes the rules set for a court by a legislature or Constitution, the formal rules and decisions made by the judges themselves about their own processes, and the norms of behavior on a particular court. How judges decide both is influenced by and influences the decision-making structure and processes. We will start with what judges think about when they decide.

1. Lee Epstein, William M. Landes & Richard A. Posner, *Behavior of Federal Judges: A Theoretical and Empirical Study of Rational Choice* (Cambridge, MA: Harvard University Press, 2013) [Epstein, Landes & Posner, *Behavior*] at 262.

Commitment and Cooperation on High Courts. Benjamin Alarie and Andrew J. Green.

## THEORIES OF HOW JUDGES DECIDE

Judges may consider very different things in making their decisions, from the relevant statutes to their relationships with other judges.[2] For our purposes, we will focus on four main explanations of how judges decide—the legal model, the attitudinal model, the strategic model, and the labor-market model.

Perhaps the most apparently common sense theory is the *legal model*. According to this theory, a judge decides cases according to the law. She may locate the correct legal answer by relying on precedents, on statutes, on the Constitution, or on a combination of all these sources.[3] In its narrowest form, the model views the judge's role as finding the law and applying it to the facts. In cases where the law does not provide a clear answer, the judge is to interpret the case law or statute in the manner most consistent with the aims of the case law or statute as a whole. As we saw in the example in Chapter 1, if the fictitious *Parks Act* prohibits "vehicles" in parks, the judge decides if a skateboard is a "vehicle" by looking at the purposes of the statute (to promote recreation? To foster quiet reflection?), what other judges have found to be "vehicles," and the nature of skateboard use. The key for the legal model is that the law decides the case without the judge attending to his or her own view of the best outcome.

The *attitudinal model*, on the other hand, sees the judge as following her own personal views of the best outcome in each case.[4] If a judge does not like skateboards in parks, he would find them to be "vehicles" under the *Parks Act*. If a judge has "liberal" policy preferences, he may be more likely to find in favor of

2. Posner has posited nine "overlapping, incomplete" theories of judicial decision-making: attitudinal, strategic (positive political theory), sociological, economic, psychological, organizational, pragmatic, phenomenological, and legal (Richard A. Posner, *How Judges Think* (Cambridge, MA: Harvard University Press, 2008), at 19, 57 [Posner, *How Judges Think*]); He then draws these theories together into a "labor-market" theory of judging (Posner, *How Judges Think, supra* note 2 at 57).

3. Posner, *How Judges Think, supra* note 2 at 41; Matthew Stephenson, "Legal Realism for Economists" (2009) 23 *Journal of Economic Perspectives* 191 at 194.

4. Jeffrey A. Segal & Harold J. Spaeth, *The Supreme Court and the Attitudinal Model Revisited* (Cambridge: Cambridge University Press, 2002) [Segal & Spaeth, *Attitudinal Model*]. The attitudinal model largely arose from US scholarship and has become a dominant model in empirical analysis. Some important early work on the attitudinal model include C. Herman Pritchett, *The Roosevelt Court: A Study in Judicial Politics and Values 1937–1947* (New York: Macmillan, 1948); Glendon Schubert, *The Judicial Mind: The Attitudes and Ideologies of Supreme Court Justices, 1946–1963* (New York: Northwestern University Press, 1965); Glendon Schubert, *The Judicial Mind Revisited: A Psychometric Analysis of Supreme Court Ideology* (Oxford: Oxford University Press, 1974); David W. Rohde & Harold J. Spaeth, *Supreme Court Decision Making* (San Francisco: W.H. Freeman, 1976).

an outcome of an appeal that encompasses a more expansive view of equality rights. The judge may consciously vote for the outcome that fits with his or her policy preferences or may unconsciously follow those preferences through unconsidered assumptions.[5] Personal preferences may not be the sole determinant of judges' decisions but they are an important influence. Judges have been found to at least partially follow their personal views on the US Supreme Court, though as we will see the influence is less clear on other high courts.[6]

How can we identify a judge's personal policy preferences? There are different indications such as the party of the individual (such as the president or prime minister) who appointed the judge, past decisions of the judge, and newspaper articles at the time of appointment.[7] However, none of these are perfect; none

5. Eric A. Posner, "Does Political Bias in the Judiciary Matter? Implications of Judicial Bias Studies for Legal and Constitutional Reform" (2008) 75 *University of Chicago Law Review* 853 (discussing the role of political bias in judicial decision-making as well as explicit and implicit bias).

6. The research on the attitudinal model in the United States is too vast to cite. See e.g. Segal & Spaeth, *Attitudinal Model, supra* note 4; Andrew D. Martin et al., "Competing Approaches to Predicting Supreme Court Decision Making" (2004) 2 *Perspectives on Politics* 761 [Martin et al, "Competing Approaches"]; Andrew D. Martin & Kevin M. Quinn, "Assessing Preference Change on the US Supreme Court" (2007) 23 *Journal of Law, Economics, and Organization* 303. In Canada, see e.g. Benjamin Alarie & Andrew Green, "Policy Preference Change and Appointments to the Supreme Court of Canada" (2009) 47 *Osgoode Hall LJ* 1 at 7–8 [Alarie & Green "Policy Preference"]; C.L. Ostberg & Matthew E. Wetstein, *Attitudinal Decision Making in the Supreme Court of Canada* (Vancouver: University of British Columbia Press, 2007) at 191–192 [Ostberg & Wetstein, *Attitudinal Decision Making*]; and Donald R. Songer et al., *Law, Ideology and Collegiality: Judicial Behaviour in the Supreme Court of Canada* (Montreal and Kingston: McGill University Press, 2012). In Australia, see Rebecca Wood Gill, Jason L. Pierce & David L. Weiden, "Empirical and Legal Trends at the High Court of Australia" (Paper delivered at Southwest Political Science Association Meetings, 2011), online: http://ssrn.com/abstract=1985814.

7. Party of the appointing president or prime minister has been a long-standing proxy for policy preference. See Nancy C. Staudt, Lee Epstein & Peter Wiedenbeck, "The Ideological Component of Judging in the Taxation Context" (2006) 84 *Washington University Law Review* 1797 (describing methods that have been used to estimate policy preferences of judges in the United States); Alarie & Green "Policy Preference," *supra* note 6. Segal and Cover developed ideology scores in the United States based on newspaper editorials at the time the justice was appointed. See Jeffrey A. Segal & Albert D. Cover, "Ideological Values and Votes of U.S. Supreme Court Justices" (1989) 83 *American Political Science Review* 557. Ostberg & Wetstein, *Attitudinal Decision Making, supra* note 6 developed similar scores in Canada. Ideal points were developed and have been applied in the United States by American political scientists Andrew Martin and Martin Quinn (see e.g. Andrew D. Martin & Kevin M. Quinn, "Dynamic Ideal Point Estimation via Markov Chain Monte Carlo for the U.S. Supreme Court, 1953–1999" (2002) 10:2 *Political Analysis* 134) and have been applied in Canada (see e.g. Alarie & Green "Policy Preference," *supra* note 6), although these scores merely situate a justice in a unidimensional policy space relative to other justices.

completely captures the range of sources or types of a judge's personal views from his political preferences (liberal versus conservative) to a bias in favor of his home state.[8]

A third explanation for how judges decide is the *strategic model*, which is related to the attitudinal model.[9] In both models, the judge decides an appeal at least in part based on her own personal policy preferences. However, under the strategic model, the judge takes into account not only her preferred outcome in the particular appeal but also the likely reaction of others such as other judges on the panel, lower courts, or the legislature. A judge may, for example, agree with a fellow judge that a skateboard is a vehicle because she wants to maintain her relationship with that judge in future cases.[10] The judge factors in these broader impacts of the decision to ensure that her personal preferences are met not just in the individual appeal but over all the decisions she cares about.

These three models describe opposite ends of the spectrum for judicial decision-making—either law controls the decision (the legal model) or the judge decides according to his or her own policy preferences directly (the attitudinal model) or more indirectly (the strategic model). However, as Posner notes, none of these models seem to capture all that influences a judge's decision.[11] The law cannot completely determine every question that a judge has to decide. There are ambiguities in statutes or precedents that do not permit a clear determination. Moreover, judges have discretion in some cases that potentially provides them with the ability to decide in accordance with other factors than the "law." Even if a judge wants to rely on precedents, she generally has a choice

8. Epstein, Landes & Posner, *Behavior, supra* note 1 at 89.

9. On the strategic model, see e.g. Lee Epstein & Jack Knight, *The Choices Justices Make* (Washington, DC: CQ Press, 1998); Segal & Spaeth, *Attitudinal Model, supra* note 4; Thomas H. Hammond, Chris W. Bonneau & Reginald S. Sheehan, *Strategic Behavior and Policy Choice on the US Supreme Court* (Stanford, CA: Stanford University Press, 2005); and Forrest Maltzman, James F. Spriggs II & Paul J. Wahlbeck, *Crafting Law on the Supreme Court: The Collegial Game* (Cambridge: Cambridge University Press, 2000) [Maltzman, Spriggs & Wahlbeck, *Crafting Law*].

10. Segal & Spaeth, *Attitudinal Model, supra* note 4 ("[t]he effort involved in these revisions [of the majority opinion to meet the dissent's points], and resentment at criticism by the dissenting judge, may impose a collegiality cost on him by making him less well liked by his colleagues, which may make it harder for him to persuade other judges to join his majority opinions in future cases" at 261); Lee Epstein, William M. Landes and Richard A. Posner, "Why (and When) Judges Dissent: A Theoretical and Empirical Analysis," (2011) 3:1 *Journal of Legal Analysis* 101. See also Lee Epstein & Tonja Jacobi, "The Strategic Analysis of Judicial Decisions" (2010) 6 *Annual Review of Law and Social Science* 341 at 344 [Epstein & Jacobi].

11. Posner, *How Judges Think, supra* note 2 at 57.

of which precedents to rely on, and in some cases judges appear to choose those cases in accordance with their ideological bent.[12]

On the other hand, judges do not appear to always rely on policy preferences. As we will see, judges in general seem to rely more on policy preferences in some areas such as civil rights and liberties than in others such as tax.[13] In addition, judges tend to vary over time in how they decide cases, rather than being perfectly predictable at the time of appointment. A judge may change, for example, because her own views have changed or because new judges have joined the court with different views.[14] Moreover, judges on some courts such as the US Supreme Court may be more influenced by their personal views than judges on other courts,[15] pointing to other factors than merely policy preferences playing a role in how judges decide, such as norms on the court.[16]

It may be, moreover, that focusing on whether a judge votes in a liberal or conservative direction blurs or obscures other important aspects of how judges decide. Fischman and Jacobi argue, for example, that there is a second dimension to judicial decision-making.[17] The judges on the US Supreme Court not only split on a liberal-conservative basis but also on legal methodology such as legalism as opposed to pragmatism. Further, Cameron and Kornhauser

12. Anthony Niblett & Albert H. Yoon, "Judicial Disharmony: A Study of Dissent" (2015) 42 *International Review of Law and Economics* 60.

13. In the United States, see Segal & Spaeth, *Attitudinal Model, supra* note 4; Martin et al., "Competing Approaches," *supra* note 6; Cass R. Sunstein et al., *Are Judges Political? An Empirical Analysis of the Federal Judiciary* (Washington, DC: Brookings Institution Press, 2006). In Canada, see Ostberg & Wetstein, *Attitudinal Decision Making, supra* note 6 at 191–99. Alarie & Green "Policy Preference," *supra* note 6; Benjamin Alarie & Andrew Green, "Charter Decisions in the McLachlin Era: Consensus and Ideology at the Supreme Court of Canada" (2009) 47 *Supreme Court Law Review* 475 at 500–501 (finding differences even across types of Charter cases).

14. See e.g. in the United States Lee Epstein et al., "Ideological Drift among Supreme Court Justices: Who, When and How Important?" (2007) 101:4 *Northwestern University Law Review* 1483 [Epstein et al., "Ideological Drift"]; in Canada, Alarie & Green "Policy Preference," *supra* note 6.

15. Ostberg & Wetstein, *Attitudinal Decision Making, supra* note 6 ("[a]lthough a substantial amount of attitudinal decision making appears in diverse areas of law in the post-Charter Court, especially in non-unanimous cases, the impact of ideology is not as crystal-clear or as systematic as that found in the US context" at 226); Alarie & Green "Policy Preference," *supra* note 6.

16. Posner, *How Judges Think, supra* note 2 at 42–43 notes that proponents of the attitudinal model and the strategic model did not claim it was the sole determinant of judicial decisions.

17. Joshua Fischman & Tonja Jacobi, "The Second Dimension of the Supreme Court" (2016) 57 *Wm. & Mary Law Review* 1671.

point to the attention a judge pays to the factual context of each case that is not accounted for in the current attitudinal approach to judicial decisions.[18]

Thus, it seems clear that judges are not solely driven either by their personal views narrowly conceived as particular policy outcomes or by legal considerations. Recognizing that these factors do not completely explain judges' decisions, Epstein, Landes, and Posner recently attempted to broaden the understanding of how judges decide through a *labor market theory* of judicial decision-making that takes account of how judges balance different factors.[19] The core of the theory is that a judge weighs all the costs and benefits of the decision. Judges take into account a wide range of factors including their job satisfaction (including a sense of accomplishment through maximizing policy preferences, and interpersonal relationships fostered by collegiality on the court), external satisfactions (such as reputation and power), leisure, wages and income from both judicial and nonjudicial work, and promotion.[20] There are cases in which ideology or values likely do not play a significant role, but there are others, such as where there is discretion or uncertainty, where they almost certainly do. The labor market theory then views judges as concerned with an additional interesting set of considerations beyond either the law or policy preferences, such as the desire for leisure or collegiality. In fact, following the law on this view may become merely a part of preferences.

Realistically, judges, as with all individuals, decide based on a complex set of factors and preferences. In this book we will in part work from something close to the labor market model of Epstein, Landes, and Posner. We view judges as consciously or unconsciously balancing a range of competing factors. Similarly to the labor market model, we assume judges make decisions just like anyone else; whether it is purchasing a car, deciding whether to exercise, dealing with a co-worker, or deciding whether to write a dissent, people try to make the best decisions possible in light of a broad range of often conflicting considerations.

## WHAT INFLUENCES A JUDGE'S DECISION?

So, what do judges take into account? If we assume people are rational, an individual decides taking into account his preferences and the relative cost of

18. Charles M. Cameron & Lewis A. Kornhauser, "Rational Choice Attitudinalism? A Review of Epstein, Landes and Posner's 'The Behavior of Federal Judges: A Theoretical and Empirical Study of Rational Choice'" (2015) *European Journal of Law & Economics.*

19. Epstein, Landes & Posner, *Behavior, supra* note 1 at 30.

20. See also Lee Epstein & Jack Knight, "Reconsidering Judicial Preferences" (2013) 16 *Annual Review of Political Science* 11–31.

the possible options. He may mistake what is the right choice or may not have complete information, but the basic notion is that the individual attempts to maximize his well-being based on his preferences and various constraining factors. In choosing a car, for example, the individual would take into account the price of the car, its size, its power, and its color in accordance with her preferences across these issues and subject to her budget. To make it simpler to understand individuals' decisions, economics often assumes these preferences are fixed (unchanging) and that individuals do not consider wider issues such as the fairness of the decision (unless they have a taste for fairness).[21]

However, individuals may also consider broader concerns than the direct effects on themselves. They may, for example, consider how their choices impact how others view them—that is, their reputation. The costs and benefits of reputation come from others. A good reputation means others will accord one esteem, and can open up opportunities such as jobs or personal relationships. A bad reputation closes opportunities.[22] In addition to such external motivations, an individual may make choices based on his own internally enforced norms or values. He may experience guilt or pride when making particular decisions. These internal motivations may be based on the individual's identity or identities.[23] Society has social categories (such as man, woman, doctor, judge) that bring with them prescriptions about the type of behavior that is expected of individuals in that category.[24] Individuals can either have positive feelings or experience anxiety because of choices that do or do not fit with these prescriptions. Individuals may be able to choose their categories in some cases, and sometimes participate in the creation of these prescriptions through either reasoning or deliberation with others in the group.[25]

21. See e.g. Amartya Sen, *Rationality and Freedom* (Cambridge, MA: Harvard University Press, 2002) [Sen, *Rationality*].

22. There is a large literature on law, norms, and reputation. See e.g. Richard H. McAdams, "The Origin, Development and Regulations of Norms" (1997) 96 *Michigan Law Review* 338; Cass Sunstein, "Social Norms and Social Roles" (1996) 96 *Columbia Law Review* 903 [Sunstein, "Social Norms"]; Eric Posner, *Law and Social Norms* (Cambridge, MA: Harvard University Press, 2000).

23. See George Akerlof & Rachel Kranton, "Economics and Identity" (2000) 115 *Quarterly Journal of Economics* 71 [Akerlof & Kranton] (setting out the main economic theory of identity). See also K.A. Brekke, S. Kverndokk & K. Nyborg, "An Economic Model of Moral Motivation" (2003) 87 *Journal of Public Economics* 1967 for a related model of choice related to self-image.

24. For Akerlof & Kranton, *supra* note 23, identity refers to "both a person's self-image as well as her assigned categories" at 718.

25. Akerlof & Kranton, *supra* note 23. See also Claire Hill, "The Law and Economics of Identity" (2007) 32:2 *Queen's LJ* 389.

In the case of both reputation and internal motivations, an individual's choice imposes a cost or provides a benefit beyond the direct effects of the choice itself. If we return to the car example, we note that an individual may benefit from buying a large car because of its roominess, comfort, or safety but may also experience broader costs or benefits. To some it may be a symbol of high social status tied to reputation, but also result in a sense of guilt due to its high fuel consumption. The individual then chooses based on the direct costs and benefits from the choice itself, from the effect on the individual's reputation and from the impact on the individual's own sense of identity.

Judges are no different. A judge's decision in a particular case is influenced by the direct costs and benefits of the decision on the judge given her preferences, the effect of the decision on her reputation, and how the decision fits with the particular judge's identity or identities. In order to understand differences across judges and high courts, we can break these factors down into five elements that affect judges' decisions: policy preferences, reputation, identity, financial/material compensation, and leisure.

## Policy Preferences

As we have seen, a judge may decide on an appeal because a particular result fits with his personal views or preferences about the outcome.[26] He may prefer the result for two main reasons: because he prefers a specific outcome in this case, or because deciding in a particular way furthers his broader goals. That a judge may prefer a specific outcome on an issue is straightforward, at least in theory. It is at the core of the attitudinal and strategic models of judicial decision-making. The judge cares about the impact of his vote—what will happen to individuals or to public policy as a result of finding for one side or the other. Will a vote overturning a search significantly limit the powers of the police? Will a development permit lead to loss of environmentally sensitive land? Will finding a skateboard not to be a vehicle lead to non-skateboarders not feeling safe in parks? These preferences may accord with political positions, but they do not have to tie into politics. It is merely how the judge would prefer the issue at the core of the case to turn out. The judge does not necessarily have to be self-interested or self-centered. She could care about how the policy will impact others but the focus is on the result of the specific issue in the appeal.

26. Preferences are not an entirely clear concept in economics. They encompass tastes, values, mental satisfaction, or some combination of these or other factors. For a discussion of the meaning of preferences, see e.g. Sen, *Rationality, supra* note 21 at 303–305; Sunstein, "Social Norms," *supra* note 22 at 938–939.

The second, broader reason a judge may prefer a particular result in an appeal stems from preferences about preferences—or what are often called second-order preferences.[27] For example, a person may have a second-order preference to be healthy, which drives other choices such as whether to drive her car or ride a bike. In the case of a judge, his second order preferences could include a preference for upholding precedent or maintaining the legitimacy of the court.[28] Such preferences then influence how he views the particular outcome. Consider *Bush v. Gore*—the US Supreme Court case about whether a recount of votes in Florida during the 2000 presidential election was constitutional. A judge may prefer the Democratic candidate (Gore) to win the election. If he only cared about this direct result, he would find the recount constitutional. However, the judge may also care about the reputation of the Court, which may make him unwilling to find the recount unconstitutional if there are prior decisions of the Court that point in the other direction. It may not overcome his concern about the direct policy outcome in the appeal but it influences his decision. The judge then will balance how the choice relates to his direct outcome preferences with the impact on the legitimacy of the court if he votes for his preferred option in the face of "clear" law or precedent.

## Reputation

People often care a lot about their reputation, and it may drive their choices. As we saw, an individual cares about how a choice will affect her reputation because others may think better or worse of her or may interact with her differently. A judge may care about how a particular decision will look to many different groups—what Baum calls "audiences."[29] For our purposes, we can separate these audiences into two groups: internal and external to the court.

The internal audience is other judges on the court. A judge may be concerned about how the other judges will react to the actual policy decision resulting from her preferred choice.[30] She may care also about how the other judges

27. These preferences may also be called meta-preferences (Sen, *Rationality, supra* note 21 at 17–18).

28. Richard A. Posner, "Judicial Behavior and Performance: An Economic Approach" (2005) 32 *Florida State University Law Review* 1259 at 1275 (arguing that judges care about following precedent in part because the strength of the system of precedent will determine whether their decisions will be followed).

29. Lawrence Baum, *Judges and Their Audiences* (Princeton, NJ: Princeton University Press, 2008).

30. Epstein, Landes & Posner, *Behavior, supra* note 1 at 42–43.

will perceive a judge who votes for her own policy preference despite a cost to the legitimacy of the court. Further, she may care about collegiality—that is, the extent to which she is viewed as seeking consensus or always dissenting. A judge's choices may impact not only what other colleagues think of her but also opportunities for her to cooperate with or persuade other judges in future cases.

A judge's external audience consists of those outside of the court, which includes a very broad range of possible groups. A judge who wishes to be viewed positively by the legal profession may be less likely to decide in accordance with her preferred policy position, if she thinks doing so would be viewed unfavorably. She may also be concerned about how she is perceived by her family or by political or interest groups—anything from the Chamber of Commerce to Friends of the Earth. Again her choices may influence the esteem in which she is held or possible future opportunities such as working as an arbitrator or on corporate boards or giving lectures after she leaves the court. In addition, a judge may be concerned about her reputation with legislators or the executive if it may impact future opportunities such as being promoted to the position of chief justice. More broadly, a judge may care about her legacy, wanting to be remembered as being on the "right side of history."

## Identity

A judge may be influenced not only by his reputation with others but also with how his choices affect his view of himself. Do certain choices provide him with a sense of guilt or pride? We will think of this factor in terms of identity. A judge may have a number of different identities that influence his decisions. He may care about how he should act as a Catholic or Republican or an American or a male. His decision in an abortion case may, for example, implicate his identity as a judge but also as a Catholic. Each of these categories brings with it assumptions about how the judge should decide a particular case and may even structure how the judge interprets the facts on which the case is based.[31]

Of particular interest is the judge's identity as a judge. A judge may feel guilt if she does not follow precedent. It may not override her concern about the ultimate policy choice or her relationship with other judges, but it may factor into her choice as a cost of a particular option. The prescriptions that come with the category of "judge" will vary across countries. A judge in the United States, for example, may view it as more acceptable to draw on her personal views than

31. See Dan Kahan et al., "'Ideology' or 'Situation Sense'? An Experimental Investigation of Motivated Reasoning and Professional Judgment" (2016) 116 *University of Pennsylvania Law Review* 349 [Kahan] (on cognitive basis for how different people view the same facts differently).

does a judge in the UK. A judge in India may see it as part of his job to find consensus and deliberate with other judges whereas, alternatively, a judge in Australia may prioritize deciding independently.

## Financial/Material Compensation

A judge on a high court should not, in theory, have to worry about the immediate financial implications of her decisions. To the extent that high courts are meant to be independent of the government of the day, a judge's salary as judge should not depend on how she decides any particular case (unlike potentially a lower court judge whose decisions could conceivably be influenced by the hope of elevation to a higher court with potentially higher pay). Of course, we can imagine institutional arrangements where a non-independent or only partially independent body determines pay increases or other aspects of judicial compensation (such as court infrastructure) or perks (such as travel, food, or housing). In such cases, judges may view the court's budget as hinging on the court's relationship with the body, which may in turn influence their decisions. Such a connection between judicial decisions and material compensation would strike at the heart of judicial independence but would not be unheard of.

As Epstein, Landes, and Posner point out, judges may also be concerned about their extrajudicial income or compensation.[32] As judges, they may be paid for speaking or other engagements or they may write books and obtain royalties. This compensation is obviously closely connected to the judge's reputation—that is, his reputation may lead to more or fewer opportunities to earn extrajudicial income.

## Leisure

Finally, a judge's choices may mean more or less work, and she may be influenced by the balance of work and leisure.[33] Deciding whether to write decisions, whether to dissent, whether to take up a particular appeal to be heard, and even the overall number of cases to be heard by the court all tilt this balance one way or the other. The balance of work and leisure may also be tipped by the willingness of a judge to rely on signals of the preferred outcome, such as the type and number of interveners in an appeal. Each judge will have her own preference for

32. Epstein, Landes & Posner, *Behavior, supra* note 1 at 30–31.

33. Epstein, Landes & Posner, *Behavior, supra* note 1 at 31. Epstein, Landes, and Posner include leisure as an explicit element in the judicial utility function.

leisure versus work, but added work has a cost that a judge will take into account to a greater or lesser extent in making different types of decisions.

We assume that a judge will take into account these different factors in making choices, including decisions in appeals. As we will see below, although judges balance these factors in the particular legal context of the appeal, the influence of each factor depends on how the particular court is designed, including both the formal rules and the informal norms. However, before we discuss the design, there is one other point about how each judge reaches a decision. Although we assume judges are essentially rational in how they balance these factors, we will also have to keep in mind two key obstacles facing judges: they are limited in how rational they can be, and they often lack full information about an appeal.[34]

Judges, like all individuals, may not make decisions that are fully rational in all cases, such as where they rely on shortcuts (or heuristics) in making decisions. For example, an individual making a potentially risky decision such as flying on an airplane may feel it is more risky if he has recently heard of a negative consequence to that choice such as an airplane accident. The individual would then be making a choice that he believes is in accordance with his preferences regarding safety, but in fact is not because he has, consciously or not, taken a single instance of a negative outcome as an indicator of the actual probability of that outcome occurring. People face all manner of hurdles to making rational decisions—from a lack of understanding of low probabilities of large harm to being overly optimistic about their own abilities.[35] Judges are similarly impeded in their decision-making, and how the court is set up can aid or hinder them in overcoming these obstacles to rational choices. For example, a judge may not rely as much on mental shortcuts if he has to decide fewer cases in a term.

Even if judges were perfectly rational, their decision-making would be hindered by a lack of complete information. Limited information is a long-standing concern in economics—how do individuals make decisions without all the relevant information? A judge may not know whether an individual intended or planned to kill someone, or whether overturning a law against brothels will increase or decrease the safety of prostitutes. Judges are hampered by this lack of information—as Vermeule terms it in relation to statutory interpretation,

34. See Adrian Vermeule, *Judging under Uncertainty: An Institutional Theory of Legal Interpretation* (Cambridge, MA: Harvard University Press, 2006) [Vermeule] (in discussing statutory interpretation, Vermeule argues for an institutional approach given that judges are both limited in the information they have and their ability to process that information (that is, boundedly rational) at 3).

35. Daniel Kahneman, *Thinking, Fast and Slow* (New York: Farrar, Straus and Giroux, 2011).

the task is "judging under uncertainty."[36] Further, different people may view the same facts differently depending on their underlying identity—such as whether there is a scientific basis for claims about climate change.[37] Again, a court's rules may help or hinder judges with this obstacle such as by permitting interveners that provide useful information beyond that provided by the parties.

## INSTITUTIONAL WEDGES

Judges then balance a range of considerations when deciding on whether to hear an appeal, what the result of an appeal will be, whether to write a dissent, and so on. This balancing will be affected by the rules of a particular court. To take a simple example, if a judge is prohibited from earning money from extrajudicial activities while on the bench (such as from speaking engagements or books), she will likely not consider immediate extrajudicial material returns in her judicial decisions. We are interested in how this balancing of factors by a judge is influenced by the fact that she is embedded in a particular institution—the high court of a given country.

We will use a broad definition of institutions. As Douglass North has famously defined them, institutions are the "rules of the game."[38] These rules can be formal, including statutes, regulations, and rules. There are also informal rules contained in the norms or conventions that exist in different contexts. The key is to examine "how institutions constrain the sequence of interaction among the actors, the choices available to particular actors, the structure of information and hence beliefs of the actors, and the payoffs to individuals and groups."[39]

We will look at institutions in two ways—how institutions influence the choices of judges, and how judges influence the shape of institutions.[40] We will spend most of the time on the former: how do formal and informal rules affect the choices made by particular judges? For example, does a judge feel more

36. Vermeule, *supra* note 34.

37. Kahan, *supra* note 31.

38. Douglass C. North, *Institutions, Institutional Change and Economic Performance* (Cambridge, UK: Cambridge University Press, 1990) at 3.

39. Barry Weingast, "Rational-Choice Institutionalism," in Ira Katznelson & Helen Milner, eds, *Political Science: The State of the Discipline* (New York: Norton, 2002) 661. See also Maltzman, Spriggs & Wahlbeck, *Crafting Law, supra* note 9 ("[r]ather than viewing justices as unconstrained actors whose behavior is dictated by their policy preferences, recent work suggested that justices are strategic actors operating in an environment defined by institutional constraints" at 13).

40. Kenneth Shepsle, "Rational Choice Institutionalism" in S. Binder, R. Rhodes & B. Rockman, eds, *Oxford Handbook of Political Institutions* (Oxford University Press, 2006) [Shepsle].

or less reputational pressure if there is a formal rule requiring a court to hear appeals *en banc* as opposed to using smaller panels? Does an appointments process that is highly political yield high court justices who have greater preference for ideological voting than would a process that is more independent of politics? The same questions arise for informal rules or norms.[41] Does a judge feel constrained to follow precedents rather than her own personal views because of the norms of a particular court? Does she seek agreement with others because the court has a "norm of consensus"?[42] These norms or conventions may connect to other issues such as whether to appoint females to the court or to rotate the selection of chief justice across different groups (such as from different parts of the country).

Part of our analysis then is how these formal and informal rules constrain or shape the choices made by judges. The rules are taken as given or exogenous. These rules provide opportunities for or limit the effect of the various factors judges take into account—they act "by affecting the justices' beliefs about the consequences of their actions."[43] Further, the formal and informal rules can either help overcome the barriers to rational decisions such as lack of information or exacerbate them.[44] Allowing interveners, for example, may help alleviate a judge's lack of information about the effect of his decision to the litigants or broader society, or it may provide a signal of how a judge will be viewed if he decides in a particular fashion (and so what will happen to his reputation). We then will look across the formal and informal rules of different high courts, taking these rules as given to see whether they influence how judges decide.

We will, however, also examine (though to a lesser extent) how judges influence their own institutional structure—that is, how judges' decisions change the rules over time. As Arvind and Stirton note, there is a need for "the creation of a proper institutionalist account of the judicial branch of government which studies the norms, conventions, aims, purposes and strategies that underlie the functioning of the judiciary, and the institutional processes by which these

41. Keren Weinshall-Margel, "Attitudinal and Neo-Institutional Models of Supreme Court Decision Making: An Empirical and Comparative Perspective from Israel" (2011) 8:3 *Journal of Empirical Legal Studies* 556 [Weinshall-Margel, "Attitudinal"].

42. Weinshall-Margel, "Attitudinal," *supra* note 41; and Ostberg & Wetstein, *Attitudinal Decision Making, supra* note 6 at 36.

43. Maltzman, Spriggs & Wahlbeck, *Crafting Law, supra* note 9 at 14.

44. Vermeule, *supra* note 34, uses an institutionalist approach to examine statutory interpretation given the lack of information and bounded rationality of judges. Similarly, we use an institutionalist approach in the context of bounded rationality and informational concerns, though examine these issues more broadly in the context of the structural rules of courts.

evolve, change, are adapted to new uses, and disappear, rather than simply starting with assumptions as to what these are."[45]

Part of the story of why institutions arise comes from the need to find cooperative solutions where otherwise there would be none.[46] For example, consider the argument that judges will vote in accordance with their personal views and ignore the "law," but everyone would be better off if the judge instead followed the "law." As Weingast notes, judges will vote in line with their own preferences unless there is some solution to bring about cooperation. One solution is to ensure that the judges interact repeatedly over time. Each judge will cooperate as long as the others do, which can lead to long-term cooperation in certain cases such as where the judges interact indefinitely. However, in other cases repeated interactions will not lead to cooperation, such as where there is no agreement on what constitutes non-cooperation or non-cooperation is not observable.[47]

Rules then may develop to either create a norm of what constitutes cooperation or to ensure that non-cooperation is punished. For example, ensuring cooperation in the sense of not voting in line with one's personal preferences requires a norm about what constitutes voting in line with one's personal views, or at very least that such voting is impermissible. Similarly, although there may be a norm of not deciding in line with personal views, it may be difficult for a judge not on the panel that hears a particular appeal to know why a judge who was on the panel actually decided as he did as the non-panel judge would need considerable information about the case and about the individual judge. Rules about court size and panel size may limit or exacerbate this constraint on how judges decide. It may be more difficult for a judge to observe and punish non-cooperation (deciding a case on personal preferences) on a large court with small panels (such as India) as opposed to a small court with no panels (such as the United States). Note however that these effects can be offsetting. Although the United States may have a weaker norm against deciding in line with one's personal views, this weakness may be counterbalanced to a certain extent by a greater ability to police the norm on the small court with no panels.

Although the design of a court may evolve to allow cooperative solutions, not all courts will evolve or do so perfectly or efficiently. It may take a leader to change an institution. Leaders may be able to create new formal or informal

45. T.T. Arvind & Lindsay Stirton, "Lawyers and the Legal Model: Judicial Ideology, Judicial Professionalism and Institutional Strategy among the Law Lords" (2012) at 44, online: https://extranet.sioe.org/uploads/isnie2012/arvind_stirton.pdf.

46. Shepsle, *supra* note 40.

47. Shepsle, *supra* note 40.

rules that others follow. On courts, chief justices may be able to play such a role. They can push for formal rules of practice for the court or for changes to these rules. Perhaps more important, they may also be able to promote norms, such as norms of consensus, through either their office or through their method of assigning cases. They may, for example, punish a judge's lack of cooperation or tendency to dissent by assigning him to fewer or less important cases.

We will spend the rest of the book attempting to draw out the influence of different institutional choices made for and by high courts in different countries. Some of this work has been done on individual countries, but there are only the beginnings of comparative work. For example, Weinshall-Margel notes that there are a number of connections between judicial decision-making and institutional norms of a high court.[48] She discusses how the method of appointment may increase or decrease the role of ideology and how both heavier caseloads and an inability to select the cases to be heard may reduce the impact of policy preferences and increase the importance of "law" in decision-making. We view these different rules as wedges that separate how judges decide in different countries—that split decision-making in different countries on two main bases: how much judges vote in line with their own personal views, and how cooperative judges are in reaching decisions. These wedges push courts into different parts of CC Space. One cannot understand patterns of voting on a court, let alone recommend altering a court's institutional structure, without understanding how these wedges alter judicial decisions and how they are created and shaped.

## JUDGES, THE LAW, AND INSTITUTIONS

Drawing this discussion together, we can then think of three interrelated categories of influences on how judges decide—whether they decide more or less "ideologically" or "cooperatively":

- *Who is the judge:* The judges that sit on the court or on a panel have certain policy preferences and identities. Even if all the institutional rules on two different courts were the same and they were deciding based on the same facts and rules, if the judges on the courts have different preferences and identities they may decide a case very differently. The identity of the judges on the court may then influence outcomes. This category ties most directly into two key court design choices. The first is the choice of the appointment process. It may be,

48. Weinshall-Margel, "Attitudinal," *supra* note 41 at 3.

for example, that some appointment processes lead to more political judges or judges with particular political or personal preferences, resulting in more political voting, all other things being equal. The second choice is whether to hear appeals in panels. If subsets of judges hear particular appeals then the choice of which judges hear those appeals may influence the outcome of the appeal.

- *The law:* As we discussed earlier, some laws or contexts may provide greater scope for a judge to apply her policy preferences because, for example, of ambiguity in the law. Differences in how judges decide cases in different contexts or across countries will then in part depend on the nature of the law underlying the appeals the court hears. A judge who tends to want to favor the accused in criminal cases may have more opportunity to acquit an accused in cases where the offense is framed in a more open-ended manner. This factor may, however, also be influenced by institutional design. For example, judges on courts with more discretion about the cases they hear may hear more cases that provide scope for application of policy preferences—either because such cases are more controversial, or because the judges prefer to hear such cases.
- *The institutional incentives or constraints on decisions:* Even given a particular set of judges and laws, different choices about the design of the court may increase or decrease the costs to a judge of making certain decisions. Think again of the judge who wants to favor accused individuals. Different institutional rules may make it more or less costly to satisfy that preference. For example, a norm against deciding in accordance with policy preferences may raise the cost of such a choice. We will examine a range of design choices that may raise or lower these costs.

It will of course be difficult to separate the influence of each of these factors in particular cases, and they may interact such as where a norm of political voting leads to a more political appointment process. We can, however, look for some indications in how judges decide that point in one direction or the other. We start with the most basic of the institutional choices—how to choose the judges who sit on the court.

3

# Planting the Seed

## *Choosing High Court Judges*

Sandra Day O'Connor announced her plan to retire as a US Supreme Court justice in July 2005. She had served since 1981 when President Ronald Reagan appointed her. She was the first female appointed to the Court and was widely viewed as a moderate by the end of her time on the bench.[1] In the United States a candidate is nominated by the president but can only be appointed with the "advice and consent" of the Senate.[2] Choosing O'Connor's successor fell to President George W. Bush, and he turned to Harriet Miers, White House counsel with whom he had a long-time close relationship. She had been his personal lawyer, and he had appointed her to a range of positions over the years as governor and then president.[3]

The nomination drew immediate criticism from both conservatives and liberals. Many Republicans felt she was not conservative enough.[4] Others

1. Julian Borger, "Bush Offers Crucial Supreme Court Seat to His Former Lawyer," *The Guardian* (October 4, 2005), online: www.theguardian.com/world/2005/oct/04/usa.topstories3 ["Bush Offers Crucial"]; "Bush Picks White House Counsel for Supreme Court," *CNN.com* (October 4, 2005), online: http://www.cnn.com/2005/POLITICS/10/03/scotus.miers/ ["Bush Picks White House"].

2. Denis Steven Rutkus, ed, *Supreme Court Appointment Process: Roles of the President, Judiciary Committee, and Senate* (New York: Nova Science, 2005) (Congressional Research Service) ["Appointment Process"] at 2.

3. "Who Is Harriet Miers," *ABC News* (October 27, 2005), online: abcnews.go.com/Politics/SupremeCourt/story?id=1170572.

4. Borger, "Bush Offers Crucial", *supra* note 1; Charles Babington & Thomas B. Edsall, "Conservative Republicans Divided Over Nominee," *Washington Post* (October 4, 2005), online: www.washingtonpost.com/wp-dyn/content/article/2005/10/03/AR2005100301468.html; David Corn, "Harriet Miers: Supreme Court Choice with Few Footprints," *The Nation* (October 3, 2005), online: www.thenation.com/blog/156205/harriet-miers-supreme-court-choice-few-footprints;

Commitment and Cooperation on High Courts. Benjamin Alarie and Andrew J. Green.

worried she was only appointed because she was a close personal friend of Bush.[5] The debate was important as O'Connor had been the "swing justice" on many cases, casting the deciding vote on decisions split between liberals and conservatives.[6] Her replacement could give the advantage for one side or the other. In the face of the strong reaction, Miers eventually withdrew her name and Bush nominated, and the Senate later confirmed, a more clearly conservative Samuel Alito.

The Miers story is not the only controversial episode in the US appointment process: Robert Bork, one of Ronald Reagan's nominees, was vilified in the press, which led to his rejection by the Senate; Clarence Thomas, nominated by George H.W. Bush, was accused of sexual harassment by a former colleague; Sonia Sotomayor, nominated by Barack Obama, was criticized for controversial views on judging—and the list goes on. The battle over who gets the nod is hard-fought because the war is seen as so important—the US Supreme Court obviously decides critical questions, often closely divided on ideological grounds. In one of the most famous examples, the Court split 5-4 on a central issue in the 2000 decision in *Bush v. Gore* about the constitutionality of a recount in Florida during the 2000 presidential election, with the five majority judges being conservative members of the Court appointed by Republican presidents.[7] The Court has been firmly divided into ideological blocs in recent years, and appointments can bolster one side or the other.[8]

And the United States is not the only nation where selection of judges is controversial. In Canada, the appointments process is more straightforward with

Thomas Lifson, "Critiques of Miers," *American Thinker* (October 3, 2005), online: www.americanthinker.com/blog/2005/10/critiques_of_miers.html.

5. See e.g. "The Great Miers Mystery; The Supreme Court," *The Economist* (October 8, 2005); Randy Barnett, "Cronyism," *Wall Street Journal* (2005), online: www.cato.org/publications/commentary/cronyism; Charles Krauthammer, "Withdraw This Nominee," *Washington Post* (October 7, 2005), online: www.washingtonpost.com/wp-dyn/content/article/2005/10/06/AR2005100601468.html (arguing that "[i]f Harriet Miers were not a crony of the president of the United States, her nomination to the Supreme Court would be a joke, as it would have occurred to no one else to nominate her").

6. Borger, "Bush Offers Crucial," *supra* note 1; "Bush Picks White House," *supra* note 1.

7. Note, however, that two of the dissenting justices were also appointed by Republican presidents.

8. Neal Devins & Lawrence Baum, "Split Definitive: How Party Polarization Turned the Supreme Court into a Partisan Court" (2014) (William & Mary Law School Research Paper No 09-276) at 38, online: http://papers.ssrn.com/sol3/papers.cfm?abstract_id=2432111 [Devins & Baum].

the power to appoint Supreme Court judges residing in the hands of the prime minister. Canadians often perceive the process at least as less overtly political than in the United States, and in fact Canada has had fewer large-scale controversies over Supreme Court appointments. However, the Supreme Court was recently in the unusual position of having to decide on the constitutionality of an appointment by Conservative prime minister Stephen Harper. Harper appointed Marc Nadon, a Federal Court of Appeal judge with conservative views, to the Supreme Court in October 2013. His appointment was immediately criticized as Canada has a constitutional requirement that three of the nine justices be Quebec judges or advocates from Quebec. Nadon had previously been a lawyer in Quebec but was not at the time of appointment. The Supreme Court eventually declared the appointment unconstitutional.[9] Despite this setback, Harper had a considerable opportunity to shape the Court, appointing seven of its current nine members.

The process can become politicized even where nominations are not made by political actors. The chief justice of India and the four most senior Supreme Court judges—known as the "collegium"—nominate candidates for the Supreme Court of India. In 2014, the collegium nominated Gopal Subramanium for a position on the Court. However, shortly after, a new party came into power in India and apparently requested the collegium to reconsider. Among other things, the government claimed Subramanium had ties to corporate lobbyists. Subramanium later withdrew his name, claiming the government was unfairly criticizing him for his independence.[10]

Appointments, and the power to make them, are contested because they have the potential to embed a set of views that will influence future law and policy. The natural question to ask is whether how one decides which judges should be on the court makes a difference to how the judges decide. Are more political processes a recipe for more political, divisive judges, pushing courts with such processes toward the Attitudinal (upper left) sector of CC Space? Much of the literature on appointment processes seems to assume such a connection. If judges decide at least in part based on political preferences or identity, the rules around appointment help determine what the preferences or identities are on the court or the judge's trade-off across factors. To see if there is a connection, we first need to examine how the appointment processes differ across countries.

9. *Reference re Supreme Court Act, ss. 5 and 6*, 2014 SCC 21; [2014] 1 SCR 433.

10. Vishnu Som & A Vaidyanathan, "Why Gopal Subramanium Is No Longer Running for Supreme Court Judge", *NDTV* (25 June, 2014), online: http://www.ndtv.com/india-news/why-gopal-subramanium-is-no-longer-running-for-supreme-court-judge-581019.

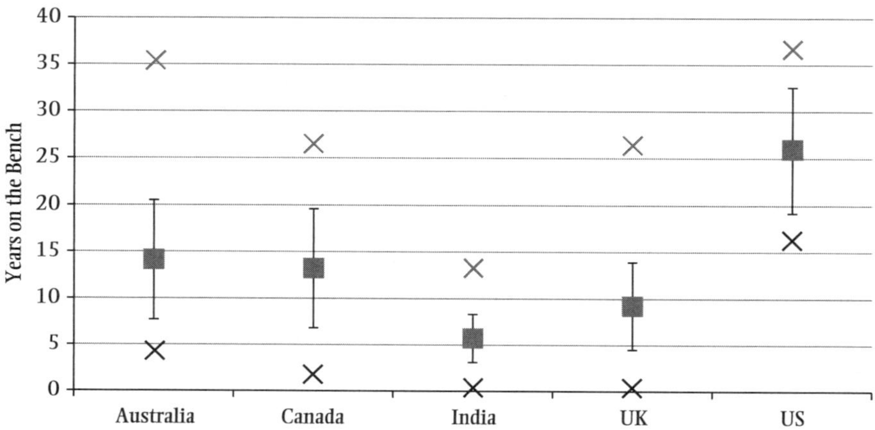


**Figure 3-1** Average tenure, standard deviation, and range of years on the bench for judges on each court between 1970 and early 2000s. US judges stayed on the bench the longest by far on average and India the shortest. Moreover, both the United States and India had narrower ranges in how long judges stayed on the court than the other three countries.

## CHOOSING THE BENCH

Given the potential for judges on high courts to influence law and policy, a country's most important choice with respect to high courts may be how judges are appointed. As we will see, countries have adopted a range of appointment processes, placing different emphasis on such values as democratic accountability and independence. Important for our analysis, these processes include not only the written requirements that are often found in constitutions or legislation but also norms about who actually chooses as opposed to who has the formal power. The process may also encompass norms about the proper criteria for choosing judges such as whether judges must be only chosen for their legal abilities or whether policy preferences are legitimately considered.

The decision about who to appoint can have long-term consequences as judges in some countries spend a long time on the bench. Figure 3-1 shows the average time on the bench for judges in different countries who were on the high court between the 1970s and the early 2000s.[11] Judges on the US Supreme Court on average sat for 26 years. In Canada and Australia judges on average were on the high court for a little under 15 years. At the other end of the spectrum, Indian Supreme Court judges on average remain on the bench for less than 6 years. Over this 30-year period, 19 different high court judges were

11. Some judges continue to sit on the high court currently, particularly in the United States, slightly skewing the data downward.

*Table 3-1.* Location of Appointment Powers in Different Common Law Countries

| Countries | Branch of Government | | |
|---|---|---|---|
| | **Executive** | **Legislative** | **Judicial** |
| Canada, Australia, pre-2005 Britain | ✓ | | |
| US | ✓ | ✓ | |
| Britain,[a] India (after legislation) | ✓ | | ✓ |
| Israel[b] | ✓ | ✓ | ✓ |
| India | | | ✓ |

[a] In Britain, two of the five members of the selection commission must be non-legally qualified, which means that members of the public also have direct power over the selection process, in addition to the executive and judicial branches of government. See section 3.3.

[b] In Israel, two of the nine members of the selection commission are elected members of the bar, in addition to judges, ministers, and parliamentarians. See section 3.3.

involved in decisions in the United States, 26 in Australia, 35 in Canada, 52 in the UK, and 131 in India.

As can be seen from Table 3-1, different branches of government appoint judges in the various countries we are studying. In order to analyze the influence of these differences, we divide the countries into four groupings depending on who has the principal appointment power: the executive (Canada, Australia, and the United Kingdom pre-2005, along with other countries such as New Zealand and South Africa); the executive and the legislature (United States alone); independent committees (United Kingdom, Israel, and, going forward, potentially India); and the judiciary (India). As we will see, these groupings are not watertight. There are formal or informal connections between the ultimate decision-maker and different parties. However, it is useful to think of the core decision-maker to understand the trade-offs made in each country.

## Executive Power

The executive's power to appoint judges is strongest in Canada and Australia. According to the *Supreme Court Act*, judges of the Supreme Court of Canada "shall be appointed by the Governor in Council by letters patent under the Great Seal."[12] The phrase "Governor in Council" in effect refers to the federal

12. *Supreme Court Act* RSC 1985, c S-26, s 4(2) [*Supreme Court Act* Canada].

cabinet delivering advice to the governor-general that generally must be followed. The prime minister has always dominated the advice giving.[13] The main constraint on the appointment power lies in regional representation. Three out of the nine justices must be appointed from amongst the judges or advocates of Quebec.[14] By convention, three justices are from Ontario, one from Atlantic Canada, and two from the four western provinces.[15]

The appointment process in Canada has always been quite secretive. The prime minister has the final say and consults with various judges and lawyers but beyond that the process has been largely closed. In 2005 the Liberal government attempted to make the process more transparent. The idea was for the minister of justice to consult with the attorney general of the province with the vacancy, and leading members of the legal community, and create a "long list" of an unspecified number of qualified candidates.[16] The Conservative government under Prime Minister Harper, which was elected in 2006, adopted this plan. A selection panel of five Members of Parliament (three government MPs, and one from each of the opposition parties as selected by the leaders of those parties) was then to assess the candidates in consultation with the chief justice, the attorney general of the province with the vacancy, and the legal community, and provide an unranked short list of three qualified candidates per vacancy to the prime minister and the minister of justice.[17] The prime minister and the minister of justice would then select a nominee, presumably from this shortlist. Following the selection, an ad hoc parliamentary committee was to question the nominee at a public hearing.[18] The committee would not have the power to delay or veto the appointment. The prime minister would formally appoint the nominees to the Supreme Court the day after these hearings.[19]

There are two concerns with this process. First, critics claim it is still too secretive. Despite the involvement of a selection panel and an ad hoc committee, the

13. Peter McCormick, "Selecting the Supremes: The Appointment of Judges to the Supreme Court of Canada" (2005) 7:1 *Journal of Appellate Practice and Process* 1 at 13 [McCormick, "Selecting the Supremes"].

14. *Supreme Court Act* Canada, *supra* note 12, s 6.

15. McCormick, "Selecting the Supremes," *supra* note 13 at 13.

16. Adam M. Dodek, "Reforming the Supreme Court Appointment Process, 2004–2014: A 10-Year Democratic Audit" (2014) 67 at 13–15, *The Supreme Court Law Review: Osgoode's Annual Constitutional Cases Conference* 111 [Dodek].

17. In 2011, Justices Moldaver and Karakatsanis were appointed at the same time. Therefore, the shortlist consisted of six candidates, rather than three candidates.

18. Dodek, *supra* note 16 at 16.

19. Dodek, *supra* note 16 at 16.

prime minister is still able to shut out any unwanted candidates and not much is known about the criteria for selection or the nature of consultations.[20] Further, the selection panel also works in secret, and the ad hoc committee has little time to prepare for the hearings.[21] In any case, Prime Minister Harper abandoned the process in his final appointments. He did not use the selection committee to arrive at a short list nor allow an ad hoc parliamentary committee to question the candidates, meaning there was no public aspect to the process or involvement of other parties for either appointment.[22] Recently elected Prime Minister Justin Trudeau has promised to reform the appointment process to make it more transparent as well as to include other criteria for selection such as bilingualism.

The executive similarly controls appointments in Australia. The Australian Constitution gives the power of appointment of justices to the governor general in council (cabinet).[23] In practice, the prime minister and cabinet decides on an appointment on the recommendation of the attorney general.[24] The attorney general, in making a recommendation, is obligated to consult with the attorney generals of the states.[25] The attorney general may also consult with the chief justice, members of the legal community, parliamentary colleagues, cabinet colleagues, and other individuals, but little is known about how the attorney general decides upon a proposed nominee.[26]

20. Dodek, *supra* note 16 at 34–38, 43.

21. Dodek, *supra* note 16 at 44.

22. The prime minister bypassed the appointments process for Justices Clement Gascon and Suzanne Côté, with his government claiming concerns about leaks in the process: Jennifer Hough, "Clement Gascon, a Quebec Court of Appeal Judge, Nominated to the Supreme Court," *National Post* (June 3, 2014), online: http://news.nationalpost.com/2014/06/03/clement-gascon-a-quebec-court-of-appeal-judge-nominated-to-supreme-court/; T. MacCharles, "Quebec Lawyer Suzanne Cote Named to Supreme Court of Canada," *Toronto Star* (November 27, 2014), online: http://www.thestar.com/news/canada/2014/11/27/quebec_lawyer_suzanne_ct_named_to_supreme_court_of_canada.html.

23. *Commonwealth of Australia Constitution Act 1900* (Cth), s 72.

24. Mita Bhattacharya & Russell Smyth, "The Determinants of Judicial Prestige and Influence: Some Empirical Evidence from the High Court of Australia" (2001) 30:1 *Journal of Legal Studies* 223–252 at 229; "Judicial Appointments: Ensuring a Strong, Independent and Diverse Judiciary through a Transparent Process," Commonwealth of Australia (2010), online: http://www.ag.gov.au/LegalSystem/Courts/Documents/JudicialApptsEnsuringastrongandindependentjudiciarythroughatransparentprocess.pdf.

25. *High Court of Australia Act 1979* (Cth), s 6 [*High Court of Australia Act*].

26. George Winterton, "Appointment of Federal Judges in Australia" (1987) 16 *Melbourne University Law Review* 185 at 186–187 [Winterton].

The prime minister may be involved in the process for the appointment of a chief justice.[27]

The executive therefore holds the appointment power in Canada and Australia. Although in each case the formal rules specify that the governor in council appoints judges, the norm is the prime minister or the attorney general plays the key role. The prime minister consults with others but there is relatively little transparency or role for other parties, elected or not, particularly as we will see relative to the United States.

## "With the Advice and Consent": Combining the Executive and Legislature

The president and the Senate share the power to appoint US Supreme Court judges because of the constitutional requirement for the president to appoint judges with the "advice and consent" of the Senate. The president nominates a candidate who then must be confirmed by the Senate. Presidents generally consult with Senate party leaders as well as members of the Senate Judiciary Committee before choosing a nominee.[28] They may also obtain advice from party leaders, interest groups, advisers within the president's administration, commentators, and sometimes sitting justices on the Supreme Court.[29]

Once the president nominates an individual, a Senate Judiciary Committee conducts an extensive investigation into the nominee and then holds a confirmation hearing.[30] At the hearing, the Committee questions the nominee on a wide range of topics including social and political issues, the Constitution, particular Court rulings, current controversies, and judicial philosophy.[31]

27. Winterton, *supra* note 26. In New Zealand, the governor general on behalf of the queen appoints Supreme Court justices. *Judicature Act 1908* (NZ), 1908/89, s 4(2). The governor general generally makes appointments on the advice of the attorney general, or the prime minister in the case of the chief justice. Richard Cornes, "Appealing to History: The New Zealand Supreme Court Debate" (2004) 24 *Legal Studies* 210 at 216. The government does not have a statutory obligation to consult with any interested parties before making its selection. Pushkar Maitra & Russell Smyth, "Judicial Independence, Judicial Promotion and the Enforcement of Legislative Wealth Transfers—An Empirical Study of the New Zealand High Court" (2004) 17 *European Journal of Law and Economics* 209 at 217.

28. Rutkus, "Appointment Process," *supra* note 2 at 7.

29. Rutkus, "Appointment Process," *supra* note 2 at 8.

30. Since 1955, each Supreme Court nominee has testified before the Judiciary Committee during his or her confirmation hearing: Rutkus, "Appointment Process," *supra* note 2 at 21.

31. Rutkus, "Appointment Process," *supra* note 2 at 29.

Although a nominee may be reluctant to answer certain questions, some senators may be persuaded to vote against confirmation based on a nominee's unresponsiveness to questions on subjects they consider important.[32] Other public witnesses, including spokespersons for advocacy groups that support or oppose a nominee, also frequently testify during confirmation hearings. After the hearings, the Judiciary Committee reports back to the Senate by making a positive or negative recommendation, or no recommendation at all.[33] A negative recommendation does not prevent a nomination from moving forward, but it communicates to the rest of the Senate that the committee members had reservations in respect of the nominee.[34]

The full Senate then debates the nominee, focusing to some extent on the nominee's judicial philosophy and ideology. These debates can become quite polarized.[35] After the floor debate, the Senate decides on a simple majority basis whether to consent to the nomination of the candidate to the Supreme Court. Most votes have been in favor of confirming the nominee's appointment by a large margin, with only a few nominees being confirmed or rejected by a close vote.[36] The Senate has confirmed 123 out of 159 Supreme Court nominations received.[37] The Senate failed to confirm three nominations in the last 40 years.[38] A justice is sworn into office after the Senate's confirmation.

The United States therefore has a process that formally requires the participation of both the executive and the legislature. Nearly all stages of the confirmation process, including the initial announcement of the nominee, confirmation hearings, committee's vote, Senate debate, and the Senate vote, are open and televised to the public.[39] All through the process, politics play a significant role in both the decision by the president to nominate a candidate, and the decision

32. Rutkus, "Appointment Process," *supra* note 2 at 30.

33. Rutkus, "Appointment Process," *supra* note 2 at 32.

34. Rutkus, "Appointment Process," *supra* note 2 at 32.

35. Rutkus, "Appointment Process," *supra* note 2 at 39–40.

36. Rutkus, "Appointment Process," *supra* note 2 at 46–47.

37. Rutkus, "Appointment Process," *supra* note 2 at 48 (the 36 nominations that were not confirmed by the Senate correspond to 31 individual nominees, 6 of whom were re-nominated and approved by the Senate later on).

38. Rutkus, "Appointment Process," *supra* note 2 at 51. One recent unconfirmed nomination was that of current chief justice John Roberts, who was first nominated to replace Justice O'Connor, before the sudden death of Chief Justice Rehnquist caused President Bush to withdraw Roberts's nomination for associate justice and resubmit it for the position of chief justice. See Rutkus, "Appointment Process," *supra* note 2 at 5.

39. Rutkus, "Appointment Process," *supra* note 2 at 56.

by the Senate to confirm or reject a candidate (or as we saw recently with the controversy about replacing Justice Antonin Scalia, even to hold a hearing). Whether a nomination is ultimately successful may depend on factors such as the Senate's perception of the nominee's ideology, timing of the nomination relative to a president's term, and presidential management of the confirmation process.[40]

## The Committee Approach

The United States tries to balance the power of the executive by requiring the involvement of the legislature. The UK and Israel have taken a different tack in addressing the political nature of the appointment process. Each maintains a connection to the executive or the legislature but grants significant power to a committee. The committee structure is different in each country, but clearly situates at least some of the appointment power in the judiciary.

The executive held the appointment power in the UK process before 2005. The Crown made judicial appointments on the advice of the prime minister, with the primary responsibility lying with the lord chancellor. The lord chancellor recommended nominees to the prime minister after consulting with various members of the bar and the judiciary.[41] In one case Prime Minister Margaret Thatcher refused to accept Lord Chancellor Hailsham's advice over her appointment of John Donaldson as master of the rolls. However, Hanretty found no systematic support for the proposition that appointments were politically motivated.[42]

After the constitutional reforms in 2005, the power to appoint judges to the UK Supreme Court shifted to an independent selection commission. The selection commission includes the president of the Supreme Court, a senior UK judge nominated by the president, and three members nominated by each of the Judicial Appointments Commissions for Scotland, Northern Ireland, and England and Wales, respectively.[43] At least two members nominated from the Judicial Appointments Commissions must be non-legally qualified.[44]

40. Rutkus, "Appointment Process," *supra* note 2 at 49.

41. Burton Atkins, "Judicial Selection in Context: The American and English Experience" (1988–89) 77 *Kentucky LJ* 477 at 591.

42. Chris Hanretty, "Political Preferment in English Judicial Appointment, 1880–2005" (2012) American Political Science Association 2012 Annual Meeting Paper 1 at 7, 11 [Hanretty, "Political Preferment"].

43. *The Supreme Court (Judicial Appointments) Regulations 2013*, SI 2013/2193, s 11 [*SC (Judicial Appointments)*].

44. *SC (Judicial Appointments), supra* note 43, s 13(3).

During the selection process, the commission must consult specific senior judges, the lord chancellor, and the first ministers of Scotland, Wales, and Northern Ireland, before recommending a single candidate to the lord chancellor.[45] The lord chancellor is then also required to consult with the same individuals before deciding whether to notify the prime minister of the commission's selection, reject the selection, or require the commission to reconsider.[46] The lord chancellor has only one opportunity to ask the commission to reconsider, and one opportunity to reject a candidate.[47] If a lord chancellor chooses to reject or require reconsideration of a selection, he must provide written reasons to the commission.[48] No lord chancellor exercised his power to reject a selection for appointment to the Supreme Court, or require its reconsideration as of 2013.[49]

Israel provides an alternative example of a committee process. A candidate for appointment to the Israeli Supreme Court must receive the approval of seven members out of a nine-member Judicial Selection Committee.[50] The candidate is then formally appointed by the president. The Judicial Selection Committee includes the president of the Supreme Court, two other Supreme Court judges who are elected by the Supreme Court, the minister of justice, another minister designated by the government, two members of the Knesset (the legislature) who are elected by secret ballot, and two elected representatives of the Chamber of Advocates.[51] The two members of the legislature typically include one member from the opposition party.[52] The minister of justice, the president of the Supreme Court, or any three Committee members can nominate candidates.[53] The president is, by convention, the most senior judge on the bench and the deputy president is the next most senior judge. The Knesset has used legislation to increase its influence in the composition of the Court. For example, in

45. *Constitutional Reform Act* 2005 (UK), c 4 [*CRA*], ss 27–28.

46. *CRA, supra* note 45, ss 28–29.

47. *CRA, supra* note 45, ss 29–31.

48. *CRA, supra* note 45, s 30(3).

49. Charles Banner, "Judicial Appointments in the Senior Courts: A Perspective from the United Kingdom" (2013) University of Hong Kong Faculty of Law Occasional Paper No 22, online: http://www.law.hku.hk/ccpl/pub/OP%20No%2022%20Charles%20Banner%20V5.pdf at 11.

50. Richard A. Posner, "Judicial Review, a Comparative Perspective: Israel, Canada, and the United States" (2010) 31 *Cardozo Law Review* 2393 at 2396 [Posner, "Judicial Review"].

51. *Basic Law: The Judiciary 1984,* s 4(b).

52. Posner, "Judicial Review," *supra* note 50 at 2397.

53. *Courts Law 1984* (Consolidated version), s 7(b).

2011, anticipating the retirement of President Dorit Beinisch on her seventieth birthday, the Knesset passed a law cancelling the requirement that a potential president have at least three years remaining until mandatory retirement. This law, dubbed the "Grunis Law," permitted Justice Asher Grunis (who was seen as less activist than Beinisch and her predecessor, Aharon Barak) to become the next president.[54]

Interestingly, the minister of justice, with the consent of the chief justice, can temporarily appoint candidates to the Israel Supreme Court.[55] Temporary appointment serves in effect as a probationary period, enabling the Appointment Committee to assess the nominees before they are permanently appointed to the Court.[56] As we will see, it may also make the temporary appointees less willing to dissent because of the power that their colleagues hold over their career. The vast majority of District Court judges who have been promoted to the Israel Supreme Court were first appointed temporarily.[57]

In effect both the UK and Israel have provided more power in the appointment process to a broader range of parties, in particular the judiciary. In the UK, the executive and the judiciary now share the power of appointing judges to the Supreme Court. In addition, members of the public also influence the appointment process as non-legally-qualified members of the commission. In Israel, the judiciary arguably has even greater power as the requirement for a nominee to receive the vote of seven of nine members of the selection committee effectively gives veto powers to the Supreme Court judges who have always voted as a bloc.[58] As we will see, India is also moving in the direction of a committee approach, although from the opposite extreme of almost complete power in the judiciary.

## Letting the Judges Decide

India is the only one of the countries we study where the judiciary holds essentially complete power to establish its own membership. According to the Indian

54. "Knesset Approves 'Grunis Law'", *Israel National News* (March 1, 2012), online: http://www.israelnationalnews.com/News/News.aspx/151335#.VVtiaUs3RD4.

55. Binyamin Blum, "To Concur or Not to Concur, That Is the Question: Theoretical and Practical Question Regarding the Judicial Independence of Judges Appointed Temporarily to the Israeli Supreme Court" (Masters Thesis, Stanford Law School, 2006) [unpublished], at 7 [Blum].

56. Blum, *supra* note 55 at 8.

57. Blum, *supra* note 55 at 8.

58. Posner, "Judicial Review," *supra* note 55 at 2398.

Constitution, the president appoints judges to the Supreme Court after consultation with judges of the Supreme Court and High Courts as he deems necessary.[59] However, as a result of some of its own decisions, the Supreme Court has de facto taken over the president's authority to appoint judges to the Supreme Court.[60] The chief justice and the four most senior judges on the Supreme Court now effectively appoint judges to the Supreme Court.

Although the judiciary has monopolized the power to appoint high court judges in India since the 1990s, it may soon share this power with the executive and the legislative branches of government. Two recent constitutional amendments, which came into force on April 13, 2015, create a National Judicial Appointments Commission.[61] The Commission would be chaired by the chief justice, and include the next two most senior Supreme Court judges, the union minister in charge of laws and justice, and "two eminent persons to be nominated by the collegium consisting of the Prime Minister, the Chief Justice of India and the leader of Opposition in the House of the People."[62] The Commission would appoint judges to the Supreme Court, including to the position of chief justice.[63] The Commission process faced a constitutional challenge that the amendments violate the basic structure of the constitution by interfering with the independence of the judiciary.[64] In 2015, the Supreme Court found that the new process was unconstitutional and began a separate set of hearings to devise reforms to make the appointment process more transparent and "responsive to the needs of the people."

## IS THERE A CONNECTION BETWEEN THE APPOINTMENTS PROCESS AND DECISION-MAKING?

The appointment processes differ in their mix of a few factors. First, the *accountability* of the decision-makers varies. In general each process has some connection to the electorate, though the identity differs, with a prime minister

59. *The Constitution of India 1950*, art 124, § (2).

60. See *S. P. Gupta v. Union of India*, AIR 1982 SC 149, 30 December 1981; *Supreme Court Advocates-on Record Association vs Union of India*, AIR 1994 SC 268, 6 October 1993; *In re Special Reference 1 of 1998*, AIR 1999 SC 1, 28 October 1998.

61. *The Constitution (120th Amendment) Bill*, 2013 (Act 120 of 2013), art 124A.

62. *Constitution (One Hundred and Twentieth Amendment) Bill, 2013; Judicial Appointments Bill, 2013* [*Judicial Appointments Bill*], s 3.

63. *Judicial Appointments Bill, supra* note 62, s 4(a).

64. *Supreme Court Advocates-on-Record v Union of India*, Writ Petition (civil), 13 November 2015.

essentially alone in some cases and elected legislators taking a role in others, and with India an outlier as the main actors are the judges themselves. Second, some countries strive for a *balance* of decision-makers such as through explicit combinations of different representatives of different groups. For others, the decision is either explicitly made by a single actor (the prime minister) or could be dominated by one party such as where the president and Senate majority are from the same party. Third, some processes are more *transparent* than others—much though not all of the US process is public as opposed to almost none in the current Canadian process. Finally, some appointment processes are more overtly *political*—with the United States again being the most extreme example.

These differing mixes may lead to different types of judges being appointed. It may be, for example, that a process with greater balance in its decision-makers leads to judges with less extreme views or more willingness to cooperate. A more political process may yield judges who are more ideological or more willing to decide in line with those views. The process therefore may alter not only who decides but how they decide. Three questions spring to mind: do some appointment processes produce judges more likely to decide in line with their political views? If we look across all the different processes, are the political views of the judges connected to the political views of whoever appoints them? Finally, are some appointment processes more likely than others to yield judges who cooperate with each other? We will examine each of these questions in turn, using both existing empirical work as well as our own analysis to answer this question.[65] As we will see, the results are not clear-cut, in part due to weaknesses in the data, but there are interesting connections between the processes and the judges.

## Do Political Processes Lead to Political Judges?

A greater number of participants in the appointments process—more appointers—may lead to more political appointments. They may be more likely to appoint individuals with stronger political preferences in order to appease their political supporters. A member of the Senate in the United States, for example, may take part in confirmation hearings and debates over nominees, and may vote to veto appointments. He may then screen candidates for their political views.[66] Depending on her view of her role and the process to be followed, an

65. See Appendix A for a description of the databases.

66. See Rutkus, "Appointment Process," *supra* note 2 at 29 for a description of the confirmation hearing process. Views on abortion, and interpretive approaches to the Constitution, are just some of the sensitive issues that have come up during these hearings.

elected executive actor such as a prime minister may also appoint individuals with strong political preferences. The converse may also be true—that is, that greater involvement of less overtly political actors such as the judiciary may lead to lesser ideological polarization on a high court. The judiciary may be less likely to choose individuals with particular policy preferences and more likely to appoint on the basis of merit or congeniality.

The process may also be important. Involving legislators in public and political processes for choosing judges may affect how judges themselves perceive their role and their professional obligations post-appointment.[67] For example, a judge appointed through the Senate confirmation process in the United States may believe that she is expected to decide in a political fashion as the process was so politically-oriented. She may not get such a signal from a less political process, though she may still vote in line with her political views anyway.

The transparency of the process potentially cuts both ways—both for and against the selected judges following particular political views. On the one hand, a transparent process allows an appointer to see the political views of the prospective appointees, and hence to have his own preferences reflected more accurately in the future decisions of the appointed judge (at least initially). The result would be greater degrees of ideological polarization on the high court between justices appointed by different actors.[68] Of course, transparency also allows the public to view this connection between the appointer and the appointed, and to punish any blatant political appointment if the public disapproves of political appointments.

Political appointers, a political process, and possibly transparency may all tilt the judiciary toward more political decision-making. Some countries have tried to counterbalance this influence through explicitly ensuring a range of viewpoints—that is, not getting rid of the politics in the appointment process but ensuring that different positions are represented. The committee process in the UK and Israel are moving toward such a balance, and the US process at least involves both parties, though power over the presidency and the Senate dictates the relative power of each party. On the other hand, there is no balance where the prime minister has complete discretion to appoint a judge to the high court,

67. Michael J. Bryant, "Judging the Judges: Judicial Independence and Reforms to the Supreme Court of Canada Appointment Process" (2004) 24 *Supreme Court Law Review* 29 (QL).

68. Benjamin Alarie & Andrew Green, "Policy Preference Change and Appointments to the Supreme Court of Canada" (2009) 47 *Osgoode Hall LJ* 1 at 45 [Alarie & Green "Policy Preference"]. In comparison, the appointment process in Canada may result in less information about judicial ideology, so prime ministers may make greater errors in their attempts to appoint judges sympathetic to their policy positions.

such as in Canada, though there may be balance over time if control over the government shifts between parties.

As a result, the diverse processes and actors involved in the appointment process may give rise to greater voting based on personal preferences in some high courts than in others. These effects on voting may be self-reinforcing. If political appointments are made and there is a norm of voting based on personal preferences, future appointments are more likely to be based on political factors—that is, there may be a "selection culture" whereby the appointment generally is made on political grounds, which may either override or be exacerbated by the formal rules.[69] Looking across factors, we expect the following connection between the appointment process and decision-making by judges:[70]

*H1: Judges will be more likely to be polarized in their voting where the appointers are political, the process is more political and there is less balance across the political views of the appointers.*

Direct comparisons across high courts are difficult because each country has a process with a mix of factors, making it hard to isolate one variable for comparison. However, some questions spring to mind. In Canada the prime minister chooses judges in a secretive process whereas in the United States the president and the Senate are involved through a very public process. Each could be connected to very political appointments, but are they? India currently allows judges to choose judges; does this correlate with less politicized appointments than where political actors are more involved? Are more balanced processes such as in Israel and the UK associated with less politicized voting than in the United States or Canada? It is possible that these different processes are not correlated with differences in judges—they could all have high or all low levels of polarization, or differences in polarization may be unrelated to the institutional structure.

69. See David Weiden, "Judicial Politicization, Ideology, and Activism at the High Courts of the United States, Canada, and Australia" 2011 64:2 *Political Research Quarterly* 335 at 336 [Weiden, "Judicial Politicization"] (arguing the formal appointment rules are less important cross-nationally than the "selection culture" establishing whether appointments may be made on partisan factors rather than merit).

70. This hypothesis is related to, though slightly different, than Weiden, "Judicial Politicization," *supra* note 69, who argues that "judges in a highly politicized judiciary will tend to engage in a greater degree of ideological decision-making" at 336. We examine the connection between the institutional rules more broadly, positing a connection between these rules and ideological voting. Weiden analyzes whether the high courts in the United States, Canada, and Australia are highly politicized by examining the ideology of the judge relative to the appointing party, and then examining if greater politicization leads to greater ideological voting.

Before we compare across countries, consider prior studies of individual high courts. One might expect the US process to result in a polarized court, given that it is highly political, with elected officials holding the power and any balance coming from the involvement of both the president and the Senate. Not surprisingly the Court has been quite divided along a liberal and conservative split. From the 1940s through the 1960s, the US Supreme Court split predictably into two groups of judges who voted consistently across economics cases and civil liberties cases.[71] In such cases, judges not only voted predictably, but the amount of disagreement and nature of dissent across the Court was also significant.[72] For example, for civil liberties cases Justice Douglas dissented from only 1.3 percent of the liberal decisions, but from 77.7 percent of the conservative decisions. In contrast, Justice Rehnquist dissented from 54.8 percent of liberal decisions, but only 0.9 percent of the Court's conservative decisions.[73]

This split has persisted over time.[74] Grofman and Brazill found that differences along a liberal-conservative line accounted for over 80 percent of the variance in voting across judges between 1951 and 1993.[75] In fact the split has

71. Herman Pritchett documented a marked division of the US Supreme Court justices into two wings from 1939 to 1941, with a "conservative" wing always supporting business and a "liberal" wing frequently favoring labor or the government. Herman Pritchett, "Divisions of Opinion among Justices of the U. S. Supreme Court, 1939–1941" (1941) 35:5 *The American Political Science Review* 890 at 895–896. Glendon Schubert examined 1946–1963 and then 1946–1969 and found the judges were consistent in their voting across economics cases (the E-scale) and civil liberties cases (the C-scale) (correlation coefficients of greater than 0.90). See Glendon Schubert, *The Judicial Mind: The Attitudes and Ideologies of Supreme Court Justices, 1946–1963* (New York: Northwestern University Press, 1965) [Schubert, *Attitudes and Ideologies*] at 122 for general conclusion on C scale; Schubert, *Attitudes and Ideologies* at 141–142 for conclusion on E scale. Schubert, *Attitudes and Ideologies,* at 80; Glendon Schubert, *The Judicial Mind Revisited: A Psychometric Analysis of Supreme Court Ideology* (Oxford: Oxford University Press, 1974) [Schubert, *Psychometric Analysis*].

72. Mark S. Hurwitz & Drew Noble Lanier, "I Respectfully Dissent: Consensus, Agendas, and Policymaking on the U.S. Supreme Court 1888–1999" (2004) 21:3 *Review of Policy* 429 at 443.

73. Jeffrey A. Segal & Harold J. Spaeth, "Decisional Trends on the Warren and Burger Courts: Results from the Supreme Court Data Base Project" (1989) 73 *Judicature* 103 at 107.

74. The literature on the politics of decision-making on the US Supreme Court is vast and growing, too vast to cite fully. It has tended to find broadly a predictable split on the Court. For an influential study, see e.g. Jeffrey A. Segal & Harold J. Spaeth, *The Supreme Court and the Attitudinal Model Revisited* (Cambridge: Cambridge University Press, 2002) at 86, setting out the principal models of judicial decision-making [Segal & Spaeth, *Attitudinal Model*], and more recently, Lee Epstein, William M. Landes & Richard A. Posner, *Behavior of Federal Judges: A Theoretical and Empirical Study of Rational Choice* (Cambridge, MA: Harvard University Press, 2013) [Epstein, Landes & Posner, *Behavior*].

75. Bernard Grofman & Timothy J. Brazill, "Identifying the Median Justice on the Supreme Court through Multidimensional Scaling: Analysis of 'Natural Courts'" (2002) *Kluwer Academic Publishers* 55 at 58.

only become more pronounced over time. Devins and Baum argue that the divide between the liberal and conservatives judges has increased since the 1990s and particularly since 2010.[76] They attribute the rising divide amongst judges to the increasing polarization of politics in the United States. Martin and Quinn have used an influential approach of identifying how judges tend to vote relative to each other and have also found a significant split on the bench over time.[77]

Thus the United States has a political process and a polarized court—is it any different when there is a sole political actor making the decision such as in Canada, Australia, or formerly in the UK? You could imagine it turning out either way—if the prime minister has complete power to select candidates and does so through a closed process, he may use the opportunity to choose highly political judges; if that were the case, the Court's composition would likely show a substantial swing in appointing judges with each change in government. On the other hand, the lack of an overtly political, public process may allow the prime minister to focus on legal competence rather than politics. It turns out that in each of the countries where the prime minister selects judges, high courts are polarized to some degree, with the debate being whether the polarization is similar to and as severe as that in the United States.

In Canada, justices on the Supreme Court of Canada could be divided into different groups as early as the 1950s and 1960s.[78] More recently, judges on the Court under Chief Justice Lamer in the 1990s split into two groups, although it is unclear whether they actually resembled the voting behavior of judges on the US Supreme Court. On the one hand, McCormick found two different voting coalitions in this period, but argued they only explained about a

76. Devins & Baum, *supra* note 8.

77. Andrew D. Martin & Kevin M. Quinn, "Assessing Preference Change on the US Supreme Court" (2007) 23 *Journal of Law, Economics, and Organization* 303 [Martin & Quinn, "Preference Change"].

78. Fouts found justices on the Supreme Court of Canada in the 1950s could be classified into four groups when voting on civil liberties and economic cases: individualists, liberals, authoritarians, and conservatives. He concluded that the Court resembled the US Supreme Court in significant respects and drew parallels to ideologies of different judges, though recognizing that not all voting could be explained by ideology. Donald E. Fouts, "Policy-Making in the Supreme Court of Canada, 1950–1960" in Glendon Schubert & David Danelski, eds, *Comparative Judicial Behavior: Cross-Cultural Studies of Political Decision-Making in the East and West* (New York: Oxford University Press, 1969) 271, 284. Peck also found three different groups on the Court from 1958 to 1967—those who supported private parties against the government, those who supported the government, and those not easily classified: Sidney R. Peck, "A Scalogram Analysis of the Supreme Court of Canada, 1958–1967" in Glendon Schubert & David J. Danelski, eds, *Comparative Judicial Behaviour: Cross-Cultural Studies of Political Decision-Making in the East and West* (New York: Oxford University Press, 1969) 293 at 320.

third of divided decisions and were not static.[79] Two other studies, however, found strong similarities between the Lamer Court and the US Supreme Court. Ostberg, Wetstein, and Ducat found justices in that period differed in three principal areas (support for communitarian values (such as social protection), procedural fairness, and judicial activism) and these differences explained 60 percent of the variance in how judges voted.[80] Similarly, Wetstein et al. found the judges divided on a liberal-conservative basis in all three areas of law that they examined: economic, criminal, and civil rights.[81] They concluded that liberal-conservative tensions appear to be as strong a force for explaining conflict with the Canadian Supreme Court as in the United States, at least in these particular areas of law.[82] Taking a slightly longer period (1984–2004), Alarie and Green found judges on the Court differ in how they vote across issues, with the difference being statistically significant but much smaller than the difference in the United States.[83]

Overall, judges on the Supreme Court of Canada appointed by prime ministers appear to be split along political grounds, though probably less so than for the US Supreme Court. The same is true for other countries where the prime minister appoints the judges. Judges on the Australian High Court appear to be at least somewhat divided into different groupings, particularly when we look at when they dissent.[84] Judges on the South African Supreme Court of Appeal

79. Peter McCormick, "Birds of a Feather: Alliances and Influences on the Lamer Court 1990–1997" (1998) 36 *Osgoode Hall Law Journal* 366. See also F.L. Morton, Peter H. Russell & Michael J. Withey, "The Supreme Court's First One Hundred Charter of Rights Decisions: A Statistical Analysis" (1992) 30 *Osgoode Hall LJ* 1 at 39 [Morton, "First One Hundred"] (finding in the 1980s, the Court had a division between activists (Wilson and Lamer) and non-activists (McIntyre and L'Heureux-Dubé)).

80. C.L. Ostberg, Matthew Wetstein & Craig R. Ducat, "Attitudinal Dimensions of Supreme Court Decision Making in Canada: The Lamer Court, 1991–1995" (2002) 55:1 *Political Research Quarterly* 235 at 240–241.

81. Matthew E. Wetstein et al., "Ideological Consistency and the Attitudinal Conflict: A Comparative Analysis of the U.S. and Canadian Supreme Courts" (2009) 42:6 *Comparative Political Studies* 763 at 781 [Wetstein et al., "Comparative Analysis"].

82. Wetstein et al., "Comparative Analysis," *supra* note 81 at 780.

83. Alarie & Green "Policy Preference," *supra* note 68 (found that the Martin Quinn scores (based on ideal policy points) for Supreme Court of Canada judges from 1984 to 2004 could be differentiated by ideology but the level of dispersion appears less than in the US Supreme Court).

84. For discussions of the Australian High Court, see R.N. Douglas, "Judges and Policy on the Latham Court" (1969) 4:1 *Politics* 20; Glendon Schubert, "Political Ideology on the High Court" (1968) 3:1 *Politics* 21; Russell Smyth, "The Role of Attitudinal, Institutional and Environmental Factors in Explaining Variations in Dissent Rates on the High Court of Australia" (2005) 40:4

from 1970 to 2000 differed significantly from each other with respect to their support for the accused in criminal cases.[85] Although the UK House of Lords and subsequently the Supreme Court have very high rates of consensus, the judges show different voting tendencies, though whether these differences are caused by different political views, openness to dissent, or other personal characteristics is unclear.[86]

Each of the countries where political actors select judges showed some polarization across judges. This connection is, however, a far cry from saying that having political actors choose judges causes more polarized courts. One obvious question is whether countries where judges are selected by balanced committees or by the judges themselves also have polarized courts. Unfortunately little empirical work has been done on this issue. Evidence from the UK does not take into account the fact that the Court only changed its appointment process to a committee-based system in 2009. Israel, which appoints its judges by committee, has a high court with some polarization at least in some areas of law—such as security and religious freedom cases.[87] More work is needed across broader areas of law, and in India where the judges themselves decide on new members.[88]

Australian Journal of Political Science) 519 [Smyth, "Role of Attitudinal"]; Russell Smyth, "Explaining Historical Dissent Rates in the High Court of Australia" (2003) 41:2 *Journal of Commonwealth and Comparative Politics* 83 [Smyth, "Explaining Historical Dissent"].

85. Kaitlyn L. Sill & Stacia Haynie, "Panel Assignment in Appellate Courts: Strategic Behaviour in the South African Supreme Court of Appeal" (2010) 37:2 *Politikon* 269 [Sill & Haynie, "Panel Assignment"]. For the South African Appellate Division evidence that judges who frequently decided emergency cases in the 1980s were less supportive of the individual in civil rights and liberties cases, see Stacia L. Haynie, *Judging in Black and White: Decision Making in South African Appellate Division, 1950–1990* (New York: Peter Lang, 2003) at 84 [Haynie, *Black and White*].

86. T.T. Arvind & Lindsay Stirton, "Lawyers and the Legal Model: Judicial Ideology, Judicial Professionalism and Institutional Strategy among the Law Lords" (2012) at 2, online: https://extranet.sioe.org/uploads/isnie2012/arvind_stirton.pdf [Arvind & Stirton]; Chris Hanretty, "Lumpers and Splitters on the United Kingdom Supreme Court" (2013) American Political Science Association 2013 Annual Meeting Paper, 4.

87. Keren Weinshall-Margel, "Attitudinal and Neo-Institutional Models of Supreme Court Decision Making: An Empirical and Comparative Perspective from Israel" (2011) 8:3 *Journal of Empirical Legal Studies* 556 [Weinshall-Margel, "Attitudinal"].

88. Judges on the Indian Supreme Court from 1950 to 1969 could be classified as liberal or conservative depending on how they decided civil liberties and economic cases. However, this period was before the cases that in effect gave the appointment power to the judges themselves. George H. Gadbois, "Selection, Background Characteristics, and Voting Behaviour of Indian Supreme Court Judges, 1950–1969" in Glendon Schubert & David J. Danelski, eds, *Comparative Judicial Behaviour: Cross-Cultural Studies of Decision-Making in the East and West* (New York: Oxford University Press, 1969) at 221–256 [Gadbois, "Background Characteristics"]. See also George H. Gadbois, Jr., "Indian Judicial Behaviour" (1970) 5:3 *Economic and Political Weekly* 149.

Although judges are polarized on high courts both in the United States and where a prime minister or president chooses the judges, there have been few empirical studies that attempt to compare decision-making across high courts. We can think of two basic ways of comparing how polarized judges are on a court. First, are the judges dispersed in their voting? A court with judges whose voting is more dispersed may indicate that the appointing process is leading to judges who are more willing to follow their personal preferences in their decisions. Second, how consistent are judges across areas of law? In terms of the US literature, for example, are judges consistently voting in a liberal or conservative direction across areas of law?

## ARE JUDGES DISPERSED?

In one of the few cross-country comparisons, Weiden studied the high courts of the United States, Canada, and Australia in the 1990s, and concluded that American judges were more than twice as influenced by political views as Canadian judges, and that Australian high court judges were situated between the United States and Canada.[89] He established the political leanings of judges, using newspaper editorials at the time each judge was appointed. These newspaper scores ranged between 0 and 1 depending on how conservative the judge seemed (with a score of 0 being most conservative).[90] American judges on average had more conservative scores (.36) than Canadian (.61), with Australian judges in-between (.47). However, in terms of the degree of polarization, the Australian judges were the most dispersed (their scores had a standard deviation of .32) followed by American (.28) and then Canadian (.22). Although the number of observations is small, on this measure the Supreme Court of Canada was the least polarized court and the Australian the most, with the United States in-between.

Our own analysis provides a different look at how dispersed judges are in different courts. In the High Courts Judicial Database, cases are coded for their "direction"—whether they are "pro" or "con" in particular types of cases.[91] For example, in criminal cases, a "con" case is against the defendant and "pro" is for the defendant; in civil rights and liberties cases, a "con" case is against and a "pro" case is for the person alleging his or her civil rights were violated (except

89. Weiden, "Judicial Politicization," *supra* note 69 at 340. See also Weinshall-Margel, "Attitudinal," *supra* note 87.

90. Weiden, "Judicial Politicization," *supra* note 69 at 338. He used existing scores for the United States and Canada and developed his own scores for Australia.

91. The HCJD (Stacia L. Haynie et al. (2007) High Courts Judicial Database. Accessed at the University of South Carolina Judicial Research Initiative, online: www.cas.sc.edu/poli/juri) also codes cases for "mixed" pro and con. In order to ensure there is a clear direction for each case, we do not use the "mixed" cases. See Appendix 1 for a more detailed description of the database.

in "reverse discrimination" cases); and in a torts case, a "con" case is against and a "pro" case is for the injured party. The directions do not line up completely with the "liberal" and "conservative" labels in the US literature, nor do these labels necessarily have the same meaning across countries. However, they do provide a measure that can be used to trace patterns of decision-making across countries. For now, we will use the labels of "liberal" and "conservative" voting to correspond to the "pro" and "con" direction, although a non-ideological name is likely more appropriate. For present purposes, then, a judge casts a "liberal" vote if she is in the majority in a decision that finds in a "liberal" direction.

Judges on a particular court may vote similarly over time, such as tending to vote for the criminal defendant as opposed to the government. Figure 3-2 provides a measure for how judges vote on different high courts. It shows the differences in the average long-term liberal voting rates of judges on a court at a given time (where a judge's long-term liberal voting rate is the number of cases she voted in

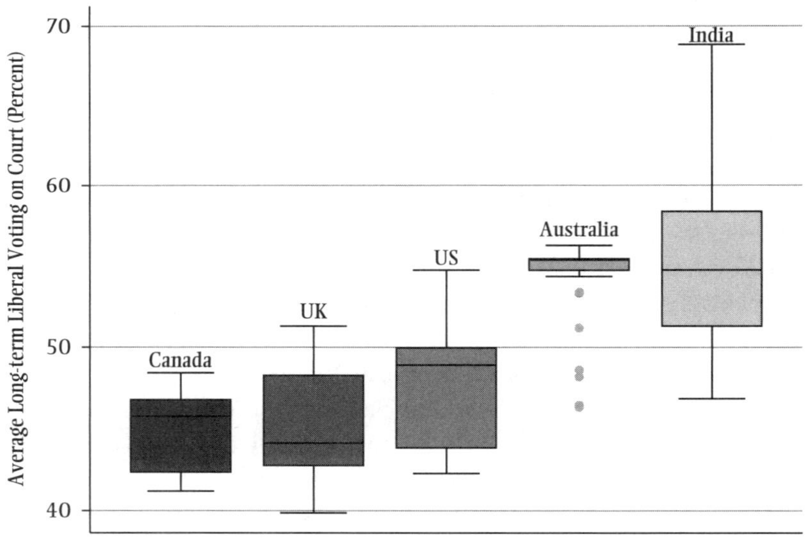


**Figure 3-2** The average long-term liberal voting rates of judges on the court in a given year over the period 1970 to the early 2000s. The box provides the middle 50 percent of the values of the annual average lifetime liberal voting rates on the court. The lines above and below show the maximum and minimum annual averages, respectively. Over the period, the average lifetime liberal voting rate of judges on the Supreme Court of Canada, the US Supreme Court, and the UK House of Lords had in general similar average long-term liberal voting rates. The Australian High Court and Indian Supreme Court tended to have higher annual average long-term liberal voting rates. In terms of the spread of these averages, Canada and Australia had less variation than the other countries.

a liberal direction divided by the total number of decisions in which she voted over the period we are studying). For example, in 2001 there were nine justices on the Supreme Court of Canada: Iacobucci (with a long-term liberal voting rate of 43.5 percent), L'Heureux-Dube (35.9 percent), Gonthier (37.8 percent), McLachlin (39.7 percent), Major (44.6 percent), Bastarache (38.9 percent), Binnie (42.9 percent), Arbour (52.9 percent), and Lebel (48 percent). For that year, the average of the liberal voting rates was 42.7 percent, and the standard deviation of these liberal voting rates was 0.054. Figure 3-2 shows this average for each court over the 30-year period, along with the maximum and minimum annual averages. The United States, Canada, and the UK have quite similar, low average long-term liberal rates whereas the averages in Australia and India are much higher. In terms of how similar are the judges on each court in the period, Figure 3-2 also shows the spread in these annual average long-term liberal voting rates. The courts in Canada and Australia had less variance over the period than the Indian or US Supreme Courts.

Interestingly, the annual average long-term liberal voting rates of the judges on the courts in the United States, Canada, and the UK track quite closely over the 30-year period starting in 1970. Figure 3-3 shows that the United States

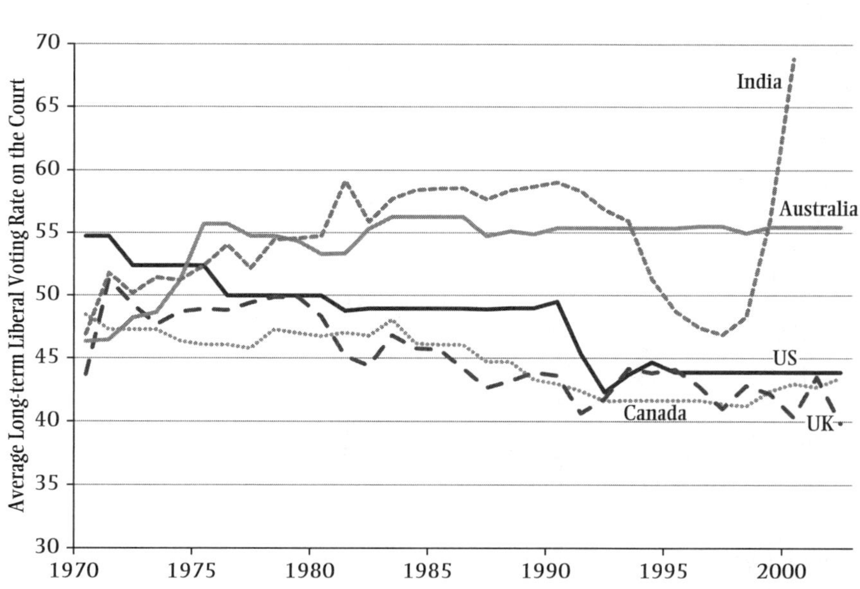


**Figure 3-3** Annual long-term liberal voting rates of judges on the court in a given year. The US Supreme Court, the Supreme Court of Canada, and the UK House of Lords averages track each other in declining over the period. The Australian High Court and the Indian Supreme Court, on the other hand, both trend upward at the beginning of the period, but the Australian average levels off whereas the average in India experiences a wild swing at the end of the period.

actually started the period with the highest average long-term liberal voting rate on the court but this average declined over the period, with the averages for the Supreme Court of Canada and the UK House of Lords tracking this decline. The average on the Australian High Court jumped at the beginning of the period and then stayed fairly uniformly high. The Indian Supreme Court average followed a similar path to the Australian court until the mid-1990s when it engaged in a quite significant swing down before shooting up by the end of the period (recall that the Indian Supreme Court data unlike the other courts is based on a sample of 100 decisions per year).

A different, though related, measure of how different are the judges on the court at a given time is how spread out are the long-term liberal voting rates of the judges on the court in a given year. Figure 3-4 shows the differences in the spread across courts by providing the standard deviation of the average long-term liberal voting rates of judges on the court in each year. Again if we return to our example of the Supreme Court of Canada in 2001, the standard deviation

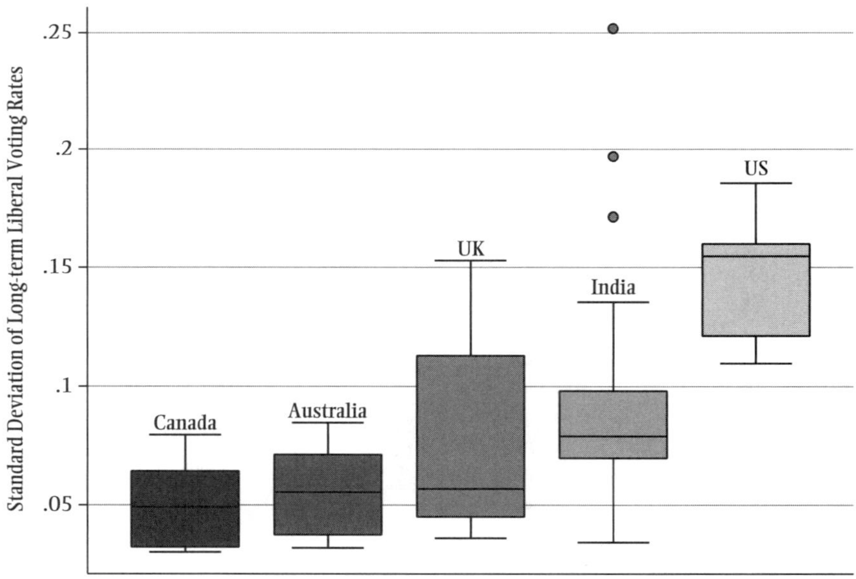


**Figure 3-4** Standard deviation of long-term liberal voting rates of judges on each court each year for the period from 1970s to the early 2000s. These standard deviations provide a measure of the spread in voting on each court. The box provides the middle 50 percent of the data for each country, with the line in the box showing the median standard deviation over the period. The lines above and below the box show the maximum and minimum annual standard deviations, respectively. The United States clearly has the greatest spread in long-term liberal voting rates across judges on this measure, whereas Canadian and Australian judges tend to be more closely concentrated in any given year.

of the long-term liberal voting rates of the nine judges was 0.054. Figure 3-4 looks at these standard deviations across time as a measure of differences in judges on a court. We can see that the greatest dispersion of liberal voting rates occurs in the United States—which had both the highest median spread and a high maximum and minimum spread. Both Australia and Canada, on the other hand, had relatively low dispersions of liberal voting rates, about a third of that of the US Supreme Court, along with correspondingly low maximum and minimum spreads. The UK and India fell in the middle, both with fairly wide ranges of maximum and minimum spreads, indicating a greater swing across sets of judges.

The high courts then differ in terms of how much spread there is across the voting of the judges on each court. The United States and India have the greatest spread in voting across judges on their courts. Canada and Australia have the most similar sets of judges with the UK in the middle. The spread in voting is not airtight evidence of political decision-making as there may be a variety of reasons for differences in voting (such as the fact that some countries have an entrenched bill of rights that may provide more or less room for ideological decision-making). We therefore also must look to other measures such as whether judges are consistent across areas of law.

## ARE JUDGES CONSISTENT ACROSS AREAS OF LAW?

Polarization possibly means a politicized court, but the difficulty is that the source of the differences is unknown. For instance, judges may be basing their decisions on legal factors but disagree as to the relevant factors. We want to know whether there is a connection between judges' personal preferences and how they decide appeals. There are a number of different ways to tease out this connection. We can look at how a judge's decisions are related to how she tends to vote on other policy issues, how she was described in newspapers at the time she was appointed, how she decided past cases, or, as we will look at later, the political party of the government actor who appointed her.[92] Although a judge's views are often labeled as either liberal or conservative in particular areas of

92. For a discussion of issues around measuring ideology, see Lee Epstein, Andrew D. Martin, Kevin M. Quinn & Jeffrey A. Segal, "Ideology and the Study of Judicial Behavior" in Jon Hanson, ed, *Ideology, Psychology, and Law* (Oxford: Oxford University Press, 2012) [Epstein et al., "Ideology"]. The newspaper scores were initially devised by Segal and Cover who coded newspaper editorials at the time of the judges' appointments on a scale denoting more or less conservative/liberal (Jeffrey A. Segal & Albert D. Cover, "Ideological Values and Votes of U.S. Supreme Court Justices" (1989) 83 *American Political Science Review* 557). These scores have been adopted by researchers on some other high courts (see e.g. C.L. Ostberg & Matthew E. Wetstein, *Attitudinal Decision Making in the Supreme Court of Canada* (Vancouver: University

law, there are other factors such as gender, regional origin, or religion that affect decisions.[93]

Not surprisingly, judges on the US Supreme Court have been found to decide cases in line with their political views despite their frequent statements to the contrary during confirmation hearings in the Senate.[94] For example, for judges on the US Supreme Court between 1962 and 1998, ideology measures derived from newspaper editorials at the time of their appointment were able to predict 70 percent of their votes in search and seizure cases, which is much higher than the prediction just based on the facts of the case.[95] In general, the ideology of US Supreme Court judges is strongly connected to how they decide cases. The strength varies over time but tends to be fairly consistent across areas of law.[96]

This connection also holds in countries with more closed processes with appointments made by a prime minister or president such as Canada and Australia, though the connection appears weaker. In Canada, for example, judges' votes were correlated with scores based on newspaper reports at the time of their appointment—judges who were described as conservative in newspapers tended to vote similarly in right to counsel, search and seizure, union, and tax cases.[97] These scores were not, however, correlated with all decisions by the judges,

of British Columbia Press, 2007) at 124 [Ostberg & Wetstein, *Attitudinal Decision Making*]; Donald R. Songer et al., *Law, Ideology and Collegiality: Judicial Behaviour in the Supreme Court of Canada* (Montreal and Kingston: McGill University Press, 2012) [Songer, *Judicial Behaviour*] for Canada; Weiden, "Judicial Politicization," *supra* note 69 for Australia).

93. Epstein et al., "Ideology," *supra* note 92.

94. Epstein, Landes & Posner, *Behavior, supra* note 74 (Justice Alito, for instance, stated that Supreme Court justices must "be careful not to inject their own views" into their decisions, and Justice Sotomayor said that "[j]udges must apply the law and not make the law" at 101).

95. Segal & Spaeth, *Attitudinal Model, supra* note 74 at 324.

96. Epstein et al., "Ideology," *supra* note 92. See also Mathew E. Wetstein, C.L. Ostberg, Donald R. Songer & Susan Johnson, "Ideological Consistency and Attitudinal Conflict: A Comparative Analysis of the U.S. and Canadian Supreme Courts" (2009) 42:6 *Comparative Political Studies* 763. See also Devins & Baum, *supra* note 8.

97. For a description of the scores, see Ostberg & Wetstein, *Attitudinal Decision Making, supra* note 92 at 49–58. See also Ostberg & Wetstein, *Attitudinal Decision Making, supra* note 92 (finding newspaper scores were significant in right to counsel, search and seizure, union, and non-unanimous tax cases but not equality or free expression cases over the period 1984–2003). C.L. Ostberg & Matthew E. Wetstein, "Search and Seizure Cases in the Supreme Court of Canada: Extending an American Model of Judicial Decision Making across Countries" (1999) 80:4 *Social Science Quarterly* 757 (examining search and seizure cases between 1984 and 1994 and finding votes were correlated with an ideology measure combining newspaper scores and the party of the appointing prime minister).

including in equality or freedom of expression cases.[98] When we look over the post-Charter period (post-1982), a judge's newspaper scores were also modestly related to his ideal point—a measure of where he sits on policy issues relative to everyone else on the Court at the time.[99] Further, judges on the Supreme Court of Canada during a natural court period (where no one left or joined the Court) in 1992–1997 were influenced by similar factors to judges of the US Supreme Court in the areas of economic, criminal, and civil liberties cases.[100] However, although a liberal/conservative divide was important for both courts, ideology seemed to play a different role or at least not as unidimensional a role in Canada, as Canadian judges could not be classified consistently as liberal or conservative in each area.[101]

Therefore, although the Supreme Court of Canada judges' political views and their decisions are correlated, they are seen as less influenced by political views than judges on the US Supreme Court.[102] They may also be influenced by other factors. For example, judges vote differently if the appeal is from their province of origin.[103] Further, female judges vote differently than male in some areas. For

98. Ostberg & Wetstein, *Attitudinal Decision Making, supra* note 92. Recently, C.L. Ostberg & Matthew E. Wetstein, "Postmaterialist Values in the Supreme Court of Canada: Empirical Analysis of Environmental Cases, 1973–2010" (Paper delivered at the annual meeting of the Canadian Political Science Association, Victoria, BC, June 6, 2013) [unpublished] found that newspaper scores were not correlated with voting on the Supreme Court on environmental matters. See Alarie & Green "Policy Preference," *supra* note 68, finding no connection between these scores and liberal voting rates of judges.

99. Alarie & Green "Policy Preference," *supra* note 68.

100. Songer, *Judicial Behaviour, supra* note 92 at 114 (using factor analysis and finding that a liberal-conservative dimension was a strong predictor of splits in economic, criminal, and civil liberties cases).

101. Songer, *Judicial Behaviour, supra* note 92 at 115; Alarie & Green "Policy Preference," *supra* note 68; Ostberg & Wetstein, *Attitudinal Decision Making, supra* note 92 at 191; Wetstein et al., "Comparative Analysis," *supra* note 81 at 780 (finding a strong inverse relationship between criminal and economic liberalism between 1992 and 1997).

102. Alarie & Green "Policy Preference," *supra* note 68; Ostberg & Wetstein, *Attitudinal Decision Making, supra* note 92 at 191; Songer, *Judicial Behaviour, supra* note 92 at 133.

103. C. Neal Tate & Panu Sittiwong, "Decision Making in the Canadian Supreme Court: Extending the Personal Attributes Model across Nations" (1989) 51:4 *Journal of Politics* 901 at 905–906 [Tate & Sittiwong] (an early study examining a range of judicial traits including regionalism, partisanship, religion, and career experience); Donald R. Songer & Susan W. Johnson, "Judicial Decision Making in the Supreme Court of Canada: Updating the Personal Attribute Model" (2007) 40:4 *Canadian Journal of Political Science* 911 [Songer & Johnson, "Judicial Decision"]; C.L. Ostberg, Matthew Wetstein & Craig R. Ducat, "Leaders, Followers, and Outsiders: Task and Social Leadership on the Canadian Supreme Court in the Early Nineties" (2004) 36:3 *Polity* 505; Songer, *Judicial Behaviour, supra* note 92 at 141–142.

example, female judges were more likely to vote in favor of rights claimants and economic underdogs and less likely to vote for criminal defendants.[104]

Australia, another country with the prime minister in control of appointments, lies between the United States and Canada in terms of the judges following their political views. As we saw, Weiden looked at judges in these three countries, measuring the views of the judges by a score based on how each judge was viewed in newspaper editorials at the time of appointment.[105] He compared this newspaper score with how likely the judge was to strike down a law, classifying the laws as either liberal or conservative. Judges in each country tended to vote in line with their political views (as measured by the newspaper scores) to some extent—that is, conservative judges were more likely to strike down liberal than conservative laws. However, judges on the US Supreme Court were more likely to be influenced by these political views than those on the Australian High Court, who in turn were more influenced than judges on the Supreme Court of Canada.[106]

Judges in the UK appear to be even less influenced in their decisions by political views. Much of the evidence relates to the House of Lords when the executive appointed judges, as opposed to the UK Supreme Court under the committee process. The Law Lords did differ in permissiveness toward the state in cases that challenge state actions; some were much more likely to uphold the state action than others.[107] They also differed in ideal points—that is, when we look at how a judge decided, we can position him on a line with the other judges depending on whether he tends to agree or disagree with each judge.[108] However, the judges may follow their political views less than other potential influences such as norm of professionalism or a greater or lesser willingness to dissent, although these norms may hide rather than replace differences in

104. Songer, *Judicial Behaviour, supra* note 92; Songer & Johnson, "Judicial Decision," *supra* note 103; Susan W. Johnson, Donald R. Songer & Nadia A. Jilani, "Judge Gender, Critical Mass, and Decision Making in the Appellate Courts of Canada" (2011) 32:3 *Journal of Women, Politics & Policy* 11; Ostberg & Wetstein, *Attitudinal Decision Making, supra* note 92 at 120 ("[r]emarkably, all five female justices serving on the Court in the period studied can be found at the liberal end of the civil rights and liberties spectrum, with five of the six most liberal voting patterns on the Court").

105. Weiden, "Judicial Politicization," *supra* note 69.

106. Weiden, "Judicial Politicization," *supra* note 69 at 340.

107. Arvind & Stirton, *supra* note 86 at 27.

108. Chris Hanretty, "The Decisions and Ideal Points of British Law Lords" (2012) 43 *British Journal of Political Science* 703 at 703 [Hanretty, "Ideal Points"] (examining ideal points of Law Lords between 1969 and 2009 and finding that the ideal points are not strongly related to ideology or to the liberal voting rate of judges).

attitudes.[109] As in other countries, judges on the UK Supreme Court may be influenced when making decisions not just by their political views but by other personal values.[110] Although there is limited work on the issue, there is then less support for the presence of political voting by judges in the UK than in the United States, Canada, or Australia.

So far we have seen that where political actors control appointments, the judges tend to be influenced by their political views, though the extent of the influence varies by country.[111] Is this also the case when a committee selects judges, as in Israel? Although justices on the Israeli Supreme Court did differ in how they voted in different areas, the differences were "not shockingly broad."[112] The individual justices differed in the extent to which they favored the defendant in criminal cases.[113] Further, in a random selection of freedom of religion cases before the Israeli Supreme Court between 1985 and 2008, justices who are religiously observant were more likely to support a freedom of religion claim.[114] Moreover, female justices were more likely to vote for the defendant than their male counterparts, though the difference was very small and seemed to depend on one justice.[115] The Israeli example therefore shows some attitudinal voting even where judges play a significant role in the appointment process.

109. Arvind & Stirton, *supra* note 86 at 27; Hanretty, "Ideal Points," *supra* note 108 at 715.

110. Rachel J. Cahill-O'Callaghan, "The Influence of Personal Values on Legal Judgments" (2013) 40:4 *Journal of Law and Society* 596. O'Callaghan undertook a content analysis of 18 UK Supreme Court decisions and found a connection between certain personal values of judges (such as universalism or traditionalism) and their decisions.

111. Judges were also influenced by political ideology in South Africa. See Glendon Schubert, "Political Culture and Judicial Ideology: Some Cross- and Subcultural Comparisons" (1977) 9:4 *Comparative Political Studies* 363; Glendon Schubert, "Subcultural Effects on Judicial Behaviour: A Comparative Analysis" (1980) 42 *The Journal of Politics* 952. Schubert found English-speaking and Afrikaans-speaking judges on the South African Appellate Division, South Africa's highest court of appeal during the apartheid era, voted very differently. See also Haynie, *Black and White, supra* note 85 at 77 (finding that Afrikaans-speaking judges on the South African Appellate Division during the apartheid era who were appointed by the apartheid government had a more conservative voting record than their colleagues).

112. Theodore Eisenberg, Talia Fisher & Issie Rosen-Zvi, "Does the Judge Matter? Exploiting Random Assignment on a Court of Last Resort to Assess Judge and Case Selection Effects" (2012) 9:2 *Journal of Empirical Legal Studies* 246 [Eisenberg et al., "Does the Judge Matter"].

113. Eisenberg et al., "Does the Judge Matter," *supra* note 112.

114. Weinshall-Margel, "Attitudinal," *supra* note 87 at 570. Weinshall-Margel employed this method to measure ideological voting because in Israel, politicians are only a minority in the appointment process, and the discussions of the nominating committee are kept secret, making more conventional methods of measuring ideology inapplicable.

115. Eisenberg et al., "Does the Judge Matter," *supra* note 112 at 248.

If we use our data to compare across countries, one measure of whether judges rely on their personal preferences is their consistency in voting across areas of law. It is not a perfect measure as a judge may have other reasons for consistency, such as reliance on a particular doctrinal or interpretative approach to legal questions that is not reflected in what we would normally think of as ideology or personal preferences.[116] Figure 3-5 shows the relationship between how judges vote across criminal, civil rights, and economic cases using long-term liberal voting rates in each of these areas. The line in each individual graph is the line that best fits how the judges on the particular court compare across the areas of law. An upward-sloping line means that there is a positive correlation between the votes of the judges in the different areas. If the judges voted exactly the same in both areas of law in the graph, the line would be the 45-degree line.

On this measure again, the US Supreme Court justices clearly lead the pack with the most consistency in voting between each of these areas, with the lines of best fit becoming successively flatter as we move from the United States through to India, indicating less of a positive relationship. We may expect to find the highest correlation in voting for each judge between criminal and civil rights cases, and that was true for each of the countries. The correlation between criminal and civil rights cases for US Supreme Court justices (with a correlation coefficient of 0.93) was far higher than for Australian (0.58), Canada (0.57), or the UK (0.5), with Indian judges having almost no correlation between votes in this area (0.03). The US justices also ranked first ahead of Australian for the correlation between their voting in both economic and civil rights cases and economic and criminal cases. Canada and the UK were fairly far behind in both these comparisons, with again Indian judges evincing almost no correlation between votes.[117]

Judges' votes in these areas then appear to be correlated in some courts. Does this relationship continue to hold if we control for (hold constant) other factors that may affect voting, such as how the lower court decided the issue before it came to the high court? We need to control for such variables as otherwise an apparent correlation may be misleading. In the case of the direction of the lower court decision, for example, it may be that judges overall tend to reverse lower court decisions. We would want to know a judge's liberal voting rate, taking into account the fact that in some cases they are reacting to liberal or conservative lower court decisions.

116. Joshua Fischman & Tonja Jacobi, "The Second Dimension of the Supreme Court" (2016) 57 *Wm. & Mary Law Review* 1671.

117. Recall that the Indian Supreme Court data was based on a sample of 100 cases for each year, leading to lower numbers of decisions by each judge in the database.

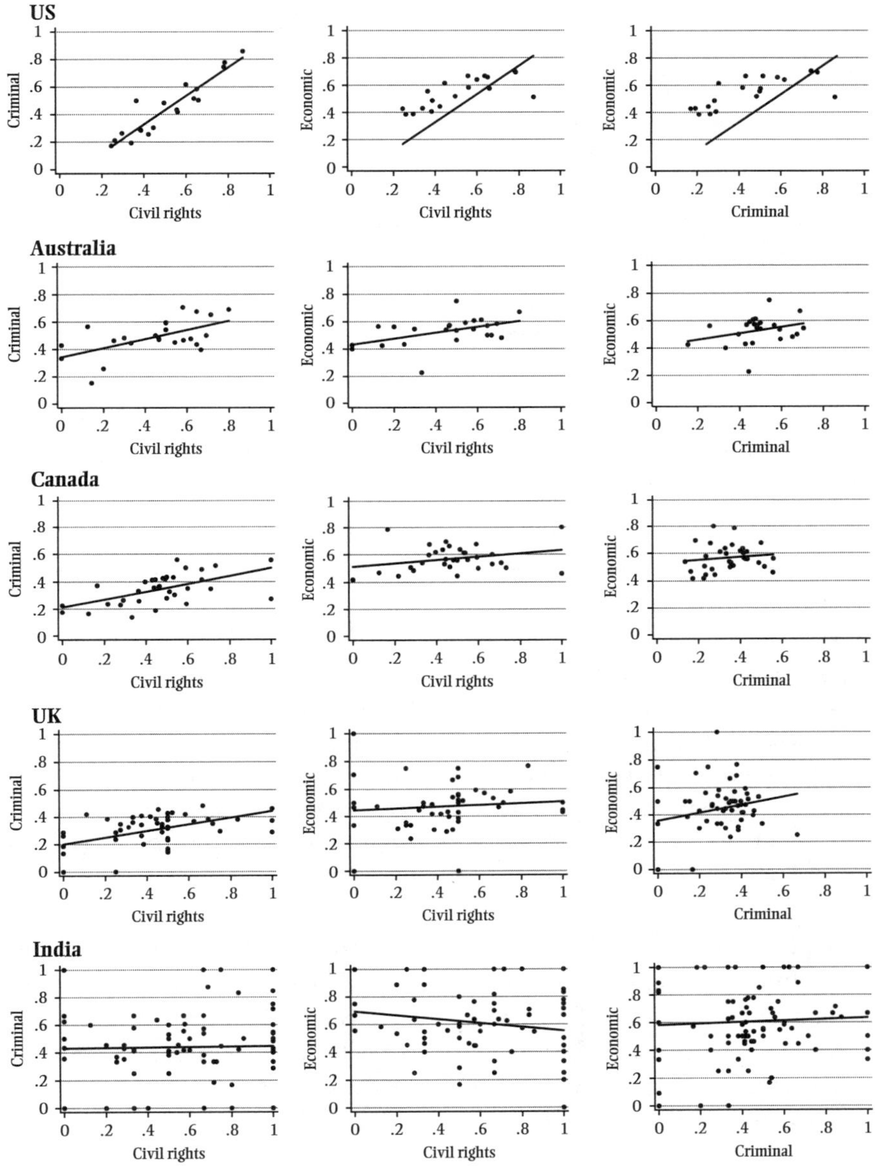


**Figure 3-5** Scatterplots of long-term liberal voting rates for judges across Criminal, Civil Rights, and Economic cases, 1970 to early 2000s. US Supreme Court judges had the highest correlation between their votes across all three of these comparisons, followed by Australian High Court justices. Judges on the Supreme Court of India showed almost no correlation in their votes across areas of law.

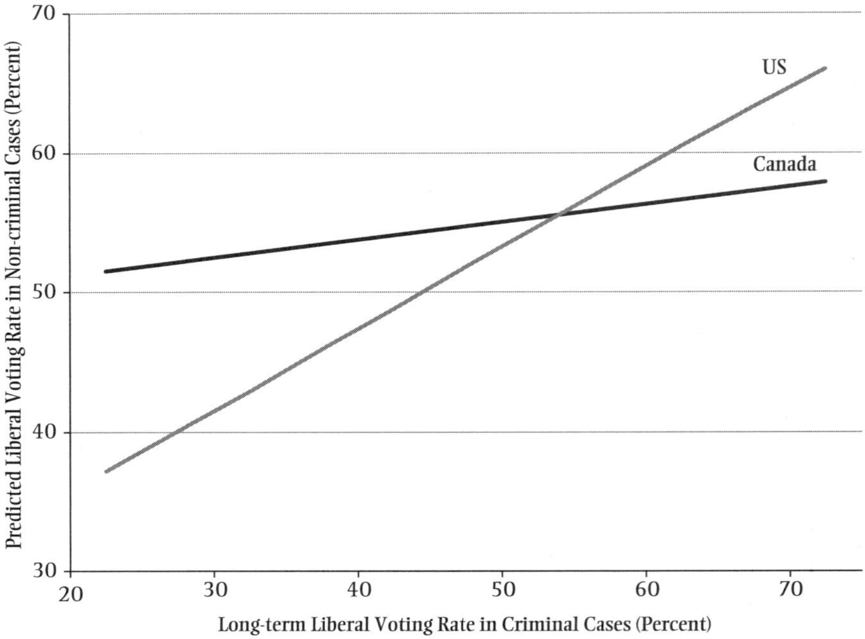


**Figure 3-6** Predicted liberal voting rate in non-criminal cases (percent) based on long-term liberal voting rates in criminal cases (percent), 1970 to early 2000s. The predictions are controlling for the direction (liberal or conservative) of the lower court decision. Justices on the US Supreme Court are much more consistent across criminal and all non-criminal cases than are justices on the Supreme Court of Canada. India, the UK, and Australia are not included as the relationship between lifetime voting on criminal cases and voting on all other cases was not statistically significant.

Figure 3-6 shows the liberal voting rate in non-criminal cases that are predicted from the long-term liberal voting rates of judges in criminal cases (controlling for the direction of the lower court decision).[118] The first point to notice is that the only two courts for which there is a statistically significant relationship between lifetime liberal voting rates in criminal cases and voting in all other cases are the US Supreme Court and the Supreme Court of Canada.[119] We cannot safely

118. Based on logit regressions with vote in non-criminal cases (liberal versus conservative) as the dependent variable and long-term liberal voting rates in criminal cases and direction of the lower court decision as the independent variables, the coefficients on long-term liberal voting rates in criminal cases were significant at the .01 level for the US Supreme Court and .05 level for the Supreme Court of Canada. The results were similar if the analysis also controlled for area of law. See Appendix 2 Table 1 for a summary of regression results.

119. Note that there is a trade-off in specifying ideology—the party of the appointer is quite a crude measure of ideology but it can be applied across all areas of law whereas judges' voting in criminal cases can only be applied to non-criminal cases.

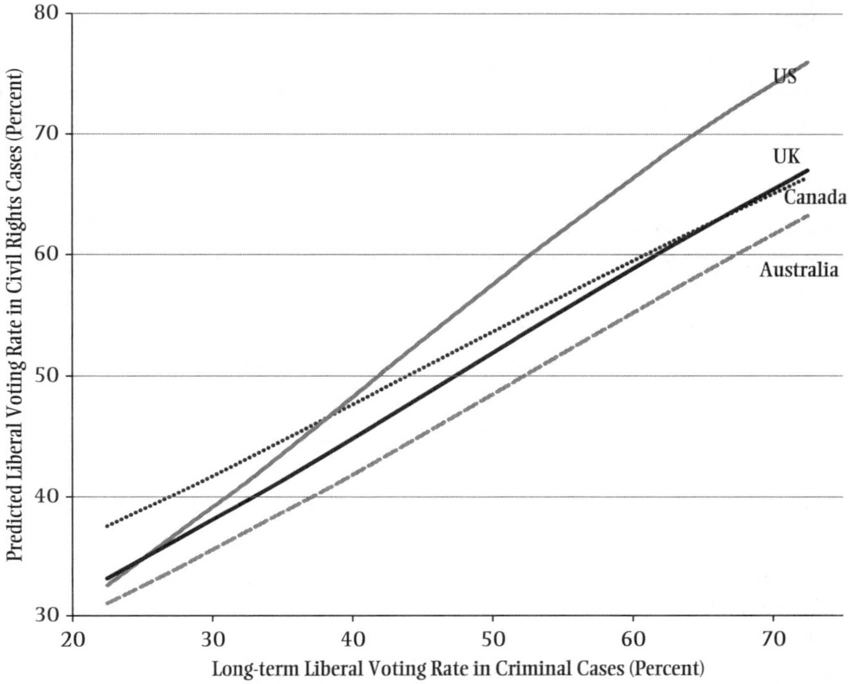


**Figure 3-7** Predicted liberal voting rate in civil rights cases (percent) based on long-term liberal voting rates in criminal cases (percent), 1970 to early 2000s. The predictions are controlling for the direction (liberal or conservative) of the lower court decision. Justices on the US Supreme Court have a greater increase in voting on civil rights cases than justices on the high courts in the UK, Canada, or Australia for equivalent increases in long-term liberal voting rates in criminal cases. India is not included as the relationship between long-term voting on criminal cases and voting on all other cases was not statistically significant.

predict the voting on non-criminal cases from the voting on criminal cases for judges in the UK, India, or Australia. Second, justices on the US Supreme Court have more consistent liberal voting rates between criminal and all other cases than do justices on the Supreme Court of Canada. For the voting to be perfectly consistent, the predicted votes would be on the 45-degree line. For justices on the US Supreme Court the relationship is positively correlated, with an increase from 40 percent to 50 percent in the long-term liberal voting rate in criminal cases related to about a 7 percent higher liberal voting rate in all other cases. Justices on the Supreme Court of Canada, on the other hand, have less of a close connection between the rates of voting, as indicated by the flatter line. An increase from 40 percent to 50 percent in lifetime liberal voting in criminal cases only corresponds to an increase of only about 1 percent in liberal voting in all other cases.

We could imagine, though, that this relationship is stronger across more controversial areas such as civil rights cases. Figure 3-7 looks at the relationship between long-term liberal voting in criminal cases and how judges vote in civil rights cases (controlling for the direction of the lower court decision).[120] Justices on the US Supreme Court have the greatest increase in predicted liberal voting in civil rights cases for equivalent increases in long-term liberal voting rates in criminal cases. An increase in long-term liberal voting rates in criminal cases from 40 to 50 percent leads to an increase in liberal voting in civil rights of about 9 percent for the US Supreme Court (51 to 60 percent) but only 6 percent for the Supreme Court of Canada (49 to 55 percent) and about 7 percent for the UK and Australia (about 43 to 50 percent and 47 to 54 percent, respectively). So justices in all these countries (other than India) have a strong positive connection in liberal voting rates between these two areas of law. In the United States judges who are conservative on criminal cases tend to be equivalently conservative in civil rights cases whereas judges who are very liberal in criminal cases are also very liberal for civil rights. For the other countries, judges who are very conservative in criminal cases tend to be relatively more liberal in civil rights cases, whereas judges who are very liberal in criminal cases tend to be relatively less liberal in civil rights cases. In none of the countries, then, is the liberal voting rate identical across the two areas of law.

In sum, judges in the United States are very consistent in their voting, based on how much of a relationship exists between their votes in criminal cases and other cases. Judges in other countries tend to be less consistent, particularly when we look at the relationship between voting in criminal cases and in all other areas. In the more controversial cases judges who vote liberally in criminal cases also tend to vote liberally in civil rights cases, and judges who tend to vote conservatively also tend to vote conservatively in civil rights cases.

Judges on the courts we study then appear to be influenced to some extent in their decisions by their political views. However, greater involvement by political actors is only weakly correlated with judges being more likely to be influenced by these views, with the main support for such a connection coming from the United States. The United States is an outlier both because its legislative branch has such a large involvement in high court appointments and because it has such a politicized appointments process. In other countries where the legislative branch has little or no power over high court appointments, the influence

120. Based on logit regressions with vote in civil rights cases (liberal versus conservative) as the dependent variable and long-term liberal voting rates in criminal cases and direction of the lower court decision as the independent variables, the coefficients on long-term liberal voting rates in criminal cases were significant at the .05 level except for India.

of political ideology over judicial decision-making is weaker. Again there is correlation but not necessarily causation.

## Do Appointers Replicate Themselves?

On a more basic level, we may think that a person who holds the appointment power is more likely to appoint a judge who thinks like her, all other things being equal. She may believe that such a choice is appropriate or may be following an unconscious bias toward individuals with similar views.[121] In either case, judges appointed by people with similar views should decide cases in similar ways, and it is likely that the preferences of appointed judges will change as the preferences of the appointer changes (such as through a change in government). The appointer does not have to be political for this connection to hold—judges in India may, for example, tend to appoint judges with similar views to their own.

For this connection between the judge and who appoints her to hold, the appointer must be able to determine at the time of appointment how an individual will vote once appointed to the bench. Even if someone wishes to appoint individuals with preferences similar to her own, she may be unable to if she can't tell how the individual will decide cases once on the court. Open hearings and questioning may provide greater evidence of the nominee's views, but may still be somewhat unhelpful if nominees are unwilling to give fulsome or non-evasive answers during the process. Appointers can look at how candidates have acted in the past—how they decided cases on the court they are on, for example—but judges may act differently on a high court than on a lower court where they feel more bound by decisions of a higher court or be concerned about potential reversal by a higher court.

Despite these variables, as a starting point, we expect that:

> *H2: A judge's voting will be positively related to the political views of whoever appointed him.*

121. Some attempts to change the composition of a high court are more transparent than others. For example, in South Africa in the 1950s, the National Party government increased the size of the Appellate Division and appointed numerous Afrikaans-speaking judges to the Court in order to move it in a more conservative direction. Judges who were appointed in the 1950s as part of this court-packing plan voted for the underdogs at a much lower frequency than other judges, suggesting that the National Party's faith in their conservatism was well placed. Lori Hausegger & Stacia L Haynie, "Judicial Decision-Making and the Use of Panels in the Canadian Supreme Court and the South African Appellate Division" (2003) 37:3 *Law and Society Review* 635 at 638.

Identifying the political views of the appointer may be quite simplistic such as coding the political party of the appointing party or parties.[122] Although such a measure has some intuitive appeal, it also has several problems. One of the largest is that it may ignore or downplay differences across appointing parties.[123] For example, different appointers (such as prime ministers or presidents) may be more or less conservative or liberal despite being from the same party. Although more sophisticated measures of ideology can be used, if how a judge votes is strongly related to the party of whoever appointed him in some countries rather than others, it provides an interesting opening to ask about the differences.

Further, despite the best efforts of some governments to influence high courts in their preferred ideological direction, these efforts are not always successful. One possible reason is that judges, once appointed, may change their judicial ideology.[124] This is important, not least because following appointment it is not possible to directly influence decision-making by appointees. In most jurisdictions it is difficult legally, not to mention risky politically, to try to remove sitting high court judges. For example, in the United States, justices on the Supreme Court are entitled to hold office "during good behavior," and once a judge is confirmed, a president has no power to remove her from office.[125] A judge's voting may be most likely to correspond to the ideology of the appointing party in the initial period on the bench and may "drift" from that position over time.[126] For example, looking at 23 US Supreme Court justices who served at least 15 terms since 1937, Epstein, Landes, and Posner found

122. See Epstein et al., "Ideology," *supra* note 92 for an overview of different measures of ideology.

123. Epstein, Landes & Posner, *Behavior, supra* note 74 at 71–72 (noting that party of appointing president in the United States, for example, has several weaknesses, including ignoring differences in ideologies of presidents from the same party, assuming presidents always appoint judges for ideological reasons rather than also thinking of personal or other reasons, and neglecting the fact that presidents do not completely control appointments).

124. Lee Epstein et al., "Ideological Drift among Supreme Court Justices: Who, When and How Important?" (2007) 101:4 *Northwestern University Law Review* 1483 at 1486 [Epstein et al., "Ideological Drift"] ("[v]irtually every Justice serving since the 1930s has moved to the left or right or, in some cases, has switched directions several times"); see also Alarie & Green "Policy Preference," *supra* note 68 re: theory of drift.

125. United States Constitution, Article III, Section 1. The only mechanism through which a justice on the US Supreme Court can be removed is through the process of impeachment. Only one justice has ever been impeached, and he was eventually acquitted by the Senate, which allowed him to remain in office. Rutkus, "Appointment Process," *supra* note 2 at 2.

126. See Epstein et al., "Ideological Drift," *supra* note 124. See also Alarie & Green "Policy Preference," *supra* note 68.

that eight of the justices became more conservative over their time on the bench, of whom Republican presidents appointed six. Democratic presidents appointed all four of the judges who became more liberal.[127] Similarly on the Supreme Court of Canada some justices became more liberal, some more conservative, and some showed no change, but there was no apparent connection to the party of the appointing prime minister; both Conservative and Liberal appointees became more conservative or more liberal or stayed the same.[128]

Unsurprisingly, American presidents tend to appoint justices with political views similar to their own, particularly in recent years. Epstein, Landes, and Posner, for example, looking at non-unanimous US Supreme Court decisions between 1937 and 2009 found that Republican appointees voted more conservatively overall than Democratic appointees. The difference was quite large in some areas of law such as in civil rights where the Republican appointees voted in a conservative fashion a little over half the time whereas Democratic appointees only about a third of the time.[129] They point out that when using more sophisticated measures of policy views, Republican presidents can be seen to sometimes appoint liberal justices and Democratic presidents conservative justices. However, the overall relationship is strong. Similarly, Devins and Baum argue that although there was a connection between the party of the appointing president and the voting of justices in the past, it was never perfect—sometimes Republican presidents appointed justices who were more liberal than some Democratic appointees.[130] However, they argue that the Court has been completely polarized since 2010 with Republican appointees as a bloc more conservative than Democratic appointees.[131]

127. Epstein, Landes & Posner, *Behavior, supra* note 74 at 116. See also Martin & Quinn, "Preference Change," *supra* note 77; Epstein et al., "Ideological Drift," *supra* note 124.

128. Alarie & Green "Policy Preference," *supra* note 68 at 40–41. Ostberg & Wetstein, *Attitudinal Decision Making, supra* note 92 found that Supreme Court of Canada judges were more stable over time in some areas (criminal at 80) than others (civil liberties at 124).

129. Epstein, Landes & Posner, *Behavior, supra* note 74 at 112–13 (examining the fraction of conservative votes in non-unanimous cases in various areas of law for the period 1937–2009). Schubert also looked at the US Supreme Court in the 1940s through the 1960s and found that the Court became more conservative in 1949–1952 when Harry Truman was in power, and then gradually became more liberal during the terms of Presidents Eisenhower and Kennedy before becoming more conservative again as a result of appointments by President Nixon. See Schubert, *Attitudes and Ideologies, supra* note 71 at 143; Schubert, *Psychometric Analysis, supra* note 71 at 89.

130. Devins & Baum, *supra* note 8.

131. Martin and Quinn used ideal point estimates to identify the median justices on the Supreme Court from 1953 to 1999, and traced the changes in attitude of the court from a conservative one in the 1950s, to a liberal one in the 1960s, and back to a conservative one during the 1970s

The relationship between the political views of the appointing party and the appointed judge is weaker in other countries. In Canada, the party of the appointing prime minister is positively related to voting by the appointed justice and the newspaper ideological scores for that justice, but the connection is not as strong as in the United States.[132] On average over the 1982–2005 period, a justice appointed by a Liberal prime minister had a 5 percent higher liberal voting record than a Conservative appointee.[133] The connection differs across areas of law—in some areas the party of the appointing prime minister has little or no connection with how the justices vote.[134] Even in Charter of Rights and Freedoms cases, Liberal appointees were considerably more likely to vote liberally in equality cases than their Conservative counterparts, but not in other types of Charter appeals.[135] Other indicators of personal views seem more closely related to how justices decide cases than the party of the appointing prime minister, and even when there is a connection, it is much more nuanced than in the United States.[136]

The justices on the High Court of Australia similarly seem to be less easily differentiated by the party that appointed them than in the United States.[137] If

and 1980s. Andrew D. Martin & Kevin M. Quinn, "Dynamic Ideal Point Estimation via Markov Chain Monte Carlo for the U.S. Supreme Court, 1953–1999" (2002) 10:2 *Political Analysis* 134.

132. Alarie & Green "Policy Preference," *supra* note 68. Some early studies of the Supreme Court of Canada also found that Liberal and Conservative appointees voted differently: Michael Bader & Edward Burstein, "The Supreme Court of Canada 1892–1902: A Study of the Men and the Times" (1970) 8:3 *Osgoode Hall LJ* 503; Tate and Sittiwong, *supra* note 103 (examining Court decisions between 1949 and 1985).

133. Alarie & Green "Policy Preference," *supra* note 68 at p 35 (note, however, they found a much smaller relationship between party of the appointing prime minister and ideal points for the judges).

134. See e.g. Ostberg & Wetstein, *Attitudinal Decision Making, supra* note 92 (finding that the party of the appointing prime minister was not significantly related to some criminal cases (right to counsel and search and seizure) or tax or union cases during the period 1984–2003); Songer, *Judicial Behaviour, supra* note 92 at 139–40 (finding that party of the appointing prime minister was weakly related in the criminal area but not for economic or civil liberties cases).

135. Benjamin Alarie & Andrew Green, "Charter Decisions in the McLachlin Era: Consensus and Ideology at the Supreme Court of Canada" (2009) 47 *Supreme Court Law Review* 475 at 491 [Alarie & Green, "McLachlin Era"]. But see Ostberg & Wetstein, *Attitudinal Decision Making, supra* note 92 at 133, 149 (finding that the party of the appointing prime minister was a weak predictor in free speech cases but not significant in equality cases).

136. Some argue that there is no connection between the party of the appointing prime minister and how judges ultimately vote: See Morton, "First One Hundred," *supra* note 79; McCormick, "Selecting the Supremes," *supra* note 13.

137. Smyth, "Explaining Historical Dissent," *supra* note 84 at 108.

we return to Weiden's attempt to compare justices in Canada, the United States, and Australia, we see he created a judicial politicization score for each country that measured the degree of correspondence between the political party of the appointing government and the newspaper ideology score of the appointed judge.[138] He found that the Canadian Supreme Court had lower judicial politicization than both the US Supreme Court and the Australian High Court during the period 1990–1999.[139] A higher judicial politicization score indicates that the appointing government in a country tends more frequently to appoint ideologically like-minded judges. The US Supreme Court had the highest judicial politicization score at 0.917, which was much higher than that of the Canadian Supreme Court at 0.5. The Australian High Court was less politicized than the US Supreme Court, but more politicized than the Canadian Supreme Court.[140]

Evidence of a tie to the politics of the appointing parties is also weak on the UK House of Lords, with studies coming to differing conclusions. Hanretty found the ideal points of Law Lords were weakly connected to the party who appointed the justice whereas Robertson found that previous partisanship affiliation was irrelevant to rates of agreements between judges.[141] Also when the Lord Chancellor made the appointments (that is before the UK changed the committee process), a judge was more likely to be appointed to the House of Lords if his decisions as a lower court judge tended to be affirmed by the House of Lords and he was not extremely anti-government.[142] However, evidence is mixed as to whether it mattered that the judge had been appointed to the Court of Appeal by the same party making the high court appointment—with Salzberger and Fenn finding it made no difference, and Hanretty finding that a judge was more likely to be appointed if he had been previously appointed by the same party.[143]

Judges themselves play a greater role in the appointment of the high court in India and Israel.[144] Israel provides an interesting opportunity to test the

138. Weiden, "Judicial Politicization," *supra* note 69 at 337.

139. Weiden, "Judicial Politicization," *supra* note 69 at 338.

140. Weiden, "Judicial Politicization," *supra* note 69 at 338.

141. David Robertson, "Judicial Ideology in the House of Lords: A Jurimetric Analysis" (1982) 12 *British Journal of Political Science* 1.

142. Eli Salzberger & Paul Fenn, "Judicial Independence: Some Evidence from the English Court of Appeal" (1999) 42 *Journal of Law and Economics* 831 [Salzberger & Fenn].

143. Salzberger & Fenn, *supra* note 142; Hanretty, "Political Preferment", *supra* note 42.

144. There have unfortunately been few studies from India of the connection between the appointing judges and those they appoint. The high court has tended to be fairly homogeneous

connection between candidates and the justices currently on the Supreme Court. As we saw, in Israel justices are typically appointed temporarily to the bench prior to a full-time appointment. Temporarily appointed judges who more frequently dissent (that is, disagree with their colleagues on the bench) were less likely to be permanently appointed to the High Court. Interestingly, temporary judges who tend to grant more applications by individuals against the state are more likely to be appointed to the bench.[145]

How does this connection between the appointer and the judge look when we use our data from the High Courts Judicial Database and the US database? It is difficult to compare across countries because of the different orientations of political parties in different countries and across time. However, Figure 3-8 shows what we find if we use a very blunt measure of "conservative" and "liberal" appointers across different countries (other than India as judges on the Indian Supreme Court appoint the new judges rather than a political party doing so).[146] It shows the difference between the liberal voting rates for conservative and liberal appointees, controlling for the direction (liberal or conservative) of the lower court decision.[147] The US Supreme Court has the highest difference with an almost 10 percent difference in liberal voting between liberal and conservative appointees in the period from 1970 to the early 2000s. Differences across judges on the Australian High Court and the Canadian Supreme Court were similar at about 5 percent with the difference for judges on the UK House of Lords the lowest at about 3 percent. These positive differences are statistically significant for Australia, Canada, and the UK, but likely as a function of the crudeness of the measure of ideology (party of the appointer) the 95 percent confidence intervals are particularly large for the United States.

in terms of background. Gadbois, "Background Characteristics", *supra* note 88 (studying the court between 1950 and 1967); Abhinav Chandrachud, "An Empirical Study of the Supreme Court's Composition" (2011) 46:1 *Economic and Political Weekly* 1 (studying judges on the court between 1985 and 2010). At least in the period 1950–1967, shared backgrounds, as opposed to ideology, did appear to be linked to greater agreement). Gadbois, "Background Characteristics", *supra* note 88 at 336.

145. Eli M. Salzberger, "Temporary Appointments and Judicial Independence: Theoretical Analysis and Empirical Findings from the Supreme Court of Israel" (2001) 35 *Israel Law Review* 480 at 503 [Salzberger, "Temporary Appointments"]. For a discussion of temporary appointments, see also Blum, *supra* note 55.

146. See Appendix 1 for a classification of the parties in each country.

147. Based on logit regressions with vote (liberal versus conservative) as the dependent variable and party of the appointer and direction of the lower court decision as the independent variables, the coefficients on party of the appointer were significant at the .01 level for the Supreme Court of Canada and .05 level for Australia and the UK. The results were similar if the analysis also controlled for area of law. See Appendix 2 Table 2 for a summary of regression results.

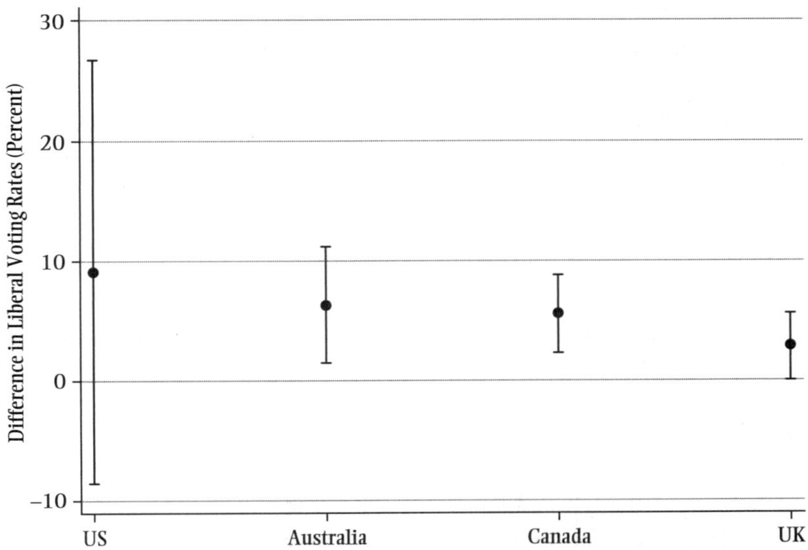


**Figure 3-8** Difference in liberal voting rates between judges appointed by conservative appointers and liberal appointers, 1970 to early 2000s. This figure shows the mean difference for each country, along with the 95 percent confidence interval, controlling for the direction (liberal or conservative) of the lower court decision. The difference for justices of the US Supreme Court is almost twice as high as the Australian High Court or the Supreme Court of Canada, and about three times greater than for the UK. Note, however, the large 95 percent confidence interval for the US Supreme Court and the fact that these confidence intervals overlap for all countries. India is not included as the judges are appointed by the chief justice rather than a political actor.

## Does a Balanced Process Lead to Cooperative Judges?

So far we have been looking at whether political appointers and a political appointment process lead to political judges. Can we get more cooperative judges from a more balanced, more cooperative process? Where committees involving different parties appoint judges, the courts may not be as polarized and there may be higher levels of unanimity, all other things being equal. Judges appointed by a cooperative process may be less politically motivated because any politically motivated or extreme candidate would not be acceptable to part of the committee. Further, as with a political process, judges appointed through a cooperative process may view their role as less tied to their political views than they would through a political process.

Of course, high levels of unanimity are still possible without a balanced process. If the executive or the legislature appoints judges and a single party holds sway for a long period of time, the judges may agree because they share the same political outlook. Unanimity may also be high where judges are in control of appointments. In India, for example, where the chief justice and existing judges select new judges, appointees may be less likely to disagree with their more senior colleagues. The ideology of the appointer is in effect the ideology of the current court. In other words, the current court would serve as a homogenizing influence, with judges seeking to appoint new judges who are similar to themselves, leading to relatively less disagreement.

We therefore formulate the following hypothesis:

> *H3: A court will have higher levels of unanimity if justices are appointed as a result of cooperation between different branches of government, or if the judicial branch has significant influence over the appointment process, all other things being equal.*

Countries such as the UK and Israel that appoint justices by committee, or India where judges appoint future judges, may then have higher rates of cooperation. Of course, once again causation will be difficult to pinpoint. As we will see in Chapter 8, unanimity may be affected by a range of factors from panel size to norms on the court. However, a first question is whether there appears to be any connection between the appointment process and the level of cooperation.[148] In Israel, for example, a committee appoints justices but the existing justices on the committee have the ability to effectively veto any appointment. We could expect the existing members of the Israeli Supreme Court to use their power over the Appointments Committee to ensure that like-minded candidates are appointed. These like-minded candidates would then be more likely to agree with their colleagues once they arrive on the Court. Justices on the Israeli Supreme Court have tended to dissent at a very low rate, with well over 90 percent of all decisions being unanimous.[149]

Table 3-2 summarizes the relevant features of these high courts and their rates of unanimity, and inserts the US Supreme Court for the sake of comparison. Israel has a low dissent rate as does India and, more recently, the UK.[150] By

148. South Africa has also used a Judicial Services Commission to appoint judges to its high court since the 1990s. However there has been no empirical literature on the South African Supreme Court of Appeal or its Constitutional Court that focuses exclusively on the post-apartheid era. Much of the study of South African judicial decision-making has focused on the apartheid era, when the executive made appointments. Haynie found a high level of consensus in the apartheid era for the Appellate Division, possibly due to the small panel sizes or lack of control over its docket. Haynie, *Black and White, supra* note 85 at 72.

149. Salzberger, "Temporary Appointments", *supra* note 145 at 504; Blum, *supra* note 55 at 37.

150. Even before the Three Judges Cases that formally allocated the power of selecting Supreme Court judges to the judiciary, the chief justice already played a central role in the selection

*Table 3-2.* Judicial and Committee Involvement in Appointment Processes and Rates of Unanimity on Selective High Courts

| Country | Judicial power over appointment process | Use of independent committee | Rate of unanimity |
|---|---|---|---|
| **Israel** | ✓ | ✓ | Very high (90%+)[a] |
| **India** | ✓ | | Very high (90%+) |
| **UK (post-2005)**[b] | ✓ | ✓ | High |
| **US** | | | Low (40%) |

[a] Effect is especially pronounced amongst judges who were temporarily appointed.

[b] Appointment process previously dominated by the executive.

comparison, the US Supreme Court reaches consensus in less than half of its total cases.[151]

A curious feature of the Israeli Supreme Court may provide some evidence of the influence of the process on the level of cooperation. As we saw, justices are often first appointed to the Court on a temporary basis before being confirmed by the Appointment Committee. Given the Supreme Court's influence on the Appointment Committee, it would seem logical for temporary appointees to refrain from disagreeing with their permanently appointed colleagues in order to maximize their chances of being promoted to a permanent position on the Court. And this holds true. Temporary appointees who agree more with the senior justices of the Court had slightly better chances of getting a permanent seat in the Court.[152] Further, between 1999 and 2005 temporary appointments

process, and the president's role was chiefly announcing the appointments. Between 1950 and 1967, 91.6 percent of decisions published by the Indian Supreme Court were unanimous. Again the high rate of unanimity is consistent with our hypothesis, though it is related to other factors such as the high caseload, small panels, and the fact that Indian judges are drawn from "a remarkably homogeneous group of men." George H. Gadbois, Jr., "Indian Supreme Court Judges: A Portrait" (1969) 3 *Law and Society Review* 317 at 149, 151, 318. For a more recent study, see Nick Robinson, "Structure Matters: The Impact of Court Structure on the Indian and U.S. Supreme Courts" (2013) 61:1 *American Journal of Comparative Law* 173 at 187. Even on constitutional cases, which are considered the most contentious cases on the Supreme Court's docket, the Court reached consensus 76 percent of the time. Nick Robinson et al., "Interpreting the Constitution: Supreme Court Constitution Benches since Independence" (2011) 41 *Economic & Political Weekly* 27 at 28.

151. Alarie & Green, "McLachlin Era," *supra* note 135 at 476.

152. Salzberger, "Temporary Appointments," *supra* note 145 at 504 (examining the period 1948–2011).

had a low dissent rate, and this dissent rate increased slightly after they were granted tenure on the Court.[153]

The UK arguably has a more balanced committee process with appointments to the Supreme Court being made by a selection commission with input from the executive, the judiciary, and lay members of the citizenry. This process was only put in place in 2009 with the advent of the UK Supreme Court, and evidence of the effect of this change is limited. The shift to a more neutral and independent appointment mechanism may partially cause an increase in consensus. However, there was a strong norm of consensus on the House of Lords even under the old appointment system dominated by the executive.[154] Further, the increased collegiality may be the result of other institutional changes such as frequent transmissions of judgments between judges, pre-meetings, and greater use of technology on the Supreme Court, especially from 2012 onward.[155]

When we look at our data for the percentage of cases that have at least one dissent across countries in the period from 1970 to the early 2000s (Figure 3-9, which reproduces Figure 1-3 for convenience), we can see that these prior indications from the literature hold. The United States has the highest rate of cases with at least one dissent and India the lowest. In this period, the executive in each of Australia, Canada, and the UK essentially made the appointment decision. They each had intermediate levels of cases with at least one dissent, though the levels varied.

As we saw in Chapter 1, another indicator of consensus is how many judges are willing to dissent, rather than just if any single judges decide to dissent. We can look to the fraction of dissenting opinions as a measure of disagreement—the number of dissenting opinions divided by the number of decisions. Figure 3-10 (which reproduces Figure 1-4 for convenience) shows the differences in fraction dissenting over the period from 1970 to the early 2000s. Again, the United States has the most disagreement with the highest fraction of dissenting opinions (that is, the most dissenting opinions for its caseload), and India was at the other end of the spectrum with a very low fraction of dissenting opinions. Australia, Canada, and the UK were in the middle. Notice that the UK House of Lords, as we discussed, had a high rate of agreement (a low fraction dissenting) even before the change in the appointments process for the UK Supreme Court.

153. Blum, *supra* note 55 at 37.

154. See Arvind & Stirton, *supra* note 86; Hanretty, "Ideal Points," *supra* note 108.

155. Alan Paterson, *Final Judgment: The Last Law Lords and the Supreme Court* (Oxford: Hart, 2013) at 196.

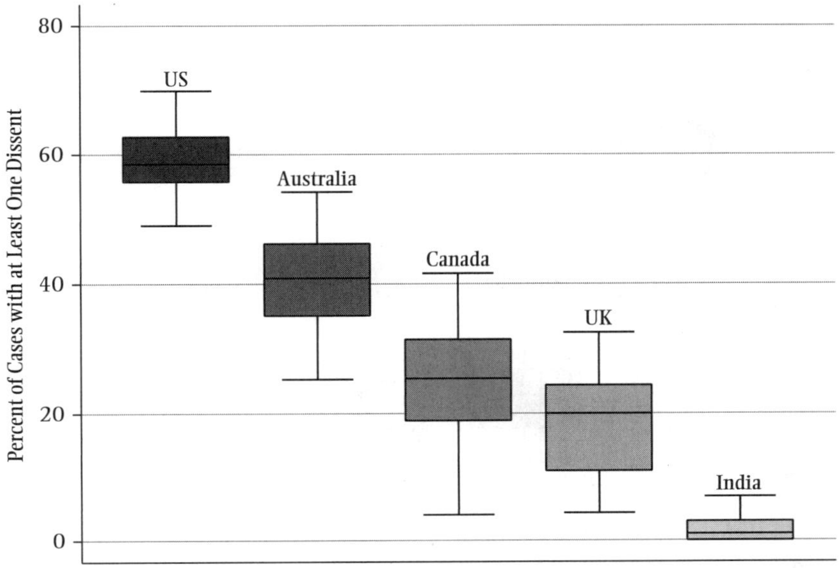


**Figure 3-9** Percent of cases per year that have at least one dissent over the period from 1970 to the early 2000s. The box shows the middle 50 percent of the data for each country, and the line in the box shows the median percentage for cases with at least one dissent over the period. The lines above and below each box provide the maximum and minimum annual percentages of opinions with at least one dissent for each country in the period. The United States had by far the highest rate of dissenting with over 50 percent of opinions having a dissent in most years. At the other extreme, most years India had less than 5 percent of opinions with at least one dissent. Canada and the UK had similar rates of opinions with dissents. Australia had the second highest level of dissent with in general over 40 percent of opinions having a dissent.

As with political voting, therefore, there is some weak, initial correlation between who appoints judges and how likely judges are to dissent. The most political process, that in the United States, has the highest dissent rate and the least political, the Indian, the lowest dissent rate. The systems with similar systems have similar dissent rates. Of course, many other factors go into dissent rates, such as norms on a court and workload. We will sort out some of the key factors in Chapter 8.

## JUDGING AND THE APPOINTMENT PROCESS

What effect can we see of the appointment process on the nature of judging? Much of the evidence is consistent with our hypotheses. Justices appointed in the United States tended to be the most polarized both in terms of how spread

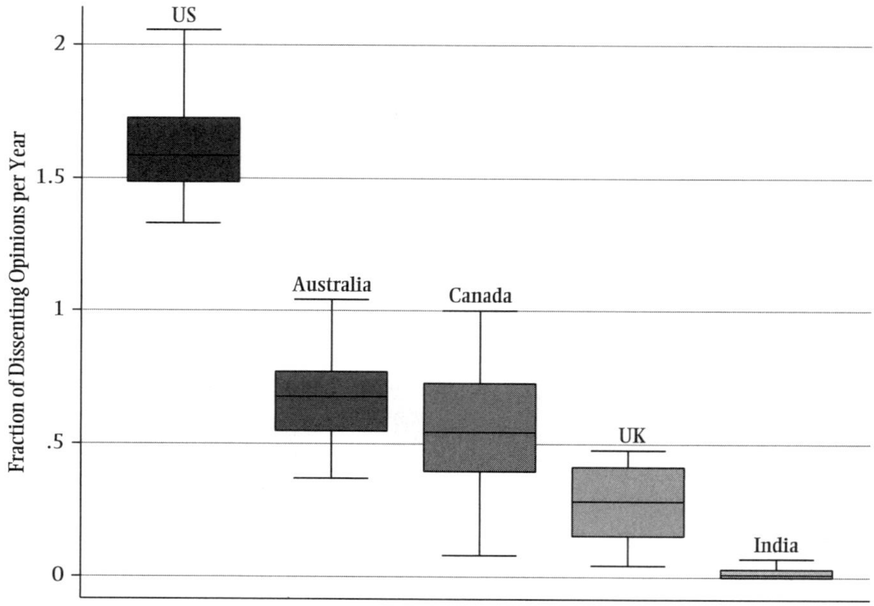


**Figure 3-10** Fraction of dissenting opinions per year (number of dissenting opinions in the year divided by the total number of decisions in the year) over the period from 1970 to the early 2000s. The box shows the middle 50 percent of the data for each country, and the line in the box shows the median value of the fraction of dissenting opinions over the period. The lines above and below each box provide the maximum and minimum fraction of dissenting opinions for each country in the period. As with Figure 1-2, the United States had by far the highest rate of dissenting over the period and India by far the lowest. Australia and Canada had similar levels of fraction of dissenting opinions, with the UK slightly less.

out and consistent they are in their voting; they also have the greatest connection between the party appointing them and markers of their voting, and dissented at by far the highest rate. The United States is an outlier on the high end on all these indicators.

India is the outlier at the other extreme in terms of the process and some aspects of judicial behavior. The judges appoint new members of the bench. They are also the least polarized in the sense that there is no indication of consistency in voting across areas of law, and they almost never dissent compared to other countries. They do, however, appear to be somewhat spread out in terms of their voting on the bench.

In between these extremes lie the UK, Canada, and Australia. For each, the executive has the power to appoint justices, and the processes are less transparent and generally less overtly political than the US process. At the same time, they have intermediate levels of polarization, connection to the party of the appointer, and dissenting. Interestingly, there are differences across these countries. Canada and Australia have less spread, are more consistent, and have more dissents than the UK House of Lords.

There then is some evidence that the design of the appointment process is correlated with differences with how judges decide, though the evidence is mixed and, obviously, correlation is not necessarily causation. We will see that other design elements influence how judges decide, particularly how norms of dissenting tie into the level of disagreement on the court. We will start with a topic that is related or at least analogous to the appointment process—the impact of hearing cases in panels rather than *en banc*.

# 4

# Who Hears the Particular Appeal?

A jury of 500 Athenians decided Socrates's fate. Socrates had been accused of refusing to recognize the gods of the state and of corrupting the youth of Athens. The jury heard arguments for and against Socrates before finding him guilty. The vote was fairly close—280 against Socrates to 220 in support of him. The jury then chose the punishment of death by a larger margin.

A jury of 500 is large but it wasn't all Athenians. So why 500, and why these 500? One possible explanation is efficiency—500 jurors could be viewed as giving a fair representation of what all Athenians would have decided, without having to subject all Athenians to the inconvenience of sitting through the trial. Yet as soon as one gets a subset of the Athenians making the decision, one may worry about how they were chosen—were these jurors selected to increase the probability of finding Socrates guilty? It turns out the 500 were selected by lot so there was some randomness as to who was making the decision. However, the lots were drawn not from the whole population but from the population of males over 30 years of age. So the choice of this jury raises issues of both efficiency and politics. Would a different jury have found Socrates not guilty? Were these the best rules for choosing the jury?

These same issues arise on high courts. We saw that the process for appointing judges may make a difference as to how a court decides. Yet it is not only who is on the bench at any given time that may matter, but which of those judges hear a particular appeal. On some high courts such as the US Supreme Court all the judges decide almost all appeals together (*en banc*). However, on many other high courts around the world only a subset of the judges on the court hears most if not all appeals. In some countries, the chief justice, or the most senior judge, has the power to determine not only how many judges will hear a given appeal but also which individual judges will be participating.

As can be seen in Figure 4-1, very different numbers of judges heard appeals on high courts in the period from 1970 to the early 2000s. All nine judges on

Commitment and Cooperation on High Courts. Benjamin Alarie and Andrew J. Green.

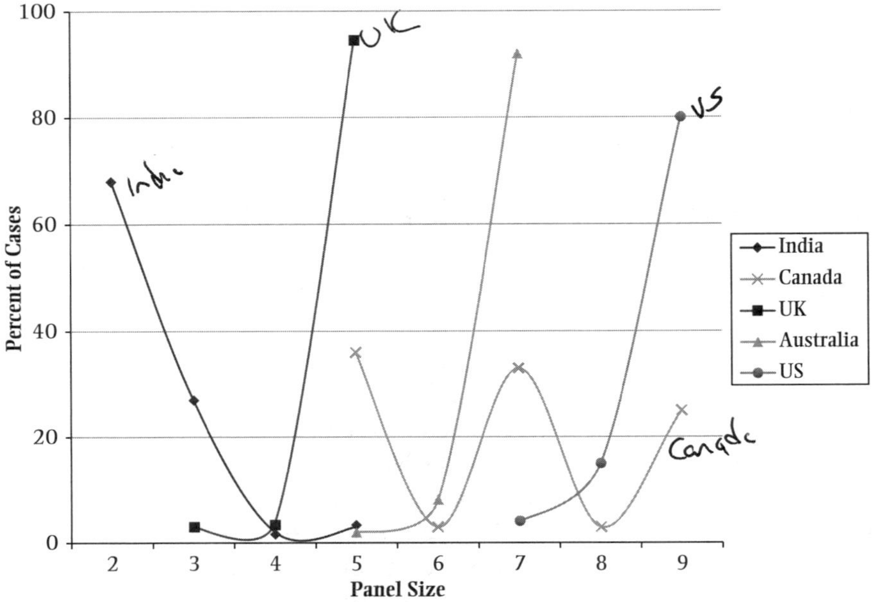


**Figure 4-1** Percent of cases at different panel sizes, 1970 to early 2000s. India and the United States are at the extremes with lower and higher panel sizes, respectively. Canada is more evenly spread across a number of panel sizes.

the US Supreme Court hear the vast majority of cases, although sometimes only eight judges will hear an appeal where, for example, there is a vacancy or conflict of interest. At the opposite extreme, only two or three of the 31 members of the Indian Supreme Court sit on most hearings. Along this range fall appellate panels in a variety of sizes. The UK House of Lords generally heard appeals in panels of five but the current UK Supreme Court with 12 judges sits in panels of five, seven, or nine judges, as does the Supreme Court of Canada with a total of nine judges. Similarly, Australia with seven judges hears appeals in panels of three, five, or seven. The Supreme Court of Canada had the most equal distribution over a number of panel sizes, with number of cases relatively evenly spread across panels of five, seven, or nine.

As with the Athenian jury, we can imagine two different stories about what happens if not all judges hear every appeal. First, tailoring the size and composition of panels hearing appeals provides a significant efficiency advantage over hearings *en banc*. A high court can hear more appeals when it divides into small panels to hear cases. India, for example, uses its large number of judges and small panel sizes to hold over 7,500 hearings in a year. Also, depending on how the panels are assigned, the workload can be evenly spread across the judges, and judges can specialize in certain types of appeals. In Israel, for instance, Justice Levi, an expert in criminal law, rendered 30 of 54 criminal law decisions by the Israeli Supreme Court between 1999 and 2002.[1]

The second story is less benign. Whoever has the power to choose the size and composition of panels that hear particular appeals has the power to influence outcomes of the appeals. If the chief justice has the power to decide the size and composition of panels, as is the case in Canada, she may be able to increase the probability of her preferred outcome on a given case if she leaves the judges who are likely to disagree with her off the panel. Consider an example from the US Federal Court of Appeal. When Chief Justice Tuttle of the Fifth Circuit assigned two or three of four particular judges to a panel in race relations cases, the plaintiff won 67 percent of the decisions as opposed to only 50 percent with other panels.[2]

Which of these stories holds for a particular court will depend on the formal and informal rules around how panels are set. Discretion to decide who hears an appeal is not necessarily a path to biasing outcomes, at least overtly. For example, former chief justice Lamer of Canada indicated that he would try to form a panel of nine justices, the maximum size possible, if he thought the outcome of a case would be different with a panel of nine compared to a smaller panel.[3] Moreover, discretion can avoid potentially quite biased panels that one would expect to sometimes arise if assignment were completely random. However, in order to get a sense of the trade-off across these stories, we start by looking at how different courts decide who decides.

## CHOOSING THE PANEL

We can break down high courts into three broad groups in terms of how they decide who hears appeals: no discretion, high discretion, and mixed. These groups are not entirely clear-cut. A court may have formal rules about potential panel sizes, such as statutory provisions setting out the minimum number of judges. Yet, even seemingly strict requirements about the size of panels may also be modified where a judge has a conflict of interest. On the other hand,

1. Binyamin Blum, "To Concur or Not to Concur, That Is the Question: Theoretical and Practical Question Regarding the Judicial Independence of Judges Appointed Temporarily to the Israeli Supreme Court" (Master's Thesis, Stanford Law School, 2006) [unpublished], at 35 [Blum].

2. Burton Atkins & William Zavoina, "Judicial Leadership on the Court of Appeals: A Probability Analysis of Panel Assignment in Race Relations Cases on the Fifth Circuit" (1974) 18 *American Journal of Political Science* 701 at 705 [Atkins & Zavoina].

3. Emmett MacFarlane, "The Supreme Court of Canada and the Judicial Role: An Historical Institutionalist Account" (PhD Dissertation, Queen's University, 2009) [unpublished], at 143.

where a chief justice has discretion to set the panel, he may still be constrained by informal rules such as, for example, a norm against making extreme panel choices to reach particular results. However, it is helpful to think of the institutional structures roughly in these three groups.

## No Discretion

The US Supreme Court is the primary example of a basic lack of discretion in the setting of panels. According to the official Court Rules, any six justices may form a quorum,[4] but in practice all justices sit on each appeal except where there are vacancies, illnesses, or recusals. A justice may recuse herself from an appeal where, for example, she was involved in the case at an earlier stage or has a conflict of interest. In the period 1970 to the early 2000s, the Court heard almost 80 percent of appeals *en banc* and about 20 percent in a panel of eight justices. Some courts in other countries have similar rules.[5]

## High Discretion

At the opposite extreme are high courts where there is considerable discretion to set the size and composition of panels. For example, only five of the nine justices of the Supreme Court of Canada are needed to hear an appeal.[6] In reality, the Court sits in panels of five, seven, or nine justices with the chief justice determining both the size and composition of the panel for any appeal. The Court has increasingly heard appeals in larger panels over time.[7] Before 1975 when the Supreme Court was required to hear a wider range of appeals, the

4. *Rules of the Supreme Court of the United States* (2010), Rule 4 (2), online: http://www.supremecourt.gov/ctrules/2010RulesoftheCourt.pdf.

5. Both the South African Constitutional Court and the Supreme Court of New Zealand have similar fairly fixed rules. The Constitutional Court of South Africa consists of the Chief Justice of South Africa, the Deputy Chief Justice, and nine other judges. *Constitution of the Republic of South Africa 1996*, s 167(1) [*RSA Constitution*]. It always hears cases *en banc*, even though the constitution only requires eight judges to hear a matter. *RSA Constitution*, s 167(2). Similarly, the Supreme Court of New Zealand, which currently consists of a total of five justices although a sixth member of the Court can be added, hears all appeals *en banc* because appeals must be heard by five judges. The *Supreme Court Act* requires that the Court consists of a chief justice and no fewer than four nor more than five other judges. *Supreme Court Act 2003* (NZ), 2003, ss 17(1), 27(1).

6. *Supreme Court Act* RSC 1985, c S-26, s 25.

7. Ian Greene et al., *Final Appeal: Decision-Making in Canadian Courts of Appeal* (Toronto: J Lorimer, 1998) at 115.

Court used mostly five-justice panels for cases.[8] After the Court gained control of its own docket with most appeals needing the Court to agree to hear them, the size of the average panel increased. From 1984 to 2005, panels of seven justices heard about half of the Supreme Court's appeals.[9]

Similarly, the relatively recently formed UK Supreme Court consists of 12 justices but does not hear cases *en banc*.[10] The Appellate Division of the House of Lords, before it was replaced by the Supreme Court in 2009, also consisted of 12 justices ("Lords of Appeal in Ordinary") and heard appeals mostly in panels of 5 but occasionally in panels of 7 or 9 justices if the appeal was considered important. According to the *Constitutional Reform Act*, Supreme Court panels must consist of an uneven number of justices, with a minimum of three.[11] Panels are assigned by the registrar, based on considerations of "availability, conflicts of interest, workload, who had sat on the Appeal Committee [PTA committee after 2009], and the needs of the Privy Council,"[12] with the most significant factor being specialization.[13] The president and deputy president of the court may override the registrar's assigned panels.[14] According to Paterson, some justices approach the registrar directly to request being assigned to cases they have a particular interest in, but the more junior justices tend to refrain from making such requests.[15] Since its inception, five-member panels have heard the overwhelming majority of UK Supreme Court cases,[16] although larger panels

8. Peter McCormick, "Selecting the Supremes: The Appointment of Judges to the Supreme Court of Canada" (2005) 7:1 *Journal of Appellate Practice and Process* 1 at 10–11.

9. Benjamin Alarie, Andrew James Green & Edward Iacobucci, "Is Bigger Always Better? On Optimal Panel Size, with Evidence from the Supreme Court of Canada" (2011) (U Toronto, Legal Studies Research Paper No 08-15) at 15, online: https://papers.ssrn.com/sol3/papers.cfm?abstract_id=1152322 [Alarie et al., "Panel Size"].

10. Glenn Dymond, "The Appellate Jurisdiction of the House of Lords" (updated November 2009) House of Lords Library Note at 22, online: http://www.parliament.uk/documents/lords-library/lln2009-010appellate.pdf.

11. *Constitutional Reform Act* 2005 (UK), s 42(1).

12. Alan Paterson, *Final Judgment: The Last Law Lords and the Supreme Court* (Oxford: Hart, 2013) at 71 [Paterson].

13. Paterson, *supra* note 12 at 71–71.

14. Paterson, *supra* note 12 at 72.

15. Paterson, *supra* note 12 at 72–73.

16. Cheryl Thomas, "Decision-Making by the United Kingdom Supreme Court and the Judicial Committee of the Privy Council: 2009–2013" 2013 *UCL Judicial Institute: UK.*

of seven or nine members have become more frequent than they were at the House of Lords.[17]

## Mixed Structures

The line between the high discretion courts and the mixed discretion courts is ill-defined. Although the chief justice or president has considerable discretion to decide on panels for the high courts of Israel, Australia, and India, formal or informal rules may significantly constrain the exercise of this discretion. The Supreme Court of Israel currently consists of up to 15 justices,[18] and only rarely sits *en banc*.[19] The president of the Supreme Court has exclusive authority to assign justices to various cases.[20] However, in practice, the Court's registrar arbitrarily composes panels, with the chief justice retaining the power of assigning justices to particularly important cases.[21] Panels must consist of at least three justices, and the most common panel size is indeed three. However, the Court may sit as a panel of a larger uneven number of justices in matters that involve fundamental legal questions and constitutional issues of particular importance.[22] In addition, members of a panel hearing an appeal may order a hearing before a larger panel and "further hearing" panels, which review prior Supreme Court decisions, must consist of at least five justices.[23]

The chief justice similarly has a high level of discretion on the High Court of Australia. At least two of the seven justices on the High Court of Australia are required to hear an appeal.[24] In reality, the Court hears appeals in panels of three, five, or seven justices, with five justices being the most common.[25]

17. Paterson, *supra* note 12 at 72.

18. "The Judges," online: http://elyon1.court.gov.il/eng/judges/judges.html.

19. Yoav Dotan, *Lawyering for the Rule of Law: Government Lawyers and the Rise of Judicial Power in Israel* (New York: Cambridge University Press, 2014) at 24.

20. *Courts Act 1984*, s 27(a) [*Courts Act* Israel].

21. Pnina Lahav, *Judgement in Jerusalem: Chief Justice Simon Agranat and the Zionist Century* (Berkeley: University of California Press, 1997) at 295, n. 25.

22. *Courts Act* Israel, *supra* note 20, s 26.

23. *Courts Act* Israel, *supra* note 20, s 26.

24. *High Court of Australia Act 1979* (Cth), s 5; The *Judiciary Act* 1903 (Cth) s 19 [*Judiciary Act*].

25. Russell Smyth, "'Some Are More Equal than Others'—An Empirical Investigation into the Voting Behaviour of the Mason Court" (1999) 6:1–2 *Canberra Law* Review 193 at 200; Vinod Mishra & Russell Smyth, "Barrister Gender and Litigant Success on the High Court of Australia" (2013) Monash University Department of Economics Discussion Paper No 15/13 at 10, online: http://www.buseco.monash.edu.au/eco/research/papers/2013/1513barristermishrasmyth.pdf.

Between 1969 and 2003, the full court decided 21 percent of the cases whereas panels of five heard about 70 percent of the cases.[26] The chief justice assigns panels.[27] However, the *Judiciary Act* requires a full court for constitutional cases, unless at least three justices concur in the decision to use a smaller panel.[28]

Finally, the chief justice of the Indian Supreme Court also determines panel size and composition.[29] The Supreme Court of India currently consists of 28 judges,[30] although since 2008, it may have up to 31 judges.[31] All panels must consist of at least two judges,[32] but at least five judges must hear cases "involving a substantial question of law as to the interpretation of the Constitution."[33] These five-judge constitution benches have become increasingly rare.[34] Further, although three-member benches used to hold the majority of the Court's hearings, two judges now decide most appeals (with norms such as of the junior judge deferring to the senior judge, thus reducing ties).[35] The largest bench was 13 judges for *Kesavananda Bharati v. State of Kerala*, a landmark case that established the "Basic Structure" doctrine for interpretation of the Indian constitution: that the legislature could not alter the Constitution's basic features (which were left undefined). The 7-6 majority in this case established judicial review in India.[36]

26. This figure is from the HCJD (Stacia L. Haynie et al. (2007) High Courts Judicial Database. Accessed at the University of South Carolina Judicial Research Initiative, online: www.cas.sc.edu/poli/juri.

27. Rebecca Wood, *Why Do High Court Judges Join? Joining Behaviour and Australia's Seriatim Tradition* (PhD Dissertation, Michigan State University, 2008) [unpublished] at 28.

28. *Judiciary Act, supra* note 241, s 23(1).

29. Nick Robinson, "A Quantitative Analysis of the Indian Supreme Court's Workload" (2013) 10:3 *Journal of Empirical Legal Studies* 570 at 591 [Robinson, "Quantitative Analysis"].

30. "List of Supreme Court Judges," Department of Justice, online: http://doj.gov.in/?q=node/24.

31. *Supreme Court (Number of Judges) Amendment Act, 2008*. In 1950 when the Supreme Court was created, the Supreme Court consisted of eight judges. This was increased to 11 in 1956, 14 in 1960, 18 in 1978, and 26 in 1986. "Constitution," *Supreme Court of India*, online: http://supremecourtofindia.nic.in/constitution.htm.

32. *Supreme Court Rules 1966*, Order VII, s 1.

33. *The Constitution of India 1950*, art 145(3) [*India Constitution*].

34. Nick Robinson et al., "Interpreting the Constitution: Supreme Court Constitution Benches since Independence" (2011) 41 *Economic & Political Weekly* 27 at 28 [Robinson, "Interpreting the Constitution"].

35. Robinson, "Quantitative Analysis," *supra* note 29 at 578; Nick Robinson, "Structure Matters: The Impact of Court Structure on the Indian and U.S. Supreme Courts" (2013) 61:1 *American Journal of Comparative Law* 173 at 180–181.

36. Robinson, "Structure Matters," *supra* note 35 at 191.

## GAMING OR EFFICIENCY? RIVAL HYPOTHESES OF PANEL SETTING

Discretion in the setting of panels may influence how a court decides cases for good or ill. As we saw, chief justices or presidents may use their panel selection power in two principal ways. The first is to optimize the allocation of the court's resources such as by increasing the number of appeals the court can hear or assigning judges to cases in their areas of expertise. A second way is for the chief justice or president to strategically use the panel-selection power to promote her preferred outcomes on appeals. We can label these two approaches to panel selection as "managerial" or "strategic," respectively.[37] We start with the managerial approach. For the moment we will leave aside the question of how a judge is affected by who else is on the panel, which are termed "panel effects." We will see in the next chapter that who a judge sits with matters. Yet it is helpful at present while discussing panel selection to assume that there are no panel effects.

## MANAGERIAL PANEL SELECTION

A chief justice taking a managerial approach to setting panels could be concerned about a number of different effects of who hears appeals. She could be concerned about hearing the most appeals possible, or at least increasing the number of decisions rendered. There is a cost to assigning larger panels—fewer appeals can be heard, all other things being equal. If a chief justice wished to select panels to optimally allocate the court's resources, she would assign smaller panels to very easy and very hard appeals, because very easy and very hard cases do not benefit as much from adding judges to the panel compared to cases of intermediate difficulty.[38] Consider a case so hard that it is essentially a flip of the coin—adding an extra judge may not give much return in terms of getting the right answer but it will have a cost in terms of appeals that he cannot hear.[39] Alternatively, the chief justice could be concerned about ensuring that the workload is not overly burdensome and is spread evenly across the judges

37. For a more thorough explanation of the different types of approaches that a chief justice can take toward panel selection, see Benjamin Alarie, Andrew Green & Edward Iacobucci, "Panel Selections on High Courts" (2015) 65:4 *University of Toronto Law Journal* 335 [Alarie et al., "Panel Selections"].

38. Alarie et al., "Panel Size," *supra* note 9 at 9.

39. Alarie et al., "Panel Size," *supra* note 9 at 11 (the notion that there are "correct" answers to every legal question is not without controversy). See Alarie et al., "Panel Size," *supra* note 9 at 6 for further discussion.

on the bench. She may set panel size and who sits on an appeal based on what other cases are on the docket at the particular time or are coming up in the future. If we think back to our framework in Chapter 2, the chief justice may be concerned that if the workload gets too heavy, his justices may be less happy or satisfied or they may spend less time on each judgment.

Setting smaller panel sizes to maximize the number of appeals heard or to spread the workload evenly across judges also has a potential cost. The more important the decision, all else being equal, the greater the social benefit in getting the answer correct. As panelists are added, the majority's chances of reaching the correct decision increases assuming each judge has a greater than 50 percent chance of getter the "correct" answer.[40] Therefore, a chief justice who seeks to allocate the court's resources to maximize social benefit would assign larger panels to more important cases. In addition, if she sets a larger panel in an important case, the public may be more likely to accept the result as a large panel would give the impression that the decision represents the views of a larger proportion of the court.

A chief justice clearly would also care about improving the quality of decisions. A managerial chief justice would want appeals to be heard by judges with expertise in the relevant law, so far as possible. Judges with a greater understanding of a particular area of law may be able to decide such appeals faster and perhaps are more likely to be "correct."[41] Similarly, a chief justice may appoint a judge to hear a case from her home region in some cases. This might have the advantage of exploiting a judge's expertise in that region's laws (which is particularly relevant in federal states) and also of potentially increasing the decision's legitimacy for the residents of the region in question. For example, in Canada, the province of Quebec's private law is based on the civil code, as distinct from the common law system used by the rest of Canada. As judges from Quebec are generally experts in civil law, in order to take account of both expertise and regionalism, the chief justice may assign justices from Quebec to private law cases originating from Quebec.[42]

40. Alarie et al., "Panel Size," *supra* note 9 at 7.

41. Alarie et al., "Panel Size," *supra* note 9 at 11.

42. Relatedly, the chief justice could be concerned about the workload and experience of new justices to the court. She may seek to minimize the opportunity cost of assigning a justice to a panel, where the opportunity cost is the lost social benefit from assigning a justice to one case and thus potentially not hearing a different case, or performing another function. The opportunity cost of assigning a first-year justice to a panel is probably higher, as a newly-appointed judge is less acclimated to the court's work and is likely capable of doing less work overall. Likewise, a chief justice generally has administrative responsibilities in addition to hearing appeals, which increases her opportunity cost of participating in a panel. She may therefore assign herself to fewer panels. Alarie et al., "Panel Size," *supra* note 9 at 7.

We therefore have the following hypothesis related to the managerial approach to panel selection:

> *H1: Panel size should vary with factors such as the importance of the case and experts in particular fields should be overrepresented on panels that hear appeals in these particular fields.*

More judges may be assigned to more important cases, in part because of concern about gaining acceptance of the result. If all judges participate in the decision, the parties and the public may see the result as more legitimate and having greater weight. As a very broad division, we could imagine civil rights as being seen as more important than criminal, economic, or other cases. However, looking at our data for the period 1970 to the early 2000s, only Canada and India had a higher average panel size for civil rights appeals. India had an average panel size of two judges for all types of cases except civil rights cases for which the average panel size was three judges. Canada had the greatest differentiation in panel size with civil rights having the highest average panel size (eight judges), followed by criminal (seven judges) and then economic and other (both with an average of six judges). The difference for India is likely at least partially due to the Court hearing constitutional cases in larger panels (often of five judges). The United States, which hears appeals *en banc*, does not differentiate across areas of law, having an average of nine judges hearing civil rights, criminal, economic, and other cases. The UK and Australia were also consistent in panel size across all areas of law, with the UK House of Lords hearings appeals with an average of five judges on the panel and Australia seven judges.

The lack of variety in panel sizes in most countries is at least inconsistent with the notion that the chief justice or the president varies the size of the panels for managerial reasons generally. Is there any evidence that he varies the composition to suit the nature of the case (rather than to meet some policy outcome) in those countries where panel size does vary? There is some. In Canada, Chief Justices Dickson and McLachlin were more likely to assign experts to panels within their areas of expertise.[43] Chief Justice Lamer, on the other hand, appeared to tend to leave experts off panels within their areas of expertise, although this result was driven almost entirely by his tendency to leave himself off panels deciding criminal appeals even though he was an expert in criminal law.[44] Chief Justice Lamer may have felt he had such a significant workload independent of deciding appeals that he had a high opportunity cost of sitting

43. Alarie et al., "Panel Selections," *supra* note 37.

44. Alarie et al., "Panel Selections," *supra* note 37.

on a panel.[45] In addition, as he was one of the most liberal judges in criminal law, he may have intentionally left both himself and Justice L'Heureux-Dubé, who was extremely conservative in criminal law issues, off criminal law panels in order to achieve balance and avoid polarization. The fact that both Lamer and L'Heureux-Dubé had workloads that were lighter than the other justices during the period 1992–1997 could be evidence of this behavior.[46]

In India, a small subset of judges were more frequently assigned to speech cases, which suggests that there may be a certain degree of specialization on the Court.[47] For example, 12 out of the 50 judges appointed to the Indian Supreme Court in the 2000s sat on more than 50 percent of the speech cases during that decade, with similar patterns in other decades starting from the 1950s.[48] Unfortunately, there is no independent evidence, beyond frequent assignment to speech cases, of any actual expertise possessed by these judges. Although chief justices on the Indian Supreme Court may be assigning speech experts to speech cases, these judges may in fact have no special expertise in speech cases at all. However, even if these justices had no expertise in speech cases before being appointed to the Court, they may acquire such expertise if they are more frequently assigned to speech cases.

In Israel, cases from 1999 to 2002 appear to have been allotted to judges in part based on their fields of expertise.[49] For example, during this period, Justice Levi, an expert in criminal law, rendered 30 of the 54 criminal cases.[50] Meanwhile, Justice Rivlin decided eight cases relating to automobile insurance, a subject on which he had authored a leading book.[51] However, this trend may be time-bound, as cases seemed to be randomly assigned from 2003 to 2005. Judges appointed after 2003 seemed to have their docket divided equally among civil, criminal, and constitutional cases regardless of their expertise.[52]

Therefore, there is some limited support for the notion that chief justices of high courts take expertise into consideration when assigning judges to panels. However, not much empirical work has been done on this issue. An alternative

45. Alarie et al., "Panel Selections," *supra* note 37.

46. Alarie et al., "Panel Selections," *supra* note 37.

47. Abhinav Chandrachud, "Speech, Structure and Behaviour on the Supreme Court of India" (2012) 25:2 *Columbia Journal of Asian Law* 222 at 251 [Chandrachud, "Speech Cases"].

48. Chandrachud, "Speech Cases", *supra* note 47 at 250.

49. Blum, *supra* note 1 at 34.

50. Blum, *supra* note 1 at 35.

51. Blum, *supra* note 1 at 35.

52. Blum, *supra* note 1 at 35.

take that we turn to now is that the selection of judges was based not on their expertise but on their policy preferences.

## DOES THE CHOICE OF PANELS INFLUENCE OUTCOMES OF APPEALS?

The most common-sense implication of the discretion to set panel size and composition is that differences in panels can lead to differences in results. A party whose appeal was heard by five judges of a nine-person court may worry that the result would have been different if the whole court or if a different set of five judges had decided the appeal. A court may have rules to overcome this concern. For example, at the federal court of appeal level in the United States a party can petition for an appeal to be heard or reheard *en banc*. The US federal government recently made use of this procedure when it lost a challenge to President Obama's healthcare act in the DC Court of Appeal in the case of *Halbig v. Burwell*, in which two (Republican-appointed) judges of a three-judge panel voted to overturn the law on the same day that three judges on the Fourth Circuit unanimously upheld the same law in a separate case. The DC Court of Appeal vacated the first judgment and scheduled a new hearing *en banc* without giving any reasons for the decision.[53] Similarly, it may be that fear of differing panels yielding different results is behind the rule in Australia that a full court is required for constitutional cases.

However, the panel selection power may not influence outcomes. If the judges on a court are similar in their personal or political views, the chief justice or president may have less scope for influencing the outcome through panel selection than a highly divided court. If all judges on the bench have the same background and the same policy views, the chief justice would not be able to use this tactic to alter outcomes at all. Moreover, panel selection may not influence outcomes overall if the panels are set randomly or if the chief justice specifically sets panels to ensure that the composition of the panel reflects the composition of the court as a whole. However, even if overall outcomes are not different from what the full bench would decide, panel selection may influence individual cases. As result, we have the following hypothesis about panel selection:

> *H2: Choice of panel composition by a chief justice will influence the outcomes of appeals.*

53. Order Granting Appellant's Pet. for Jacqueline Halbig et al. v. Sylvia Mathews Burwell, No.14-5018 (DC Cir., Sept. 4, 2014), 2014 WL.

There is some evidence that the ability to choose the panel makes a difference as to how a court decides. On the UK House of Lords, for example, a third of possible alternate bench compositions would have produced a majority of justices favoring a different outcome in *Bancoult (no 2)*,[54] an important administrative law and human rights case.[55] Similarly, which justices heard the appeal was very influential to the outcome of Charter claims before the Supreme Court of Canada between 1983 and 1989.[56] Justices had very different approaches to the Charter, and Charter claims had a much better chance of being accepted when the majority of the deciding panel were justices who were more receptive to Charter claims.[57] Panel selection was also important in mandatory criminal jurisdiction cases before the Israeli Supreme Court. Different combinations of justices varied widely in how they decided these cases.[58] The panel most favorable to defendants decided 33.3 percent of its cases in their favor, whereas the panel least favorable to defendants only decided 2.8 percent of its cases in their favor.[59]

On the other hand, strategic panel assignments by South African chief justices on the South African Appellate Division during the apartheid era may have had only limited effects on the outcomes of cases.[60] Different chief justices did not appear to cause different results through their panel selection.[61] For example, despite Chief Justice Rabie's attempts to appoint more Afrikaans-speaking judges and fewer liberal judges to civil rights cases, Rabie's tenure as chief justice was not statistically correlated with more conservative outcomes in this area of law.[62]

54. *R (Bancoult) v Secretary of State for Foreign and Commonwealth Affairs* [2008] UKHL 61, [2009] 1 AC 453.

55. T.T. Arvind & Lindsay Stirton, "Lawyers and the Legal Model: Judicial Ideology, Judicial Professionalism and Institutional Strategy among the Law Lords" (2012) at 30, online: https://extranet.sioe.org/uploads/isnie2012/arvind_stirton.pdf.

56. Andrew Heard, "The Charter in the Supreme Court of Canada: The Importance of Which Judges Hear an Appeal" (1992) 24:2 *Canadian Journal of Political Science* 289 at 305 [Heard].

57. Heard, *supra* note 56 at 305.

58. Theodore Eisenberg, Talia Fisher & Issie Rosen-Zvi, "Does the Judge Matter? Exploiting Random Assignment on a Court of Last Resort to Assess Judge and Case Selection Effects" (2012) 9:2 *Journal of Empirical Legal Studies* 276 [Eisenberg et al., "Does the Judge Matter"].

59. Eisenberg et al., "Does the Judge Matter," *supra* note 58 at 276.

60. Stacia Haynie, "Judicial Decision-Making and the Use of Panels in the South African Appellate Division, 1950-1990" (2002) 29:2 *South African Journal of Political Studies* 147 at 154.

61. Hausegger & Haynie, "Use of Panels," *supra* note 60 at 155.

62. Hausegger & Haynie, "Use of Panels," *supra* note 60 at 155.

A chief justice or president may not influence outcomes overall through panel selection where panels are set to achieve the same result as if the full bench heard the appeal. If there is no ideological diversity on the bench the chief justice will not even be able to influence individual cases. Even assuming a chief justice wishes to influence the outcomes of appeals through manipulating the composition of panels, she might not succeed, even if there is some ideological diversity across the judges on the court. It depends on the court's minimum bench size and the total number of judges. In order for her to influence the outcome, there must be enough judges who would support her preferred outcome for her to form a majority of the minimum allowable bench size. For instance, in Canada where the minimum bench size is five justices, the chief justice could appoint herself and two others who support her preferred result to a five-judge panel. If the Canadian Supreme Court decides a case on a 7-0, or 9-0 basis, no other combination of judges could have produced a majority in favor of the opposite outcome on a different panel.[63] A 6-3 decision, on the other hand, could have been decided differently if the three dissenters on the actual decision had been placed on a panel of five judges with any two of the other judges on the majority.

One measure of the extent to which a chief justice can alter outcomes then is the proportion of cases that could potentially have been decided differently with a differently constituted panel. We term this measure the Gaming Prospect Ratio (GPR)—the potential for a chief justice or president to "game" the panel selection by using panel selection rules to achieve a preferred outcome. We construct the GPR by dividing the number of decisions that could have been decided differently with a different panel by the total number of cases heard by the court.[64] More ideologically divisive courts will exhibit higher GPRs, because in such courts, more cases are likely to be decided by a close split, which opens the door for potential gaming.

Figure 4-2 sets out the GPR for various high courts—the percentage of cases that could potentially have been gamed through panel selection. Note that for India and the UK Houses of Lords, the GPRs are 100 percent—that is, all the cases could potentially have been decided differently with a different set of justices on the bench at the time. Because of the size of the court and the sizes of panels, all cases could be heard by a completely different set of justices, which means that if there is any ideological diversity (and the case would turn on ideological voting by the justices), the chief justice could rearrange the panels to influence any decision. Even in countries that ostensibly are in the mixed

63. This assumes the lack of panel effects, which will be discussed in Chapter 5.

64. Again assuming no panel effects.

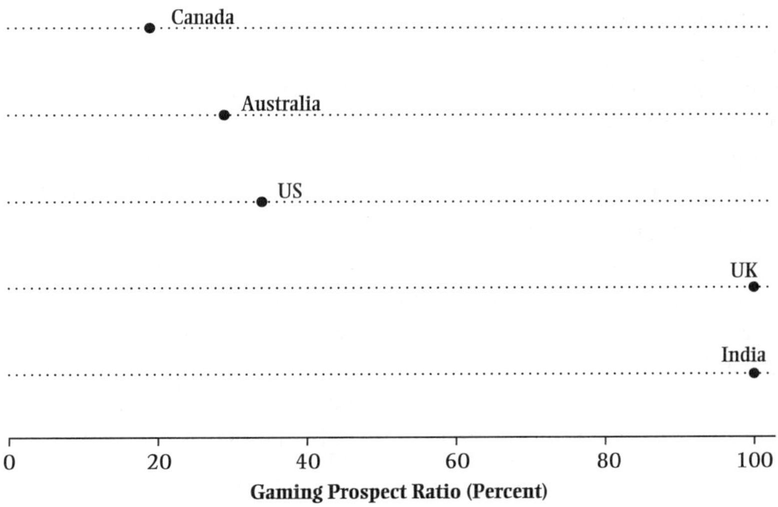


**Figure 4-2** Gaming Prospect Ratios (GPR) for various countries for 1970 to the early 2000s. A country's GPR is the number of decisions that could have been decided differently with a different panel, divided by the total number of cases heard by the court (the figure converts this rate to a percentage). Because of the small panels and large bench, India and the UK have 100 percent GPR—all the cases could potentially come out differently with a different panel. Canada has the lowest GPR. The US GPR is hypothetical, assuming the US Supreme Court heard cases in panels of five, seven, or nine judges.

category such as India, the chief justice has essentially unconstrained powers to set panels; with 31 judges on the Court, the chief justice has a wide range of panels of two, three, or five from which to choose.

The other three countries have lower GPRs. Canada has the lowest of these GPRs, with about 20 percent of cases potentially coming out differently with differently constituted panels. Australia has a slightly higher GPR of 30 percent. Although the United States hears appeals *en banc* (with a resulting GPR of 0), we also looked at what the GPR would be in a hypothetical scenario where it heard cases in panels of five, seven, or nine judges as in Canada. It would have the highest GPR at about 34 percent, meaning that given the justices on the bench about a third of the cases would be decided differently. The ratio would be even higher if the court could use panels of two or three judges as in India.

The GPR then is a function not only of the rules directly relating to panel selection but broader institutional rules relating to the size of the court, the appointments process (how ideologically split the court is), and the jurisdiction of the court (which may determine how contentious the cases before the court are, with higher GPRs for more contentious dockets). It will also likely depend on norms about consensus and dissents. However, interestingly, the GPRs have been relatively stable in recent years both in Canada and in the hypothetical US hearing in panels. Figure 4-3 shows the differences in the GPR at the Supreme Court of Canada and the US Supreme Court over time. The GPR for the US Supreme Court ranged from a low of 34 percent during the Warren Court to a high of 41 percent during the Burger Court. It has, however, stayed fairly consistent for the last two chief justices (that is, since 1986). The GPR for the Canadian Supreme Court was much lower, generally ranging from 12 to 15 percent since 1973. Again, the GPR of the Supreme Court of Canada has been fairly stable since the mid-1980s (after Canada adopted the Charter of Rights and Freedoms).

Although the GPR shows the proportion of cases that theoretically could have been decided differently, many of these in fact may not have been decided

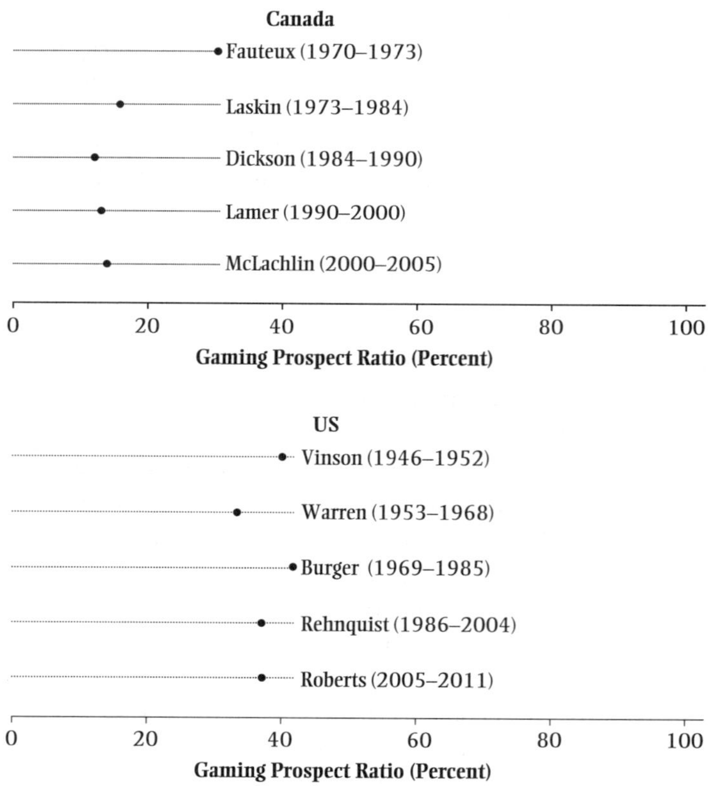


**Figure 4-3** Gaming Prospect Ratio (GPR) for Canada and the United States over time (percent). The GPR for both countries has been fairly constant over the past few decades, with the Canadian rate about a third of the hypothetical US rate.

differently. The most obvious example is the US Supreme Court, which decides all cases *en banc*, and hence does not provide opportunities for gaming through panel selection. In addition, a chief justice may choose to forgo the opportunity to game the outcome of appeals by choosing to hear the appeal with a full court instead of a smaller panel.

To what extent is a chief justice or president willing to take up this potential to alter outcomes? To look at this, we use a measure we call the Gaming Resistance Ratio (GRR). It is the proportion of cases that could have been decided differently by a smaller panel but were instead heard by a larger panel. For example, in Canada panels of nine where the votes were 6-3 could have been decided differently as a panel of five, and where the votes were 5-4 could have been decided differently as panels of five or seven. As seen in Figure 4-4, the GRR of the US Supreme Court is approximately 100 percent, because the potential gaming possibilities are essentially eliminated by the fact that the court decides all cases *en banc*. Conversely, the GRR for India, South Africa, and the UK were essentially zero as they did not hear decisions in panels large enough to alter the probability of gaming.

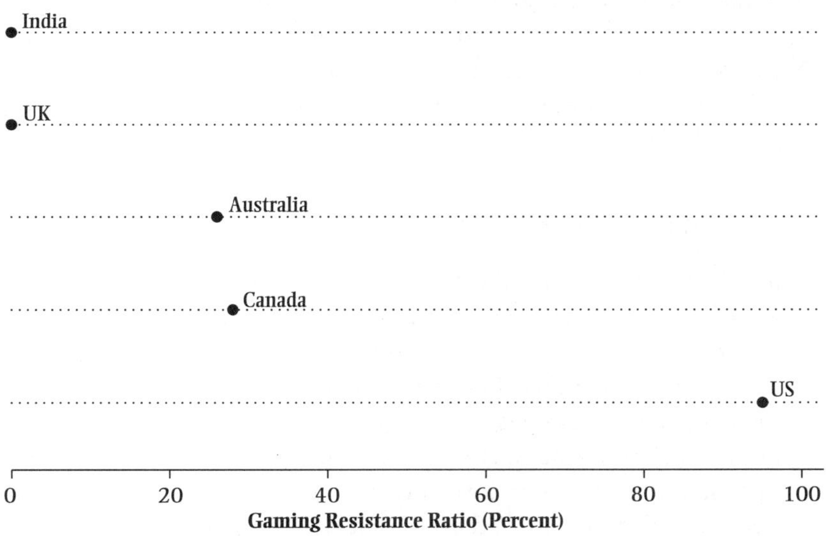


**Figure 4-4** Gaming Resistance Ratios (GRR) for various countries for 1970 to the early 2000s. A country's GRR is the number of cases that could have been decided differently by a smaller panel but were heard by a larger panel. For Canada and Australia, about 30 percent of cases could have come out differently if the Court had used smaller panels. Because of the small panels, India and the UK have a GRR of 0. The United States has an almost 100 percent GRR because it never hears decisions in smaller panels.

The GRR in Canada and in Australia, on the other hand, are more informative. The GRR is slightly higher for the Supreme Court of Canada than for the Australian High Court (28 percent versus 26 percent). For each court, the chief justice resisted the opportunity to potentially influence the outcome in about a third of the cases where he or she had the opportunity to do so. However, as with the GPR, the GRR changes over time, but the changes were much more extreme. In Canada, the gaming resistance ratio varied from a low of 15 percent under Chief Justice Dickson to a high of 69 percent under Chief Justice McLachlin, raising the possibility that different chief justices may have had different tastes for influencing outcomes through panel selection. Chief Justice McLachlin, for example, appears to have largely refrained from using the power to game outcomes through using smaller panels. Alternatively, she may have either faced a set of cases for which it was more difficult to predict the resulting votes or, even with a similar set of cases, been less able to predict how the justices on her court will vote than other chief justices.

Therefore, chief justices in high courts outside of the United States have scope within which to try to influence the outcomes of appeals via panel selection. For some countries such as India, there are almost unlimited opportunities for gaming the system through panel selection, though it is difficult to tell from the evidence whether these opportunities were taken. For other countries such as Canada and Australia, the nature of the court provides the chief justice with potential for influencing outcomes through panel selection but she sometimes resists, pointing perhaps at differences in norms concerning the legitimacy of influencing outcomes through panel selection.

## STRATEGIC PANEL SELECTION

If the panel selection power influences outcomes, whoever has this power may attempt to further her own preferred policy outcome. A chief justice may be able to increase the probability of her preferred result if she assigns a panel with similar views to her own. In India, Chief Justice Subba Rao was in dissent more than any other judge before he became chief justice, and had a distinctive anti-government ideology. However, after he became chief justice, Rao was never in dissent whereas the entire Court gave more anti-government decisions than ever before.[65] As mentioned earlier, on the US Court of Appeals for the Fifth Circuit during the 1960s, former chief judge Tuttle assigned a minority of judges to hear a disproportionately large number of race relations cases. This

65. George H. Gadbois, Jr., "Indian Judicial Behaviour" (1970) 5:3 *Economic and Political Weekly* 149 at 166.

panel selection made a difference to the pattern of outcomes, with decisions usually in support of the black plaintiffs.[66]

One way to see this effect would be if judges who are ideologically similar to the chief justice are more regularly assigned to panels that hear important cases. Alternatively, the chief justice could choose just enough judges to win. Chief justices in apartheid South Africa repeatedly assigned ideologically proximate minimum winning coalitions, rather than whole panels, in order to maximize the probability of their preferred outcome.[67] Even if the whole panel does not exclusively consist of judges ideologically proximate to the chief justice, the median judge on the assigned panels will be more in line with the chief justice's ideology than the court median. According to this theory a liberal chief justice would assign panels with more liberal medians than the court median, and vice versa for a conservative chief justice.

On the other hand, even the most strategically minded chief justice or president would not likely assign judges who are ideologically close to him to all panels. A chief justice likely cares not only about immediate outcomes of particular cases but the legitimacy of the court as a whole or of her time as chief justice. Her reputation may suffer either within the court or external to the court if she blatantly stacks panels. However, assuming chief justices care about policy outcomes to some extent and have some discretion to set panels, our hypothesis is:

> *H3: Chief justices will try to assign panels that are ideologically close to themselves for important cases.*

When we look across all cases in Canada, chief justices Dickson, Lamer, and McLachlin set panels that were slightly different from each other in terms of the median judge on the panels—the median judges on average had different liberal voting rates during the tenure of each of these chief justices.[68] However, the differences were exceedingly small, and the majority of panels had medians that were close to the Court median.[69] Further, somewhat surprisingly, some chief justices in Canada (1986–1997) and South Africa (1950–1990) were significantly

66. Atkins & Zavoina, *supra* note 2 at 709.

67. Kaitlyn L. Sill & Stacia Haynie, "Panel Assignment in Appellate Courts: Strategic Behaviour in the South African Supreme Court of Appeal" (2010) 37:2 *Politikon* 269 [Sill & Haynie, "Panel Assignment"].

68. Alarie et al., "Panel Selections," *supra* note 37. For example, Dickson set slightly more conservative panels than the median, whereas McLachlin set more liberal panels.

69. Alarie et al., "Panel Selections," *supra* note 37.

more likely to select for panels individuals who were ideologically further away from themselves.[70] Therefore, at least for Canada and South Africa, chief justices do not appear to have used their panel selection powers to promote their preferred policy outcomes across all cases.

However, not all cases are equally important, and a chief justice may save judges who have similar views to her for panels that hear the most important ones. Table 4-1 shows examples of the direction of ideological bias in panels that were set in "important" cases. A "pro-civil rights" bias indicates that a chief justice disproportionately assigned judges who were favorable to civil rights claims to panels, whereas a "pro-chief justice" bias indicates that a chief justice disproportionately assigned judges who were ideologically close to herself to panels.

The strongest evidence of strategic panel setting comes from South Africa. Chief justices of the South African Appellate Division from 1950 to 1990 disproportionately assigned judges who were ideologically close to themselves to the more salient cases that involved civil rights and liberties.[71] Further, although chief justices in South Africa do not attempt to group entire panels of judges who are similar to themselves, likely because of workload constraints, they do appear concerned with the minimum number of judges necessary to decide the case, or the minimum winning coalition.[72] Chief justices repeatedly assigned whole panels of judges in civil liberties cases, which were considered more important compared to other types of cases.[73] In these cases, panels that were ideologically further from the chief justice were less likely to be repeatedly assigned to future cases.[74]

Looking at how the conservative Chief Justice Rabie and more liberal Chief Justice Corbett used these powers starkly shows differences in the use of panel selection powers.[75] Chief Justice Rabie struck more conservative panels in civil

70. Hausegger & Haynie, "Use of Panels," *supra* note 60 at 651.

71. Hausegger & Haynie, "Use of Panels," *supra* note 60 at 651. One possible explanation for chief justices appearing to appoint judges who are ideologically close to themselves is that centrist judges are more likely to be appointed as chief justices compared to their more ideologically strident colleagues, and that as a result, there is a greater pool of judges who are ideologically close to a centrist chief justice from which they can draw for panels. On the other hand, a rare counter-example happened in South Africa from 1994 to 2000, when the South African chief justice, Ismail Mahomed, was extremely liberal compared to the rest of the court, and hence had very few ideologically proximate judges from whom he could select. Sill & Haynie, "Panel Assignment," *supra* note 67 at 280.

72. Sill & Haynie, "Panel Assignment," *supra* note 67.

73. Sill & Haynie, "Panel Assignment," *supra* note 67 at 278.

74. Sill & Haynie, "Panel Assignment," *supra* note 67 at 281.

75. Stacia L. Haynie, *Judging in Black and White: Decision Making in South African Appellate Division, 1950-1990* (New York: Peter Lang Pub Incorporated, 2003) at 83 [Haynie, *Black and White*].

*Table 4-1.* Summary of the Literature Regarding Panel Selection Bias in Important Cases

| Jurisdiction | Time | Important cases | Panel bias | Authors |
|---|---|---|---|---|
| **Canada** | 1986–1997 | Charter cases | Pro-chief justice | Hausegger & Haynie |
| **Canada** | 1986–2005 | Discretionary appeals | More liberal | Alarie & Green |
| **India** | 1947–2009 | Constitution cases | Pro-chief justice | Robinson |
| **South Africa (Appellate Division)** | 1950–1990 | Civil rights cases | Pro-chief justice | Hausegger & Haynie |
| **South Africa (Appellate Division)** | 1985–1990 | Emergency cases | Anti-individual | Haynie |
| **United States** | 1972–2004 | Specialty Courts | Republican | Ruger |

rights and liberties cases, whereas his successor, Chief Justice Corbett, created more liberal panels in civil rights and liberties cases than would be created by chance.[76] Moreover, it is commonly thought that during South Africa's state of emergency in the late 1980s Chief Justice Rabie frequently selected an "emergency team" of five justices, who were presumed to be more conservative, in order to ensure government victories in cases relating to the state of emergency.[77] The evidence bears this out. The judges on the "emergency team" selected by Chief Justice Rabie were indeed less supportive of the individual in civil rights and liberties cases compared to their colleagues on the Court at the time.[78]

The evidence from Canada is more mixed. A chief justice may appoint different types of panels to cases heard as of right as opposed to with leave of the Court. Appeals heard as of right should on average be less important than appeals heard with leave as the appeals heard as of right may not have passed the threshold to be heard with leave. Chief justices from 1986 to 2005 did set slightly more liberal panels to appeals heard with leave.[79] However, the chief

76. Hausegger & Haynie, "Use of Panels," *supra* note 60 at 153.

77. Stephen Ellmann, *In a Time of Trouble: Law and Liberty in South Africa's State of Emergency* (New York: Oxford University Press, 1992) at 64.

78. Haynie, *Black and White, supra* note 75 at 84.

79. Alarie et al., "Panel Selections," *supra* note 37.

justices did not consistently lean in a liberal direction.[80] They may then not have been setting panels strategically or only doing so in a more finely grained set of important cases. For example, from 1986 to 1997, chief justices disproportionately assigned judges who were ideologically close to themselves to cases involving a Charter of Rights and Freedoms issue.[81]

How chief justices choose panels may also change over time. For example, the Indian Constitution requires that the Court sit in larger benches of at least five judges to hear cases "involving a substantial question of law as to the interpretation of the Constitution."[82] Since independence, a chief justice has only dissented 10 times on a constitution bench, which may indicate that chief justices have used their panel-setting powers to assign like-minded judges to constitutional cases to obtain outcomes they favor.[83] However, the difference between the dissent rates of the chief justice and other judges in constitutional cases has decreased in recent years. The dissent rate of the chief justice on constitutional benches was 27 times less than that of other judges in the 1960s, but only four times less in the 2000s.[84] This change in the dissent rate may indicate either that chief justices are less likely to attempt to strategically set panels or that they are less successful than in the past at predicting how their colleagues will decide cases.[85]

Although the chief justices of the US Supreme Court do not select panels to hear appeals, they do fill a wide range of offices within the judicial bureaucracy,

80. Benjamin Alarie & Andrew Green, "Policy Preference Change and Appointments to the Supreme Court of Canada" (2009) 47 *Osgoode Hall LJ* 1 at 27. Chief Justice Dickson's votes were slightly conservative, Chief Justice Lamer's votes were slightly liberal, and especially so in criminal cases, whereas Justice McLachlin's votes were slightly conservative. However, the reliability of these measures, which were based on a one-dimensional policy space, may be questioned, partly because the results of some other justices seem inconsistent with conventional expectations.

81. Hausegger & Haynie, "Use of Panels," *supra* note 60 at 651.

82. *India Constitution, supra* note 33, art 145(3).

83. Robinson, "Interpreting the Constitution," *supra* note 34 at 31.

84. Robinson, "Interpreting the Constitution," *supra* note 34 at 31.

85. Note that it would be helpful to also know the relative dissent rate of chief justices in other types of cases although, in other cases, dissent rates are extremely low in India. An alternate explanation of dissent rates of chief justices is that upon becoming chief justice, a judge becomes more focused on consensus-building as a result of the demands of the job, and as a result, appears to become more centrist. For example, Canadian chief justice McLachlin's level of dissent activity decreased after she became chief justice (Matthew Wetstein & C.L. Ostberg, "Strategic Leadership and Political Change on the Canadian Supreme Court: Analyzing the Transition to Chief Justice" (2005) 38:3 *Canadian Journal of Political Science* 653).

including specialty courts such as courts established in the *Foreign Intelligence Surveillance Act*.[86] A chief justice may select judges for these specialty courts for policy reasons, just like chief justices in other common law countries may use their panel-selection powers to enhance their own policy preferences. For example, chief justices Rehnquist and Burger both appointed more Republicans than Democrats to judicial offices that were more political in nature. Further, Chief Justice Burger placed most of his Democratic appointees onto courts that were "confined to relatively specific fields and perhaps also channelled by relatively more neutral technical standards."[87]

One measure of how a chief justice might change the composition of a panel is to look to see if she tends to set panels to reflect her own policy preferences rather than the mean liberal voting rates of those on the court at any given time. Figure 4-5 looks at the relationship between the difference between the court mean and the panel mean, and the difference between the court mean and the chief justice's lifetime liberal voting rate.[88] If there is a positive relationship, then when the chief justice is more liberal than the court mean, she tends to set panels more liberal than the court mean (and if more conservative, more conservative than the court mean). There was a consistently positive relationship for the UK, India, and Australia courts (although for civil rights for Australia, the estimate is not significant at the .05 level), pointing toward gaming of panel selection in each of these countries. Interestingly, it is only positive for civil rights in Canada, whereas it was not significant (and in fact had a negative estimate) for both criminal and economic cases. Further, the effect is much larger in Canada for civil rights than for any other area of law in other countries.

Overall, then, there is some evidence that chief justices assign judges who hold similar views to their own, at least to important appeals. Examining the relationship between the chief justice's voting tendencies and the panel means provides some evidence of a correlation, but it is far from perfect. More work is needed to control for various factors, which may alter the panel composition over time that are not related directly to the chief justice. Moreover, we may be more concerned about the median judge or creating a minimum winning

86. James E. Pfander, "The Chief Justice, the Appointment of Inferior Officers, and the 'Court of Law' Requirement" (2013) 107:3 *Northwestern University Law Review* 1125 at 1126–1127.

87. Theodore Ruger, "The Judicial Appointment Power of the Chief Justice" (2004) 7:2 *Journal of Constitutional Law* 341 at 394.

88. This figure is based on linear regressions with the left-hand variable being the difference between the mean of the lifetime liberal voting rates of the judges on the court in the year of the appeal and the mean of the lifetime liberal voting rates of the judges on the panel. The right-hand side variable is the difference between the court mean and the lifetime liberal voting rate of the chief justice at the time of the appeal.

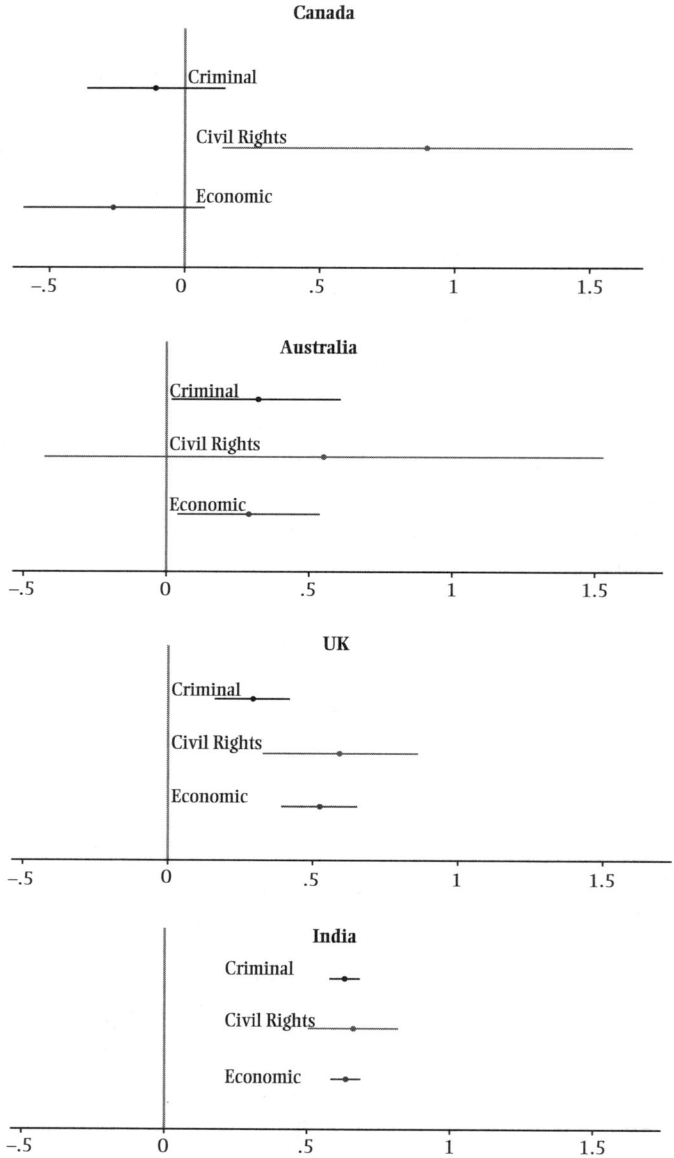


**Figure 4-5** The relationship between the difference between the court mean lifetime liberal voting rate and the panel's mean lifetime liberal voting rate, and the difference between the court mean and the chief justice's lifetime liberal voting rate, over 1970 to the early 2000s. The lines show the 95 percent confidence intervals. A positive value means that if a chief justice is more liberal than the court mean, she tends to set panels that are more liberal than the court mean—and if the chief justice is more conservative than the mean, she sets panels that are more conservative than the mean. The relationship is positive for the UK, India, and Australia across criminal, civil rights, and economic cases (although not statistically significant for civil rights cases in Australia). The relationship is positive and statistically significant in Canada only for civil rights but the effect is stronger than in other countries. The US Supreme Court is not included, as it does not hear appeals in panels.

coalition, neither of which are captured by this analysis. It also points to the importance of the selection of the chief justice, which as we saw in Chapter 1 varies across countries with, for example, the president choosing the chief justice directly in the United States, and a tradition of the most senior judge becoming chief justice in India.

## SETTING PANELS

As we note above, the chief justice has more or less room to set such panels depending on the size of the court, the size of the panels, and the degree of heterogeneity in voting across judges on the court. The United States of course has avoided all the concerns about the chief justice using the panel-setting powers to game outcomes by having a norm of hearing all appeals *en banc* (unless there is a vacancy or a conflict of interest). It does so at the potential expense of efficiency—of hearing more cases or using expertise to its best advantage.

At the other extreme is India. Instead of attempting to control the number of cases that come before the Court, the Court was expanded over time, and the panel size was set small. There is not a large variance in panel sizes, though there is some increase for constitutional cases. As a result, however, chief justices have the greatest potential for composing panels to meet their own policy preferences. As we saw in Figure 4-5, there is some evidence that they did so in past decades.

In between these extremes, again, are Canada, the UK, and Australia. As in India, the senior law lord in the UK had significant potential for setting panels to accord with his own views, given the size of the court and the panels. Figure 4-5 provides some limited evidence that senior law lords did so to a small extent across different areas of law. The chief justices in both Canada and Australia had less scope for gaming than the senior law lord in the UK, and there is some evidence that they resisted this temptation at least in some cases. Further, they were less likely to structure panels according to their own views across all areas of law, though chief justices in Canada may have done so to a greater extent in civil rights cases. Finally, chief justices in Canada were most likely to use this power to vary the size of the panel according to the nature of the case, potentially taking advantage of the efficiency gains from the panel-setting power.

However, judges may not vote solely because of the appeal in front of them. They may also take into account their relationship with others—either with other judges on the bench or with other institutions. It is to these relationships that we now turn.

# 5

# Do Judges Care About Others?

So far we have largely taken judges as caring about their own policy goals. The appointment process may produce high courts populated with judges with particular policy preferences, influencing outcomes in particular cases. The chief justice or others may have particular policy preferences that influence their choice of the size or composition of panels that hear particular appeals. However, not surprisingly a judge may care about other things than the direct policy effects of his decisions, such as how various groups may view him if he votes in favor of or against abortion rights or enhanced national security measures.[1]

How much do judges care about or respond to other people when making decisions? For example, do judges think about their interactions with their colleagues on the high court when deciding cases? They appear to in at least some cases. For example, a Democratic appointee on the US federal courts of appeal who is sitting on a panel with two other Democratic appointees will vote in a liberal direction 64 percent of the time but only 44 percent of the time when sitting with two Republican appointees.[2] A judge may for a number of reasons decide differently based on the policy preferences or personal characteristics of the others on the panel or bench. A judge who is in an ideological minority on a panel may, for example, act as a "whistleblower" on extreme ideological voting by the others—holding them to account for voting inappropriately in line with

1. See e.g. Lee Epstein & Jack Knight, *The Choices Justices Make* (Washington, DC: CQ Press, 1998) at 159 (plurality decision in a Planned Parenthood case apparently strictly following precedent from *Roe v. Wade*); Lee Epstein & Tonja Jacobi, "The Strategic Analysis of Judicial Decisions" (2010) 6 *Annual Review of Law and Social Science* 341 at 344 [Epstein & Jacobi]; Lawrence Baum, *Judges and Their Audiences* (Princeton, NJ: Princeton University Press, 2008).

2. Cass R. Sunstein et al., *Are Judges Political? An Empirical Analysis of the Federal Judiciary* (Washington, DC: Brookings Institution Press, 2006) [Sunstein et al., *Are Judges Political*] at 23–24. These differences varied across areas of law.

their own personal views.[3] Whatever the reason, however, who is on the panel may matter more than simply adding together each judge's vote according to his direct policy preferences.

Judges may care not only about their colleagues on the bench but also about how other branches of government such as the legislature will react to their decisions.[4] For example, US Supreme Court judges did not simply vote what would appear to be their policy preference in civil rights decisions involving constitutional issues between 1953 and 1992. Instead they adapted their voting based on the political preferences of members of the other branches of government who might react to their decisions.[5]

In addition to the direct effect of her decision on law and policy, a judge may care about her long-term reputation with other judges or institutional actors, and how it might be affected by such behavior as frequently dissenting. Moreover, she may take into account the broader reputation of the court as a whole—will the public view the court as less legitimate if the judges blatantly vote based on their preferred policy outcome?

In this chapter, we will look at whether three different types of relationships alter how judges decide cases. First, as we saw, judges may be influenced by the policy preferences or personal characteristics of other judges on the bench, or more narrowly on the panel hearing a particular appeal. Do high court judges vote differently if they are on a panel with judges of similar policy preferences versus judges of opposing preferences? Does diversity in personal characteristics on a panel make a difference to outcomes? Second, a judge's relative status within the court may matter as to how the judge or the panel votes, such as whether the judge is the chief justice or a new appointee (or freshman) on the bench. Finally, a judge may care about how the legislature or government will react to his decision. To what extent do high court judges appear to be influenced by the political preferences of the current government or legislature? We begin with how a judge is affected by her colleagues.

## OTHER JUDGES ON THE PANEL

A court may reach different outcomes depending on the diversity of its membership. The diversity may be in policy preferences, ideological outlook, or more

3. Sunstein et al., *Are Judges Political, supra* note 2 at 15.

4. Epstein & Jacobi, *supra* note 1 at 351. We will discuss other actors such as interest groups further in Chapter 7.

5. Lee Epstein, Jack Knight & Andrew Martin, "The Supreme Court as Strategic National Policymaker" (2001) 50:2 *Emory Law Journal* 583 at 610 [Epstein et al., "National Policymaker"] ("[t]ests at both the individual and the aggregate levels support the proposition that the Justices adjust their decisions in anticipation of the potential responses of the other branches of the government").

personal characteristics such as gender or race. Diversity, or the lack thereof, will depend on the appointment process to the bench as a whole as well as the nature of the panel-setting process. It may also vary for a given bench depending on the area of law, such as where a court is composed of judges who are uniformly conservative on economic issues but mixed on criminal matters.

If a judge compromises on his ideal outcome despite being in the majority on a panel, it might be because the minority judge simply raises considerations that would not have occurred to him otherwise.[6] Alternatively, the minority judge may serve as a "whistleblower" who threatens to expose the rest of the panel's ideological extremity or disregard for legal doctrine by writing a dissenting opinion.[7] The potential whistleblower motivates the majority to base their decision more firmly on doctrinal grounds rather than personal preference.

Similarly, a minority judge may persuade others to adopt her position if she feels more strongly about the outcome of a particular case than they do.[8] The majority may find her conviction persuasive, or may choose to partly cooperate in hopes of unanimity (as a judge with strong preferences will be more willing to bear the costs of dissenting) or her voting their way in cases they find particularly important. The author of the majority opinion usually enjoys an agenda-setting advantage, but may have to compromise her position in order to obtain a majority coalition.[9] Conversely, judges sitting on a panel of like-minded judges

6. There are other factors that may affect the influence of other panelists on a judge's decision. In part the impact of diversity may depend on how decisions are made on a court. The process generally involves some post-hearing conference such as in Canada where the judges discuss the appeal in reverse order of seniority. It may also depend on who writes the opinion. Again in Canada, the chief justice is formally responsible for assigning opinion writing, though the actual process has been described as collegial (Peter McCormick, "Was It Something I Said? Losing the Majority on the Modern Supreme Court of Canada, 1984–2011" (2012) 50:1 *Osgoode Hall Law Journal* 93). Opinions are assigned by collective agreement at the House of Lords (Alan Paterson, *Final Judgment: The Last Law Lords and the Supreme Court* (Oxford: Hart, 2013) at 93 [Paterson]. In India, the senior judge decides whether to write the opinion himself or assign it to another panel member (Abhinav Chandrachud, "From Hyderbad to Harvard: How U.S. Law Schools Make Clerking on India's Supreme Court Worthwhile" (2014) HLS Program on the Legal Profession Research Paper at 22, online: http://ssrn.com/abstract=2413576).

7. Frank B. Cross & Emerson H. Tiller, "Judicial Partisanship and Obedience to Legal Doctrine: Whistleblowing on the Federal Courts of Appeals" (1998) 107:7 *Yale Law Journal* 2155 at 2155 [Cross & Tiller]; Sunstein et al., *Are Judges Political, supra* note 3 at 15.

8. See e.g. Richard A. Posner, *How Judges Think* (Cambridge, MA: Harvard University Press, 2008) at 32–33 [Posner, *How Judges Think*].

9. See e.g. Lawrence Wrightman, *The Psychology of the Supreme Court* (New York: Oxford University Press, 2006) at 81–82; Forrest Maltzman, James F. Spriggs II & Paul J. Wahlbeck, *Crafting Law on the Supreme Court: The Collegial Game* (Cambridge, UK: Cambridge University Press, 2000) at 72. The author of a decision may be content with obtaining a bare majority (for example, five justices on the US Supreme Court), though in some cases they may care

may be more likely to follow their policy preferences because they don't need to consider complex strategies.[10]

Differences on panels may then influence whether a judge dissents. A judge on a mixed panel may be less likely to dissent, because the majority opinion will be more likely to rest on doctrinal considerations if they fear the minority judge will act as a whistleblower.[11] Moreover, as we discussed in Chapter 2, writing a dissenting opinion requires effort and potentially imposes reputational costs with colleagues, and so a judge may not dissent unless he anticipates a benefit that offsets that cost.[12] He may then shirk the additional work by assenting to the majority opinion despite not agreeing entirely with its reasoning. However, he may consider the costs of writing the dissent to be justified if the differences between panel members are wide enough to preclude acceptable compromises.[13]

not only about winning but the size of the majority (Epstein & Jacobi, *supra* note 1 at 348). David W. Rohde, "Policy Goals and Opinion Coalitions in the Supreme Court" (1972) 16:2 *Midwest Journal of Political Science* 208 at 671–672 [Rohde, "Policy Goals"]. Rohde argued that this was the reason for the predominance of 5-4 rulings in civil liberties cases decided by the Warren Court. Alternative theories predict that cases with ideologically extreme decisions by lower courts are likelier to result in broad majorities. The rationale for this argument is that the likelihood of a particular judge joining the majority opinion increases in relation to his ideological closeness to the median justice within the majority coalition. In cases where the median of the majority aligns with the median of the court, judges with extreme preferences in either direction are more likely to dissent or concur, whereas opinions that favor a particular policy direction can gain support from judges who share that preference and those who occupy the center of the court. See Tonja Jacobi, "Competing Models of Coalition Forming and Case Outcome Determination" (2009) 1:2 *Journal of Legal Analysis* 411 [Jacobi, "Competing Models"]; Cliff Carrubba et al., "Who Controls the Content of Supreme Court Opinions?" (2012) 56:2 *American Journal of Political Science* 400 (arguing that the decision is most heavily influenced by the median justice in the majority). See Chapter 8 for a discussion of consensus.

10. The diversity of the panel may interact with the size of the panel. For example, a judge on a smaller panel may be less likely to vote in line with her personal preferences if smaller groups make greater efforts to compromise. Further, as the majority grows larger (and the minority correspondingly decreases), judges in both groups may be less likely to compromise with each other because they have less to gain by doing so. See e.g. Lee Epstein, William M. Landes & Richard A. Posner, *Behavior of Federal Judges: A Theoretical and Empirical Study of Rational Choice* (Cambridge, MA: Harvard University Press, 2013) [Epstein, Landes & Posner, *Behavior*] at 145 (n. 9). Alternatively, however, larger majorities may not lead to an increased number of dissents if smaller minorities incur greater costs by dissenting—such as weakening of their reputation with their colleagues. They then may be more likely to conform to the majority's decision. Epstein, Landes & Posner, *Behavior*, at 146–149 (n. 9) (finding, however, that this effect does not hold for the US Supreme Court).

11. Cross & Tiller, *supra* note 7 at 2156, n. 7.

12. Epstein, Landes & Posner, *Behavior, supra* note 10 at 256. For a further discussion of dissenting, see Chapter 8.

13. Some work has been done in the United States on "voting fluidity," which looks at when a judge changes her vote between the initial conference and the final decision. For example, see

The influence of panel diversity may vary by area of law. Judges may be less affected by their colleagues in ideologically divisive cases.[14] Further, if members of the high court are strongly divided on political issues, they may be more likely to form coalitions with their ideological allies in order to prevent their "foes" from reaching a majority.[15] The reasonably stable split between Democratic and Republican appointees on the US Supreme Court may provide an illustration of this phenomenon.[16] Conversely, on the less politically diverse courts in Canada and the UK, certain pairs of judges may be more likely to vote together, but these coalitions are not as consistent as they are in the United States, and do not have a significant effect on final outcomes.[17]

These potential impacts of panel diversity and panel size lead to the following hypothesis:

> *H1: Judges will be more likely to reach ideologically extreme decisions when sitting with ideologically similar judges than on more diverse panels.*

e.g. Robert H. Dorff & Saul Brenner, "Conformity Voting on the United States Supreme Court" (1992) 54:3 *The Journal of Politics* 762 [Dorff & Brenner]; Forrest Maltzman & Paul J Wahlbeck, "Strategic Policy Considerations and Voting Fluidity on the Burger Court" (1996) 90:3 *The American Political Science* 581 [Maltzman & Wahlbeck, "Burger Court"]; Saul Brenner, Timothy Hagle & Harold J Spaeth, "Increasing the Size of Minimum Winning Original Coalitions on the Warren Court" (1990) 23:2 *Polity* 309.

14. Cass Sunstein et al. suggest that ideological voting is most pronounced in some areas of law, such as abortion and capital punishment cases, and rarely occurs in others, including criminal appeals, takings claims, challenges to punitive damage awards, and standing issues. Correspondingly, they find that panel effects have a more significant influence in the latter categories. Sunstein et al., *Are Judges Political, supra* note 3 at 55, n. 6.

15. Judges often appear to value coalitions for reasons that extend beyond simply "winning" in a particular case or promoting consensus: Jacobi, "Competing Models," *supra* note 9; Epstein & Jacobi, *supra* note 1 at 348, n. 1. See Chapter 8 for a detailed examination of consensual norms and their influence on high court decision-making.

16. See e.g. Neal Devins & Lawrence Baum, "Split Definitive: How Party Polarization Turned the Supreme Court into a Partisan Court" (2014) (William & Mary Law School Research Paper No 09-276) at 38, online: http://papers.ssrn.com/sol3/papers.cfm?abstract_id=2432111.

17. T.T. Arvind & Lindsay Stirton, "Lawyers and the Legal Model: Judicial Ideology, Judicial Professionalism and Institutional Strategy among the Law Lords" (2012) at 39, online: https://extranet.sioe.org/uploads/isnie2012/arvind_stirton.pdf [Arvind & Stirton]; Brice Dickson, "Close Calls in the House of Lords" in James Lee, ed, *From House of Lords to Supreme Court: Judges, Jurists and the Process of Judging* (Oxford: Hart, 2011) 283 at 284. Benjamin Alarie & Andrew Green, "Should They All Just Get Along? Judicial Ideology, Collegiality, and Appointments to the Supreme Court of Canada" (2008) 58 *University of New Brunswick LJ* 73.

Most of the literature regarding these panel effects has focused on the US Federal Courts of Appeals, which hear cases in three-judge panels. The judges have been found to reach "ideologically amplified" decisions when the rest of the panel shares their political views. Conversely, the presence of a judge with conflicting preferences is associated with an "ideological dampening effect."[18] Sunstein et al. found that the effect of both individual preferences and panel composition varies depending on the area of law involved. Judges were influenced by their partisan commitments as well as the dispositions of other panel members in several areas, including affirmative action, sex discrimination, disability discrimination, sexual harassment, piercing the corporate veil, campaign finance, racial discrimination, contract violations, and environmental regulations.[19] In these fields, Democratic judges were substantially more likely to vote for outcomes classified as "liberal" than their Republican colleagues. Moreover, both groups of judges were more likely to support liberal decisions when the other two panel members were Democrats, and correspondingly less likely to vote liberally when sitting with two Republicans. However, neither individual nor panel preferences appears to influence judicial voting in cases that involve criminal appeals, federalism, or takings claims.[20] A third group of decisions, including abortion and capital punishment issues, was dominated by ideological voting. In these contentious areas, Democratic- and Republican-appointed judges voted in a predictable ideological pattern that was not affected by which colleagues they sat with.[21]

Similarly, Cross and Tiller found that judges on divided panels are almost twice as likely to follow legal doctrine that conflicts with the majority's policy preferences.[22] In DC Circuit Court of Appeals decisions citing *Chevron USA v. Natural Resources Defense Council Inc.*[23] (a key US administrative law decision), in order to reach their preferred outcome, politically unified panels did not follow the principle of deference established in *Chevron* two-thirds of the time. In contrast, almost the same percentage of politically divided panels followed *Chevron* despite a conflict with the majority's policy goals.[24] These results

18. Cass R. Sunstein, David Schkade & Lisa Michelle Ellman, "Ideological Voting on Federal Courts of Appeals: A Preliminary Investigation" (2004) 90:1 *Virginia Law Review* 301 [Sunstein, Schkade & Ellman].

19. Sunstein, Schkade & Ellman, *supra* note 18, at 319, n. 64.

20. Sunstein, Schkade & Ellman, *supra* note 18 at 325, n. 64.

21. Sunstein, Schkade & Ellman, *supra* note 18 at 319, n. 64.

22. Cross & Tiller, *supra* note 7, n. 7.

23. *Chevron USA, Inc. v. NRDC*, 467 U.S. 837 (1984).

24. Cross & Tiller, *supra* note 7 at 2172, n. 7.

may show a strategic response to the minority judge's potential role as a "whistleblower" who reveals the majority's disobedience by writing a dissent.[25]

Panel effects also appear to play a significant role in the decision-making of judges on the Ontario Court of Appeal. Applying the methodology used by Sunstein et al., Stribopoulos and Yahya found that judges' decisions vary significantly depending on which party appointed them; however, on panels composed of both Liberal and Conservative appointees, the influence of political ideology is dampened. This was particularly evident in cases involving Charter claims or criminal appeals.[26] Stribopoulos and Yahya suggest that this trend reflects a tendency for judges to engage in more deliberation on heterogeneous panels, and thus reach different results.[27]

The composition of the rest of the court (not just the panel) may also matter. Kastellec found that the probability of reaching a liberal decision increases in relation to the number of Democratic judges sitting on the panel, and that the presence of a single Republican "counterjudge" had significantly more influence when the rest of the circuit was similarly aligned.[28] In Democratic circuits, panels with two Democrats and one Republican voted liberally 52 percent of the time, whereas those composed entirely of Democrats reached liberal outcomes 62 percent of the time. In contrast, Democrats in a Republican circuit were 67 percent likely to vote liberally on an ideologically homogenous panel, but only did so 48 percent of the time when one Republican judge was on the panel. Interestingly, Republican majorities in Democratic circuits voted liberally in 35 percent of cases, regardless of whether the panel included a Democrat; however, in Republican circuits, adding a Democratic counterjudge increased the chances of a liberal vote from 27 percent to 34 percent.[29]

25. This effect may in part be accounted for by the risk of reversal. For example, the likelihood of a minority panel member voting counter-ideologically in sex discrimination cases is predicted to fall from 75.1 percent to 64.1 percent when she is more closely aligned with the full circuit, whereas counter-ideological voting by the majority increases from 45.1 percent to 57.1 percent. However, the political preferences of the US Supreme Court do not appear to have any impact on appellate judges. Pauline Kim, "Deliberation and Strategy on the United States Courts of Appeals: An Empirical Exploration of Panel Effects" (2009) 157:5 *University of Pennsylvania Law Review* 1319 at 1363–1364.

26. James Stribopoulos & Moin A. Yahya, "Does a Judge's Party of Appointment or Gender Matter to Case Outcomes? An Empirical Study of the Court of Appeal for Ontario" (2007) 45:2 *Osgoode Hall Law Journal* 315 at 346–347 [Stribopoulos & Yaha].

27. Stribopoulos & Yahya, *supra* note 26 at 348.

28. Jonathan P. Kastellec, "Hierarchical and Collegial Politics on the U.S. Courts of Appeals" (2011) 73:2 *Journal of Politics* 73 345 [Kastellec, "Hierarchical"].

29. Kastellec, "Hierarchical," *supra* note 28 at 357, n. 73.

Judges may be influenced not only by the political leanings of their colleagues but also by diversity in personal characteristics such as gender or race.[30] For instance, both the ideology and race of judges on a panel appeared to influence federal appellate cases involving affirmative action programs.[31] The difference between panels that included a black judge and those that did not was striking: panels with three non-black judges voted in favor of affirmative action in 53 percent of cases, yet adding a single black judge to the panel increased the chances to 81 percent. More surprisingly, two non-black Republican judges sitting with a black colleague were 86 percent likely to vote in favor of affirmative action—significantly higher than the 67 percent likelihood of a Republican casting a pro-affirmative action vote when sharing the panel with two non-black Democrats, even though the former judges constitute a majority and the latter does not.[32]

Similarly, both race and ideology have been found to influence judges' decisions in cases involving the *Voting Rights Act* in the United States.[33] In fact, the racial composition of a panel appears more significant than its partisan alignment in these cases. Black judges were found to rule in plaintiffs' favor a little over half of the time, regardless of their political party,[34] and the presence of a black judge increased the probability of non-black panel members voting for the plaintiff by nearly 19 percent.[35]

The presence of female judges may also have a significant effect on case outcomes. In employment discrimination cases, for example, female judges were 20 percent more likely to rule in favor of plaintiffs. Their effect on other panel members is similarly significant, as the probability of a male judge voting for the plaintiff increases by 19 percent when he sits with a female colleague.[36] Boyd, Epstein, and Martin found female judges also influenced their colleagues

30. Epstein, Landes & Posner, *Behavior, supra* note 10 (n. 9).

31. Jonathan P. Kastellec, "Racial Diversity and Judicial Influence on Appellate Courts" (2013) 57:1 *American Journal of Political Science* 167 [Kastellec, "Racial Diversity"].

32. Kastellec, "Racial Diversity," *supra* note 31 at 173, 175, 179.

33. Adam B. Cox & Thomas J. Miles, "Judging the Voting Rights Act" (2008) 108 *Columbia Law Review* 1 [Cox & Miles].

34. Cox & Miles, *supra* note 33 at 30. Democratic judges voted for plaintiffs in 36 percent of these cases, whereas Republicans did 21 percent of the time. The likelihood of Democratic judges casting a pro-plaintiff vote increased 23 percent when the panel was composed entirely of Democrats, as opposed to when they sat with two Republicans. Cox & Miles, *supra* note 33 at 42.

35. Cox & Miles, *supra* note 33 at 35.

36. Sean Farhang & Gregory Wawro, "Institutional Dynamics on the U.S. Court of Appeals: Minority Representation under Panel Decision Making" (2004) 20:2 *Journal of Law, Economics, and Organization* 299 at 320 [Farhang & Wawro].

in sex discrimination cases, but did not find evidence of sex-based panel effects in any other relevant areas, including sexual harassment.[37] They argue that their findings support an informational theory of group decision-making, which presumes that female judges have knowledge about specific issues that influences how they and their male colleagues vote in gender-related issues.[38] Panels on the Ontario Court of Appeal including male and female judges also displayed unique voting trends, especially in criminal cases involving a gender or violence-related component, sentencing appeals, and family law cases.[39]

There is, however, inconsistency in results in the panel effects literature.[40] Fischman recently reviewed 11 major studies and used a new empirical model to interpret their results.[41] His analysis assumes that judges are influenced by their colleagues' votes rather than the presence of judges with divergent preferences or characteristics. Doing so shows consistent evidence of panel effects across several areas, including several fields in which Sunstein et al. claimed judges were not influenced by their colleagues, such as criminal appeals and capital punishment cases.[42] Fischman reports that each vote cast by a colleague increases by approximately 40 percent the likelihood that a particular judge will vote in the same direction. Most significantly, his results remain true regardless of whether panel members are distinguished on the basis of party affiliation, gender, race, or other characteristics.[43] Based on these results, he concludes that prior studies on panel effects can be explained at least in part by a strong norm of consensus.[44]

37. Christina L. Boyd, Lee Epstein & Andrew D. Martin, "Untangling the Causal Effects of Sex on Judging" (2010) 54:2 *American Journal of Political Science* 389 at 400–402.

38. But see Peresie finding that being female increases the chances that a judge will vote for the plaintiff by 86 percent in sexual harassment cases and 65 percent in sex discrimination cases. Likewise, sitting on a mixed panel hugely increased the chances of a male judge voting for the plaintiff in sexual harassment cases (from 16 percent to 35 percent) and sexual discrimination cases (from 11 percent to 30 percent). Jennifer L. Peresie, "Female Judges Matter: Gender and Collegial Decisionmaking in the Federal Appellate Courts" (2005) 114:7 *Yale Law Journal* 1759 at 1776–1778.

39. Stribopoulos & Yahya, *supra* note 26 at 349–352, n. 90.

40. See e.g. Sunstein, Schkade & Ellman, *supra* note 18 at 320; Farhang & Wawro, *supra* note 36 at 321, n. 79 (finds no panel effects re: race in employment discrimination cases).

41. Joshua B. Fischman, "Interpreting Circuit Court Patterns: A Social Interactions Framework", (2015) 31:4 *Journal of Law, Economics, and Organization* 808 at 810 [Fischman, "Interpreting Circuit"].

42. Fischman, "Interpreting Circuit," *supra* note 41 at 810.

43. Fischman, "Interpreting Circuit," *supra* note 41 at 810.

44. This explanation is consistent with the high rate of unanimity on the US Federal Courts of Appeals, which has a dissent rate of approximately 6 percent.

So far, little research has been done regarding panel effects on high courts. However, analyses from Canada, the UK, and Israel suggest that judges from these countries may be similarly influenced by their colleagues' views. Jilani, Songer, and Johnson argue that the appointment of female justices to the Supreme Court of Canada had a significant influence on the voting patterns of male judges.[45] Studying the court's decisions from 1967 to 2007, they found that with the addition of each female colleague, male judges became 9 percent more likely to vote for liberal outcomes in cases involving equality and discrimination, criminal law, or civil liberties. However, non-Charter criminal appeals were an exception to this trend—with each female appointee, male judges reportedly became only 3 percent more likely to vote conservatively (in favor of the prosecution).[46]

The law lords on the UK House of Lords also appear to be influenced by which colleagues sat on a panel with them. For example, Lord Templeman's participation in a tax-related case correlated with a 65 percent chance that the state would prevail; yet in cases decided without him, the state's success rate dropped to 11 percent.[47] Further, a particular judge's influence over the disposition of a case varies depending on the other panel members' identities. For example, in cases heard by Lord Lowry, but *not* Lords Ackner or Keith, the likelihood that the weaker party will succeed is approximately 80 percent (whereas the average success rate of weaker litigants is 43 percent). Interestingly Lord Keith did not have a significant effect on case outcomes unless he was accompanied by Lord Ackner.[48]

Similar analyses of the Supreme Court of Israel also offer some evidence that panel effects influence the justices' behavior. For instance, the voting trends of frequently occurring panels appear to vary more significantly than those of the individual judges, suggesting that certain combinations result in amplified decision-making.[49] Eisenberg, Fisher, and Rosen-Zyi also find weak support for

45. Nadia A. Jilani, Donald R. Songer & Susan W Johnson, "Gender, Consciousness Raising, and Decision Making on the Supreme Court of Canada" (2010) 94:2 *Judicature* 59 [Jilani, Songer & Johnson].

46. Jilani, Songer & Johnson, supra note 45 at 66–67, n. 88.

47. David Robertson, *Judicial Discretion in the House of Lords* (New York: Oxford University Press, 1998) at 36–37 [Robertson, *Judicial Discretion*].

48. Robertson, *Judicial Discretion, supra* note 47 at 62–68, n. 92.

49. Theodore Eisenberg, Talia Fisher & Issie Rosen-Zvi, "Does the Judge Matter? Exploiting Random Assignment on a Court of Last Resort to Assess Judge and Case Selection Effects" (2012) 9:2 *Journal of Empirical Legal Studies* 246 at 275 [Eisenberg et al., "Does the Judge Matter"].

the theory that female judges influence their colleagues' voting behavior; however, excluding a single judge from these results (Justice Naor) seems to negate the influence that gender has on final outcomes.[50]

Examining panel effects on high courts is difficult because, unlike for the US Court of Appeals, judges are not randomly assigned to panels. As we saw, some individual such as the chief justice has the power to alter the composition, meaning that we cannot tell directly if who was on the panel influenced how a judge voted, or if a judge was assigned to a panel because of how she was likely to vote. However, it is interesting to look to see if there are correlations between the characteristics of different panels of judges and outcomes.

If we look at our data for the period from 1970 to the early 2000s, there is some limited evidence that the composition of panels is related to how the panel decides. Although we could imagine that a judge would be more likely to vote in a liberal direction as the fraction of liberal appointees she is sitting with increases, such a connection is not borne out for all countries. A Supreme Court of Canada judge on a panel of all liberal appointees has a 4.5 percent higher probability of voting in a liberal direction than if the panel is composed of all conservative appointees. Similarly, for the UK House of Lords a judge on an all-liberal panel has a 7 percent higher probability of a liberal vote than if there was an all-conservative panel.[51] However, there was no effect in the United States or Australia.

What seems more important is the average lifetime liberal voting rates of the other panelists. One way to look at the effect of how liberal are the other panelists is to look at the probability of a judge voting in a liberal direction when the other panelists have the lowest average lifetime liberal voting rates as opposed to the highest rates for that country. In Canada, a judge had just over a 50 percent probability of voting in a liberal direction if she is sitting with judges with the highest average lifetime liberal voting records, as opposed to just under 40 percent when sitting with judges with the lowest average lifetime liberal voting rate. Similarly, an Australian judge's probability of voting in a liberal direction fell by nine percentage points. For the UK the difference was much more extreme. A judge whose other panelists had the lowest average lifetime liberal

50. Eisenberg et al., "Does the Judge Matter," *supra* note 49 at 280.

51. The probabilities were found using logit regressions with whether the judge voted in a liberal direction as the dependent variable and the independent variables being the fraction of judges on the panel appointed by a liberal appointer, the party of the appointer of the particular judge, the direction (liberal or conservative) of the lower court decision, and the area of law. The fraction of liberal appointees was significant at the .05 level for Canada and the UK but was insignificant for the United States and Australia. When ideology was measured using the liberal voting rate in criminal cases (and looking at non-criminal cases), the fraction of liberal appointees was insignificant for all countries.

voting rate (which was about 30 percent) had only an 11 percent probability of voting in a liberal direction whereas if she was sitting other panelists having the highest average lifetime liberal voting rate (which was about 70 percent), she had an over 90% probability of voting in a liberal direction.[52]

The composition of the panel is then related to the rate at which a judge votes in a liberal direction (again remembering that we cannot sort out causation given the data). Does it also relate to how likely a judge is to dissent? The answer seems to be yes. Figure 5-1 shows the difference in dissent rates for judges whose lifetime liberal voting rate is at the average lifetime liberal voting rate of the other panelists as compared to one whose lifetime liberal voting rate is higher or lower by 20 percent (e.g., a judge with a panel average lifetime liberal voting rate of 45 percent is compared to a judge whose lifetime liberal voting rate is either 25 percent or 65 percent). The greatest effect is for Canada and Australia. A Supreme Court of Canada judge's probability of dissenting jumps from about 5 percent if she is similar to the average of the other panelists up to a third if she has a 20 percent higher or lower liberal voting rate than the average. For Australia the increase is from about a 10 percent probability of dissenting to about a third for a similar difference of the judge from the average of the other panelists. The increase in probabilities of dissenting was less for judges on the US Supreme Court though from a higher base rate of dissenting (from about 15 percent to about 35 percent) and much less for UK lords (from about 5 percent to 9 percent). Therefore, judges whose liberal voting tendencies are further from the average of others on the panel tend to dissent at a greater rate. The greater difference in dissent rates in Canada and Australia from a similar departure from panel averages may be related to the tighter spread of liberal voting rates in those countries.

As with most of us, judges are influenced by whom they are talking to when making decisions. There seems clear evidence of this effect at the lower court level. It would be surprising if this effect did not also play a role at the high court level, particularly as the composition of panels on many high courts can vary widely. The correlation between some measures of panel diversity and

52. These probabilities were found using logit regressions with the dependent variable being whether the judge voted in a liberal direction as the dependent variable and the independent variables being the average lifetime liberal voting rates of the other judges on the panel, the party of the appointer of the particular judge, the direction (liberal or conservative) of the lower court decision, and the area of law. For Canada the probability of voting in a liberal direction fell from 50.8 percent to 38.7 percent from the highest average lifetime liberal voting rates of the other panelists (56 percent) to the lowest (34 percent). For Australia, it fell from 54.8 percent for the lowest average lifetime liberal voting rate for other justices (about 60 percent) to 45.6 percent for the lowest (about 40 percent). The average lifetime liberal voting rates of the other justices coefficient was significant at the .01 level for the UK and Australia and .05 level for Canada. For the United States, which does not sit in panels, the coefficient was significant but negative.

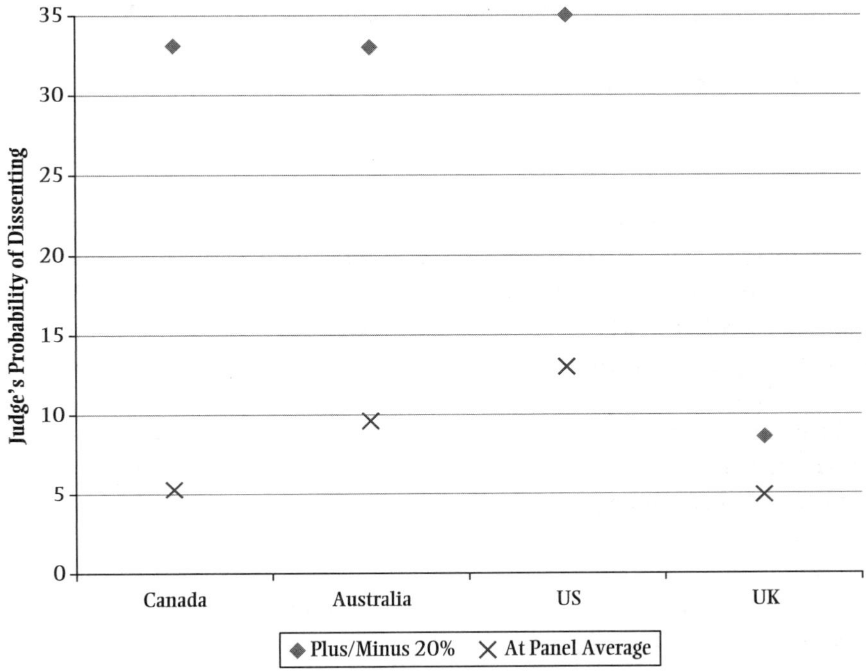


**Figure 5-1** Difference in probability of a judge dissenting if further from average lifetime liberal voting rate of other panel members. These probabilities were found by regressing whether or not a judge dissents on the difference between the judge's lifetime liberal voting rate and the average lifetime liberal voting rates of the others on the panel, the party appointing the particular judge, the direction (liberal or conservative) of the lower court decision, and the area of law. In each case the effect of the difference from the panel average is significant at least at the .01 level except the UK, which is only significant at the .1 level. The difference between the judge and the rest of the panel is related to a greater increase in the dissent rate in Canada and Australia than the United States or the UK.

either voting or dissenting points in this direction, though more work is needed on both the measures of diversity and a means for clarifying causation. What about another aspect of how judges may relate to each other—their position on the bench?

## A JUDGE'S ROLE

A judge may act differently depending on her formal or informal role on the court or on a specific panel. Take, for example, what could be seen as the two opposite ends of the spectrum—a newly appointed judge and the chief justice. Are newly appointed judges less willing to express themselves either through dissents or more extreme voting? Does a chief justice dissent less than other judges, perhaps because she seeks out consensus on the court or because she is able to stack panels in her favor? We will examine both these roles in turn.

## Freshman Judge

Consider a judge who is a "freshman"—newly appointed to the bench. Judges may go through an acclimation period while they adjust to a new set of institutional norms. During this phase, he may be more equivocal and less decisive than his more experienced colleagues, displaying less extreme preferences.[53] He may take time to become comfortable with the type of work and authority that comes with the role. He may also face internal norms of deference to more senior colleagues, as in India. How much he is influenced by this freshman effect may depend on other features of the court such as whether he was appointed by the judges on the court itself, which may at least initially make him less willing to conflict with their opinions. This analysis leads to the following hypothesis:

> *H2: Freshman judges are likely to dissent less than their more experienced colleagues and to be more ideologically moderate.*

As with most of these empirical questions, the so-called "freshman effect" has received most scholarly attention in the United States but this attention has provided only mixed evidence of such an effect. For example, a freshman judge on the US Supreme Court does not appear to be any more likely to remain unaligned with a voting coalition (either liberal or conservative or moderate) than their more experienced colleagues.[54] Further, freshman judges may be subject to greater "vote fluidity"—that is, changing views between those

53. Saul Brenner, "Another Look at Freshman Indecisiveness on the United States Supreme Court" (1983) 16:2 *Polity* 320 [Brenner, "Another Look"]; Maltzman & Wahlbeck, "Burger Court," *supra* note 13 at 589, n. 22; Dorff & Brenner, *supra* note 13 at 770, n. 22; Timothy M Hagle, "'Freshman Effects' for Supreme Court Justices" (1993) 37:4 *American Journal of Political Science* 1142 at 1145 [Hagle, "Freshmen"].

54. Snyder's 1958 investigation of the US Supreme Court constitutional cases found that freshman justices were more likely to align with a moderate voting bloc than more senior justices. Eloise C. Snyder, "The Supreme Court as a Small Group" (1958) 36 *Social Forces* 232 at 237–238. However, more recent studies have identified weaknesses with this study, and Heck and Hall found no evidence of such an effect on the Warren Court and the Burger Court. Terry Bowen & John M. Scheb, "Reassessing the 'Freshman Effect': The Voting Bloc Alignment of New Justices on the United States Supreme Court, 1921–90" (1993) 15:1 *Political Behaviour* 1; Robert L. Dudley, "The Freshman Effect and Voting Alignments: A Reexamination of Judicial Folklore" (1993) 21:3 *American Politics Quarterly* 360. See e.g. Edward V. Heck & Melinda Gann Hall, "Bloc Voting and the Freshman Justice Revisited" (1981) 43:3 *Journal of Politics* 852.

initially expressed in the judges' conference and their final vote—than more senior judges, but the evidence is mixed. [55]

However, a different effect of longer time on the high court has received greater support.[56] Many judges change their ideological positions or vote differently after their first two terms. Freshman judges may be more moderate than judges who are more senior.[57] Further, Hagle found that a substantial number of judges appointed to the US Supreme Court between 1953 and 1989 showed initial signs of voting instability—that is, their ideological positions on a number of issue areas changed significantly after their first two terms.[58] More recently, Epstein et al. found that the vast majority of US Supreme Court justices exhibit "ideological drift"—a significant change between their first term voting preferences and the ideological positions they adopt later in their careers.[59] They claim that their results provide "strong corroborating evidence" for Hagle's research

55. Maltzman & Wahlbeck, "Burger Court," *supra* note 13 at 589 (finding freshman had higher rates of voting fluidity on the Burger Court); Dorff & Brenner, *supra* note 13, n. 22. See also Brenner, "Another Look," *supra* note 53 at 324, n. 35 (finding weak evidence that freshman judges were more likely to change their views between the conference and the final votes than judges who had been on the bench for more than three years). But see Timothy M. Hagle & Harold J. Spaeth, "Voting Fluidity and the Attitudinal Model of Supreme Court Decision Making" (1991) 44:1 *Political Research Quarterly* 119 (finding that freshman had higher rates of voting fluidity than their colleagues on the Burger Court).

56. Freshman justices on the US Supreme Court may also write fewer opinions and rely more heavily on precedents. On opinion writing see Saul Brenner & Timothy M. Hagle, "Opinion Writing and Acclimation Effect" (1996) 18:3 *Political Behaviour* 235 at 254, n 104 [Brenner & Hagle, "Opinion Writing"]; Terry Bowen, "Consensual Norms and the Freshman Effect on the United States Supreme Court" (1995) 76:1 *Social Science Quarterly* 222; but see Forrest Maltzman, James F. Spriggs II & Paul J. Wahlbeck, "The Politics of Dissent and Concurrences on the US Supreme Court" (1999) 27:4 *American Politics Research* 488 at 503–504, n. 103 [Maltzman et al., "Politics of Dissent"] (finding freshman judges are no less likely to join or author a concurring or dissenting opinion). For precedents, see Mark S. Hurwitz & Joseph V. Stefko, "Acclimation and Attitudes: 'Newcomer' Justices and Precedent Conformance on the Supreme Court" (2004) 57:1 *Political Research Quarterly* 121.

57. Brenner, "Another Look," *supra* note 53 at 324, n. 35.

58. Hagle, "Freshmen," *supra* note 53 at 1147, n. 114 for Supreme Court justices. Wood et al. and Shippen found freshman do appear to undergo voting instability, though conclude that the behavior is not widespread enough to confirm Hagle's hypothesis. Sandra L. Wood et al., "'Acclimation Effects' for Supreme Court Justices: A Cross-Validation, 1888–1940" (1998) 42:2 *American Journal of Political Science* 690; Charles R. Shipan, "Acclimation Effects Revisited" (2000) 40:2 *Jurimetrics* 243 at 255 ("[t]he results indicate that some new Justices exhibit acclimation effects, but most do not . . . . Thus, this study demonstrates that no general effect exists for newcomers to the Court").

59. Lee Epstein et al., "On the Perils of Drawing Inferences about Supreme Court Justices from Their First Few Years of Service" (2008) 91:4 *Judicature* 168 [Epstein et al., "Perils"].

on voting instability;[60] however, they also note that some justices continue to change their preferences after this initial acclimation period, and that neither the direction nor significance of these changes is predictable.

When we look at our data for high courts in the period 1970 through the 2000s, there is little evidence of a freshman effect in the other countries we are studying. Take, for example, the claim that freshman judges may be more moderate than senior colleagues.[61] In Canada, judges who were on the Court for less than three years did not vote differently overall than more senior judges—judges who were seen as "liberal" were not more likely to vote in a liberal direction than their more senior liberal colleagues, nor were "conservative" freshman more likely to vote in a conservative direction than senior conservatives.[62] The same was true for the Australian High Court in this period as well as the Indian Supreme Court.[63]

The lack of a voting difference for freshman on the Supreme Court of Canada is consistent with the limited study by other researchers of this issue. For example, although there is a positive correlation between a judge's ideology scores based on newspaper articles and how he voted in criminal cases in his first year on the bench, there is no significant overall correlation between how a first year judge votes and these scores.[64] Further, as in the United States, many Supreme

60. Epstein et al., "Perils," *supra* note 59 at 179, n. 126.

61. To study whether freshman judges are more moderate, we ran logit regressions with the dependent variable being whether the judge voted in a liberal direction and the independent variables being whether the judge was a "freshman" (had been on the court for less than three years) along with the party of the appointer, the direction (liberal or conservative) of the lower court decision, the area of law, a time trend, and both with and without an interaction term between the party of the appointer and whether the judge was a freshman.

62. Both the freshman coefficient and the interaction term were insignificant at the .05 level. For the United States, when the regression included whether the judge had been on the Court for less than three years but not the interaction term, the coefficient on the freshman variable was significant at the .05 level and negative (-0.095), but when the interaction term was included in the regression neither the freshman nor the interaction term was significant.

63. For Australia, the freshman coefficient and the interaction term were insignificant at the .05 level. For India, as there is no "party" of the appointer, we used the lifetime liberal voting rate in criminal cases and the freshman variable as independent variables along with all the other control variables except the interaction term and ran the regression on non-criminal cases. The coefficient on the freshman variable was not significant at the .05 level.

64. Benjamin Alarie & Andrew Green, "Policy Preference Change and Appointments to the Supreme Court of Canada" (2009) 47 *Osgoode Hall LJ* 47 1 at 7–8. See also C.L. Ostberg, Matthew E. Wetstein & Craig R. Ducat, "Acclimation Effects on the Supreme Court of Canada: A Cross-Cultural Examination of Judicial Folklore" (2003) 84:3 *Social Science Quarterly* 704 at 714 [Ostberg et al., "Acclimation Effects"] (finding that freshman judges did not dramatically change their ideological position).

Court of Canada judges change how they vote over time; there is no predictable pattern as to whether a judge will become more conservative, more liberal, or stay the same.[65] Ostberg, Wetstein, and Ducat did find one significant difference between freshmen and non-freshmen—freshmen judges participated in fewer panels. They argue that "modern Chief Justices of the Canadian Court have utilized a powerful acclimation tool to help ease the transition for justices in the initial stages of their tenures. This is an important finding because it suggests that an institutional feature such as panel assignment can have a profound effect on a justice's acclimation to a Court."[66]

Although there was no evidence of freshman voting differently on an ideological basis than senior colleagues for Canada, Australia, and India, the UK House of Lords was different. Freshman at the House of Lords actually appear to vote more "extremely" than those who have been on the Court longer. Freshman judges appointed under a more conservative government were about 3 percent less likely to vote in a liberal direction than more senior conservative appointees. Similarly, freshman liberal appointees were about 2 percent more likely to vote in a liberal direction than more senior liberal appointees.[67] As we discuss in Chapter 8, the UK House of Lords may have had a fairly strong norm of consensus, which could dampen the tendency to vote in particular directions over time.

The story is the same if we look not at how extreme judges are but at whether freshman judges are less willing to dissent than their more senior colleagues because, for example, they need time to become accustomed to the bench. When we look at our data for the 1970s through the 2000s, there is no evidence of freshman (again defined as being on the bench for less than three years) being less likely to dissent than their senior colleagues except new justices on the US Supreme Court who were slightly less willing to dissent (by about 5 percent) than more senior judges.[68] Similarly, Ostberg, Wetstein, and Ducat found newly appointed justices on the Supreme Court of Canada were no more likely

65. Alarie & Green "Policy Preference," *supra* note 64.

66. Ostberg et al., "Acclimation Effects," *supra* note 64.

67. The coefficients on the freshman and the interaction terms were significant at the .05 level.

68. We ran logit regressions with the dependent variable being whether the judge dissented and the independent variables being whether the judge was a freshman (less than three years on the court), the ideology of the judge (either the party of the appointer or the lifetime liberal voting record in criminal cases), the direction (liberal or conservative) of the lower court decision, the area of the law, and a time trend variable. The freshmen coefficients were not significant at the .05 level for the UK, India, or Australia. The freshman coefficient was significant at the .1 level in Canada and was negative as predicted but small (-1.85%). For the United States, the freshman coefficient was significant at the 0.05 level and showed about a 5.5 percent lower probability of dissenting for freshman. We also ran these regressions using liberal voting rates in criminal

to join or write the majority opinion.[69] Further, for India, a strong norm of seniority may similarly reduce the applicability of the freshman theory. In his analysis of the Supreme Court of India, Robinson notes that split decisions are rare, despite the frequent use of two-judge panels, because "tradition dictates that the junior judge generally defer to the opinion of the senior."[70]

There is therefore limited evidence of a freshman effect outside the United States. Recall, of course, that the assignment of judges to panels outside the United States is not necessarily random, which makes it difficult to interpret the results. The freshman judges may be appointed to different types of cases than more senior judges (such as being less likely to be placed on contentious cases than their more senior colleagues). However, it is interesting that freshman judges do not appear to vote differently or dissent less frequently than their more senior colleagues except potentially in the UK.

## The Chief Justice

The chief justice may be more likely to be part of the majority in a given decision. Like other high court judges, chief justices may aim to produce particular outcomes that align with their preferences. She may be better able to persuade others to agree with her preferred outcome due to the informal influence of her position (such as her ability in some cases to decide who hears interesting cases or writes particular opinions). As we saw in the last chapter, she may also select panels to ensure she sits with a winning coalition of like-minded judges. Alternatively, a chief justice may be more inclined to compromise her own position to promote consensus because she places a higher value on collegial norms than other judges, believing that dissenting will undermine her leadership or the court's institutional legitimacy.[71] These differing goals lead to the following hypotheses:

> *H2: The Chief Justice is more likely to write or join majority opinions than other judges.*

cases as the measure of ideology (and ran the regressions on non-criminal cases) and the freshman coefficient was negative and significant at the .05 level but smaller (about 2 percent).

69. Ostberg et al., "Acclimation Effects," *supra* note 64 at 714.

70. Nick Robinson, "Structure Matters: The Impact of Court Structure on the Indian and U.S. Supreme Courts" (2013) 61:1 *American Journal of Comparative Law* 173 at 186.

71. Pamela C. Corley et al., "Extreme Dissensus: Explaining Plurality Decisions on the United States Supreme Court" (2010) 31:2 *Justice Systems Journal* 180 at 186–187 [Corley et al., "Extreme Dissensus"]; Maltzman & Wahlbeck, "Burger Court," *supra* note 13 at 589.

We found no evidence of the chief justices dissenting at a greater rate in most of the countries studied in our data over the period 1970 to the early 2000s—that is, whether or not the judge voting was the chief justice did not impact the probability that the judge would dissent.[72] The only exception was the United States where there was some limited evidence that chief justices had dissented at a lower rate than other justices.[73] However, more detailed studies have found that chief justices act differently from other judges. For example, Wetstein and Ostberg examined the behavior of the three most recent chief justices of the Supreme Court of Canada, and found that their opinion writing and voting strategies changed significantly after assuming leadership of the court.[74] Both Dickson and Lamer wrote a significantly higher percentage of majority opinions after becoming chief justice, although McLachlin did not.[75] Wetstein and Ostberg claim that increased authorship of majority opinions is an indicator of "task leadership," or influence over the court's output. Conversely, McLachlin reduced her dissent activity to a much greater extent than either of her predecessors. Moreover, her dissent authorship rate dropped from 9.9 percent to approximately 2.8 percent.[76] They argue that McLachlin is a "social leader," whose primary goal is to increase collegiality and consensus on the court.[77]

72. We ran logit regressions for each country with the dependent variable being whether the judge dissented and the independent variables being whether the judge was the chief justice, the ideology of the judge (either the party of the appointer or the lifetime liberal voting rate in criminal cases), the direction (liberal or conservative) of the lower court decisions, the area of law, and a time trend. None of the chief justice coefficients were statistically significant for Canada, Australia, or the UK.

73. The only significant coefficient was on the chief justice variable in the United States when we used party of the appointing president for the judges' ideology. The effect was significant at the .05 level and, as predicted, negative (–5.7%). However, the coefficient was not statistically significant when we used lifetime liberal voting records in criminal cases as a proxy for ideology.

74. Matthew Wetstein & C.L. Ostberg, "Strategic Leadership and Political Change on the Canadian Supreme Court: Analyzing the Transition to Chief Justice" (2005) 38:3 *Canadian Journal of Political Science* 38 653 [Wetstein & Ostberg, "Strategic Leadership"]).

75. Wetstein & Ostberg, "Strategic Leadership," *supra* note 74 at 664–665, n. 97.

76. Wetstein & Ostberg, "Strategic Leadership", *supra* note 74 at 671, n. 3.

77. Wetstein & Ostberg, "Strategic Leadership", *supra* note 74, n. 97 (applying models of judicial leadership from David J. Danelski, "The Influence of the Chief Justice in the Decisional Process of the Supreme Court" in Sheldon Goldman & Austin Sarat, eds, *American Court Systems: Readings in Judicial Process and Behavior* (San Francisco: W.H. Freeman, 1978) 506.

Chief justices of the US Supreme Court also have different writing and dissenting patterns than other justices.[78] Chief justices are more likely to write majority opinions than other judges, particularly in important cases.[79] Moreover, chief justices were less likely to dissent than other justices. For example, Chief Justice Burger's dissent rate between 1969 and 1985 was 9.5 percent, while the other justices dissented 15.4 percent of the time. Although the judges were similarly willing to write or join a "regular concurrence" that agreed with the majority's disposition and reasons, Burger was significantly less likely to write a "special concurrence" that criticized the majority reasoning.[80] If we look at the Vinson, Warren, Burger, and Rehnquist courts, chief justices authored a similar number of majority opinions per term as associate justices, yet wrote fewer opinions overall. Associate justices wrote approximately 2.4 times more concurrences and 2.5 times more dissents than the chief justices during this period, with 23 percent being dissents for chief justices and 37 percent for associate justices.[81] Of course, some of this effect may be due to how the chief justice chooses to assign opinion writing.[82]

The chief justice of the Indian Supreme Court also appears more likely to be part of the majority coalition. For example, on the Supreme Court between 1950 and 1967, Subba Rao was the most frequent dissenter prior to his appointment as chief justice, joining the minority in 48 of the 702 hearings he participated in and writing a total of 42 solo dissents.[83] After assuming leadership of the court, Subba

78. Recall that the practice of assigning opinions varies across countries. In the United States, the justices vote in the conference following the hearing and then the practice is that the most senior justice in the majority (or the chief justice if that person is in the majority) assigns the opinion writing, including possibly to him- or herself. In Canada, the chief justice assigns the opinion writing, although the practice is collegial, as it was at the House of Lords. In India, the most senior judge on the panel decides who writes the opinion.

79. Saul Brenner & Eric S. Heberlig, "'In My Opinion . . .': Justices' Opinion Writing in the U.S. Supreme Court, 1946–1997" (2002) 83:3 *Social Science Quarterly* 762 at 769–770; Elliot E. Slotnick, "The Chief Justices and Self-Assignment of Majority Opinions: A Research Note" (1979) 31:2 *Political Research Quarterly* 219 at 220.

80. Maltzman et al., "Politics of Dissent", *supra* note 56 at 503, 506.

81. Brenner & Hagle, "Opinion Writing," *supra* note 56. A similar study by Corley et al. on the US Supreme Court between 1953 and 2006 found that the chief justice was, on average, twice as likely to join a plurality opinion and significantly less likely to write or join a special concurrence: Corley et al., "Extreme Dissensus," *supra* note 71 at 188, 391–407, n. 34; see also Melinda Gann Hall & Paul Brace, "Order in the Courts: A Neo-institutional Approach to Judicial Consensus" (1989) 42 *Western Political Quarterly* 391 at 403 (reports a 22 percent higher dissent rate on courts that randomly assign opinions than those where the chief justice assigns the opinion).

82. Corley et al., "Extreme Dissensus," *supra* note 71 at 195, n. 34.

83. George H. Gadbois, Jr., "Indian Judicial Behaviour" (1970) 5:3 *Economic and Political Weekly* 149 at 151–153 [Gadbois, "Indian Judicial Behaviour"].

Rao participated in another 77 reported decisions and was in the majority every time.[84] Between 1950 and 1959, chief justices dissented at a rate far lower than the Court's average, with the five chief justices in office during this period only dissenting in 8 percent of the non-unanimous decisions in which they participated while 26 percent of the votes in non-unanimous cases were dissents.[85] Although the dissent rate more recently is extremely low, one place to look for differences in dissents is constitutional cases, which may be heard in larger panels. In these cases, the chief justices dissented in only 0.8 percent of cases, compared to a dissent rate overall in these cases of 5.2 percent.[86] However, more recently, chief justices have begun to dissent at a similar rate to other Supreme Court judges: whereas the chief justice was 27 times less likely to dissent during the 1960s, he was only four times less likely to dissent during the 2000s.[87]

Similarly, Hanretty's analysis of the UK Supreme Court found that agreement between pairs of judges was more likely when one member of the dyad was president or deputy president of the Court.[88] He notes that this trend may suggest either that leaders of the court are more likely to agree with their colleagues, or that they are better at persuading others to support their own opinions. A similar analysis by Arvind and Stirton suggests that senior law lords were most willing to adopt a wide range of acceptable outcomes in order to promote group consensus.[89]

Chief justices may then be less willing to dissent than other judges on the court. They may be able to use their influence to encourage other judges to join them, or may be less willing to foster dissension on the court, which may reduce its legitimacy. However, as with the other issues in this chapter, causation is difficult to tease out. At least outside the United States, the chief justice may be in the majority not because of how she votes but because she establishes which judges hear particular cases.

84. Gadbois, "Indian Judicial Behaviour," *supra* note 83 at 166.

85. George H. Gadbois, "Selection, Background Characteristics, and Voting Behaviour of Indian Supreme Court Judges, 1950–1969" in Glendon Schubert & David J. Danelski, eds, *Comparative Judicial Behaviour: Cross-Cultural Studies of Decision-Making in the East and West* (New York: Oxford University Press, 1969) at 240–241.

86. Nick Robinson et al., "Interpreting the Constitution: Supreme Court Constitution Benches since Independence" (2011) 41 *Economic & Political Weekly* 27 at 31 [Robinson, "Interpreting the Constitution"].

87. Robinson, "Interpreting the Constitution," *supra* note 86 at 31.

88. Chris Hanretty, "Lumpers and Splitters on the United Kingdom Supreme Court" (2013) American Political Science Association 2013 Annual Meeting Paper, 4 [Hanretty, "Lumpers and Splitters"] at 15, 19.

89. Arvind & Stirton, *supra* note 17 at 41, n. 17.

## OTHER BRANCHES OF GOVERNMENT

In addition to his relationship with the other judges on the bench, a high court judge may be influenced by his particular institutional context—in particular by the relationship of the court and the legislature.[90] A high court judge may decide based on different considerations than the rest of the judiciary. Unlike most lower court judges, a high court judge will not typically consider the possibility of career advancement, or the risks of being removed from office or having her rulings reversed.[91] Instead, the factor external to the court that may primarily constrain her may be the risk of political backlash by other branches of government, which can take a variety of forms.

The legislature may retaliate against the judiciary by enacting new laws or rules that respond to or reverse prior decisions. In Canada, for example, the judiciary has the power to review the constitutionality of primary and delegated legislation; however, section 33 of the *Canadian Charter of Rights and Freedoms* allows the federal and provincial legislatures to declare that a statute shall operate notwithstanding a violation of the fundamental freedoms, legal rights, or equality rights. In the United States, the formal separation-of-powers doctrine prevents other branches of government from directly interfering with the judiciary. However, Congress can enact new legislation or constitutional amendments that effectively nullify the Supreme Court's interpretation of a provision. Congress can potentially even suspend or withdraw the Court's jurisdiction to review particular statutes or decisions.[92] A judge may be partly motivated by a desire to avoid such action by legislatures.[93]

90. Epstein & Jacobi, *supra* note 1.

91. Posner, *How Judges Think, supra* note 8.

92. US Const. art. III (provides that the Supreme Court's appellate jurisdiction is granted "with such Exceptions, and under such Regulations as the Congress shall make" at § 2, cl 2). In *Ex parte McCardle*, 74 U.S. 506 (1869), the US Supreme Court affirmed that Congress had the authority to suspend its statutory jurisdiction to review the denial of habeas corpus petitions.

93. Other countries lack similar constitutional guarantees of judicial review. The UK, for example, lacks a written constitution as the basis for judicial review. The court's role has been expanded by the *Human Rights Act 1998*, which allows the court to issue a declaration that an Act of Parliament is incompatible with the European Convention on Human Rights. However, declarations of invalidity do not invalidate the Act, nor are they binding to the parties in the proceedings that give rise to them. *Human Rights Act 1998*, (UK), c 42, s 4(6) [*Human Rights Act*]. They have not been used frequently; more often a court will merely interpret a statute in such a way that it is compatible. Paterson, *supra* note 6 at 282; *Human Rights Act, supra* note 499, s. 3 (1).

A legislature or the executive may also retaliate against an unpopular decision by high courts in other ways, such as imposing indirect burdens through budget constraints or altering the appointments process. A famous American example is the "switch in time that saved nine": in order to prevent the Supreme Court from striking down his New Deal legislation, President Roosevelt threatened that he would enlarge the bench and appoint new justices with more favorable inclinations. To avoid that, Justice Owen Roberts changed his position and voted to uphold the legislation.[94] The retaliation may be more personal. For example, in New Zealand, where many justices are knighted but not all, the conferral of knighthoods is a potential way for the government to reward or sanction justices if it wishes.[95]

If judges are partly motivated by a desire to influence public policy, they will have clear incentives to avoid reversal or backlash, and may attempt to make decisions that reflect the policy agendas of the political parties currently in power. It may be that "given the institutional constraints imposed upon the Court, the Justices cannot effectuate their own policy and institutional goals without taking account of the goals and likely actions of the members of the other branches."[96] However, although this approach seems rational, it is not clearly the case. Richard Posner, for example, argues that it is unrealistic to claim that judges strategically base their statutory interpretations on such specific extralegal factors.[97] Supreme Court justices may not be constrained by other political actors, either because these institutions are likely to share the same policy goals,[98] or due to the institutional safeguards that insulate the

94. Chris Hanretty, "The Appointment of Judges by Ministers: Political Preferment in England, 1880–2005" (2012) American Political Science Association 2012 Annual Meeting Paper 1 at 7–11.

95. In the 1930s Depression, the attorney-general asked superior court judges to refund a portion of their salary and, after they refused, none of them received a knighthood including the senior judge. Philip A. Joseph, "Appointment, Discipline and Removal of Judges in New Zealand" in H.P. Lee, ed, *Judiciaries in Comparative Perspective* (New York: Cambridge University Press, 2011) at 93.

96. McNollgast, "The Political Economy of Law: Decision-Making by Judicial, Legislative, Executive and Administrative Agencies" in A. Mitchell Polinsky & Stephen Shavel, eds, *Law And Economics Handbook* (North Holland, 2007), n. 2; Epstein et al., "National Policymaker," *supra* note 5 at 585 (finding the US Supreme Court interprets statutes differently based on the likelihood that a particular decision will be effectively reversed via new legislation, which varies depending on factors such as the ideological distance between the Supreme Court and Congress and between the Supreme Court and the president, or whether the political party that enacted the statute is currently in power).

97. Posner, *How Judges Think*, *supra* note 8 at 29–30; William N. Eskridge Jr., "Overriding Supreme Court Statutory Interpretation Decisions" (1991) 101:2 *Yale LJ* 331 [Eskridge].

98. Robert A. Dahl, "Decision-Making in a Democracy: The Supreme Court as a National Policy-maker (2001) 50:2 *Emory Law Journal* 563.

court from external interference and allow justices to advance their sincere preferences.[99]

This tendency to be concerned about how other institutions will react may depend on a range of factors beyond just the party in power.[100] High courts may be more willing to intervene in the decision-making of other governmental branches in countries that have recently introduced a new constitutional framework. For example, the policy-making roles of the South African Constitutional Court, and Indian and Israeli Supreme Courts have been linked to their relatively recent establishment.[101] As their institutional roles have not been formally delimited to the same extent as high courts in other nations, these courts may be less constrained by other branches of government, and able to play a more active role in shaping their emergent political systems. Relatedly, internal governmental tensions may provide an opportunity for high courts to advance specific policy goals while bolstering their own legitimacy. Several authors suggest that the Supreme Courts of India and Israel became particularly influential by establishing an active role during periods of political instability.[102] Further, during periods of political tension such as a national security crisis, judges may alter their behavior and become more or less willing to intervene against government decisions.[103]

99. See e.g. Jeffrey A Segal, "Separation-of-Powers Games in the Positive Theory of Congress and Courts" (1997) 91:1 *American Political Science Review* 28.

100. Further, this theory assumes that decisions supported by large majorities are more likely to be perceived as legitimate by other governmental actors and members of the public. Therefore, judges that would otherwise concur or dissent may be more likely to join the majority during especially important or salient cases that are likely to be subject to increased institutional backlash. Rohde, "Policy Goals," *supra* note 9 at 215. We will discuss this issue further in Chapter 8.

101. Theunis Roux, "Legitimating Transformation: Political Resource Allocation in the South African Constitutional Court" (2003) 10:4 *Democratization* 92; Eli M. Salzberger, "Judicial Appointments and Promotions in Israel: Constitution, Law, and Politics" in Kate Malleson & Peter H. Russell, eds, *Appointing Judges in an Age of Judicial Power: Critical Perspectives from around the World* (Toronto: University of Toronto Press, 2006) 241 at 241; Venkat Iyer, "The Supreme Court of India" in Brice Dickson, ed, *Judicial Activism in Common Law Supreme Courts* (New York: Oxford University Press, 2007) 121 [Iyer].

102. Iyer, *supra* note 101, n. 41; Yoav Dotan, "Judicial Accountability in Israel: The High Court of Justice and the Phenomenon of Judicial Hyperactivism" in Moshe Maor, ed, *Developments in Israeli Public Administration* (London: Routledge, 2002) 87 at 88–89.

103. See e.g. John Dugard, "The Judiciary in a State of National Crisis: With Special Reference to the South African Experience" (1987) 44:2 *Washington and Lee Law Review* 477; Lee Epstein et al., "The Supreme Court during Crisis: How War Affects Only Non-war Cases" (2005) 80:1 *New York University Law Review* 1 [Epstein et al., "Crisis"]. See also Menachem Hofnung & Keren Weinshall-Margel, "Judicial Setbacks, Material Gains: Terror Litigation at the Israeli High Court of Justice" (2010) 7 *Journal of Empirical Legal Studies* 664 [Hofnung &

As a general matter, we will start with the most basic hypothesis relating to the risk of retaliation or override by the government of the day:

*H4: Judges will alter their votes depending on the political leanings of the government in power at the time of the court decision.*

Justices on the US Supreme Court appear at least at times to take into account the preferences of other branches of government. For example, the Court was more likely to adjust its policy goals to reflect the preferences of the current Congress and president than it was to accommodate the enacting Congress in the period 1967 to 1990, which may be due to a desire to avoid legislative override.[104] A similar constraint or influence occurred with respect to the Court's interpretation of the National Labor Relations Act between 1949 and 1988, affecting the likelihood of a pro-union decision.[105] Although judges with strong ideological positions tend to vote in line with their personal goals, congressional preferences appear to at least influence the behavior of moderate justices.[106]

The judges may be more closely attuned to the preferences of other governmental actors in particular cases. For example, judges may be sensitive to both

Weinshall-Margel, "Judicial Setbacks"]; Yoav Dotan, "Judicial Rhetoric, Government Lawyers, and Human Rights: The Case of the Israeli High Court of Justice during the Intifada" (1999) 33:2 *Law and Society Review* 319 [Dotan, "Judicial Rhetoric"]; Epstein et al., "Crisis", *supra* note 103, n. 42 (finding the US Supreme Court was significantly more likely to curtail individual liberties during periods of war or other security crises in the period 1941–2001).

104. Eskridge, *supra* note 97 at 390 (also finding that the Court's interpretations of federal statutes were more likely to be reversed by Congress when they revealed an ideologically divided Court, relied on the statute's plain meaning, and ignored legislative signals, or ruled against federal or state governments (at 334)).

105. Pablo Spiller & Rafael Gely, "Congressional Control or Judicial Independence" (1992) 4:3 *Rand Journal of Economics* 463, n. 137. Another early study by Rohde supports the idea that split decisions may be subject to further scrutiny, and suggests that the justices may strategically respond by forming larger majority coalitions when they perceive a threat to the judiciary. Studying civil liberties decisions during the Warren era, he found that 40 percent of the majority coalitions were minimum-winning (*i.e.*, composed of five judges) and only 8 percent were unanimous. However, when a threat was perceived, the unanimity rate rose to 26 percent and minimum-winning coalitions only occurred 23 percent of the time. Rohde, "Policy Goals," *supra* note 9 at 212, 218, n. 20.

106. Epstein et al., "National Policymaker," *supra* note 5 at 610. See also Mario Bergara, Barak Richman & Pablo T. Spiller, "Modeling Supreme Court Strategic Decision Making: The Congressional Constraint" (2003) 28:2 Legislative Studies Quarterly 247 (also finding that both judicial ideology and political constraints influence the Supreme Court's decision-making, and that the Court's decisions reflect strategic responses to the preferences of both Congress and the president).

the risks and implications of non-compliance or backlash. Justices on the US Supreme between 1951 and 2007 appeared to be more likely to take into account the preferences of Congress, the president, and the general public in cases that require compliance by the other branches of government.[107] US Supreme Court justices were more likely to vote ideologically during constitutional challenges to legislation (as opposed to mere statutory interpretation) in the civil rights and liberties cases decided from 1953 to 2004, particularly when a state enacted the impugned statute rather than the federal government.[108] Judges may have been more willing to advance their preferences when there was greater authority for the Court's decision, whereas deference to the federal government and the risk of legislative override or non-compliance prompted more moderate results.

Conversely, however, exercising the Court's constitutional authority to strike down a federal statute is likely to create hostility between Congress and the Court (although possibly less so where a different party controlled Congress at the time of enactment and the time of the Court's decision). Although it will be more difficult for Congress to overrule the decision, any attempts to do so may seriously damage the Court's perceived legitimacy, making the Court more sensitive to the general preferences of the sitting Congress and the president in constitutional cases.[109] Further, the constitutional provisions themselves in some cases may constrain such ideological voting, such as where conservative judges on the Supreme Court of Canada were less likely to vote attitudinally in the immediate aftermath of the passage of the Canadian Charter of Rights and Freedoms.[110] Moreover, although the Canadian Charter has a section

107. Matthew E.K. Hall, "The Semiconstrained Court: Public Opinion, the Separation of Powers, and the U.S Supreme Court's Fear of Nonimplementation" (2014) 58:2 *American Journal of Political Science* 352. See also Anna Harvey & Barry Friedman, "Pulling Punches: Congressional Constraints on the Supreme Court's Constitutional Rulings, 1987–2000" (2006) 31:4 *Legislative Studies Quarterly* 533 (finding the likelihood of the Rehnquist Court striking a statute enacted by a liberal Congress increased dramatically (between 47 percent and 288 percent, depending on the legislative model used) following the 1994 congressional election, when conservatives took control of both the House and Senate).

108. Brandon L. Bartels, "Choices in Context: How Case-Level Factors Influence the Magnitude of Ideological Voting on the U.S Supreme Court" (2011) 39:1 *American Politics Research* 142, n. 143.

109. See also Jeffrey A. Segal, Chad Westerland & Stefanie A. Lindquist, "Congress, the Supreme Court, and Judicial Review: Testing a Constitutional Separation of Powers Model" (2011) 55:1 *American Journal of Political Science* 89 at 101. See also Bryan W. Marshall, Brett W. Curry & Richard L. Pacelle, Jr., "Preserving Institutional Power: The Supreme Court and Strategic Decision Making in the Separation of Powers" (2014) 42:1 *Politics and Policy* 37 at 40–41; Keith E. Whittington & Tom S. Clark, "Ideology, Partisanship, and Judicial Review of Acts of Congress, 1789–2006" (2009), online: http://ssrn.com/abstract=1475660 at 12.

110. Susan W. Johnson, "The Supreme Court of Canada and Strategic Decision Making: Examining Justices' Voting Patterns during Periods of Institutional Change" (2012)

(section 33) permitting the legislature to override court decisions under the Charter,[111] the Court may have been felt less constrained in imposing its policy agenda at times when there was lower support for legislative use of the override.[112]

In examining our data for 1970 through the early 2000s, we found little evidence of a connection between how judges on high courts vote and a simple measure of the politics of the government in power at the time of the decision. One possibility is that judges, either liberal or conservative, would be more likely to vote in a liberal direction if the government of the day is liberal. However, we did not find any such effect except in the UK.[113] In the UK, a judge was more likely to vote in a liberal direction if a liberal government was in power, though the effect was small (about 3.5 percent).[114] The results remained the same even if we

42:2 *American Review of Canadian Studies* 236 (also examining the impact of the elimination of appeals from the Supreme Court of Canada to the Privy Council in 1949).

111. Peter W. Hogg & Allison A. Bushell, "The *Charter* Dialogue between Courts and Legislatures (Or Perhaps the *Charter of Rights* Isn't Such a Bad Thing after All)" (1997) 35:1 *Osgoode Hall Law Journal* 75; Peter W. Hogg, Allison A. Bushell Thornton & Wade K. Wright, "*Charter* Dialogue Revisited: Or 'Much Ado about Metaphors'" (2007) 45:1 *Osgoode Hall Law Journal* 1; Kent Roach, "Dialogic Judicial Review and Its Critics" (2004) 24 *Supreme Court Law Review* 49.

112. Christopher P. Manfredi, "Strategic Behaviour and the Canadian Charter of Rights and Freedoms" in Donald E Abelson, Patrick James & Michael Lusztig, eds, *The Myth of the Sacred: The Charter, the Courts, and the Politics of the Constitution in Canada* (Montreal: McGill-Queen's University Press, 2002) 147 (using a strategic model to explain the Supreme Court of Canada's decisions in two politically contentious cases decided a decade apart (*R v Morgentaler,* [1988] 1 SCR 30, 44 DLR (4th) 385 and *Vriend v Alberta,* [1998] 1 SCR 493, 156 DLR (4th) 385) and finding the Court was more willing to impose its policy agenda on legislative actors in the latter case, with the most influential factor appearing to have been the declining popularity of section 33 of the Charter). Similarly, Supreme Court of Canada justices invalidated legislative or regulatory acts in about a third of constitutional rights cases between 1982 and 2008 but the Court was significantly more likely to uphold the statute when intervening government actors or organized interest groups opposed invalidation. Nedeljko Radmilovic, "Between Activism and Restraint" in Donald E Abelson, Patrick James & Michael Lusztig, eds, *The Myth of the Sacred: The Charter, the Courts, and the Politics of the Constitution in Canada* (Montreal: McGill-Queen's University Press, 2002), at 75, n 49 [Radmilovic].

113. We ran logistic regressions with the dependent variable being whether the judge voted in a liberal direction, and the independent variables being whether the government was liberal (see Appendix A for a description of our coding of governments), the ideology of the judge (using either the party of the appointer or the judge's lifetime liberal voting rates in criminal cases), the direction (liberal or conservative) of the lower court decision, the area of law, and a time trend. The government variable was not statistically significant at the .05 level in the regressions for Canada, the United States, Australia, or India.

114. This result was significant at the .01 level using either the party of the appointer or the lifetime liberal voting rate as a measure of the judge's ideology (and the effect being slightly larger when using lifetime liberal voting rate (almost 5 percent).

looked for whether liberal or conservative judges reacted differently to different orientations of the government—that is, did liberal judges react differently to a conservative government than a conservative judge did to a liberal government.[115]

Another possible effect of a judge considering the preferences of the government in power would be that she would be more likely to vote in favor of a government whose preferences are not aligned with her own, controlling for the underlying nature (liberal or conservative) of the lower court decision being appealed. In our data, we found that judges' votes in favor were not affected by the nature of the government in power, except in Canada.[116] However, in Canada, the judges were influenced in a direction consistent with the proxy for their ideology. Conservative judges were about 4 percent less likely to find in favor of the government if a liberal government was in power as opposed to a conservative government; a liberal judge was about 1 percent more likely to find in favor of a liberal government than a conservative government.[117]

The data we have for these high courts between 1970 and the early 2000s, then, do not provide strong evidence of judges being influenced by the preferences of the government in power at the time of the decision. Part of the reason for the lack of a correlation between voting and the political leanings of the government of the day may of course be due to the crude measure of politics used. However, it may also stem from other mechanisms the court may use to avoid backlash and yet still allow voting that does not accord with the preferences of the current government. For example, the court may tend to shift toward viewing the question as constitutional if the judges are worried about the legislature not complying with a ruling. In US Supreme Court cases involving federal statutes between 1953 and 2000, the Court was more likely to base a decision on constitutional grounds as its ideological distance from Congress increases. Given the difficulty of challenging the court's constitutional interpretation, the court may be responding to the risk of legislative override by

115. We operationalized this effect with an interaction term between the party appointing the judge and the orientation of the government in power.

116. We ran logistic regressions on all cases involving the government as a party (but only as appellant or respondent, not both), with the dependent variable being whether the government won, and the independent variables being the government in power (liberal or conservative), the party appointing the judge (liberal or conservative), an interaction term between the government in power and the party appointing the judge, the direction (liberal or conservative) of the lower court decision, the area of law, and a time trend variable. The government and interaction terms were not significant at the .05 level for the UK and Australia. For the United States, the government in power coefficient was significant at the .01 level but very small (with a 0.5 percent lower win rate for "liberal" governments) and not significant for the interaction term. We did not run this regression for India as judges appoint their fellow judges.

117. These effects were significant at the .01 level.

strategically choosing legal instruments that increase the costs of congressional retaliation.[118]

A court may also soften the blow of not agreeing with the current government. For example, the Supreme Court of Canada has increasingly used suspended declarations of invalidity (that is, delaying the time until the legislation is declared invalid) to minimize institutional conflict: 10.5 percent of the Court's invalidations were suspended in the 1980s, 27.5 percent in the 1990s, and 60 percent in the 2000s.[119] The chances of the court issuing a suspended declaration rather than an immediate declaration increased significantly when government interveners opposed invalidation.[120] When reviewing governmental acts at the High Court of Justice, justices on the Israeli Supreme Court reduce institutional tensions by rejecting petitions for judicial review but pushing parties to settle out of court,[121] or by dismissing applications after the government has agreed to modify its initial position.[122] These strategies may allow the justices to indirectly attain their preferred results while avoiding conflicts that may damage their perceived legitimacy.

Finally, although legislative override is typically seen as a threat to the judiciary, there is also evidence that the US Supreme Court occasionally invites override of its decisions. A majority of the Court may, for example, favor the application of a particular legal rule but disagree with the resulting policy outcome. Instead of compromising to avoid negative policy implications, the Court can maximize its preferences by applying its preferred doctrine if it anticipates that Congress will find the policy result similarly unacceptable and develop a superior response.[123] One study found that approximately 11 percent of the

118. Chad M King, "Strategic Selection of Legal Instruments on the U.S Supreme Court" (2007) 35:5 *American Politics Research* 621 at 637–638.

119. Radmilovic, *supra* note 112 at 63.

120. Radmilovic, *supra* note 112 at 65–66, n. 49.

121. Dotan, "Judicial Rhetoric," *supra* note 103, n. 43; Yoav Dotan, "Judicial Activism and Government Practises in Litigation at the Israeli High Court of Justice 1970–2000" in Yun-chien Chang, ed, *Empirical Legal Analysis: Assessing the Performance of Legal Institutions* (Abingdon, UK: Routledge, 2014) 159 at 172.

122. Hofnung & Weinshall-Margel, "Judicial Setbacks," *supra* note 103, n. 43; Hofnung & Weinshall-Margel, "Judicial Setbacks", *supra* note 103 at 686–687 (Justice Procaccia noted in a decision overturning a state confiscation of land: "[d]uring the hearings on the petition, we suggested different paths in the hope of obtaining an agreement which would balance between the needs and the different interests of the sides, but, unfortunately, these offers were not accepted . . . and so there is no escape from judicial decision in the petition").

123. Pablo T. Spiller & Emerson H. Tiller, "Invitations to Override: Congressional Reversals of Supreme Court Decisions" (1996) 16:4 *International Review of Law and Economics* 503 at 504–505.

Court's interpretations of federal statutes between 1986 and 1990 included an invitation to override.[124] Such invitations were more likely when the decision's policy outcome diverged from the ideal points of the justices forming the majority coalition. The Court may then be attempting to balance its competing interests in "good policy" and "good law" by prompting the legislature to correct conflicts.[125]

## JUDGES AND OTHER ACTORS

Judges do seem to care about other judges on the bench or panel hearing the appeal, whether to further their own policy goals or for other relationship reasons. On the other hand, there is at best mixed evidence that judges are influenced by their position on the bench (such as whether they are freshman or the chief) or by other branches of government. The high court data we have for the countries we are studying makes it difficult to tease out strong relationships, let alone causation. However, we have seen that at least some aspects of the design of the court—such as whether the court sits in panels and how these panels are chosen, or whether the chief justice can shield freshman judges from the immediate pressure of a high caseload—may alter the influence of these relationships. We will return to a form of relationship in Chapter 7 when we discuss whether judges are influenced by particular litigants such as interveners or the government. Before that, though, we turn to a discussion of how these litigants actually get before the high court.

124. Lori Hausegger & Lawrence Baum, "Inviting Congressional Action: A Study of Supreme Court Motivations in Statutory Interpretation" (1999), 43:1 *American Journal of Political* 162 at 165 [Hausegger & Baum, "Inviting Congressional Action"].

125. Hausegger & Baum, "Inviting Congressional Action," *supra* note 124 at 169.

# 6

# Slipping Through the Screen

## *How Do Courts Choose the Cases They Hear?*

Imagine you are suing a hospital arguing that the doctors were negligent in treating your father. You win at trial, but the hospital appeals and you lose at the first appellate level. You then decide to appeal to the highest court in the country but you need the court to agree to hear your case. How likely are you to get your appeal heard? It turns out that if you just look at the bare percentages of requests to be heard, your chances differ widely depending on the country.[1] If you are in Canada, the Supreme Court grants about 10 percent of all applications to have appeals heard—in 2013, it granted 53 requests from the 509 applications.[2] If you are in the United States, on the other hand, the Supreme Court hears about the same number of appeals but they amount to less than 1 percent of appeals that seek a hearing (for 2009/2010, the Court heard 82 of 8,800 cases seeking to be heard).[3] In terms of straight numbers, the Indian Supreme Court hears the most appeals (about 7,500), and by one estimate has about twice the acceptance rate of the Supreme Court of Canada.[4]

The courts do not pick cases randomly from those that apply. Whether the court decides to hear certain appeals is important to the individuals involved

1. We are abstracting for the moment from the issue of jurisdiction—that is, whether this particular type of appeal is even open to be heard in all the countries we consider. We are also abstracting from differences in the cost of initiating an appeal in each country.

2. "Category 2: Applications for Leave Submitted," *Supreme Court of Canada Statistics from 2005 to 2015*, online: http://www.scc-csc.gc.ca/case-dossier/stat/cat2-eng.aspx.

3. Ryan C. Black & Christina L. Boyd, "Selecting the Select Few: The Discuss List and the U.S. Supreme Court's Agenda-Setting Process" (2012) 94:4 *Social Science Quarterly* 1124 [Black & Boyd, "Selecting"].

4. Nick Robinson, "A Quantitative Analysis of the Indian Supreme Court's Workload" (2013) 10:3 *Journal of Empirical Legal Studies* 570 at 588 [Robinson, "Quantitative Analysis"].

Commitment and Cooperation on High Courts. Benjamin Alarie and Andrew J. Green.

but also to how the law develops in a particular country. If a court hears only constitutional cases, lower courts will be the key players in other areas of law such as contracts or family law. If a court only hears criminal appeals that favor the accused and overturns a very high percentage of these appeals, it could be a sign that the lower courts are incompetent or biased or that the high court has a particular view of how the law should develop.

So how do courts decide which cases to hear? As we will see, the rules and processes differ across courts, although the main explicit factor tends to be whether a case raises issues of public or legal significance. We can, however, imagine different ways courts can choose cases. A court may give priority to certain types of cases such as constitutional ones or cases involving the national government. The court may take into account other factors, such as the importance to other potential plaintiffs of the suit against the hospital, but whether or not the case is constitutional or involves the national government carries more weight.

Judges may, however, select cases according to their own personal views of which cases should be heard. Most simply, a judge may want the court to hear a case if she wants to either affirm or reverse the result in the lower court. If she wants you (or people in similar situations) to be able to successfully sue for medical malpractice, she will want the court to hear your appeal of the case against the hospital. A judge may be even more strategic in reaching her goals and take into account not just the result she wants but the probability that her view wins when the case is heard. A judge would potentially need to have considerable information about the case and her colleagues to calculate her odds of being on the winning side before voting for the court to hear a particular case.

These differing approaches to choosing which cases to hear have another implication. As the approaches become more or less strict or allow different types of parties to succeed, the types of parties who apply or don't apply will change. If you know the court tends not to hear medical malpractice suits, you may be less likely to appeal. Further, of course, the court may change the test to account for a greater number of applications. If the number of applications increases, the court will have to become more selective to keep the number of cases heard by the court relatively constant.[5]

Which cases a court chooses to hear will result from a combination of these different approaches to selecting cases and the particular rules and processes that the court follows. In this chapter, we analyze which approach different high

5. We have seen, however, that there are other ways to deal with an increase in applications. In India, the number of judges was increased and the panel size decreased to enable the Court to hear more cases.

courts follow and how the various rules and processes influence this approach. To do this, we must first lay out how the rules and processes differ across courts.

## WHO GETS TO DECIDE WHICH CASES TO HEAR?

High courts differ in terms of selecting the cases they hear in two broad ways. First, some courts have more discretion to refuse to hear certain cases. At one extreme are the high courts in Australia, New Zealand, and the United States, which effectively have full control over which cases they hear.[6] Parties who wish the court to hear their appeal must ask permission of the court.[7] At the other extreme, some courts must hear a wide range of cases, such as the Israeli Supreme Court, which acts as the first level of review for several types of disputes.[8]

Other countries fall somewhere in-between these extremes, providing a right to appeal in limited circumstances while requiring most appeals to obtain consent of the court. In Canada, for example, approximately 20 percent of the Supreme Court's docket consists of appeals heard "as of right," meaning that the court has no choice but to hear those appeals.[9] An individual has a right to have her appeal heard by the Supreme Court in criminal cases where a judge dissents at the court of appeal or the court of appeal has overturned an acquittal. In addition, both the United Kingdom Supreme Court and the South African Supreme Court of Appeal are required to hear cases that have been certified for appeal by the lower courts, although for most cases the courts themselves usually grant permission directly.[10]

6. *Judiciary Amendment Act (No. 2) 1984* (Cth) s. 3(1) [Australia]; *Supreme Court Act 2003* (NZ), 2003, s 13; Black & Boyd, "Selecting," *supra* note 3 at 1124–1126.

7. Although most high courts exclusively hear appeals (or, in some cases, resolve disputes or questions referred to them by the government), some common law countries, including India, Israel, and South Africa, and civil law countries, such as Germany, allow members of the public to submit applications directly to the high court: Brice Dickson, *Judicial Activism in Common Law Supreme Courts* (New York: Oxford University Press, 2007) at 7 [Dickson, *Judicial Activism*]. These public petitions are often permitted in cases regarding the enforcement of constitutional rights, or judicial review of government actions.

8. *Courts Law 1984* (Consolidated version), s 41(a).

9. Benjamin Alarie & Andrew James Green, "Docket Control at the Supreme Court of Canada: What's Behind the Screen?" (July 21, 2014) [unpublished] online: https://ssrn.com/abstract=2469326 [Alarie & Green, "Docket Control"].

10. See e.g. Brice Dickson, "The Processing of Appeals in the House of Lords" (2007) 123:4 *Law Quarterly Review* 571–601 [Dickson, "Processing"]; "A Guide to Bringing a Case to the Supreme Court," online: https://www.supremecourt.uk/docs/a-guide-to-bringing-a-case-to-the-supreme-court.pdf; Kaitlyn L. Sill & Stacia Haynie, "Panel Assignment in Appellate

The second way high courts differ is in how they select the cases to hear when they do have a choice. Although most courts have some similar form of test to be heard based on the importance of the appeal (for example, whether it is of "national importance"), courts vary in terms of who decides if the test is met. The full bench of the US Supreme Court votes on whether to hear cases (which they call granting certiorari or "cert"), based on a "discuss list" of potential applications compiled by the chief justice.[11] The Court follows a Rule of Four—four judges must vote to hear the case for it to go on the Court's agenda.[12] Other courts allow subsets of judges to decide which cases to hear. In Canada and the United Kingdom, a panel of three justices decides whether the Court hears an appeal (grants "leave to appeal"), subject to review by the entire Court (which in most cases is perfunctory).[13] Going even further, a single justice of the Israeli Supreme Court generally reviews petitions to be heard by the Court, although that judge may refer the decision to a three-justice panel.[14] As individual justices rarely accept applications outright, the Israeli Supreme Court effectively relies on two levels of screening.[15]

A further difference across courts is whether law clerks are involved in the selection process. Some courts, such as in the United States,[16] Canada,[17] and the UK,[18] allow clerks to write memoranda concerning upcoming petitions. The

Courts: Strategic Behaviour in the South African Supreme Court of Appeal" (2010) 37:2 *Politikon* 269 at 271–272.

11. H.W. Perry, *Deciding to Decide: Agenda Setting in the United States Supreme Court* (Cambridge, MA: Harvard University Press, 1991) at 85.

12. In one case, the Rule of Four was subverted when four judges voted to hear a case involving capital punishment, but they could not persuade one more judge to be the fifth vote needed to grant a stay of execution. The Texas inmate was executed while waiting for his Supreme Court hearing, and the case was declared moot. *Hamilton v. Texas*, 497 U.S. 1016 (1990).

13. See Roy Flemming, *Tournament of Appeals: Granting Judicial Review in Canada* (Vancouver: UBC Press, 2004) at 59 [Flemming, *Tournament of Appeals*].

14. Theodore Eisenberg, Talia Fisher & Issi Rosen-Zvi, "Case Selection and Dissent in Courts of Last Resort: An Empirical Study of the Israeli Supreme Court" in Yun-chien Chang, ed, *Empirical Legal Analysis: Assessing the Performance of Legal Institutions* (Abingdon, UK: Routledge, 2014), 181 at 192 [Eisenberg et al., "Case Selection"].

15. Eisenberg et al., "Case Selection," *supra* note 14.

16. Todd C. Peppers & Christopher Zorn, "Law Clerk Influence on Supreme Court Decision Making: An Empirical Assessment" (2008) 58 *DePaul Law Review* 51 at 52.

17. Lorne Sossin, "The Sounds of Silence: Law Clerks, Policy Making and the Supreme Court of Canada" (1996) 30 *University of British Columbia Law Review* 279 at 289.

18. Dickson, "Processing," *supra* note 10 at 577.

judges may ultimately rely on these memoranda to make the crucial decision to grant or deny review. Other high courts do not allow clerks as large a role. In India[19] and Australia,[20] for example, the petition process relies less on written memoranda and more on oral presentations, in which clerks do not take part. Although we do not differentiate across courts on this basis in our analysis, reliance on clerks may be an important area for future analysis of how courts decide which cases to hear.

## HOW DO JUDGES DECIDE WHICH CASES TO HEAR?

Although courts generally select cases for review based on some sense of whether they raise issues of public or legal significance, the vagueness of this threshold allows judges considerable scope in their choice. Before we discuss how judges decide, however, it is important to point out that not only do the judges screen out cases they do not want to hear but the parties themselves decide whether to appeal to the high court or not.[21] As a result, neither the petitions to be heard by a court nor the set of cases actually heard by the court is random. The parties will decide to appeal or not in part based on the probability of succeeding on appeal. which, following the Priest-Klein hypothesis, should in general mean that cases with a very high (or very low) probability of success should not actually result in a hearing on the merits. We do not consider this private screen of cases coming before high courts but instead focus on the public screen of the judge selection of cases to hear.

We will consider four main theories of how judges make this choice, each of which may be partially true and operate along with the others:[22]

- Workload—judges decide on cases to hear at least in part with a view to ensuring they control the amount of work they have to do;
- Cue Theory—judges decide based on easily identified signals from the case that it raises important legal issues;

19. Abhinav Chandrachud, "From Hyderbad to Harvard: How U.S. Law Schools Make Clerking on India's Supreme Court Worthwhile" (2014) HLS Program on the Legal Profession Research Paper at 24, online: http://ssrn.com/abstract=2413576 [Chandrachud, "Hyderbad"]).

20. Jonathan Horton, "Justices' Associates: Some Observations" (2002) 22:1 *University of Queensland Law Journal* 114 at 120 [Horton].

21. For a good examination of this connection between how the parties decide whether to appeal and ideological voting on a court, see Jeff Yates & Elizabeth Coggins, "The Intersection of Judicial Attitudes and Litigant Selection Theories: Explaining U.S. Supreme Court Decision-Making" (2009) 29 *Wash. U. J. L. & Pol'y* 263 [Yates & Coggins].

22. For example, Epstein, Martin, and Segal propose a "bounded discretion" model under which some petitions to be heard should obviously be granted and some obviously denied, but there are

- Simple Ideology—judges vote to hear cases based solely on their own personal views about the outcome; and
- Sophisticated Ideology—judges vote to hear cases not simply on their own personal views but whether their views will win out when the case is heard by the court.

We start with the simplest premise—that judges consider their overall workload when deciding whether to hear an appeal.

## WORKLOAD: HOW WILL ACCEPTING A PARTICULAR CASE AFFECT A JUDGE'S WORKLOAD?

Judges may care about how much work they have to do. Docket control is a key mechanism by which high courts can moderate their own workloads. A court can only hear so many appeals. Judges may be more selective about which cases merit review based on the overall number of applications they receive. A greater number of applications to be heard may mean that the acceptance rate declines.[23] Relatedly, as the number of cases appealed as of right increases (that is, the number of appeals the court is obliged to hear), high courts may be more reluctant to grant leave to cases they are not required to hear. Increasing a court's mandatory

others where the answer is not so clear. They argue it is only in these less clear cases that the personal preferences or ideology of the judge matters. Lee Epstein, Andrew D. Martin & Jeffrey A. Segal, "Must Grants, Clear Denials and Mid-level Politics: The First Step towards a Bounded Discretion Model of Certiorari Decisions" (Paper delivered at the 2nd Annual Conference on Institutions and Law-Making, Emory University, 14 February 2012) [unpublished] [Epstein et al., "Must Grants"].

23. Efficiency theories may tie in the cue theory. Clark and Strauss suggest that the ideal scope of a court's mandatory jurisdiction depends on the perceived quality of lower court decisions. If lower courts tend to reach "correct" outcomes, high courts can maximize their institutional efficiency by granting discretionary review to a small number of difficult or important cases, rather than auditing a wide array of decisions. Therefore, there may also be a connection between the number of petitions that a high court accepts and both the areas of law it chooses to prioritize and the rate at which it reverses lower court decisions. (Tom Clark & Aaron Strauss, "The Implications of High Court Docket Control for Resource Allocation and Legal Efficiency" (2010) 22:2 *Journal of Theoretical Politics* 247). In addition, there is evidence that high courts aim to maximize their efficiency by making strategic decisions to audit lower court decisions. For instance, although cue theory suggests that lower court conflicts are a consistently positive indicator of petition success, judges may prefer to deny leave when it is not clear which position is correct (Lawrence Wrightman, *The Psychology of the Supreme Court* (New York: Oxford University Press, 2006) at 64). This allows other lower courts to weigh in on the question. Judges will therefore aim to balance the costs of allowing these disagreements to persist with the informational benefits gained by allowing lower courts' deliberations on a complex legal issue to persist (Tom Clark & Jonathan Kastellec, "The Supreme Court and Percolation in the Lower Courts: An Optimal Stopping Model" (2013) 75:1 *Journal of Politics* 150 at 166).

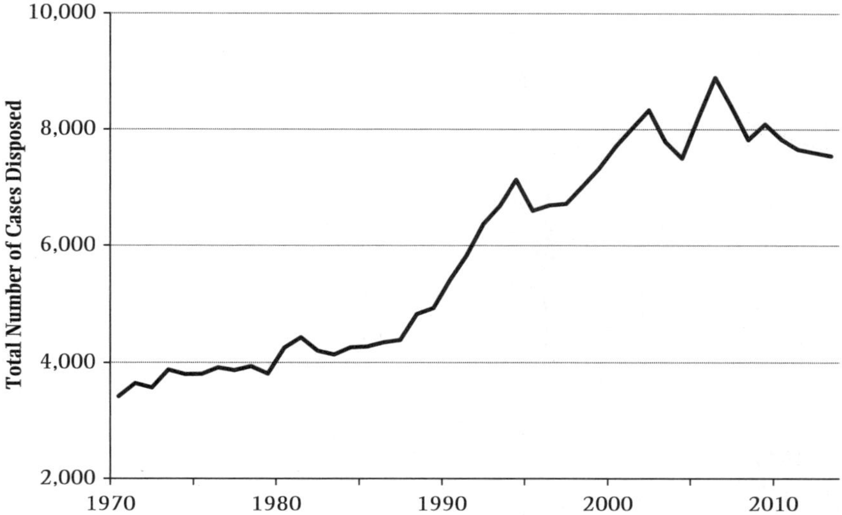


**Figure 6-1** Total cases disposed by the US Supreme Court, 1970–2012. Cases disposed is a measure of how many petitions to be heard the Court heard in a given year. The number of petitions rose slowly in the 1970s and 1980s before rising dramatically in the 1990s. SOURCE: Federal Judicial Center: Supreme Court of the United States, "Supreme Court, 1878–2012", accessed February 5, 2016, http://www.fjc.gov/history/caseload.nsf/page/caseloads_Sup_Ct_totals.

jurisdiction may thus increase access to the court, but also make judges more likely to deny petitions that would otherwise deserve review on the merits.[24]

There are other ways to deal with an increase in petitions. The number of judges could be increased, or appeals could be heard in smaller panels. More judges and smaller panels mean a court can hear more cases than a court that hears all appeals *en banc*. However, an initial hypothesis is:

> *H1: Acceptance rates will decline as the total number of petitions to be heard increases and as the number of cases that the court has to hear increases.*

The US Supreme Court is a good place to start to see if judges respond to workload because it has long had nine justices and heard appeals *en banc*. As seen in Figure 6-1, petitions to be heard by the Court since 1970 can be broken down

24. Similarly a particular court's acceptance rates (the rate at which it agrees to hear appeals) will vary depending on its available resources. When a court is not at full capacity, maintaining its prior caseload would place additional burdens on each sitting judge. Vacancies may therefore create disincentives for individual judges to vote in favor of granting leave.

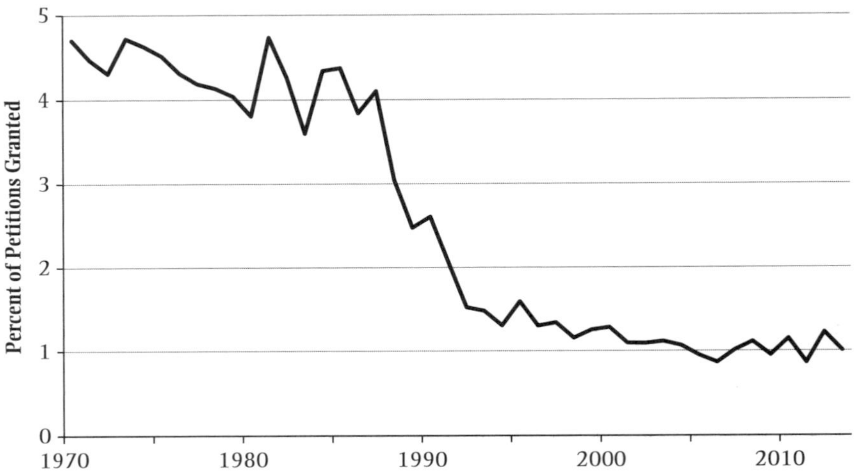


**Figure 6-2** Percent of petitions for cert and appeal granted by the US Supreme Court, 1970 to 2012. The Court significantly reduced the percentage of petitions it agreed to hear starting in the late 1980s, leveling off by 2000.

SOURCE: Percent Granted was calculated by dividing Petitions for Certiorari and Appeals Granted Plenary Review by Cases Disposed, from Federal Judicial Center: Supreme Court of the United States, "Supreme Court Dispositions, 1970–2012", http://www.fjc.gov/history/caseload.nsf/page/caseloads_Sup_Ct_Methods_of_Disposition_2, accessed February 5, 2016, and Federal Judicial Center: Supreme Court of the United States, "Supreme Court, 1878–2012," http://www.fjc.gov/history/caseload.nsf/page/caseloads_Sup_Ct_totals, accessed February 5, 2016, respectively.

into two basic periods—the 1970s/1980s where petitions were increasing slowly but were fairly steady, and then the 1990s onward where petitions increased dramatically. Interestingly, in 1988, right at the break between the two periods, the US Supreme Court obtained virtually complete control of its docket with the ending of most of its mandatory caseload.[25]

If judges were concerned at least in part about workload, they would agree to hear a lower percentage of these petitions as the number increased, particularly in the later period. This decline is seen in Figure 6-2, which shows that the percent of petitions that the Court agreed to hear. The percentage has a slight downward trend (though with a significant variance) in the pre-1988 period. In fact, this downward trend was an extension of a precipitous drop in the grant rate during the 1940–1970 period, when the number of petitions more than

25. Jeffrey A. Segal, Harold J. Spaeth & Sara C. Benesh, "The Supreme Court in the American Legal System" (New York: Cambridge University Press, 2005) at 276.

tripled. As recently as 1949 the Court accepted 15 percent of petitions for certiorari, and in 1932, the Court agreed to hear a full 28 percent of petitions for certiorari.[26]

Jucewicz and Baum argue that the Court may have dropped the acceptance rate before 1970 in order to maintain a reasonable workload—that is, the judges adjusted to the large increase in petitions.[27] To see if judges also adjusted to small fluctuations in petition levels, they examined the terms from 1975 to 1984, which was a period of relative stability in petitions.[28] They found the Court's standards for accepting cases remained fairly constant during this period. For the most part, the more cases that came to the Court, the more it accepted.[29] Thus during the period of relative stability they examined, justices did not feel the need to adjust their case-screening criteria to relatively small changes in total number of petitions.[30]

The period after 1988 clearly saw another dramatic increase in people asking the Court to hear their appeals. The number of petitions for leave to appeal disposed of by the Court jumped from between 4,000 and 5,000 to an average of just over 8,000 between 2002 and 2012 (Figure 6-1). As the workload theory would predict, Figure 6-2 shows a corresponding dramatic drop in the percentage of these petitions the Court agreed to hear. Interestingly, however, maintaining a steady workload is likely not the only factor in this decline. As the number of applications increases, the percentage that are truly worthy of being heard by the Supreme Court may drop. Further Figure 6-3 shows that judges also have been hearing fewer appeals in recent years—dropping from over 150 in the 1970s and 1980s to under 100 by the 2000s. The drop in the acceptance rate was therefore a combination both of agreeing to hear a lower percentage of the ever-expanding number of petitions in order not to be overwhelmed and of hearing fewer cases per year. Clearly more is going on here than just maintaining a constant workload in terms of number of cases.[31]

26. "History of the Federal Judiciary: Supreme Court of the United States, Method of Disposition 1932–1969," *Federal Judicial Center*, online: http://www.fjc.gov/history/caseload.nsf/page/caseloads_Sup_Ct_method_of_disposition.

27. Joseph Jucewicz & Lawrence Baum, "Workload Influences on Supreme Court Acceptance Rates" (1990) 43:1 *Western Political Quarterly* 123 [Jucewicz & Baum] (they quote Chief Justice Rehnquist as stating "[t]oday we decline to review cases involving important questions of federal law not previously decided by our Court, cases which the Court would have unquestionably heard and decided as little as thirty years ago" at 125).

28. Jucewicz & Baum, *supra* note 27 at 126.

29. Jucewicz & Baum, *supra* note 27 at 130.

30. Jucewicz & Baum, *supra* note 27 at 133–134.

31. As we will see, Owens and Simon argue that the drop in the number of cases that the US Supreme Court hears may be in part due to an increasingly ideological split on the Court,

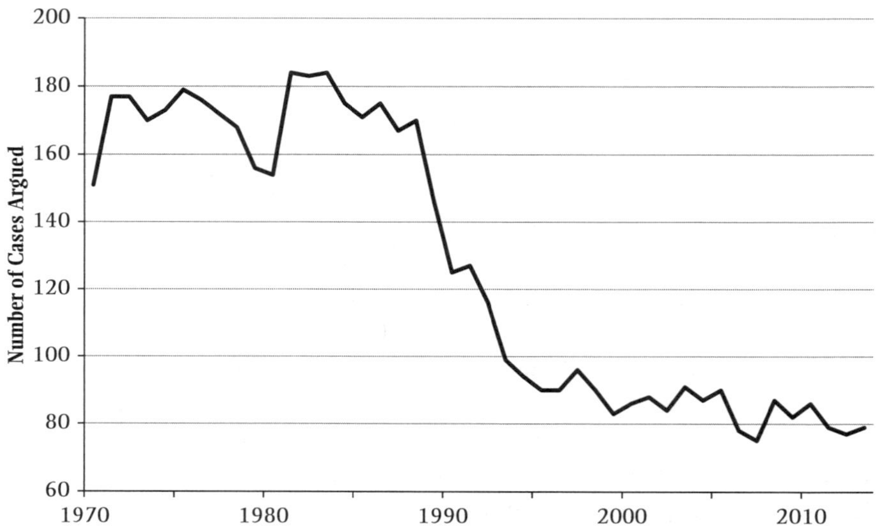


**Figure 6-3** Number of cases heard per year by the US Supreme Court, 1970 to 2012. Not only did the percentage of petitions the Court agreed to hear drop in the late 1980s, but the total number of cases it heard per year also dropped significantly.
SOURCE: Cases argued from Federal Judicial Center: Supreme Court of the United States, "Supreme Court Dispositions, 1878–2012," accessed February 5, 2016, http://www.fjc.gov/history/caseload.nsf/page/caseloads_Sup_Ct_Methods_of_Disposition_2.

Do other courts exhibit a concern for workload? The Supreme Court of Canada also has considerable control over its docket, although less so than in the United States. The Canadian Supreme Court obtained substantial control over its own docket in the late 1970s, with today about 80 percent of the cases it hears annually arising from the leave-to-appeal process. As in the United States, there have been changes in the petition rates and acceptance rates for the Court but the levels are much lower. As Figure 6-4 shows, more petitioners have sought access to the Court in recent years—from an average of 493 in the 1990s to 548 after 2000. Justices at the same time granted leave to appeal to a lower percentage of applications over time, from an average of 15 percent in the 1990s to less than 12 percent after 1990 (Figure 6-5). As in the United States, the acceptance rate dropped both due to the increase in applications but also due to a slight decrease in the number of cases accepted. In the 1990s, the Supreme

which makes them less able to agree on hearing appeals: Ryan J. Owens & David A. Simon, "Explaining the Supreme Court's Shrinking Docket" (2012) 53:4 *William and Mary Law Review* 1219 at 1265 [Owens & Simon].

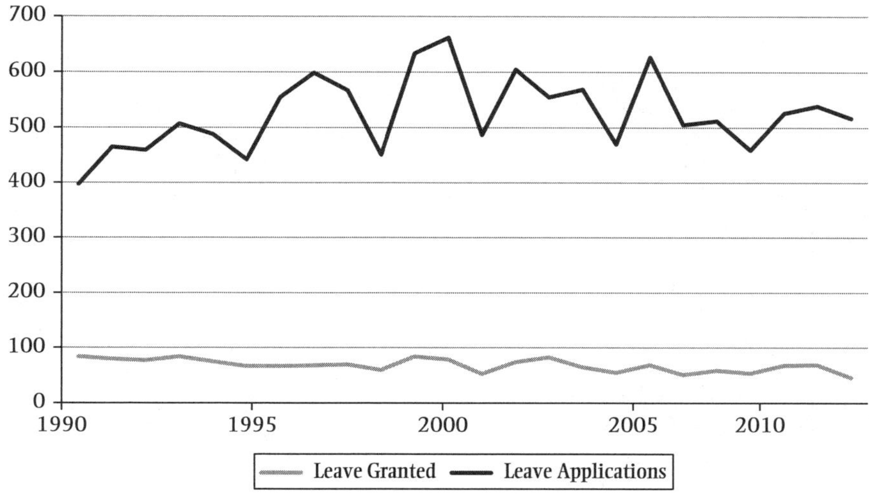


**Figure 6-4** Number of applications for leave to appeal and number of leave applications granted for the Supreme Court of Canada, 1990–2013. The number of applications rose over the period, though more slowly in the United States.
SOURCE: Benjamin Alarie & Andrew James Green, "Docket Control at the Supreme Court of Canada: What's Behind the Screen?" (July 21, 2014) [unpublished] online: https://ssrn.com/abstract=2469326

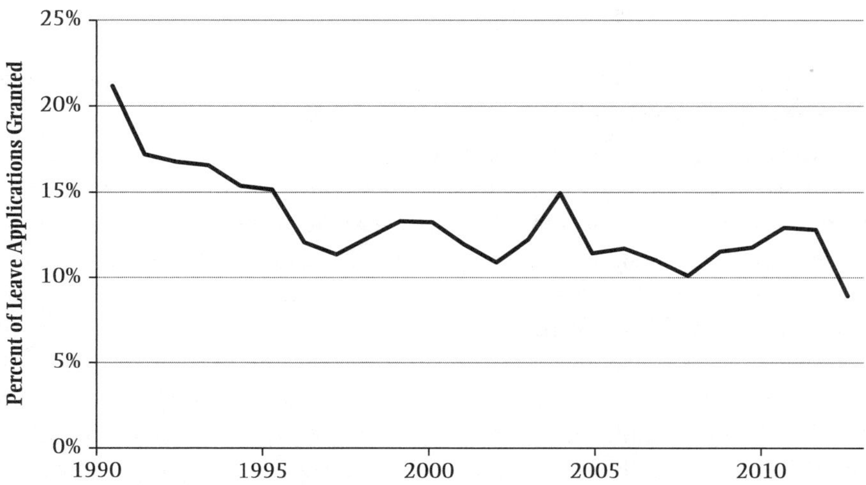


**Figure 6-5** Grant rate (percent) for applications for leave to appeal, Supreme Court of Canada, 1990–2013. The grant rate drops markedly through the 1990s before leveling off somewhat by 2000.
SOURCE: Benjamin Alarie & Andrew James Green, "Docket Control at the Supreme Court of Canada: What's Behind the Screen?" (July 21, 2014) [unpublished] online: https://ssrn.com/abstract=2469326.

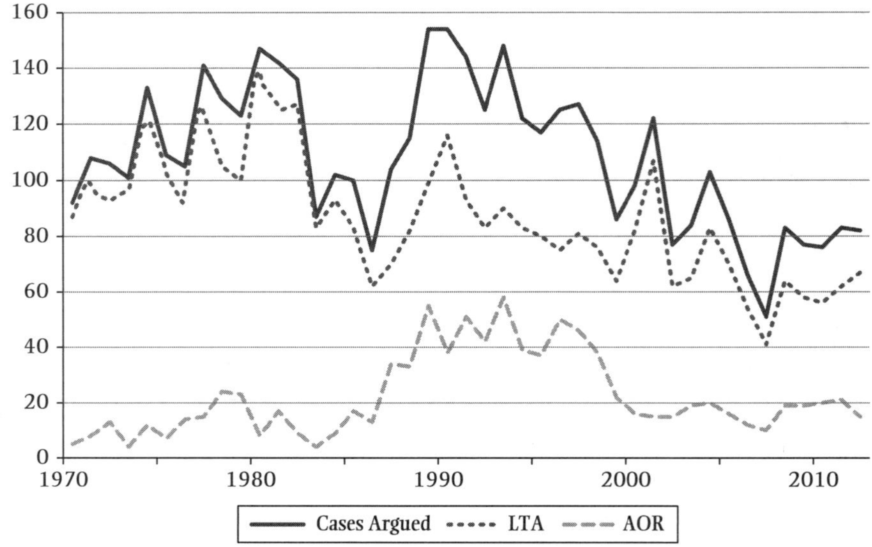


**Figure 6-6** Number of cases argued before the Supreme Court of Canada in total, by leave and as of right, 1970–2012. The Court has heard fewer cases in recent years after climbing up in the 1970s and then the early 1990s. The late 1980s saw an increase in total cases but the increase was related to an increase in as of right cases rather than a large increase in cases heard with leave.
SOURCE: Alarie and Green database.

Court agreed to hear on average 73 cases per year (in addition to appeals as of right), but after 1990 that number fell to 65 per year (Figure 6-4).

Two other influences on workload are important in Canada beyond the number of cases that the justices agree to hear. First, as we saw, the Court has to hear certain criminal cases, and therefore its workload includes both those it has to hear and those it agrees to hear. A justice deciding whether to agree to the Court hearing an appeal may base her choice at least in part on both the number of applications to be heard and the general level of appeals the Court has to hear. Figure 6-6 divides the cases argued in a term into those for which leave was granted and those that were heard as of right.[32] There is a slight downward trend in the total number of cases heard since 1980. We can also see that when we look over a slightly longer time frame, the Supreme Court has agreed to hear fewer cases after it obtained greater control over its docket in the late 1970s and headed into the Charter era (the Charter of Rights and Freedoms being adopted in 1982). Although there was a significant increase in the number of

32. Note that these numbers will be different from those cases that were granted leave during a given year as there is a lag between when an appeal is granted leave and when it is argued.

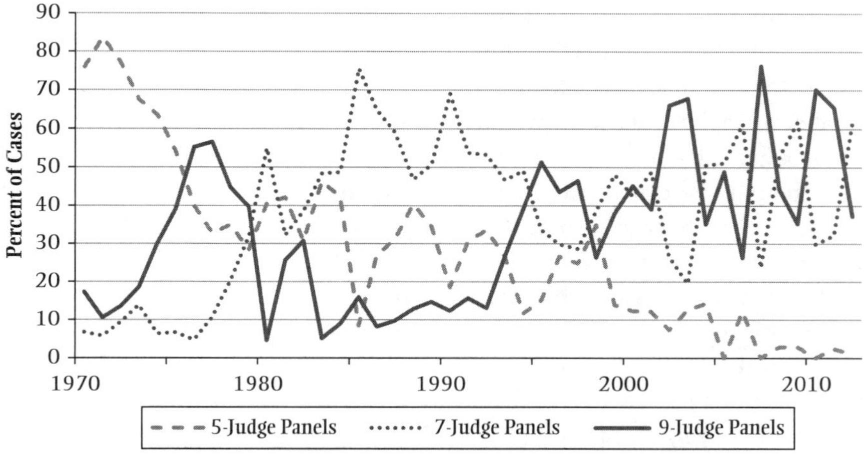


**Figure 6-7** Percentage of different Panel Sizes, Supreme Court of Canada, 1970–2012. The number of panels of five justices have declined steadily over the period whereas panels of nine have been increasing in the post-Charter era.
SOURCE: Alarie and Green database. Note that these totals do not include panels of six or eight.

cases argued in the late 1980s, a large part of the increase was due to an increase in as of right cases in that period (possibly due to criminal cases with Charter implications working their way through the system). There was, however, no significant reduction in the number of cases heard with leave in this period. This lack of response to the variation in the number of as of right cases implies that the workload theory does not fit for the Supreme Court of Canada (at least assuming that the changes over time in the as of right cases are not correlated with the quality or quantity of the other cases).

Second, in Canada and a number of other countries the chief justice has a tool for moderating caseload that is not available to the chief justice of the US Supreme Court. The chief justice of the Canadian Supreme Court can set small panels to hear certain cases and therefore reduce the workload of the justices in terms of the total number of cases they need to hear.[33] The Court may then have offsetting ways to deal with the increasing number of applications to be heard. The justices can reduce the percentage of applications they agree to hear or the chief justice can reduce the average panel size that hears each case. Interestingly, if we look at the distribution of panel sizes since 1970 in Figure 6-7, chief justices do not appear to have used panel size in this manner. Instead, as the applications have risen, the number of cases granted leave has declined

33. See Chapter 4 for a discussion of how the chief justice sets panel size.

but the average panel size has increased. Panels of five have declined steadily as panels of nine have risen. Chief Justice McLachlin, the current Canadian chief justice, for example, has decreased the number of five judge panels even as the number of applications for leave increased. She therefore has not responded to the increased demand by increasing the number of appeals the Court hears, even though she can moderate the load by using panels of five judges. She instead appears to be absorbing the extra time from the fewer cases by ensuring the full court hears more cases.

The UK Supreme Court has not been in existence for long, but the patterns are interesting. As can be seen from Figure 6-8, in its first five full years of operation the Court disposed of a much lower (though increasing) number of applications for leave to be heard by the Court than in the United States or Canada—rising from a little under 200 to almost 300 by 2014. The Court granted leave at a much higher rate than either the US Supreme Court or even the Supreme Court of Canada, rising over the period though not as rapidly as the number of applications. The Court granted leave to 67 applications in 2010 but over 80 per year in the last three years, with a grant rate of about 30 to

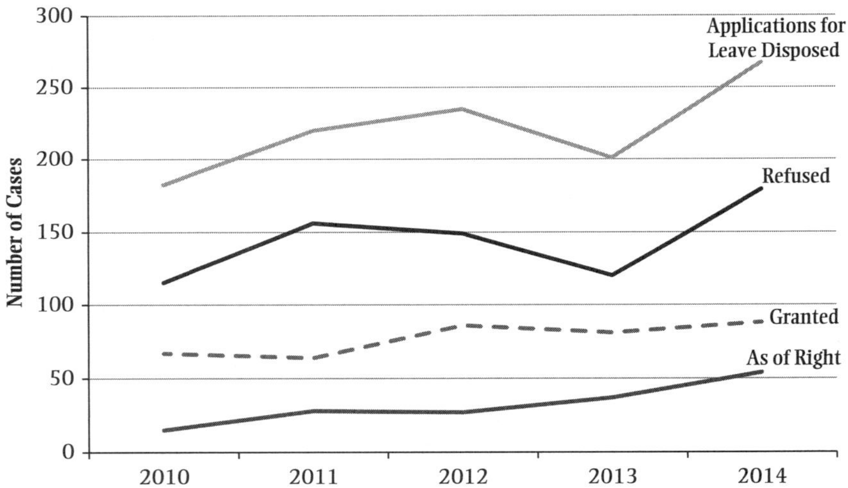


**Figure 6-8** Number of applications for leave to appeal in total, granted and refused, as well as number of applications for appeal filed as of right, UK Supreme Court 2010–2014. All of these applications have increased over the period, though the number of applications for leave granted may have leveled off. The number of applications for leave disposed is found by adding those refused and granted (as opposed to the number of applications filed, as some were not disposed of within the year).
SOURCE: UK Supreme Court Annual Reports found at www.supremecourt.uk/news/the-supreme-court-annual-reports-and-accounts.html, last accessed February 9, 2016.

40 percent over the period. Finally, the number of appeals filed as of right has increased over the period. It will be interesting to see if the number of cases granted leave continues to hold steady if there continues to be increasing applications for leave as well as applications filed as of right.

The Indian Supreme Court took a different path. In India, the number of people wanting their appeals heard by the Supreme Court rapidly increased following independence. According to Robinson, the number of admission matters the Court instituted increased five times (from 1,037 to 5,549) between 1950 and 1976 and then another five times again in the next five years due to the 1975–1977 state of emergency ("the Emergency").[34] After a small drop, the number of matters seeking admission rose steeply and consistently through the 1990s and 2000s.

The Indian Supreme Court did not cap or even reduce its acceptance rate in the same way that the United States and Canada seem to have done. Instead it responded to the increased demand in three ways. First, it tolerated backlogs—as the court admitted more cases, the average wait time to hear cases increased.[35] For example, by 2011, 43 percent of regular hearing matters were heard within two years of being commenced, but 40 percent took from two to five years to be heard, and 17 percent were older than five years.[36] Second, the number of judges on the Indian Supreme Court increased dramatically over time. The Court started with eight judges in 1950 but increased to 11 in 1956, then 14 in 1960, 17 in 1977, 26 in 1986, and finally up to 31 in 2008.[37] Third, the Court reduced its average panel size. As Figure 6-9 shows, the Court heard more appeals in panels of two and fewer large panels, including a dramatic decline in five-judge panels that hear constitutional matters.[38] The Court therefore changed how it heard appeals in order to help satisfy at least some of the increasing demand (although the increases in the number of judges and reduction in panel size may also have spurred some demand by increasing the capacity of the Court). Robinson's data shows a "rush of litigants toward the top of the system," which he suggests may be due to even more severe backlogs in the lower courts, which litigants seek to avoid.[39] The Supreme Court, he points out, has been "quite willing to oblige."[40]

34. Robinson, "Quantitative Analysis," *supra* note 4 at 578.

35. Robinson, "Quantitative Analysis," *supra* note 4 at 589.

36. Robinson, "Quantitative Analysis," *supra* note 4 at 591.

37. Nick Robinson, "Structure Matters: The Impact of Court Structure on the Indian and U.S. Supreme Courts" (2013) 61:1 *American Journal of Comparative Law* 173 at 182.

38. Robinson, "Quantitative Analysis," *supra* note 4 at 578.

39. Robinson, "Quantitative Analysis," *supra* note 4 at 582.

40. Robinson, "Quantitative Analysis," *supra* note 4 at 582.

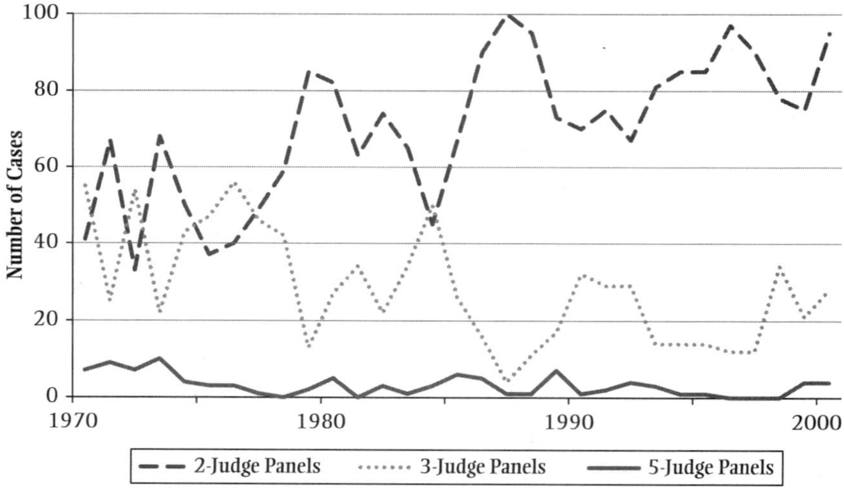


**Figure 6-9** Number of cases of differing panel sizes (from sample per year of about 100 cases), Indian Supreme Court, 1970–2000. The number of five-judge panels has stayed low over the period, whereas the number of two-judge panels increased.
SOURCE: High Courts Judicial Database.

Judges may then care about workload when they are considering whether to hear appeals. However, it is clearly not the only factor. First, courts may use other methods to moderate workloads such as changing the number of judges on the bench or using smaller panels. Second, even if workload does play a role, the judges still have to have some method to select the appeals they want to hear, be it cues of importance or ideology. It is to these explanations that we now turn, starting with whether judges use cues.

## Cue Theory: What Kind of Case Is This?

Judges may look for certain features or "cues" in an appeal petition that signal that the petition does or does not present important legal issues. If judges can identify these cues easily or at low cost, they can efficiently sort large numbers of petitions to determine which ones deserve closer scrutiny.[41] Judges on this view are primarily motivated by legal considerations and concerns about efficiency. We can think of cues as falling in two broad groupings: those related to the case itself, and those related to the players or parties.

41. Black & Boyd, "Selecting," *supra* note 3.

Consider first cues related to the case itself. A judge may ask, for example, whether there was a dissent at the lower court, conflicting holdings across lower courts, or conflicts with supreme court precedents; if an appellate court reversed the original decision; or if an application raises important or novel legal issues.[42] Each of these factors may indicate a controversial or important decision. Judges may also look for cues that the case is not important, such as if the lower opinion is unpublished or if the petition emphasizes fact-specific concerns.[43]

A cue that may be the most easily identifiable for judges is whether the appeal involves certain fields of law.[44] Judges may assume these fields are likely to involve significant legal issues, or provide an opportunity to influence specific policy areas. Judges on a particular high court may, for example, be more likely to agree to hear appeals involving constitutional and civil liberties issues. Alternatively, although the number of constitutional benches declined over 1993–2011 in India, the Court has started to accept a higher percentage of tax, service, labor, and land adjudication appeals.[45] The cues may change over time, depending on broader policy considerations. For instance, the Emergency period in India was marked by a decline in the high courts' willingness to intervene against the government, as was Israel during national security crises.[46]

42. See e.g. Roy Flemming & Glen Krutz, "Selecting Appeals for Judicial Review in Canada: A Replication and Multivariate Test of American Hypotheses" (2002) 64:1 *Journal of Politics* 232 at 24, n. 16 [Flemming & Krutz, "Selecting Appeals"]; S. Sidney Ulmer, "Conflict with Supreme Court Precedents and the Granting of Plenary Review" (1983) 45:2 *Journal of Politics* 474; S. Sidney Ulmer, "The Supreme Court's Certiorari Decision: Conflict as a Predictive Variable" (1984) 78:4 *American Political Science Review* 901; S. Sidney Ulmer, William Hintze & Louise Kirklosky, "The Decision to Grant or Deny Certiorari: Further Consideration of Cue Theory" (1972) 6:4 *Law and Society Review* 637; Margaret Meriweather Cordray & Richard Cordray, "The Philosophy of Certiorari: Jurisprudential Considerations in Supreme Court Case Selection" (2004) 82:2 *Washington University Law Quarterly* 389. In their seminal study of case selection at the US Supreme Court, Tanenhaus et al. identified three factors correlationally associated with successful certiorari applications: (1) petitions filed by the federal government, (2) dissenting opinions in the lower courts' decision or conflicting rulings across lower courts, and (3) cases raising civil liberties issues: J. Tanenhaus et al., "The Supreme Court's Certiorari Jurisdiction: Cue Theory" in Glendon Shubert, ed, *Judicial Decision Making* (New York: The Free Press of Glencoe, 1963) at 111.

43. Black & Boyd, *supra* note 3 at 1135, n. 2; Flemming & Krutz, "Selecting Appeals," *supra* note 42 at 41, n. 16.

44. Wrightman, *supra* note 23, n. 5.

45. Robinson, "Quantitative Analysis," *supra* note 4 at 572.

46. Menachem Hofnung & Keren Weinshall-Margel, "Judicial Setbacks, Material Gains: Terror Litigation at the Israeli High Court of Justice" (2010) 7 *Journal of Empirical Legal Studies* 664; Robinson, "Quantitative Analysis," *supra* note 4. Alternatively, however, there may be an increased willingness to find for the government if the governments during this period chose judges who they know will be favorably disposed to their initiatives.

As we will see, cues related to the case itself may be more influential on courts with less explicit ideological motives or fewer strategic opportunities. However, we adopt the following as an initial hypothesis relating to cues:

*H2: The rate at which high courts agree to hear appeals varies significantly across different areas of law.*

The other grouping of cues relates to the parties involved in the appeal. Judges may, for example, be more likely to agree to hear appeals from parties with greater resources, filed by high profile "repeat litigators," or supported by amici curiae.[47] Each of these factors may for certain judges point to the appeal being more likely to have important public or political implications. Further, having the government involved, either as a party or intervening in the appeal, may point toward greater importance. The status of the parties involved may then influence judges into hearing an appeal on the merits, although there may be an overlap with ideology in that judges with different personal preferences may react differently to different types of parties. For example, a judge who tends to favor the underdog may be more likely to want to hear appeals involving parties with fewer resources. However, our initial hypothesis concerning parties to the appeal is as follows:

*H3: Judges are more likely to agree to hear appeals involving the government, repeat litigators and parties with greater resources.*

If a high court tends to hear more cases in some areas of law than others, the difference may result from the number of applications in an area or from the grant rate. For example, a court may hear more constitutional than property law appeals because although it agrees to hear about 15 percent of both types of cases, more people apply to have appeals heard that involve constitutional matters. It may also be, however, that similar numbers of applications to be heard are brought in each area but the court agrees to hear a higher proportion of constitutional than property appeals. These explanations may be related—a higher grant rate for constitutional appeals may elicit more applications in that area.

47. See e.g. Kevin McGuire, *The Supreme Court Bar: Legal Elites in the Washington Community* (Charlottesville: University Press of Virginia, 1993) [McGuire, *Supreme Court Bar*]; Kevin McGuire, "Amici Curiae and Strategies for Gaining Access to the Supreme Court" (1994) 47:4 *Political Research Quarterly* 821; Gregory Caldeira & John Wright, "Organized Interests and Agenda Setting in the U.S. Supreme Court" (1988) 82:4 *American Political Science Review* 1109 [Caldeira & Wright, "Organized Interests"].

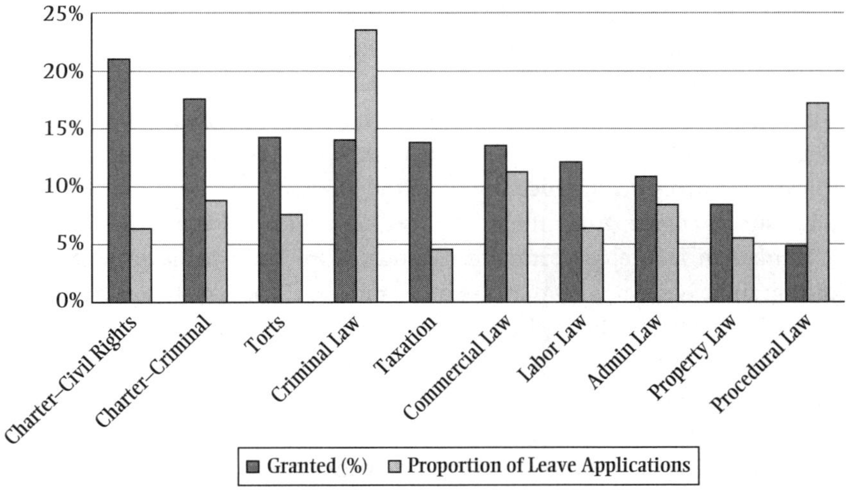


**Figure 6-10** Relative Proportion of Leave to Appeal Applications and Grant Rates, Top Ten Areas of Law, Supreme Court of Canada, 1990–2011.
SOURCE: Alarie & Green, "Docket Control," *supra* note 9.

Take the Supreme Court of Canada as an example. It differentiates across areas of law. Figure 6-10 looks at the 10 areas of law with the highest number of applications for leave to appeal since 1990. It shows that both the proportion of leave applications (and therefore the number of applications) and the rate at which leave is granted vary considerably across these areas. Criminal law and procedural law make up the highest proportion of applications for leave to appeal with tax and property law the lowest in the top 10 areas. The differences are quite stark. Over 2,300 applications for leave were launched involving criminal law but less than 500 for tax law.[48] However, the grant rates vary considerably, with the Court most likely to hear appeals involving the Charter of Rights and Freedoms, tort law, and criminal law. The Court did agree to hear a higher percentage of appeals in other areas but for these areas there were few applications to be heard. For example, the Court granted leave to appeal in over 30 percent of cases involving federalism issues but these cases made up a mere 8 percent of applications for leave.[49]

Courts are more likely to agree to hear appeals not only in certain areas of law but also if particular parties are involved. Governments are especially successful at getting their appeals heard by high courts. In the United States, for

48. Alarie & Green, "Docket Control," *supra* note 9.

49. Alarie & Green, "Docket Control," *supra* note 9.

example, the US Supreme Court agreed to hear about 46–80 percent of appeals when the US solicitor general was the petitioner—that is, when the US government was asking the Court to hear the appeal.[50] In part this high success rate may be due to the US government becoming more selective in the appeals it brings, as the number of cases for which the federal government petitioned to be heard has dropped significantly since the 1980s.[51]

This success of the government at being heard also holds in other countries. The Canadian federal government is much more likely to have the Supreme Court grant leave to appeal than are other parties.[52] The Israeli government has also been effective at being heard, with the government obtaining review in about 70 percent of criminal cases in which it sought to be heard in 2006–2007, compared to a 6 percent rate for defendants. In civil cases it was less successful, obtaining review in just under 50 percent of the cases in which it sought to be heard, but still more effective than other parties who obtained review less than 15 percent of the time.[53]

So governments are generally the best at getting their cases heard across countries. High courts tend to differ, however, in whether they differentiate between nongovernment petitioners. This difference may in part be due to how each court decides which cases to hear and how many applications they receive.

As we have seen, the United States attracts a very large number of petitions to be heard—in the order of 8,000 per year—and all judges may vote on whether to hear each petition. The chief justice reduces this workload somewhat through the creation of the "discuss list" of petitions that are more seriously considered, but it is still a large number of petitions each year. Judges on the Court do appear to take into account the relative resources of the parties in deciding whether an appeal will be heard on the merits. Individuals are generally taken

50. David C. Thompson & Melanie F. Wachtell, "An Empirical Analysis of Supreme Court Certiorari Petitions Procedures: The Call for Responses and the Call for the Views of the Solicitor General" (2009) 16:2 *George Mason Law Review* 237 at 277 [Thompson & Wachtell]. Similarly, Caldeira and Wright also found a high success rate for the US government, with the Court agreeing to hear two-thirds of appeals when the solicitor general was the petitioner. Caldeira & Wright, "Organized Interests," *supra* note 47 at 1117.

51. Margaret Cordray & Richard Cordray, "The Solicitor General's Changing Role in Supreme Court Litigation" (2010) 51:5 *Boston College Law Review* 1323 at 1353. At the same time, Cordray and Cordray found that the solicitor general was more likely to become involved in appeals at the merit stage as amicus.

52. Flemming, *Tournament of Appeals*, *supra* note 13 at 57.

53. Theodore Eisenberg, Talia Fisher & Issi Rosen-Zvi, "Israel's Supreme Court Appellate Jurisdiction: An Empirical Study" (2011) 96:3 *Cornell Law Review* 693 at 718–719 [Eisenberg et al., "Empirical Study"].

to have the smallest number of resources when they are involved before the Supreme Court; businesses come second thanks to greater resources available and better organization. The government and government organizations, with their "nearly limitless pool of resources and the frequency with which they litigate," are considered the most powerful.[54]

Parties with relatively fewer resources tended to be more likely to bring petitions to be heard by the Court but less successful in getting heard. Black and Boyd found, for example, that the petitioner had fewer resources than the responding party (such as an individual petitioning and a business responding) in 62 percent of cases and more resources 31 percent of the time (in the remaining 7 percent the parties were at an equal level).[55] They explain their results through cue theory. Of course, it may not just be that the judge sees the party with greater resources as more likely to have an important case but that high resource petitioners such as the government and big business had the knowledge and ability to craft briefs including clear cues.[56]

Another indication of the importance of resources in the United States stems from how the petition to be heard came before the Supreme Court. The Court receives two kinds of petitions: for paid petitions, the petitioner must pay a fee and follow various other requirements, whereas for petitions *in forma pauperis* (literally, in the form of a pauper), there are no fees and many of the other requirements are waived.[57] Most of the petitions *in forma pauperis* are submitted by prisoners. This is the simplest way in which the US Supreme Court can identify the status of petitioners. Over the 10 years leading up to the 2011–2012 term, the Supreme Court granted on average 4.3 percent of all paid petitions, but only 0.2 percent of all *in forma pauperis* petitions.[58]

The disadvantage of petitioners without resources can be mitigated somewhat if the party has support from interest groups. Such support comes in a form called amicus briefs in the United States—materials provided to the Court by someone who is not a party to the case. By one estimate, if a petitioner with few resources, such as an individual, seeks to be heard by the Court but has no

54. Ryan Black & Christina Boyd, "US Supreme Court Agenda Setting and the Role of Litigant Status" (2010) 28:2 *Journal of Law, Economics, and Organizations* 286 at 293 [Black & Boyd, "Agenda Setting"].

55. Black & Boyd, "Agenda Setting," *supra* note 54 at 297.

56. Black & Boyd, "Agenda Setting," *supra* note 54 at 289, 305.

57. Saul Brenner, "Granting Certiorari by the United States Supreme Court: An Overview of the Social Science Studies" (2000) 92:2 *Law Library Journal* 193 at 195.

58. Kedar S. Bhatia, "Likelihood of a Petition Being Granted" (10 January 2013), *Daily Writ* (blog), online: http://dailywrit.com/2013/01/likelihood-of-a-petition-being-granted/.

support from interest groups, his odds of success are about 0.1 percent—with a 97 percent chance of being denied leave to appeal without even making the chief justice's discuss list. However, the same petitioner with two amicus briefs in support had a 7 percent chance of being granted review.[59] Similarly, amicus curiae briefs filed in support of a petition to be heard by the Court increased the estimated probability that the Court would grant that petition by 50–60 percent (starting from the baseline certification rate of less than 1 percent). For cases with a reasonable chance of acceptance in the first place, amicus curiae briefs seem often to make the difference between success and failure.[60]

The governments, both federal and state, are listened to even when they are not the petitioner. The Court can ask for the input of the American government in cases in which the government is not directly involved. This is a privilege extended to no other party in the American court system. If the Court asks for advice from the government on whether to hear a case, it is likely to follow the advice it receives—between 1998 and 2004, when the solicitor general recommended a straight grant or denial of a petition, the Supreme Court followed the recommendation almost 80 percent of the time.[61] If a state government supports a petition, the Court is also more likely to agree to hear the appeal. During the 2001–2010 terms, where three or more states filed an amicus brief, the Court granted certiorari 44.4 percent of the time, far more often than the baseline grant rate.[62] This effect was larger when more states were in support of the petition and when the states that support the brief were more diverse in terms of

59. Black & Boyd, "Selecting," *supra* note 3 at 1139. Ryan Black and Christina Boyd also recently found that the influence of amici briefs supporting a petition was contingent on both judicial ideology (as the positive effect on liberal judges was substantially greater) and party status (with weaker parties benefitting the most from intervener submissions, whereas much stronger parties were actually disadvantaged). Black & Boyd, "Agenda Setting," *supra* note 54 at 303–305 (this result conflicts with the earlier findings of Caldeira & Wright, "Organized Interests," *supra* note 47, n. 13, which found that interveners were consistently a positive cue).

60. Caldeira & Wright, "Organized Interests," *supra* note 47 at 1122.

61. Thompson & Wachtell, *supra* note 50 at 245.

62. Greg Goelzhauser & Nicole Vouvalis, "Amicus Coalition Heterogeneity and Signaling Credibility in Supreme Court Agenda Setting" (2014) *The Journal of Federalism*, Forthcoming at 8 [Goelzhauser & Vouvalis]. They note that the overwhelming majority of state-filed amicus petitions support the granting of review. Gregory A. Caldeira, John R. Wright & Christopher Zorn, "A Unified Model of Supreme Court Voting" (Paper delivered at the Conference on Institutions and Law-Making, Emory University, Atlanta, GA, February 25–26, 2011) [unpublished] [Caldeira, Wright & Zorn, "Unified Model"] (suggest that it's a bad idea to ever file a brief against cert "[t]hat is, because such briefs represent nontrivial investments by the groups filing them, they indirectly signal the importance of the case, thus raising the likelihood of certiorari in spite of the arguments presented therein" at 3).

ideology.[63] Diversity in the states supporting the petition may send credible cues to the Court about the importance of a case.

In the United States, then, parties without resources are less successful in getting the Supreme Court to hear their appeals, although this disadvantage is reduced if they can get support from interest groups or governments. Similarly, in Israel, other than the government that as noted before has been very successful at being heard by the Court, there is some limited evidence of the petitioner's resources making a difference when the Court is deciding whether to hear an appeal. After the government, a corporate petitioner that lost at the lower court to an individual had the highest success rate of being heard by the Supreme Court.[64] Beyond this, however, a party's resources did not appear to influence the Court's decision to hear an appeal.

This resource advantage, however, does not appear to be consistent across high courts, in part potentially due to differences in how courts decide which cases to hear and the number of applications. As we discussed earlier, the Canadian Supreme Court, for example, receives vastly fewer requests to be heard per year than the US Supreme Court, and accepts a much higher percentage of those it does receive. Further, unlike its American counterpart that votes on all certiorari petitions *en banc*, the Canadian Supreme Court votes on petitions in panels of three judges. Flemming argues that these differences mean that Supreme Court of Canada justices do not have to use resources of the petitioner as a cue in their decision to grant or deny leave to appeal, beyond the relative success of the government we noted earlier.[65] Due to the lower volume of cases, justices can obtain and work through enough information to make informed decisions when voting on leave-to-appeal petitions and can rely less on these cues.[66]

Judges, in deciding whether to hear an appeal, then are influenced by the area of law of the appeal and whether it is the government that is asking to be heard. Aside from government success, whether a judge relies on cues depends on how the court decides which cases to hear. Being the stronger party in the case appears to increase a petitioner's chance of being heard in the United States, and to a lesser extent in Israel, though not in Canada, which raises interesting questions about inequality and access to justice. Similarly, the experience of the lawyers involved may influence how likely an appeal is to be heard in different

63. Goelzhauser & Vouvalis, *supra* note 62 at 12–13.

64. Eisenberg et al., "Empirical Study," *supra* note 53 at 719.

65. Flemming, *Tournament of Appeals, supra* note 13 at 57, 59–60.

66. Flemming & Krutz, "Selecting Appeals," *supra* note 42 at 246.

countries such as the United States and India,[67] but does not appear to matter in others such as Canada.[68] Moreover, different judges may respond differently to these cues. For example, liberal justices on the US Supreme Court tended to favor "underdog" litigants, whereas their conservative colleagues had the opposite inclination.[69] Whether or not a court will hear an appeal therefore appears correlated with at least some cues arising in the appeal.

## Simple Ideology: Do I Want to Overturn This Decision?

A judge, however, may not simply want to spot important appeals but to target cases she cares about. She may want to pursue certain appeals in order to satisfy her personal view on particular issues. A liberal judge may, for example, vote to grant a hearing in an appeal because she wants to overturn a lower court decision limiting a union's right to strike, regardless of whether there are any other cues about the appeal's importance. Ulmer argues there may be little difference between the review by a court of whether to hear an appeal on the merits and the review on the merits, as judges essentially decide at the petition stage how they would ultimately dispose of the case.[70] This theory is variously called "simple ideological voting" or "error correction": a judge decides whether the court should hear an appeal on its merits based on her preferences as to whether it is appropriate to "correct" the lower court's ruling.[71] As an example of simple ideological voting, Justices Brennan and Marshall of the US Supreme Court often used "stock" dissents from refusals to grant certiorari in capital punishment cases: "Adhering to our views that the death penalty is in all circumstances cruel and unusual punishment . . . we would grant certiorari and

67. McGuire, *Supreme Court Bar, supra* note 47, n. 13; Mark Galanter & Nick Robinson, "India's Grand Advocates: A Legal Elite Flourishing in the Era of Globalization" (2013) Harvard Law School Program on the Legal Profession Research Paper No. 2013-5.

68. Flemming & Krutz, "Selecting Appeals," *supra* note 42 at 246; Roy Flemming & Glen Krutz, "Repeat Litigators and Agenda Setting on the Supreme Court of Canada" (2002) 35:4 *Canadian Journal of Political Science* 811.

69. S. Sidney Ulmer, "Selecting Cases for Supreme Court Review: An Underdog Model" (1978) 72:3 *American Political Science Review* 902.

70. S. Sidney Ulmer, "The Decision to Grant Certiorari as Indicator to Decision 'On the Merits'" (1972) 4:4 *Polity* 4 429–447 [Ulmer, "Grant Certiorari"].

71. Saul Brenner, "Rational Choice and Supreme Court Decision Making: A Review Essay" (1998) 26:2 *Southeastern Political Review* 361 at 370 (argues that "[v]irtually all Supreme Court scholars maintain that the justices on the Court generally vote in accord with the error-correcting strategy").

vacate the death sentences in these cases."[72] A judge who agrees with and wishes to affirm a lower court ruling would, on the "simple ideological voting" view, have less incentive to vote for the court to hear the appeal as this risks the overturning of a lower court ruling he finds favorable. [73] This view therefore leads to the following hypothesis:

> *H4: A judge who votes in favor of granting leave will be more likely to vote to overturn the lower court's decision during a hearing on the merits.*

High courts overturn lower court decisions at very different rates. In the United States, for example, the Supreme Court has recently tended to reverse about 7 out of every 10 cases it hears.[74] In stark contrast, the Supreme Court of Canada in recent years has tended to affirm more lower court rulings than it has reversed, although in 2013 it affirmed the same number as it reversed.[75] The first five years of the UK Supreme Court has seen the Court affirm a little under half of the appeals it heard.[76] The question is, however, whether judges on a particular court are more likely to agree to hear an appeal when they want to reverse a lower court decision, even taking account of these different overall reversal rates.

The clearest evidence of judges agreeing to hear an appeal in order to reverse it comes from the US Supreme Court. For example, in the 1950, 1952, 1963, 1965,

72. Michael Mello, "Adhering to our Views: Brennan and Marshall and the Relentless Dissent to Death as a Punishment" (1995) 22:3 *Florida State University Law Review* 591 at 693.

73. Songer argues that the persuasive force of cue theory comes from its recognition that judges lack the resources to thoroughly review each petition they receive, and must rely on low-cost informational cues to make their initial assessments. Donald Songer, "Concern for Policy Outputs as a Cue for Supreme Court Decisions" (1971) 41:4 *Journal of Politics* 1185 at 1186. Further, Black and Owens found that US Supreme Court justices vote to hear appeals based both on the policy direction of the decision itself and on whether the lower court judges had similar policy preferences to themselves (that is, if a majority of the justices of the Supreme Court are conservative, they are more likely to review decisions by liberal lower courts, and vice versa): See e.g. Ryan Black & Ryan Owens, "Consider the Source (and the Message): Supreme Court Justices and Strategic Audits of Lower Court Decisions" (2012) 65:2 *Political Research Quarterly* 385 [Black & Owens, "Consider the Source"].

74. In the 2014–2015 term the US Supreme Court reversed 72 percent of lower court decisions. See Kedar Bhatia, "Final Stat Pack for October Term 2014: Merits Cases by Vote Split" (June 30, 2015) *SCOTUSblog* (blog), online: http://sblog.s3.amazonaws.com/wp-content/uploads/2015/07/SB_votesplit_OT14.pdf at 3–4.

75. "Category 4: Appeal Judgements", *Supreme Court of Canada Statistics from 2005 to 2015*, online: http://www.scc-csc.ca/case-dossier/stat/cat4-eng.aspx.

76. UK, HC, *The Supreme Court Annual Reports* (various years) (we used the number of appeals affirmed divided by the number of judgments per year).

1967, 1972, and 1974 terms, US Supreme Court justices who voted to reverse on the merits had voted to agree to hear the appeal over three-quarters of the time, whereas justices who wished to affirm the decision had voted to hear the appeal only about 60 percent of the time.[77] Boucher and Segal found that the error correction hypothesis was correct for the 1946–1952 period (the Vinson Court), concluding that, for most justices, "... the simple desire to reverse a lower court decision is a crucial factor in whether they will vote to grant certiorari."[78] Further, because the Court has been fairly conservative, judges on the Court have been more likely to agree to hear an appeal if the lower court produced a liberal decision than if it was a conservative decision.[79]

Not all cert petitions make for difficult decisions: a small number are very obvious candidates for review, whereas a very large number should clearly be denied. Epstein, Martin, and Segal argue that only in cases with neither strong pulls to grant or deny would the justices' preferences about the lower court's decision come into play.[80] Only for this third category of cases—that are neither cases that should clearly be heard nor clearly ones that should not be heard—did they find liberal justices were more likely to agree to hear conservative lower court decisions, and vice versa. The differences are stark. If the court below reached a liberal decision, a very conservative judge was likely to agree to hear the appeal almost 70 percent of the time whereas an extreme liberal would do so less than 60 percent of the time. It is even clearer with conservative lower court decisions, with the conservative judge being over 20 percent less likely to agree to hear the appeal than the liberal judge.[81]

Justices on the Supreme Court of Canada also appear more likely to agree to hear an appeal if they want to overturn it, although not to the same extent as in the United States. Recall that panels of three justices decide whether

77. Saul Brenner & John F. Krol, "Strategies in Certiorari Voting on the United States Supreme Court" (1989) 51:4 *Journal of Politics* 828 at 833 [Brenner & Krol].

78. Robert Boucher & Jeffrey Segal, "Supreme Court Justices as Strategic Decision Makers: Aggressive Grants and Defensive Denials on the Vinson Court" (1995) 57:3 *Journal of Politics* 824 at 835 [Boucher & Segal]. See also Ulmer, "Grant Certiorari," *supra* note 70 at 440 (finding for 8 of the 11 justices on the Vinson Court (1947–1956) there was a statistically significant relationship between the vote for certiorari and the vote to reverse the decision of the lower court on the merits); Jan Palmer, "An Econometric Analysis of the U.S. Supreme Court's Certiorari Decisions" (1982) 39:3 *Public Choice* 387 at 396 [Palmer] (examining successful petitions from 1947 to 1956 and finding a positive relationship between voting to grant certiorari and voting to reverse the lower court's decision).

79. Epstein et al., "Must Grants," *supra* note 22 at 13.

80. Epstein et al., "Must Grants," *supra* note 22 at 4.

81. Epstein et al., "Must Grants," *supra* note 22 at 18.

the Court will hear an appeal in Canada. We looked for whether justices on a panel that decided whether or not to hear an appeal voted to reverse more frequently than justices who were not on the panel. Taking into account both whether the lower court decision could be termed liberal or conservative and the ideology of the justices, justices who were not on the leave-to-appeal panel voted to reverse the lower court decision about half the time.[82] A justice on the leave panel, on the other hand, was more likely to reverse the appeal on the merits than a justice not on the leave panel, but the difference was small—the justice on the leave panel was about 3 percent more likely to reverse the lower court decision.[83]

Given that there are three justices on the leave-to-appeal panels, we can also look to see if justices on the leave panel vote on the merits differently depending on their personal preferences. We could imagine, for example, that if two justices on the panel were conservatives and the third liberal, that the conservative judges were more likely to reverse an appeal the panel voted to hear on the merits than the third (liberal) judge—their desire to hear a case to overturn it would overcome the reluctance by the liberal judge. This difference does in fact exist, but again the difference is small. When a judge is on the leave panel, and in the majority in terms of policy preferences for that panel (that is, one of either two conservative judges or two liberal judges on the panel), she is about 2.5 percent more likely to reverse the lower court decision than a justice who was not on the leave panel. Conversely, when the justice on the leave-to-appeal panel is in the minority on the panel (that is, the only liberal judge or only conservative judge), he is about 5 percent less likely to reverse the decision of the lower court. Judges in the majority on the leave panel are therefore more likely to agree to hear the appeal in order to reverse it, whereas a judge who is isolated ideologically on the panel does not appear to share that desire to reverse the lower court decision.[84]

Judges, at least on the US Supreme Court, tend to look not only at whether they agreed with the lower court decision but also at who sat on the lower court. Judges are more likely to agree to hear decisions that they disagree with if the decisions are from a court whose judges are ideologically different than from one whose judges are ideologically similar to themselves. For example, a conservative Supreme Court justice is more likely to agree to hear an appeal from a

82. Alarie & Green, "Docket Control," *supra* note 9 at 14–15, 18 (these results were consistent whether the judges' ideology was measured by the party of the prime minister who appointed them, their lifetime liberal voting average, or their lifetime ideal point measures).

83. Alarie & Green, "Docket Control," *supra* note 9 at 18.

84. Alarie & Green, "Docket Control," *supra* note 9 at 19.

liberal decision of a court whose judges are liberal than from a liberal decision by conservative judges. Judges, therefore, appear to pay attention both to the decision and to the judges who made it.[85]

Another way to test this simple ideological or error correction view is to see if judges act differently when hearing appeals that the court has no choice but hear (that is, the appellant has a right to be heard) as opposed to when they have granted leave to appeal. A judge may be no more or less likely to overturn a criminal case he was obliged to hear, but if he has voluntarily chosen to hear it he may be more likely to overturn it. For example, in 2006–2007 the Israeli Supreme Court overturned 25 percent of mandatory criminal appeals (appeals they had to hear) but 45 percent of discretionary criminal cases (cases they could choose to hear or not).[86] Canada had a similar pattern, though a higher affirmation. The Supreme Court of Canada affirmed a little over 60 percent of appeals that it had to hear (appeals as of right) as opposed to affirming just 53 percent of appeals overall and 55 percent of criminal cases for which they granted leave to appeal.[87] If judges do choose appeals in order to correct errors, courts with greater docket control should have higher reversal rates than those that permit appeals as of right.

Overall, the evidence for the error correction hypothesis is stronger in the United States than in Canada. In the United States justices who vote to hear an appeal are more likely to vote to overturn the lower court ruling at the merits stage. Liberal justices are more likely to review decisions coming from conservative lower courts, and to tolerate conservative decisions rendered by liberal lower courts, and vice versa for conservative justices. This tendency to agree to hear decisions that they eventually overturn also exists in Canada, but the effect is much smaller. As we will discuss in the next section, the difference may in part arise because of differences in how the courts decide which cases to hear.[88]

85. Black & Owens, "Consider the Source," *supra* note 73 at 390. Black and Owens found large differences—the probability that a conservative Supreme Court justice, for example, would vote to hear an appeal of a liberal decision fell from 21 percent if the decision was by a liberal lower court to 6 percent if it was a conservative lower court.

86. Eisenberg et al., "Empirical Study," *supra* note 534 at 713–714.

87. These figures are derived from an analysis conducted by the authors of the judgments of the Supreme Court of Canada from 1958 to 2011.

88. Flemming & Krutz, "Selecting Appeals," *supra* note 42 at 246, n. 16 argue that the Supreme Court of Canada is primarily influenced more by jurisprudential factors in deciding whether to hear a case than by party status, judicial preferences, or strategic concerns, in part because the Court hears appeals in panels of differing sizes and compositions, making it difficult to predict how the full Court will decide any appeal on the merits.

## Sophisticated Ideology: Can I Win?

Unfortunately there is a problem at the core of the error correction view of how judges decide which appeals to hear. For the most part, a judge does not advance his interests if he votes for the court to hear an appeal, but then cannot get a majority of judges lined up in favor of his preferred outcome. In deciding whether the Court should hear an appeal, he may therefore consider not only what outcome he would prefer but attempt to predict whether he would be in the majority if the appeal is heard on the merits. This is known as "sophisticated ideological voting" or an "outcome prediction strategy."[89] Being in the majority allows the judge to be in a position to set an important precedent and influence the evolution of legal doctrine.[90]

Judges who wish to affirm a lower court ruling (that is, agree with the result) may be more likely to follow the outcome prediction strategy.[91] They will evaluate the potential costs and benefits of hearing an appeal differently than those who wish to reverse a decision. Although affirming the lower court's decision has the benefit of extending its precedential influence, voting to grant leave to appeal also creates the risk that the court will overturn a favorable result. Affirm-minded justices therefore may choose to strategically make either "aggressive grants" (voting to grant leave in order to affirm the decision) or "defensive denials" (voting not to hear an appeal rather than risk reversal of an agreeable result).[92] For instance, in *Bowers v. Hardwick*, an appeal from a ruling that a law criminalizing sodomy was unconstitutional, the US Supreme Court

89. One of the first scholars to explore certiorari strategies was Glendon Shubert, whose research established that judges vote to grant or deny leave to appeal based on the likeliness of achieving their preferred results at a hearing on the merits. Glendon Schubert, "The Study of Judicial Decision Making as an Aspect of Political Behaviour" (1958) 52:4 *American Political Science Review* 1007 [Schubert, "Study of Judicial"]; see also, Glendon Schubert, "The Certiorari Game" in *Quantitative Analysis of Judicial Behaviour* (Glencoe, Illinois: The Free Press, 1959); Glendon Schubert, "Policy Without Law: An Extension of the Certiorari Game" (1962) 14:2 *Stanford Law Review* 284.

90. A judge may also want to minimize conflict with colleagues, as a more united court may be perceived as more legitimate. We will consider this point in more detail in Chapter 8, as docket control can influence consensual norms.

91. See e.g. Saul Brenner, "The New Certiorari Game" (1979) 41:2 *Journal of Politics* 649 [Brenner, "New Certiorari Game"]; Boucher & Segal, *supra* note 78; Sara C. Benesh, Saul Brenner & Harold J. Spaeth, "Aggressive Grants by Affirm-Minded Justices" (2002) 30:3 *American Politics Research* 219, n. 26 [Benesh et al., "Aggressive Grants"]; see also Gregory Caldeira, John Wright & Christopher Zorn, "Sophisticated Voting and Gate-Keeping in the Supreme Court" (1999) 15:3 *Journal of Law, Economics and Organizations* 549 [Caldeira et al., "Sophisticated Voting"].

92. Benesh et al., "Aggressive Grants," *supra* note 91, n. 26; Boucher & Segal, *supra* note 78, n. 32; Brenner, "New Certiorari Game," *supra* note 91, n. 32.

initially did not have enough votes to grant certiorari, and Justice White wrote a dissent from the denial. Two liberal judges, Justices Brennan and Marshall, then joined White, apparently believing that White wished to affirm the decision to spread its precedential value (an aggressive grant). However, when Justice Rehnquist, a conservative, also joined them, Justice Brennan changed his vote, "presumably because Rehnquist's 'join' made him aware that White was actually pursuing a reversal strategy."[93] Conversely, as the risks of reviewing a disagreeable outcome are less significant, judges who wish to reverse a lower court decision are more likely to follow a simple error-correction strategy. On this theory, then, judges making aggressive grants are most likely to join the majority during the final vote, as they perform the most thorough risk assessments before granting leave to appeal.

For the outcome prediction strategy to work, a judge must be able to make some reasonable prediction of how the court will vote on the merits. She will be better able to predict the outcome where the membership on the court is stable so she is able to build a reasonable assessment of the voting by the other judges. Further, a judge may find the outcome prediction strategy more successful if she is ideologically aligned with the majority of her colleagues and be more willing to grant certiorari than a judge whose preferences conflict with the majority.[94] The existence of stable ideological coalitions may then increase the accuracy of outcome predictions, leading judges to use it more consistently than other strategies.

In addition, to predict outcomes, a judge needs to be able to have a good sense of which judges will hear the appeal, such as on the US Supreme Court, which hears all appeals *en banc*. Judges in other countries may have more difficulty. For example, Flemming and Krutz have argued that strategic concerns do not play a significant role in leave decisions at the Supreme Court of Canada, largely because for each appeal the chief justice decides not only the size of the panel that will hear the appeal but also who will sit on the panel. A judge on the Supreme Court of Canada hearing a petition for leave to appeal will have difficulty predicting how a case will be decided during a full hearing.[95]

93. Lee Epstein & Jack Knight, *The Choices Justices Make* (Washington, DC: CQ Press, 1998) at 61, 122 (a fourth judge eventually joined in, and the Supreme Court went on to reverse the lower court's decision). In another case, *Miller v. California*, 413 U.S. 15 (1973), the US Supreme Court upheld laws banning certain sexually explicit works. For a subsequent case, *Lilies v. Oregon*, 425 U.S. 963 (1976) (in which a lower court followed *Miller*, Justice Stevens voted to deny certiorari, saying that "[r]egardless of how I might vote on the merits after full argument, it would be pointless to grant certiorari in case after case of this character only to have *Miller* reaffirmed time after time").

94. Caldeira et al., "Sophisticated Voting," *supra* note 91 at 566, n. 32.

95. Flemming & Krutz, "Selecting Appeals," *supra* note 42 at 235, n. 16.

However, hearing appeals in panels may not mean the outcome prediction strategy is invalid for a court. For the Israeli Supreme Court, final outcomes seem to reflect the same preferences as leave-to-appeal decisions, despite the Court's use of small panels, as the desire to reverse a lower court decision is an important factor in granting of leave.[96]

Judges' votes during leave decisions may therefore rest on strategic factors that reflect their unique institutional constraints. We will therefore examine the following hypothesis:

> *H7: Judges who vote to grant review are more likely to be in the majority during a hearing on the merits, particularly if the lower court decision accords with their personal views.*

On this view, a justice first determines her preferred outcome for a given case, then the probability of such a resolution carrying the day, given the composition of the court as a whole, and only then decides whether to vote to grant or to deny certiorari—voting to grant only when the justice is reasonably confident that her preferred outcome will be the resolution on the merits. For this strategy to work, the justices must have sufficient familiarity with their colleagues' inclinations to enable them to predict how they will vote on the merits.[97]

Although justices of the US Supreme Court do pay attention to non-strategic cues or signals, whether or not they agree to hear an appeal is related to outcome on the merits. Caldeira, Wright, and Zorn, for example, examining the 1968, 1982, and 1990 terms found that if a judge voted to hear an appeal, he would be significantly more likely to be in the majority.[98] Further, Brenner and Krol found that justices who both voted to reverse and won on the merits voted for cert almost 80 percent of the time, compared to about 40 percent for those who lost on the

96. Eisenberg et al., "Case Selection," *supra* note 14, n. 8; Eisenberg et al., "Case Selection," *supra* note 14 ("[w]ith respect to both criminal and civil cases, the table offers evidence that disagreement with the ruling in the district court is an important criterion in referring cases for all justices. Full reversal occurs in over 65 percent of both criminal and civil cases reviewed on the merits" at 196).

97. Caldeira, Wright & Zorn, "Unified Model," *supra* note 62 at 4, note ("for justices to vote strategically on certiorari, they require some reasonably good idea of the likely outcome of a particular case should that case reach the merits. If this is the case, and if justices both have and use this information in making their certiorari decisions, then justices who vote for certiorari should ceteris paribus, be more likely to be on the winning side on the merits").

98. Caldeira, Wright & Zorn, "Unified Model," *supra* note 62 at 5 (this effect remains even when controlling for the ideology of the judges). See also Schubert, "Study of Judicial," *supra* note 89; Palmer, *supra* note 78 at 396.

merits and voted to affirm, whereas no such pattern occurred when the grant rates of reverse-minded judges who won were compared with those who lost.[99]

Another way to test whether a judge is predicting outcomes when she is deciding whether the court should hear the appeal is to look at how she fits in with the rest of the court. Caldeira, Wright, and Zorn, for example, found that on a conservative court, the more liberal a given justice is, the less likely he is to vote to grant certiorari. Conversely, on a liberal court, increasing liberalism of a justice is positively correlated with the net probability of voting to grant certiorari.[100] Thus a conservative judge on a conservative court votes to hear appeals at a much higher rate than when on a very liberal court—as would a liberal judge on a liberal court.[101] They argued that these findings supported the existence of sophisticated voting amongst justices, be they liberal or conservative.[102]

Although justices on the US Supreme Court seem to act strategically when deciding whether to hear an appeal, Canadian Supreme Court justices do not. If we look at the Supreme Court of Canada in the period 1984 to 2011, justices on the panel deciding whether to grant leave were no more likely to be in the majority on the merits than justices who were not on the leave panel.[103] Further, it makes no difference if a judge on the three-justice leave panel is sitting with other justices with the same preferences or with different preferences—a conservative justice, for example, is no more likely to be in the majority on the merits decision than a justice not on the leave panel, whether or not the panel included one or two other conservative justices or two liberal justices. As a result, Canadian justices do not appear to decide whether to grant leave based on their assessment of whether their preferred outcome will win on the merits.[104]

To summarize, US Supreme Court justices appear to base their decision on whether the Court should hear an appeal at least in part on whether they feel their views will win when the case is heard, particularly if they want to affirm the lower court decision. Affirm-minded justices risk much more than

99. See also Brenner & Krol, *supra* note 77 at 833; Brenner, "New Certiorari Game," *supra* note 91 at 653–654; Boucher & Segal, *supra* note 78 at 831 (finding each justice on the Vinson Court was significantly less likely to vote for cert when he eventually voted to affirm the lower court's decision, although there was evidence that justices would take a chance and grant cert if they had a high level of support from other members of the Court).

100. Caldeira et al., "Sophisticated Voting," *supra* note 91 at 564.

101. Caldeira et al., "Sophisticated Voting," *supra* note 91 at 565.

102. Caldeira et al., "Sophisticated Voting," *supra* note 91 at 566.

103. Alarie & Green, "Docket Control," *supra* note 9 at 20.

104. Alarie & Green, "Docket Control," *supra* note 9 at 24.

reverse-minded justices when voting to grant cert, and thus have more incentive to employ strategic voting. Canadian Supreme Court justices, on the other hand, do not appear to vote strategically. A key difference between the Canadian and American Supreme Courts may lie in institutional design choices. It is more difficult to game the system in Canada. Unlike in the United States where all justices hear the merits decision, a justice on the Supreme Court of Canada has to predict not only how particular justices will vote, but also the chief justice's choice of both the size and composition of the panel that will ultimately hear the decision on the merits.[105]

## WHICH FACTORS MATTER?

Judges take into account a wide range of factors in deciding whether the court should hear an appeal—workload, signals of the importance of the appeal, and the judge's view of the preferred outcome all seem to play a role. As we discussed earlier, these factors may all play a role but to a different extent depending on the appeal. All judges can agree that some cases must be heard whereas the vast majority clearly ought to be denied review; it is the middle category between these groups that sparks debate.[106] For petitions to the US Supreme Court with strong anti-grant or pro-grant factors, a judge's ideology did not affect his decision on whether the Court should hear the appeal. Only for those petitions with few compelling reasons to either grant or deny a hearing (*i.e.*, in the middle category) is there evidence of ideological voting.[107]

This mixed influence of factors is consistent with other studies. Cordray and Cordray, for example, found that justices on the US Supreme Court who voted together most frequently on the merits also tended to vote together on certiorari. However, the great majority of justices agreed with each other less often on certiorari votes than they did on the merits.[108] Of petitions granted certiorari unanimously, over a quarter resulted in 5-4 decisions on the merits, meaning

105. Flemming & Krutz, "Selecting Appeals," *supra* note 42 at 235 argue that Canadian Supreme Court justices cannot act strategically because this prediction is too difficult. See also Alarie & Green, "Docket Control," *supra* note 9 at 25; Flemming, *Tournament of Appeals, supra* note 13 at 85.

106. Epstein et al., "Must Grants," *supra* note 22 at 4.

107. For such petitions, for example, if the court below reached a liberal decision, the predicted grant probability for a very conservative justice was 67 percent; for an extreme liberal, the rate was 58 percent. Epstein et al., "Must Grants," *supra* note 22 at 18.

108. Richard Cordray & Margaret Cordray, "Strategy in Supreme Court Case Selection: The Relationship between Certiorari and the Merits" (2008) 69:1 *Ohio State Law Journal* 1 at 2–3 [Cordray & Cordray, "Strategy"].

that many of the justices probably voted to hear the case without being confident in advance of winning on the merits. Conversely, for petitions granted with just the minimum number of four cert votes, the Court was unanimous about one-third of the time on the merits. In these cases five of the justices voted against granting cert, even though they might have foreseen a high probability of being in the majority on the merits. Cordray and Cordray argue that it is unlikely that the justices simply misjudged their colleagues' likely voting behavior in so many instances; they suggest, rather, that these differences between the vote on whether to hear the appeal and the decision on the merits indicate justices having a strong sense of the Court's institutional responsibility to hear certain cases unrelated to their chances of success on the merits.[109]

Whether a judge will attend to different factors will depend on how the particular court is designed: how many judges a court has, whether it hears appeals in panels, and whether all judges are involved in deciding which appeals to hear. It is also related to how judges are appointed. How judges feel about their roles—whether it is permissible to consider their own views on the outcome, for example—and whether they can follow their own views will depend on who gets appointed to the court and how. Consider the US Supreme Court again. Owens and Simon argue that as justices on the Court become more ideologically dispersed, they will decide fewer cases. When justices hold divergent ideological interests—as on the current Court—they face challenges in achieving desired outcomes, which often results in "fractured relations, lethargy, and stalemate."[110] When justices are ideologically alike, the Court will grant cert to between 145 and 190 cases, but when the Court becomes ideologically divided, it will permit only 102 to 147 cases.[111] The justices are both less willing to agree on which cases to hear and potentially less able to predict the outcome on the merits. Justices on the Supreme Court of Canada may also face this difficulty with prediction, not only because the chief justice can vary who and how many judges sit on the merits decision, but because the justices are less clearly ideologically aligned than in the United States.

We will return to how judges perceive their role and relationship with other judges in Chapter 8 when we examine the role of norms on different high courts. Before we get there, however, there is one more key difference in the rules across high courts: who gets to argue appeals before the judges?

109. Cordray & Cordray, "Strategy," *supra* note 108 at 28–29.

110. Owens & Simon, *supra* note 31 at 1265.

111. Owens & Simon, *supra* note 31 at 1277.

7

# The Influence of the Parties on Judges

## *Accuracy or Affiliation?*

We have seen that high courts differ across appointment processes, the use of panels, and how they choose cases to hear. Once a case is before a court and the panel is chosen, the judges must react to the facts of the case before them and the relevant law. They are also faced with the parties involved in the dispute—most obviously the appellants and the respondents. However, the judges may also hear from parties who want to join in the appeal to help one side or the other by providing a broader perspective or alternate viewpoint—such as an environmental group seeking to participate in an appeal in order to help the court understand the long-term implications of a broader or narrower interpretation of environmental legislation.

At first glance, judges appear to be influenced more by some parties than others. Take the litigants themselves—those who are appealing or responding to the appeal. It turns out that, among the different types of parties that might be involved in an appeal—such as the government, businesses, other groups (such as environmental groups) and individuals—the government tends to win appeals more than other parties. Figure 7-1 shows the percentage of cases in which each group won at high courts (whether as appellant or respondent) in the period from 1970 to the early 2000s. In Canada, for example, the federal government won over 60 percent of appeals it was involved in compared to less than 40 percent for individuals.[1] In the United States the government's advantage was similar—with the federal government prevailing in 60 percent

1. Peter McCormick, *Canada's Courts* (Toronto: J. Lorimer, 1994) at 164 has the government winning 62 percent of the time and individuals 44 percent of the time [McCormick, *Canada's Courts*].

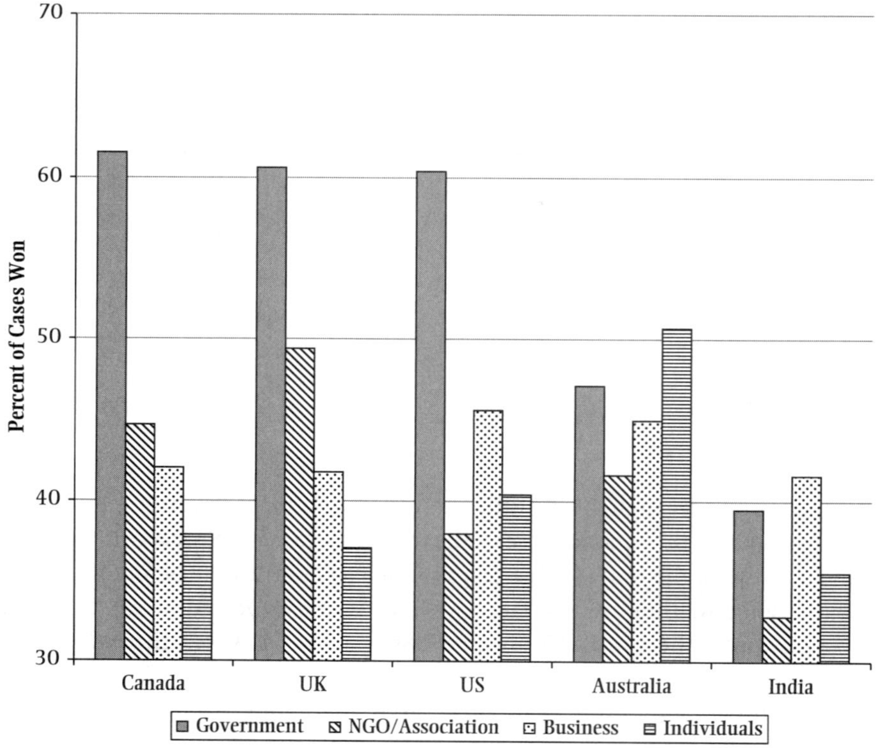


**Figure 7-1** Percentage of Cases That the Party Wins, 1970 to early 2000s. These win rates are calculated by dividing the number of cases in which the group was successful by the total number of cases in which the group was involved on one side. These win rates exclude cases in which both the appellants and respondents are members of the group (for example, the win rate for individuals does not include cases in which both the appellants and respondents are individuals). Government tends to have a high win rate relative to other parties and individuals a relatively low win rate, with Australia being an outlier in terms of individuals.
SOURCE: High Courts Judicial Database.

of the appeals it was involved in and individuals only 40 percent.[2] In fact in all countries except Australia, the government was very successful before the high court and individuals much less so. Why is there this difference across different groups? Is there something about the party that influences the judges?

At the same time as the judges deal with different groups as the litigants, they face an increasing number of other parties who want to give them information

2. Reginald S. Sheehan, William Mishler & Donald R. Songer, "Ideology, Status, and the Differential Success of Direct Parties before the Supreme Court" (1992) 86:2 *American Political Science Review* 464 at 465 [Sheehan et al., "Ideology"].

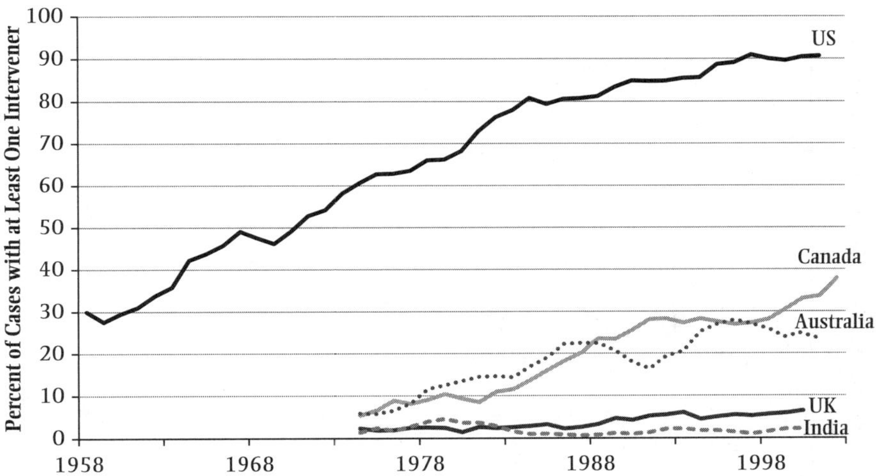


**Figure 7-2** Percent of cases with at least one intervener. We used a five-year rolling average of the number of cases with at least one intervener per year, in order to smooth out the trends. The proportion of cases with interveners increased in all countries during this period, though by the end of the period still only a small percentage of cases involved interveners in India and the UK. By the early 2000s, about 90 percent of cases before the US Supreme Court involved at least one intervener.
SOURCE: High Courts Judicial Database.

on the appeal. Figure 7-2 shows the tremendous rise in the number of cases where groups intervene who are not the direct parties. These parties are called different things in different countries—for example, interveners in Canada and amicus curiae in the United States.[3] We will generally refer to them as interveners. Canada and the United States most freely allow interveners to participate and have seen the greatest increase, though by 2000 the proportion of cases with interveners in Canada only reached the level of the United States in the early 1960s. However, the number of interveners has gone up in all countries to some extent. Moreover, the number of interveners per case has gone up in most countries, as we can see in Figure 7-3. The question is whether judges are influenced by this flood of interveners, and if so, how?

3. Note that for the intervener numbers in this chapter and in all other analysis in the book, the Spaeth database did not have information on interveners (Harold J. Spaeth et al. 2016, Supreme Court Database, Version 2016 Release 01. online: http://Supremecourtdatabase.org [Spaeth database]). As a result, we relied on the HCJD (Stacia L. Haynie et al. (2007) High Courts Judicial Database. Accessed at the University of South Carolina Judicial Research Initiative, online: www.cas.sc.edu/poli/juri [HCJD]) for this information.

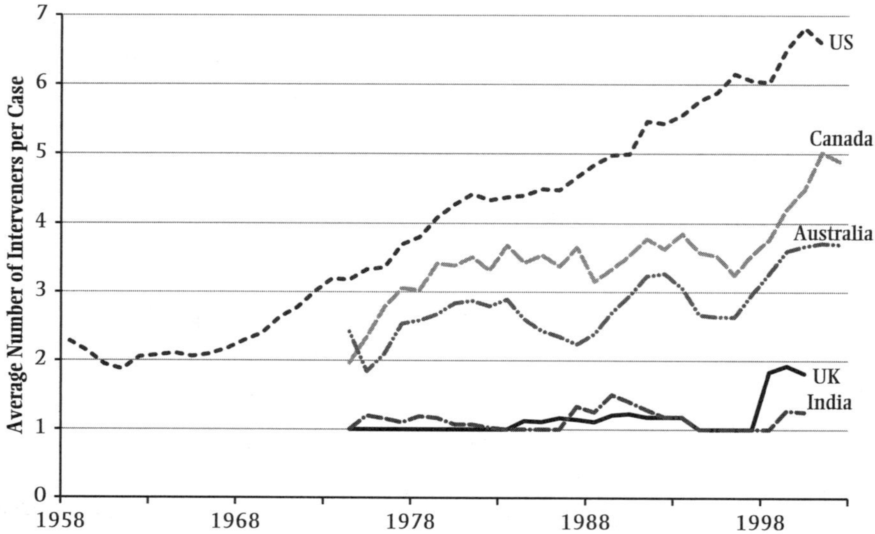


**Figure 7-3** Average number of interveners in cases with at least one intervener. We used a five-year rolling average of the number of interveners per case with at least one intervener, in order to smooth out the trends. The United States again led with the most interveners per case. Canada and Australia also saw large increases in the average number of interveners over the period.

These different parties may sway judges in various ways but two are central—*accuracy* and *affiliation*. A judge may be influenced in a particular direction by a party because she feels that party more likely leans toward the correct result—a more accurate outcome. She may believe that having a party she sees as credible on one side makes that side more likely to provide the better answer. A judge may have a good idea, for example, for how well reasoned decisions are from judges from her home province or state. Alternatively, she may be getting more or better information from certain parties, independent of her feelings about these parties.

A judge may, on the other hand, be pushed in a direction by certain parties because she feels an affiliation with those parties. She may, for example, share a taste for conservation values with an environmental group or for freedom from government influence with a libertarian group. She may lean in favor of an underdog such as a poor individual, regardless of the quality of the case or information coming from that party. She may be swayed by a connection with litigants she knows or who come from the same place.

Before we examine how judges take into account accuracy and affiliation in their dealings with different parties, we first need to lay out briefly how the different parties may be included in appeals on the various high courts.

## WHO IS BEFORE THE COURT?

The high courts we have been looking at mainly hear appeals from lower courts. These courts may be courts of appeal with national scope, such as the Federal Court of Appeal in Canada that hears most matters relating to the federal government's use of its powers. Others may be more geographically based, as is the case for the UK Supreme Court, which hears appeals from courts in England, Wales, Northern Ireland, and to some extent Scotland.[4] When hearing appeals, then, high court judges will be reacting to how other judges have viewed the case. Not all decisions of high courts, however, are on appeals. Some high courts are also the first court to hear certain cases. For example, the Israeli Supreme Court is the first court to hear administrative law matters, and the Indian Supreme Court the first court to address cases involving certain fundamental rights and disputes between the federal and state governments.[5]

Perhaps not surprisingly, individuals appear most as parties before high courts, with the exception of the United States. Figure 7-4 shows the percentage of cases involving the different groupings of parties. Individuals quite starkly lead the pack as appellants in all countries, with businesses also bringing a high percentage of appeals. Government's involvement is most prominent as a respondent in high court cases, responding to appeals more than any other party. Individuals and businesses also respond but in general to a much lesser extent. Overall, individuals play a particularly active role in India where they make up the largest percentage of appellants and act as respondents to a greater extent than in the other countries.[6]

As we saw, judges hear not only from the direct litigants but from other parties who want to intervene in the appeal. The various high courts tolerate interveners to very different degrees. In the United States, the Court is extremely lenient in allowing third parties to intervene. It allows for "essentially unlimited

4. Chris Hanretty, "Lumpers and Splitters on the United Kingdom Supreme Court" (2013) American Political Science Association 2013 Annual Meeting Paper, at 4 [Hanretty, "Lumpers and Splitters"], the exception being certain criminal appeals from Scotland.

5. Yoav Dotan, "Do the 'Haves' Still Come Out Ahead? Resource Inequalities in Ideological Courts: The Case of the Israeli High Court of Justice" (1999) 33:4 *Law & Society Review* 1059 at 1061 [Dotan, "Resource Inequalities"]. For India, see *The Constitution of India 1950*, art. 131.

6. The Spaeth database, *supra* note 3, does not provide comparable information. Instead it provides the type of the primary party listed (as opposed to the number of each type of party whether or not listed first). If we use the Spaeth database for the United States and look at the percentage of cases where each type of party is first listed, we obviously find lower percentages: of appellants, individuals make up 28.9 percent, business 14.6 percent, government 38.8 percent, and private non-profits 1 percent whereas of respondents, individuals comprise 34.8 percent, business 13.5 percent, government 33.1 percent, and private non-profits 1.5 percent.

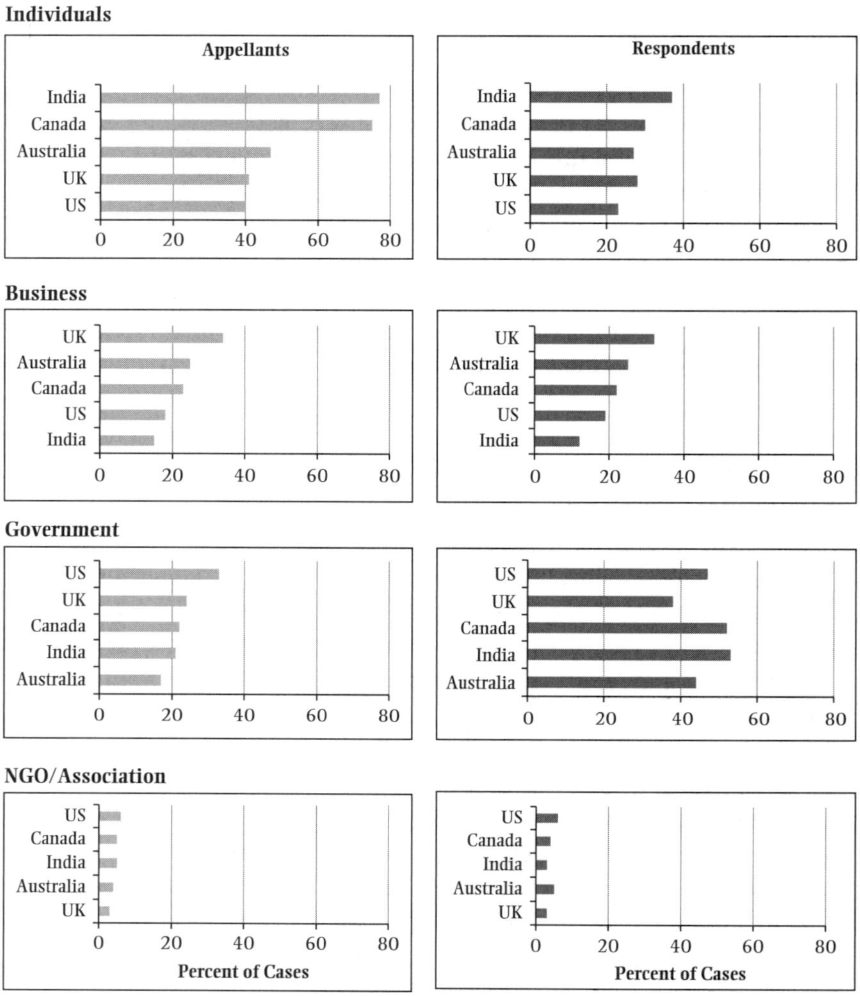


**Figure 7-4** Percentage of cases of different parties as appellant and respondent, 1970 to the early 2000s. Individuals by far appealed the most whereas governments were most often the respondents. These percentages were based on the number of decisions with at least one of the particular type of appellant or respondent for all countries.
SOURCE: HCJD.

amicus participation."[7] A private party such as an individual or business seeking to intervene must obtain the agreement of the parties to the appeal. If those parties refuse, it may ask the Court for permission to join in. In practice, the

7. Paul M. Collins, Jr, *Friends of the Supreme Court: Interest Groups and Judicial Decision Making* (New York: Oxford University Press, 2008) at 45 [Collins].

Court almost always gives permission.[8] The solicitor general and certain other government representatives do not need permission to intervene in an appeal.[9] Figure 7-2 shows that the result of the lenient approach has been a striking growth in interventions.[10]

For the high courts in Canada,[11] the UK,[12] India,[13] Israel,[14] and Australia,[15] a party seeking to intervene in an appeal must go straight to the Court for permission. In general the party must identify its position on a relevant issue, and set out why it would be helpful to the Court to allow the party to

8. See *Rules of the Supreme Court of the United States* (2010), Rule 37(b), online: http://www.supremecourt.gov/ctrules/2010RulesoftheCourt.pdf. See also Collins, *supra* note 7 at 42.

9. The solicitor general on behalf of the federal government, by an authorized representative of an agency of the United States, by an attorney general on behalf of a state, or by an authorized law officer on behalf of a city or smaller entity do not need permission to file an amicus brief.

10. The South African Constitutional Court and Supreme Court have very similar rules to the United States, with the intervener needing to seek permission of the parties first, and if that is refused, permission of the chief justice. See *Rules of the Constitutional Court* (S Afr) 2003, Rule 10; *Rules of the Supreme Court of Appeal* (S Afr) 1998, Rule 16. In one of the first cases before the South African Constitutional Court, deciding the constitutionality of the death penalty, the president of the Court, Chaskalson J., took the initiative to invite a variety of potential interveners on each side of the issue to participate in the case. George Williams, "The Amicus Curiae and Intervener in the High Court of Australia: A Comparative Analysis" (2000) 28 *Federal Law Review* 365 at 374 [Williams, "Amicus Curiae"].

11. *Rules of the Supreme Court of Canada*, SOR/2002-156 [*Rules of the SCC*] (states that "any person interested in an application for leave to appeal or a reference may make a motion for intervention to a judge", r 55). Under *Rules of the SCC, supra* note 11, r 57(2), a motion for intervention must identify the intervener's position with respect to the issue, and set out the submissions and the reasons for believing they will be useful. Justice Sopinka softened the test for intervention by declaring that *any* interest would be sufficient to satisfy the test: *Reference re Workers' Compensation Act, 1983 (Nfld.)* [1989] 2 SCR 335.

12. *Rules of the SCC, supra* note 11 (dealing with intervention during a petition to appeal, states that "any person and in particular (a) any official body or non-governmental organization seeking to make submissions in the public interest or (b) any person with an interest in proceedings by way of judicial review may make written submissions to the Court in support of an application for permission to appeal" at r 15(1)). In similar terms, *Rules of the SCC, supra* note 11, r 26(1) allows for intervention during an appeal as well.

13. *Code of Civil Procedure 1908*, Order I, Rule 8A, Supreme Court of India [*Civil Procedure* India].

14. Israel's intervention procedures arise from case law: Israel Doron & Manal Totry-Jubran, "Too Little, Too Late? An American Amici in an Israeli Court" (2005) 19 *Temp. International & Comp LJ* 105 at 112–114 [Doron & Totry-Jubran].

15. *High Court Rules 2004* (Cth), r 44.04. New Zealand is similar. Intervention at the New Zealand High Court is not codified, but Clark argues the Court's power to allow intervention would stem from "the inherent jurisdiction of a court to request assistance in its deliberations

intervene. Some courts have an explicit test that must be met, such as the Supreme Court of India where the Court must be satisfied that "it is necessary in the public interest to allow" the party to state its opinions.[16]

As Figure 7-2 shows, despite these similarities in the rules, interveners take part at very different rates across the high courts. The Supreme Court of Canada grants leave to intervene very frequently, and "interveners have been active at an unprecedented level."[17] Similarly, interventions rose in the 1990s in the UK, but rates are still much lower than in Canada and the United States.[18] In Australia, the rates of interventions also rose, with Justice Kenny noting that interveners are rare, but should be allowed in cases where they have "more than mere intellectual or emotional concern."[19] The Indian Supreme Court, on the other hand, had very low rates of interventions.

## ACCURACY OR AFFILIATION?

How does a judge react to the parties in front of her? Does she decide based on which side clearly has the stronger arguments, more information, and better advocates—or does she side with the party with whom she feels an affiliation? It is likely some combination of the two—although some judges may be clinical in separating out any personal views, others may be almost irrationally blinded to the weakness of their side.

### Accuracy

Some parties may be able to provide judges with better information and arguments, all other things being equal. Galanter, for example, argued that parties

from members of the legal profession." Edward Clark, "The Needs of the Many and the Needs of the Few: A New System of Public Interest Intervention for New Zealand" (2005) 36 *Victoria University of Wellington Law Review* 71 at 76, 81, n. 23.

16. *Civil Procedure* India, *supra* note 13, Order I, Rule 8A.

17. Benjamin Alarie & Andrew Green, "Interventions at the Supreme Court of Canada: Accuracy, Affiliation, and Acceptance" (2010) 48 *Osgoode Hall LJ* 381 at 382 [Alarie & Green, "Interventions"].

18. Lorne Neudorf, "Intervention at the UK Supreme Court" (2013) 2:1 *Cambridge Journal of International and Comparative Law* 16, at 24.

19. Susan Kenny, "Interveners and Amici Curiae in the High Court" (1997) 1 *Federal Judicial Scholarship* (arguing that "[f]or interveners the test should be whether the 'special interests' of the applicant are, or are likely to be, affected by a decision in the proceeding. For amici, the test should be whether the applicant has some expertise, knowledge, information, or other insight which is not available to the parties and which is likely to assist the Court in arriving at a correct determination").

with greater or superior resources (the "haves") are more likely to win than those with fewer or inferior resources (the "have-nots").[20] It is not only wealth that matters. As Wheeler et al. note, "the greater resources of stronger parties presumably confer advantages beyond hiring better lawyers on appeal. Larger organizations may be more experienced and thus better able to conform their behaviour to the letter of the law or to build a better trial court record, matters on which we have no evidence. Experience and wealth also imply the capacity to be more selective in deciding which cases to appeal or defend when the lower court loser appeals."[21] On this view, governments would fare better than businesses, and businesses better than individuals, based on the relative resources of each type of party.[22]

Further, as experience itself is a kind of resource, litigants who are repeat players—that is, have been before the court before—should have an advantage. The expectation is that repeat players should win more consistently than "one-shotters." Repeat players may have an informational advantage as they may know better what kind of information judges want to hear. It is not an entirely clear story, however. Repeat players may also benefit from affiliation, which we will discuss later, in that judges learn to recognize and agree with certain parties or counsel over time. Either way, the government should be the most powerful repeat player, not only because it is frequently involved in litigation, but also because it has the expertise required to "self-select" the cases that are most likely to succeed.

Which groups are successful in front of a high court may change over time. In Canada, for instance, after the advent of the *Charter* in 1982, the status of individuals before the court was fundamentally changed in cases relating to fundamental rights and freedoms. Any change over time in a party's success will have to take account of changes in law in determining whether particular litigants—individuals, businesses, government—have become more or less successful, and whether that success is attributable to their inherent characteristics or to evolving societal norms.[23]

The alternate view, apart from the affiliation story we will discuss below, is that inequality of party resources should not matter in appellate courts. By the time the appeal reaches the highest level, the cases should be evenly matched

20. Marc Galanter, "Why the 'Haves' Come Out Ahead: Speculations on the Limits of Legal Change" (1974) 9 *Law & Society Review* 95 [Galanter, "Come Out Ahead"].

21. Stanton Wheeler et al., "Do the 'Haves' Come out Ahead? Winning and Losing in State Supreme Courts, 1870–1970" (1987) 21:3 *Law & Society Review* 21 403 at 441 [Wheeler et al.].

22. Donald R. Songer, *The Transformation of the Supreme Court of Canada: An Empirical Examination* (Toronto: University of Toronto Press, 2008) at 86 [Songer, *Transformation*].

23. See Songer, *Transformation, supra* note 22 for a discussion of the influences on the Supreme Court of Canada over time.

(or else the parties would have settled out of court).[24] Smyth further suggests the opposite of Galanter's thesis, namely that the *weaker* party should win in some situations. The party with more resources may have other motives than just winning the particular case: "testing the waters" for future cases, or appealing as a delaying tactic. Further, stronger parties may be less selective in which cases to litigate if they have ways to keep costs low.[25]

A party's resources include the money it can put toward gathering information and hiring counsel. However, parties may rely not only on their own resources but also on those of interveners. A party backed by an intervener, or more interveners than the other side, may have more information, more sophisticated (or at least more) arguments, and greater persuasive power. For instance, in the leading American case of *Mapp v. Ohio,* the Supreme Court adopted an argument that had been submitted only by the American Civil Liberties Union as an amicus, not by the parties, that the Constitution requires the exclusion of illegally seized evidence in criminal trials.[26] Comparing across parties to see if judges are influenced by resources therefore needs to take account of any added help from interveners.

The first question to ask then is whether parties with greater resources win more, all other things being equal: Does the government generally fare better than businesses, and do businesses generally fare better than individuals? All other things being equal means in particular that judges are more likely to vote for the party with the greater resources, even taking into account any affiliation the judge may have with the parties—for example, that a judge would be more likely to vote for a business than an individual pursuing the same argument regardless of whether the judge had a conservative or liberal orientation. We would expect some variation in the power of resources from country to country, and even from court to court within a single country.[27] We therefore will look to see if:

> *H1: Judges are more likely to vote in favor of the litigant with the greatest resources including number of interveners, controlling for the judge's personal preferences.*

24. Russell Smyth, "The 'Haves' and the 'Have Nots': An Empirical Study of the Rational Actor and Party Capability Hypothesis in the High Court 1948–99" (2000) 35:2 *Australian Journal of Political Science* 255 at 257 [Smyth, "The 'Haves' and the 'Have Nots' "].

25. Smyth, "The 'Haves' and the 'Have Nots,'" *supra* note 24 at 257.

26. Williams, "Amicus Curiae," *supra* note 10 at 376.

27. In the Tax Court of Canada, for instance, resources matter a great deal. See Benjamin Alarie & Andrew James Green, "Policy Preferences and Expertise in Canadian Tax Adjudication" (2014) 62:4 *Canadian Tax Journal* 985.

## Affiliation

If a judge is influenced more by affiliation than accuracy, she likely takes some signal of like-mindedness from the party, and at least in part bases her decision on that signal. The easiest example is a conservative judge voting in favor of a party with conservative leanings. A judge who has worked in the government may favor the government's position, or a former defense lawyer may tend to find for the accused. A judge from Nebraska may be more likely to favor a litigant from that state or neighboring states. In each case, of course, it will be necessary to separate out other factors that influence voting, such as the party's resources or the government's ability to select stronger cases to appeal.

Judges may not only feel an affiliation with the direct litigants but with the interveners. Judges may allow interveners in order to improve the accuracy of their decisions—because the interveners are thought to add some value in terms of information or perspective to what the parties would otherwise argue. However, a judge may also use interveners as either sources of information about the outcome that best suits their personal views or of arguments to support their preferred outcome.[28]

If judges are influenced by affiliation, voting may be more extreme as interveners may push judges toward preferred policy positions. For example, on a court evenly split with left-leaning and right-leaning judges, interveners on each side may make it more difficult for these judges to find agreement, as they are encouraged to move in different directions. In countries with a more lenient intervener process, such as the United States and Canada, interveners may then generate disharmony on the bench.[29] Other countries, such as Australia, may only allow interveners where the court anticipates that the intervener will be of significant assistance in deciding the case correctly.[30]

28. Alarie & Green, "Interventions", *supra* note 17 at 383 (arguing that judges may use interveners to improve accuracy or as a source of information to further views they wish to be affiliated with, but may also allow interveners so these parties feel they have had their voices heard by the court and the public (which Alarie and Green call "acceptance")). See also Joseph D. Kearney & Thomas W. Merrill, "The Influence of Amicus Curiae Briefs on the Supreme Court" (2000) 148:3 *University of Pennsylvania Law Review* 743 at 747–748 [Kearney & Merrill, "Influence"] (arguing that interveners may be providing new information and legal arguments to the judges (a legalist view), providing information about how different groups in society would react to a particular decision (an interest group theory) or not influencing judges at all as they have fixed positions (an attitudinal view)).

29. See also Collins, *supra* note 7 at 173.

30. Simone Cusack & Cecilia Riebl, "International Human Rights Law in Australian Courts: A Role for Amici Curiae and Interveners" (2006) 31 *Alternative Law Journal* 122 at 124.

Thus interveners may have a greater effect in those few cases, but a lesser effect overall.[31]

If on the other hand judges rely on interveners for high quality information rather than as signals of affiliation, the ideology or personal views of the judges should not be connected to the ideology or other markers of policy views of the interveners. Judges may in such cases be open to persuasion by information. Relatedly, interveners may help judges minimize mistakes by providing additional information.[32] Judges will likely rely on interveners for both accuracy and affiliation, depending on the country, the time period, and the ideological complexion of the court, among other factors.

Following on the idea that judges decide partly from affiliation with parties before them, we will examine the following hypothesis: [33]

> *H2: Judges will tend to vote in line with like-minded parties, whether litigants or interveners.*

## HOW DO JUDGES RELATE TO THE LITIGANTS?

In theory then there are two very different ways in which judges may take into account the litigants in front of them—as clear-eyed calculators taking in the best information from whatever source, or as loyal followers searching for signals of which party represents their preferred view. The truth likely lies in a mix and

31. Interestingly, because interveners in Australia submit their petition for leave to appeal at the same time as their submissions in case leave is granted, they might influence the justices even if leave is denied. In *Attorney-General (Cth) v Breckler* [1999] HCA 28; 197 CLR 83, an intervener was denied leave to appeal, but Justice Kirby stated that "We have, of course, received [their] written submissions, and I have read them, and I will find that difficult to put out of my mind." Williams, "Amicus Curiae," *supra* note 10 at 389–390.

32. Doron & Totry-Jubran, *supra* note 14 at 117–118.

33. A judge may also consider affiliation with the lower court judges who made the decision being appealed. See e.g. Russell Smyth & Vinod Mishra, "The Transmission of Legal Precedent across the Australian State Supreme Courts over the Twentieth Century" (2011) 45:1 *Law & Society Review* 139; Peter McCormick & Tammy Praskach, "Judicial Citation, the Supreme Court of Canada, and the Lower Courts: A Statistical Overview and the Influence of Manitoba" (1996) 24 *Manitoba Law Journal* 335. A judge may, for example, be more likely to affirm decisions from judges who sit in her home state or province—what McCormick refers to as the "homer" effect. Peter McCormick, "Judicial Citation, The Supreme Court of Canada, and the Lower Courts: The Case of Alberta" (1996) 34:4 *Alberta Law Review* 870 at 888. Similarly, the judge may be more willing to agree with lower court judges with whom she shares views about policy—such as a conservative judge being more likely to affirm a decision by a conservative lower court. This affiliation effect may also relate to prior courts as where a conservative judge is more likely to cite conservative precedent or potentially decisions by other conservative judges. See Anthony Niblett & Albert H. Yoon, "Friendly Precedent" (February 21, 2015) [unpublished], online: http://ssrn.com/abstract=2268707 (discussing citation practices and ideology).

may vary depending on how the particular court is set up or who is on the court. Looking across high courts, a few similarities emerge.

## Judges Are More Likely to Vote in Favor of the Litigant with the Greatest Resources, Sometimes

As we saw in Figure 7-1, looking just at which parties win more before courts, some patterns emerge. In the United States, Canada, and the UK in the period 1970 to the early 2000s, resources appear to matter—government wins more than businesses, which win more than associations, which in turn win more than individuals. The relative win rates are strikingly similar. Government wins about 60 percent of the time it is involved in an appeal whereas individuals do only a little less than 40 percent. In other countries, however, although government still does relatively well, its success rate is less than 50 percent and some other party does even better. For India, for example, the government is successful only around 40 percent of the time, and businesses have a slightly higher success rate. Individuals in Australia are the most successful, winning about 50 percent of the time with government slightly behind with about a 45 percent success rate.

This story of resources is consistent with the existing empirical work on how judges on particular high courts respond to different types of litigants.[34]

34. For US studies, see e.g. Wheeler et al., *supra* note 21; Donald J. Farole, Jr, "Reexamining Litigant Success in State Supreme Courts" (1999) 33:4 *Law & Society Review* 1043 [Farole]; Donald R. Songer, Reginald S. Sheehan & Susan Brodie Haire, "Do the 'Haves' Come Out Ahead over Time? Applying Galanter's Framework to Decisions of the U.S. Courts of Appeals, 1925–1988" (1999) 3:4 *Law & Society Review* 811 [Songer et al., "Ahead over Time"]; Joel B. Grossman, Herbert M. Kritzer & Stewart Macaulay, "Do the 'Haves' Still Come Out Ahead?" (1999) 33:4 *Law & Society Review* 803 [Grossman, Kritzer & Macaulay]; Donald Songer, Ashlyn Kuersten & Erin Kaheny, "Why the Haves Don't Always Come Out Ahead: Repeat Players Meet Amici Curiae for the Disadvantaged" (2000) 53:3 *Political Research Quarterly* 537 [Songer, Kuersten & Kaheny]; Paul Brace & Melinda Gann Hall, "'Haves' versus 'Have Nots' in State Supreme Courts: Allocating Docket Space and Wins in Power Asymmetric Cases" (2001) 35:2 *Law & Society Review* 393 [Brace & Hall, "Versus"].

For Canada, see e.g. Ian Brodie & F.L. Morton, "Do the 'Haves' Still Come Out Ahead in Canada?" (The University of Western Ontario, 2004) [Brodie & Morton]; Peter McCormick, "Party Capability Theory and Appellate Success in the Supreme Court of Canada, 1949–1992" (1993) 26:3 *Canadian Journal of Political Science* 523 [McCormick, "Party Capability"].

For the UK, see e.g. Chris Hanretty, "Haves and Have-Nots before the Law Lords" (2014) 62 *Political Studies* 686 [Hanretty, "Haves"]; Burton M. Atkins, "Party Capability Theory as an Explanation for Intervention Behavior in the English Court of Appeal" (1991) 35:4 *American Journal of Political Science* 881 [Atkins, "Party Capability"].

For Israel, see e.g. Dotan, "Resource Inequalities," *supra* note 5.

However, these differences may be due to other factors. For example, litigants may have differing success rates in different areas of law. Once we control for the area of law, much of the government advantage appears to disappear. Figure 7-5 shows the differences in the win rates of different parties relative to the putatively weakest party—individuals. Canadian governments most clearly have greater success whether they are appellants or respondents, with an almost 20 percent greater probability of success than individuals.[35] Businesses and associations, on the other hand, do not really have any apparent greater success in Canada than individuals despite in theory having greater resources.[36]

The story is comparable at the US Supreme Court.[37] Prior studies had found that the federal government is really the only party that consistently comes out ahead, winning about two-thirds of the time overall compared to a little under

For Australia, see e.g. Smyth, "The 'Haves' and the 'Have Nots,'" *supra* note 24.

For a more complete listing of such articles, see Brian Glenn, "The Varied and Abundant Progeny" in Herbert M. Kritzer & Susan S. Silbey, eds, *In Litigation: Do the "Haves" Still Come Out Ahead?* (Stanford, CA: Stanford University Press, 2003) 371.

35. These findings are consistent with prior work both on Canadian Courts of Appeals and the Supreme Court of Canada. On the courts of appeal, see McCormick, *Canada's Courts, supra* note 1 at 158. McCormick as well as Haynie et al. also found that justices on the Supreme Court of Canada were more likely to favor litigants with more resources—and in particular government, which as in the United States tended to win about two-thirds of the time in the 1990s. McCormick, *Canada's Courts, supra* note 1 at 164 (finding the federal government won about 62 percent of the time, large business about 57 percent of the time, and individuals about 45 percent). Stacia Haynie et al., "Winners and Losers: Appellate Court Outcomes in a Comparative Context" (Paper delivered at the annual meeting of the American Political Science Association, Washington, DC, September 1, 2005) [unpublished] at 108 [Haynie, "Winners and Losers"]; McCormick, "Party Capability," *supra* note 34.

36. However, see Songer, *Transformation, supra* note 22 at 94–95 (finding individuals actually fare well against businesses).

37. Galanter, who initially worked on this resource story, confirmed that resources matter in US trial courts. Galanter, "Come Out Ahead," *supra* note 20. Resources do appear to also matter at the State Supreme Court level (Brace & Hall, "Versus," *supra* note 34 at 409 (finding a have-not with a lawyer is more likely to succeed); Grossman, Kritzer & Macaulay, *supra* note 34 at 806 (factors that may indicate a shift in favor of have-nots include the rise of contingency fees and punitive damages and the increasing specialization of lawyers). Resources have also been found to be influential at the Courts of Appeal (Susan Brodie Haire, Roger Hartley & Stefanie A. Lindquist, "Attorney Expertise, Litigant Success, and Judicial Decisionmaking in the U.S. Courts of Appeals" (1999) 33:3 *Law & Society Review* 667 (finding in products liability cases that non-specialized lawyers have a lower success rate at the Court of Appeals than specialized lawyers). Songer and Sheehan argue that at least at the Courts of Appeal, a lack of control over the cases they hear results in weak appeals by individuals that governments and business can overcome (Donald R. Songer & Reginald S. Sheehan, "Who Wins on Appeal? Upperdogs and Underdogs in the United States Courts of Appeals" (1992) 36:1 *American Journal of Political*

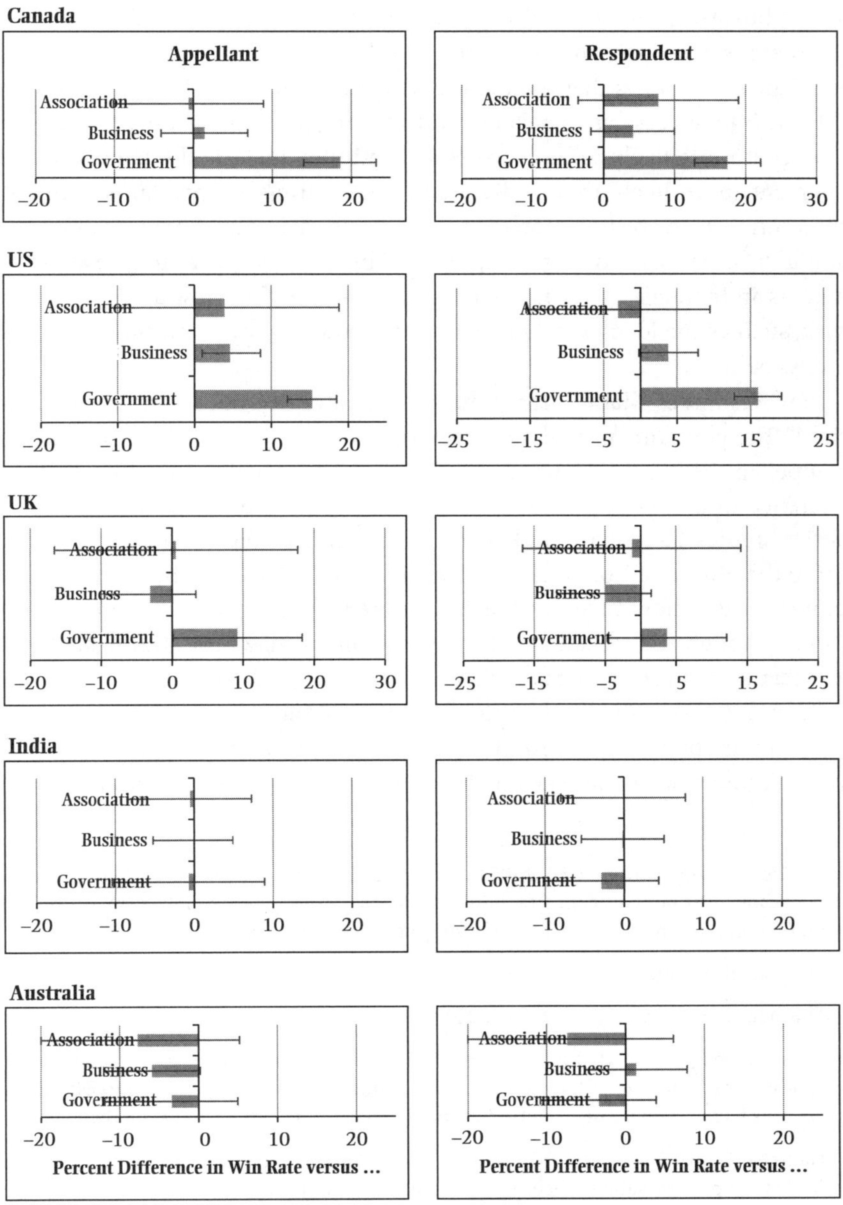


**Figure 7-5** Difference in win rates of governments, businesses, and associations as opposed to individuals whether as appellants and respondents (percent), 1970 to early 2000s. The bars represent the estimated percent difference whereas the lines are the 95 percent confidence intervals. These differences were found by regressing whether the appellant or respondent won on the type of party, controlling for the area of law and a time trend. Government most clearly dominated individuals and other litigants in the United States and Canada as appellant or respondent, followed by the government as appellant in the UK. The government appears to have no advantage over other litigants in India and Australia.

half for businesses and individuals (and about a third for poor individuals), but that there is no consistency over time.[38] When we take account of the area of law, Figure 7-5 shows that the picture becomes more complicated if we break it down into success as appellants and respondents. Governments are about 15 percent more likely to be successful than individuals, and businesses about 5 percent more likely than individuals when acting as appellants. Similarly, when acting as the respondent, government wins at about 15 percent more than individuals, whereas both associations and businesses appear to fare about the same as individuals as respondents. Other factors than resources may be at work, such as the ideological makeup of the court at any given time, which we discuss below.[39]

The "Resources Matter" story does not really play out in the other countries.[40] The government had about a 9 percent greater probability of winning as appellant before the House of Lords, but there is no statistically significant difference in the win rates for any other parties as appellants or respondents. Earlier studies had also found that the government has a distinct advantage before the House of Lords, although there is little difference between all other actors.[41] Given how recently the UK Supreme Court was formed, data are scarce—though the advantage of the government may have diminished, with the exception of certain areas such as criminal law and tax.[42]

Figure 7-5 shows that there is no real difference across any of the parties acting either as appellants or respondents in either India or Australia.[43] Similarly, Smyth found that for judges on the Australian High Court resources of the

*Science* 255). Farole, *supra* note 34 at 1054–1055 (arguing the main advantage is held by government litigants over nongovernmental litigants and that businesses had only a small advantage over individuals (with larger businesses having a greater advantage)).

38. Sheehan et al., "Ideology," *supra* note 2 at 468.

39. Sheehan et al., "Ideology," *supra* note 2 at 468.

40. In Israel, on a basic level, the "have-nots" lose consistently. Still, there are certain complexities. For instance, the *kind* of have-not matters in Israel: prisoners have a low success rate, but immigrants have a higher one. Dotan, "Resource Inequalities," *supra* note 5 at 1069, 1071.

41. Hanretty, "Haves," *supra* note 34 at 695. Atkins, "Party Capability," *supra* note 34 at 897 found that the party capability theory played out at the Court of Appeal.

42. Alan Paterson, *Final Judgment: The Last Law Lords and the Supreme Court* (Oxford: Hart, 2013) at 57.

43. But see Reginald S. Sheehan & Kirk A. Randazzo, "Explaining Litigant Success in the High Court of Australia" (2012) 47:2 *Australian Journal of Political Science* 239 at 246 [Sheehan & Randazzo] (finding that when we look only at success as appellants, the order is national government (52.9%) > individual (50.5%) > subnational government (47.6%) > business (41.2%)).

litigating parties don't matter.[44] However, more recently, as an appellant, the national government in Australia has had an advantage over other actors, whereas individuals are second in the hierarchy.[45] In India, differences in success rates across parties are non-existent, once area of law is taken into account (Figure 7-3), in line with other work that found that gaps in success rates between parties are not large.[46]

In sum, the resource story does not play out clearly across courts if we differentiate by whether the parties are appealing or responding and we control for different areas of law.[47] Part of the problem may be that comparing the success rates of the various parties across high courts is difficult as a party's influence on judicial decision-making may depend on institutional factors. For instance, caseload, docket control, the role of the court, and the length of oral argument are all factors that potentially affect a judge's decision; predictably, the relative capabilities of parties will interact differently with these factors depending on the institutional context.

There is some limited support for a further application or implication of the resource theory—that repeat players should win more.[48] We would expect, from the resources story, repeat players to have a noticeable advantage over infrequent users of the court system.[49] They may have greater knowledge of how to use the system, which arguments work, or which cases to bring forward. All this experience can be viewed as a form of resource.

44. Smyth, "The 'Haves' and the 'Have Nots,'" *supra* note 24 at 267. Similarly, in South Africa, the gap in success rates between individuals and government is not particularly large; furthermore, the success rate of corporations is lower than that of individuals. South Africa's institutional structure may limit the advantage gained by party resources—as the Supreme Court does not have docket control and there is a cab-rank rule, whereby lawyers cannot readily decline cases, meaning judges may not be easily swayed by the fact that a prestigious lawyer took a particular case. Stacia L. Haynie, "Oral Advocacy and Judicial Decision-Making in the South African Appellate Courts" (2005) 21 *South African Journal on Human Rights* 473 at 483–484.

45. Sheehan & Randazzo, *supra* note 43 at 246, 254. See also Haynie et al., "Winners and Losers," *supra* note 35 at 21 (finding that the national government used to have the lowest success rate whereas subnational governments had the highest success rate, with individuals second highest).

46. Herbert Hirsch & Gene L. Mason, "A Systems Analysis of the Indian Supreme Court" (1971) 6:42/43 *Economic and Political Weekly* 2201 at 2207; George H. Gadbois, Jr., "Indian Judicial Behaviour" (1970) 5:3 *Economic and Political Weekly* 153.

47. See also Haynie et al., "Winners and Losers," *supra* note 35.

48. One other implication is that parties with interveners should win more than they would otherwise, as interveners bring added resources to the case. We will discuss interveners in the next section.

49. Galanter, "Come Out Ahead," *supra* note 20.

Government in particular may be the ultimate repeat player.[50] In the United States, there is no doubt that the government is a powerful repeat player.[51] However, it is difficult to isolate the reason for the government's success: its experience, or some other reason. There may, for example, be an element of deference; courts in the United States frequently defer to government representatives, such as the solicitor general, certain prosecutors, or government agencies in administrative law.[52] However, the government's repeated interaction with high courts may in part explain their success rate beyond resources and other issues such as deference.

Even beyond government, other parties may gain an advantage from appearing more often before the courts.[53] In Canada, since the advent of the *Charter of Rights and Freedoms*, Brodie and Morton found that certain groups that used to be disadvantaged have since been given the resources required to become repeat players and start winning, in particular, official language minority groups, feminists, and homosexual rights groups.[54] The government in Canada does *not* have a consistent advantage in the equality area, but Charter issues overshadow factors such as resources and repeat player status—individuals are using their rights and freedoms successfully against the government.[55] Similarly, in the UK, Hanretty found that experience is a more important indicator of future

50. Haynie, "Winners and Losers," *supra* note 35 at 16. A similar explanation is proposed by Stacia L. Haynie & Kaitlyn L. Sill, "Experienced Advocates and Litigation Outcomes: Repeat Players in the South African Supreme Court of Appeal" (2007) 60:3 *Political Research Quarterly* 443 at 446–447 [Haynie & Sill, "Experienced Advocates"]. See also Kevin T. McGuire, "Explaining Executive Success in the U.S. Supreme Court" (1998) 51:2 *Political Research Quarterly* 505 at 522.

51. C.L. Ostberg & Matthew E. Wetstein, "Equality Cases and the Attitudinal Model in the Supreme Court of Canada" (Paper delivered at the annual meeting of the Canadian Political Science Association, 2004) [unpublished] [Ostberg & Wetstein, "Equality Cases"].

52. Farole, *supra* note 34 at 1056.

53. Haynie and Sill, on the contrary, found that being a repeat player before the South African Supreme Court of Appeal is not the best predictor of future outcome. Past *success* is a much better predictor, as many repeat players are also repeat losers. Haynie & Sill, "Experienced Advocates," *supra* note 50 at 450.

54. Brodie & Morton, *supra* note 34 at 25.

55. Ostberg & Wetstein, "Equality Cases," *supra* note 51 (finding that government did have a slight numerical advantage in equality cases but that the difference was not statistically significant). It may also be the lawyer's status that matters as Szmer, Johnson, and Sarver found that a lawyer's previous litigation experience, as well as the size of the litigation team, has a statistically significant positive effect on judges: John Szmer, Susan W. Johnson & Tammy A. Sarver, "Does *the* Lawyer Matter? Influencing Outcomes on the Supreme Court of Canada" (2007) 41:2 *Law & Society Review* 279 at 298.

outcome than prior rates of success.[56] Repeat players before the Israeli Supreme Court have a much higher success rate than infrequent petitioners.[57] Among the most successful repeat players are interest groups, with their success due in part to their specialization.[58]

Overall, the "resources matter" story has only limited support when we look across courts. Parties with more resources, including experience, do tend to do better before some courts, such as the Supreme Court of Canada. In part, however, even when resources appear to matter, the success rates show what Kritzer calls the "government gorilla", that is, that it is not *all* the "haves" who come out ahead, but really just the government.[59] As we saw, governments may succeed not only because of resources but other factors such as judges deferring to government, or government selecting its cases more carefully and appealing only those that are most likely to succeed.[60] It is also difficult to separate out resources from other factors such as law or institutional choices.

## Judges Do Not Clearly Tend to Vote in Line with Like-Minded Litigants

A judge may share a number of characteristics with a party. They may have similar ideological or political views, a common province or state of origin, or even a shared personal trait such as professional background.[61] We may expect, for example, that in general conservative judges are more likely to vote in favor of business

56. Hanretty, "Haves," *supra* note 34 at 695.

57. Yoav Dotan & Menachem Hofnung, "Interest Groups in the Israeli High Court of Justice: Measuring Success in Litigation and in Out-of-Court Settlements" (2001) 23:1 *Law & Policy* 1 at 14 [Dotan & Hofnung, "Interest Groups"].

58. Dotan & Hofnung, "Interest Groups," *supra* note 57 at 15–16. Similarly, Dotan found that "cause lawyers" are becoming effective as repeat player litigators in Israel as they are a highly committed and specialized group: Yoav Dotan, "Public Lawyers and Private Clients: An Empirical Observation on the Relative Success Rates of Cause Lawyers" (1999) 21:4 *Law & Policy* 401 at 416–417.

59. Herbert M. Kritzer, "The Government Gorilla: Why Does Government Come Out Ahead in Appellate Courts?" in Herbert M. Kritzer & Susan S. Silbey, eds, *In Litigation: Do the "Haves" Still Come Out Ahead?* (Stanford, CA: Stanford University Press, 2003) 342.

60. Songer, *Transformation, supra* note 22 at 109.

61. For example, Tabarrok and Helland write that "judges have an incentive to service their constituency" in states where the judiciary is elected (Alexander Tabarrok & Eric Helland, "Court Politics: The Political Economy of Tort Awards" (1999) 42 *Journal of Law and Economics* 157 at 186). Smyth argues this home bias is not an issue in Australia. Smyth, "The 'Haves' and the 'Have Nots,'" *supra* note 24 at 271.

or perhaps government. Obviously this influence is related to our earlier discussion of ideological voting by judges but looks to the relationship of the judge and the party as opposed to the issue specifically. It is reasonable to suspect that judges may wish to affiliate themselves with a party who is representative of their own worldview or align with that view. In practice, however, it is not so clear.

In the United States, ideology has been called a strong predictor of party success.[62] Individuals enjoy greater success during liberal periods on the court, whereas state and local governments, typically prioritizing order over individual rights, suffer during those same periods. The federal government wins consistently, with some evidence that the success rate is higher when a conservative court is aligned with a conservative administration.[63] However, judges may be more likely to look to the ideology of the party where the appeal is not as important. Where an issue is very important policy-wise, a judge may be more likely to rely on his own ideology than that of the litigant, and vote for the party that best represents his worldview.[64]

There has been relatively little research conducted on the interaction between judges' ideology and parties' success rates outside of the United States. Justices on the Supreme Court of Canada have tended not to favor unions—McCormick notes that North American judges may have a normative and ideological bias against unions.[65] In Israel, the High Court of Justice appears to be a "protector of the little person," and sides with minority causes in order to increase its legitimacy.[66] In Australia, on the other hand, the judges' personal views do not appear to play as significant a role in case outcomes.[67]

62. Sheehan et al., "Ideology," *supra* note 2. Brace and Hall argue that ideology has only "very modest explanatory power" in state supreme courts when examining the success rates of different parties, although they see 'haves' and 'have nots' as very crude labels: Brace & Hall, "Versus," *supra* note 34 at 410. Studies of Courts of Appeals are similarly inconclusive: Songer et al., "Ahead over Time," *supra* note 34 at 828.

63. Sheehan et al., "Ideology," *supra* note 2.

64. Andrea McAtee & Kevin T. McGuire, "Lawyers, Justices, and Issue Salience: When and How Do Legal Arguments Affect the U.S. Supreme Court?" (2007) 41:2 *Law & Society Review* 259 at 275.

65. McCormick, *Canada's Courts, supra* note 1 at 159.

66. Dotan, "Resource Inequalities," *supra* note 5 at 1075. Dotan also notes that a small group of about 10 lawyers representing the government appears almost daily before the High Court and that they may have formed a common ideology with the judges, aligning with this ideology perhaps even more than catering to the government. In South Africa the ideology of the Court is "significantly related to outcomes": Haynie & Sill, "Experienced Advocates," *supra* note 50 at 448 (noting "liberal lower court decisions were significantly likely to be reversed, even when controlling for both the status of the litigant and the experience and success of the appellant's advocate").

67. Smyth, "The 'Haves' and the 'Have Nots,'" *supra* note 24 at 268.

If we look at whether a judge votes for the appellant or the respondent (as opposed to whether the appellant or respondent wins as in Figure 7-5), we find little consistent evidence of a connection between the ideology of a judge and broad groupings of parties (government, business, associations, and individuals).[68] In Canada, conservative judges vote in favor of the government at a much higher rate than liberal judges, whether the government was the appellant or respondent (in each case conservative judges were about 23 percent more likely to find in favor of the government than an individual appellant as opposed to about 10 percent for liberal judges).[69] Interestingly, in Canada, conservative judges also tended to favor business and association respondents over individual respondents to a greater extent than liberal judges.[70] Other than Canada, we found no other pattern of connection. Such connection may be difficult to find with broad proxies of ideology and groupings of parties. More detailed analysis is necessary to tease out any such connection that may exist.

## HOW DO JUDGES RELATE TO INTERVENERS?

Although judges may be influenced by the direct litigants in an appeal, we saw in Figures 7-2 and 7-3 that there is another important player before the courts—interveners. Do judges react in the same way to interveners as they do to the litigants? Judges may rely on interveners to increase the accuracy of their decision, possibly because the intervener brings greater information and resources to the resolution of the dispute. Alternatively, they may see interveners more as a signal of the nature of the outcome, and tend to favor interveners who align with their own policy preferences.

68. Using data on judge votes, we used logit regressions for each country where the dependent variable was whether the judge voted for the appellant (defined as a vote in the majority where the appellant won or in dissent where the appellant lost) and the independent variables were the type of litigant (government, business, association, or individual, using individual as the default), party appointing the judge, the direction (liberal or conservative) of the lower court decision, an interaction term between each type of litigant and the party appointing the judge, area of law, and a time trend. Similar regressions were run for votes for the respondent.

69. These results were significant at the .01 level. In no other country were judge votes statistically significantly different for the government than for individuals, except Australia where conservative judges were about 6 percent less likely to vote for the government appellants than individual appellants.

70. Conservative judges found for business respondents about 6 percent more often than individual respondents (significant at the .05 level) whereas there was no difference for liberal judges. They also found in favor of association respondents about 14 percent more often whereas liberal judges found for association respondents about 2 percent more often (significant at the .01 level). There were no statistically significant differences for appellants. The results for the other countries was mixed without a clear ideological story.

Prior studies point toward the accuracy story. One way to see such an effect would be for judges to vote against their apparent preferences in cases involving interveners. In Canada, for example, conservative interveners make for a more conservative judgment, whereas liberal interveners make for a liberal judgment, though conservative interveners have a greater effect.[71] The judges appear to primarily take information from the interveners as "in the presence of interveners, judges in some cases vote in a direction different than would be predicted from general indicators of their ideology."[72]

Similarly, in the US Supreme Court, Collins found that "amicus briefs serve to attenuate the justices' reliance on their attitudes . . . leading to more variable behavior", to the point that "amicus briefs are the single strongest predictor of increased variance in judicial decision making."[73] Kearney and Merrill, too, find that amicus briefs affected voting patterns particularly during the Warren Court and the Burger Court, though the increasing number of such briefs may have reduced their effectiveness in later periods.[74] Both studies conclude that judges look to interveners for the provision of information.[75] If judges were basing their votes on the desire for affiliation with a particular intervener's ideological position, interveners would not attenuate the judges' attitudinal voting; rather, judges would merely vote in favor of the party supported by like-minded interveners.[76]

If the accuracy story holds for interveners, interveners should mitigate the disadvantage of the relatively under-resourced party—having an intervener as an ally should increase the range of arguments and bring added experience, and also may help allay the costs of the appeal.[77] Kearney and Merrill propose an informational story, namely that interveners can make up for inexperienced

71. Alarie & Green, "Interventions," *supra* note 17 at 407–408. Unexpectedly, they also found neutral interveners make judges vote more liberally than do liberal interveners.

72. Alarie & Green, "Interventions," *supra* note 17 at 409. Anecdotal evidence also appears to support this, as anonymous judge has stated that interveners are "often valuable" because they bring a fresh perspective, though another found interveners less helpful as they were "too political' ": Donald R. Songer et al., *Law, Ideology, and Collegiality: Judicial Behaviour in the Supreme Court of Canada* (Montreal: McGill-Queen's University Press, 2012) at 87 [Songer et al., *Law, Ideology*].

73. See also Collins, *supra* note 7 at 173.

74. Kearney & Merrill, "Influence," *supra* note 28.

75. See also Collins, *supra* note 7 at 173.

76. See also Collins, *supra* note 7 at 173.

77. Songer, Kuersten & Kaheny, *supra* note 34. Donald R. Songer & Ashlyn Kuersten, "The Success of Amici in State Supreme Courts" (1995) 48:1 *Political Research Quarterly* 31 (the presence of amici also increases the chances of success in state supreme courts, regardless of whether they support the appellant or the respondent).

counsel, insofar as amicus briefs provide legal arguments that a more experienced lawyer could have offered independently.[78] Not all US studies have found amicus briefs to have an influence on litigant success. Songer and Sheehan conclude that litigants tend not to fare better when supported by briefs; in fact, some even fare worse.[79] One possible reason for these findings is that the authors do not distinguish between types of interveners. Certain interveners, such as the solicitor general, are much more successful than others.

An alternative indicator of an influence of interveners is the dissent rate. As we discussed earlier, interveners may push judges to more extreme positions, making it harder to find common ground. Songer et al. found that interveners decreased the odds of a unanimous decision at the Supreme Court of Canada, but the effect was only slight, and was a less meaningful predictor of lack of unanimity than the presence of constitutional issues or statutory interpretation.[80] Interestingly, in the UK, Hanretty found that interveners lead to less divided voting, also suggesting an accuracy story that the presence of interveners "reduces complexity by accentuating different sides to the debate."[81]

When we look across high courts in the 1970s through the 2000s, we find that judges on a number of high courts had a modestly higher dissent rate in the presence of interveners. In Canada, the UK, and Australia, judges were about 2–3 percent more likely to dissent if there was at least one intervener involved in the case, but the presence of an intervener did not appear to influence the dissent rate in the United States.[82] Of course, it is difficult to know if something about the interveners' submissions increased the likelihood that a judge would dissent, or whether more controversial cases (those so more likely to be divisive) were more likely to attract interveners. We did, however, control for the area of law (such as whether the case was a civil rights case) in looking for an influence of interveners, which may in part control for the nature of the case.

Interveners may only be persuasive to a certain point. One party may gain an advantage by having one or two more briefs than another, but a greater

78. Kearney & Merrill, "Influence," *supra* note 28 at 830.

79. Donald R. Songer & Reginald S. Sheehan, "Interest Groups Success in the Courts: Amicus Participation in the Supreme Court" (1993) 46:2 *Political Research Quarterly* 339 at 346.

80. Songer et al., *Law, Ideology, supra* note 72 at 161–163.

81. Hanretty, "Lumpers and Splitters," *supra* note 4 at 19.

82. We used a logit regression with the dependent variable being whether the judge dissented, and the independent variables being the presence of an intervener, the ideology of the judge (party appointing the judge), the direction (conservative or liberal) of the lower court decisions, and the area of law. The effects in Canada and Australia were significant at the .01 level and in the UK at the .05 level. Recall that for the United States, the Spaeth database did not include information on interveners so for the United States regressions in this case we used the HCJD, *supra* note 3.

disparity will lead to diminishing returns, and may even be counterproductive.[83] More interveners do not necessarily continue to add a large benefit. This declining impact is consistent with some evidence that judges do not look to interveners for new evidence but for reinforcement of arguments already raised by the parties,[84] although also with the idea that there is only a certain amount of new information to be added such that there is diminishing marginal returns to each new intervener. Finally, as with litigants, the most influential amicus is the government—the solicitor general increases the success rate of appellants by almost 17 percent, and that of respondents by almost 26 percent.[85]

Judges then may be somewhat influenced by interveners, but the effect does not appear to be large. Judges in Canada and the United States seem to draw information from interveners rather than support for personal views.[86] However, interveners may slightly increase the likelihood of a dissent in a particular case. Studies of the influence of interveners on high courts other than the US Supreme Court and the Supreme Court of Canada are unfortunately scarce.

## DO PARTIES MAKE A DIFFERENCE?

The story about the influence of parties on judges is mixed. Resources appear to matter in certain situations, such as when the government is litigating, but this is not necessarily true across time and across countries. Repeat players do seem to do better overall, but, again, there are other factors at work such as a tradition of deference to the executive. Further, interveners may have a modest impact on judges through providing information about the case, but may modestly increase the propensity of a judge to dissent. Both the value of dissents and the factors that lead judges to dissent are controversial. It is to this issue we turn in the next chapter.

83. Kearney & Merrill, "Influence," *supra* note 28 at 829.

84. Spriggs and Wahlbeck analyze the content of amicus briefs, and examine which arguments judges actually rely on in their judgments. They find that 75 percent of the amicus briefs reiterated the arguments of the parties themselves, and that 33 percent provide no new information at all. Moreover, judges are less likely to adopt an argument from an amicus brief if that argument was not also presented by the party. Thus they concluded that the benefit of amicus briefs is not in the provision of new arguments, but rather in the reinforcement of existing ones. James F. Spriggs II & Paul J Wahlbeck, "Amicus Curiae and the Role of Information at the Supreme Court" (1997) 50:2 *Political Research Quarterly* 365 at 382–383.

85. Kearney & Merrill, "Influence," *supra* note 28 at 803–804.

86. In Israel, Doron and Totry-Jubran looked at interveners but did not test their effect empirically: Doron & Totry-Jubran, *supra* note 14. Similarly, in Australia, Williams discussed the "entrenched preference" for governmental input as interveners but again did not systematically examine the impact of interveners empirically: Williams, "Amicus Curiae," *supra* note 10 at 396.

# 8

# Norms, Leadership, and Consensus

> Lord Ackner was supposed to have observed that one only dissents when one's sense of outrage at the majority decision outweighs one's natural indolence, so it could be said that I am recommending more indolence.
>
> —Lord Neuberger, *President of UK Supreme Court (2012)*[1]

So far we have mainly discussed how different rules influence voting by judges, such as rules about appointment processes, jurisdiction of courts, or interveners. Norms may also be very influential. The Supreme Court of India, for example, has a norm that junior judges on panels defer to the senior judge, which is powerful given the prevalence of two-person panels.[2] In the UK there may have been a norm of making "professional" as opposed to political appointments to the House of Lords, which would affect the nature of the ideological division on the court. These norms may change over time. For example, there may have been a radical shift in norms of consensus on the US Supreme Court in the early 1940s, playing a part in a sharp rise in the number of dissents.[3]

Norms then lie in the background of the formal rules but can have a large effect. By "norms," we generally mean, following McAdams, "informal social regularities that individuals feel obligated to follow because of an

1. Lord Neuberger, "No Judgment—No Justice" (Paper delivered at First Annual BAILII Lecture, 20 November 2012), online: http://www.bailii.org/bailii/lecture/01.html.

2. Nick Robinson, "Structure Matters: The Impact of Court Structure on the Indian and U.S. Supreme Courts" (2013) 61:1 *American Journal of Comparative Law* 173 at 186.

3. Cass R. Sunstein, "Unanimity and Disagreement on the Supreme Court" (2015) 100 *Cornell L.R.* 769 at 772 [Sunstein, "Unanimity"].

Commitment and Cooperation on High Courts. Benjamin Alarie and Andrew J. Green.

internalized sense of duty, because of a fear of external non-legal sanctions, or both."[4] These norms then have a "normative" content—that is, a sense they should be followed—and can be enforced through internal shame, guilt, or pride or through the esteem or disesteem of others.[5] They can reinforce, contradict, or fill in the gaps in more formal rules and may change as the context changes.[6]

This chapter examines how norms may influence voting by judges. It is hard to observe norms and to identify their effects.[7] We focus on one particular norm—the norm of consensus. Different courts may have different norms about the need for the judges to agree on a particular result or a set of reasons. Although some studies have defined a norm of consensus as meaning that a court has a high level of agreement,[8] countries can have a norm that favors a high level of agreement (a norm of high consensus) or that tolerates significant disagreement (a norm of low consensus).[9]

Figure 8-1 returns to an issue we discussed briefly in Chapter 1—the difference in the percent of cases per year that involved at least one dissent. The median dissent rates varied widely over the 1970s through the early 2000s, from less than 2 percent in India to about 40 percent in Australia and over 50 percent in the US Supreme Court. Canada and the UK had more intermediate levels of dissents. Differing norms of consensus may be part of the explanation for these varying dissent rates, though as we will see other factors are also important. The ordering of countries is similar in recent years—with

4. Richard H. McAdams, "The Origin, Development and Regulations of Norms" (1997) 96 *Michigan Law Review* 338 at 340. Caldeira and Zorn argue that norms may represent an equilibrium in which "no actor, given current information and its current position, can improve its position on its own" and therefore may also be followed out of self-interest. Gregory Caldeira & Christopher Zorn, "Of Time and Consensual Norms in the Supreme Court" (1998) 42:3 *American Journal of Political Science* 874 at 876 [Caldeira & Zorn, "Of Time"].

5. Richard H. McAdams & Eric B. Rasmusen, "Norms in Law and Economics" (2005), online: http://papers.ssrn.com/sol3/papers.cfm?abstract_id=580843 at 12–13.

6. Caldeira & Zorn, "Of Time," *supra* note 4 at 876.

7. Caldeira & Zorn, "Of Time," *supra* note 4 at 875.

8. Russell Smyth, "Historical Consensual Norms in the High Court" (2002) 37:2 *Australian Journal of Political Science* 255 [Smyth, "Historical Consensual"]; Thomas G. Walker, Lee Epstein & William J. Dixon, "On the Mysterious Demise of Consensual Norms in the United States Supreme Court" (1988) 50:2 *The Journal of Politics* 361 [Walker, Epstein & Dixon].

9. Caldeira & Zorn, "Of Time," *supra* note 4 at 875; Paresh Kumar Narayan & Russell Smyth, "The Consensual Norm on the High Court of Australia: 1904–2001" (2005) 26:2 *International Political Science Review*) 147 at 148.

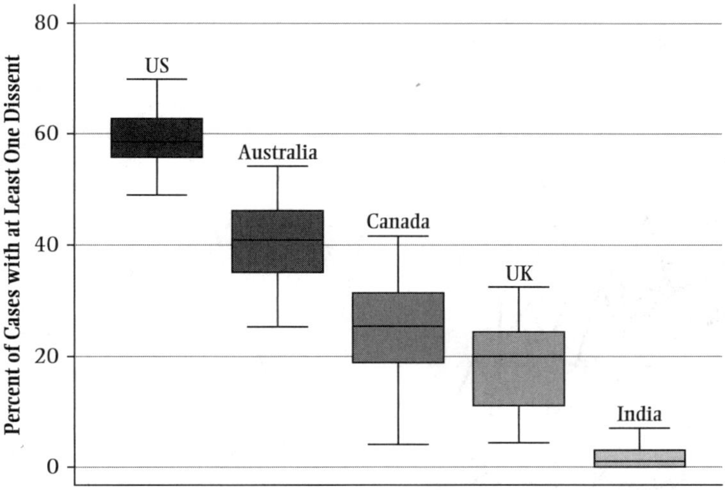


**Figure 8-1** Percent of cases per year that have at least one dissent over the period from 1970 to the early 2000s. The box shows the middle 50 percent of the data for each country, and the line in the box shows the median percentage for cases with at least one dissent over the period. The lines above and below each box provide the maximum and minimum annual percentages of opinions with at least one dissent for each country in the period. The United States had by far the highest rate of dissenting, with over 50 percent of opinions having a dissent in most years. At the other extreme, most years India had less than 5 percent of opinions with at least one dissent. Canada and the UK had similar rates of opinions with dissents. Australia had the second highest level of dissent with in general over 40 percent of opinions having a dissent. Note that this Figure is the same as Figure 1-3.

the US Supreme Court on the high side with at about 60 percent for 2014–2015,[10] Australia at about a third of the cases in 2012,[11] the Canadian Supreme Court about 30 percent in 2015,[12] and the UK Supreme Court having about 24 percent of cases with at least one dissent between 2009 and 2013.[13]

10. Kedar Bhatia, "Final Stat Pack for October Term 2014: Merits Cases by Vote Split" (June 30, 2015) *SCOTUSblog* (blog), online: http://sblog.s3.amazonaws.com/wp-content/uploads/2015/07/SB_votesplit_OT14.pdf at 5.

11. Andrew Lynch & George Williams, "The High Court on Constitutional Law: The 2012 Statistics" (2013) 36:2 *U. New South Wales LJ* 514.

12. "Category 4: Appeal Judgements," *Supreme Court of Canada Statistics from 2005 to 2015*, online: http://www.scc-csc.ca/case-dossier/stat/cat4-eng.aspx#cat4c.

13. Alan Paterson, "A Scarcity of Dissents?" (February 19, 2014), *UKSC Blog*, online: http://ukscblog.com/scarcity-dissent/.

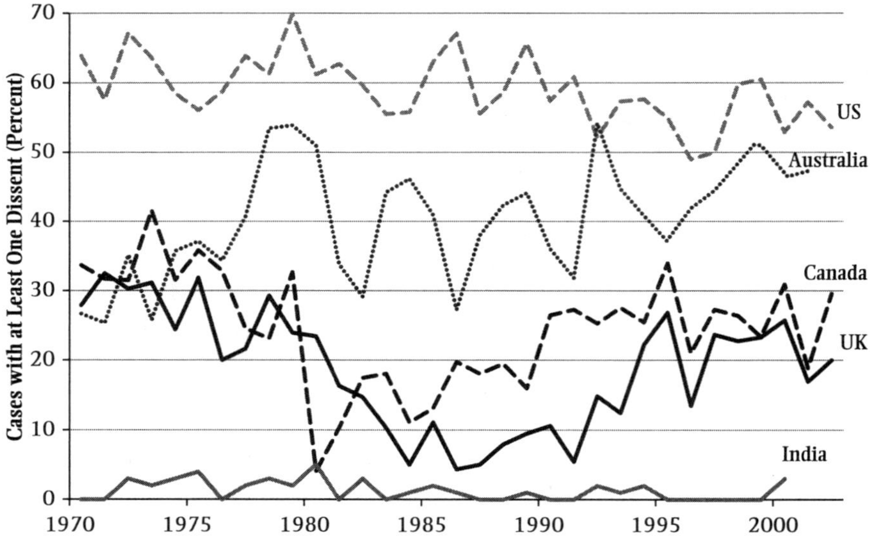


**Figure 8-2** The percentage of cases with at least one dissent for each country, 1970 through the early 2000s. The United States had uniformly high and India uniformly low dissent rates over the whole period. Australia, Canada, and the UK started the period with about a third of cases having at least one dissenting opinion, but diverged in the mid-1970s. Australia rose to US levels by the end of the period. Canada and the UK followed similar patterns, with the percent of cases with a dissent dipping before rising again in the 1980s.

These dissent rates may change over time. Figure 8-2 shows how the percent of cases involving at least one dissent varied across the countries between 1970 and the early 2000s. The United States had some variation in the dissent rate but was almost always over 50 percent. Interestingly prior to 1941, justices on the US Supreme Court dissented at an even lower rate than the current UK Supreme Court with a US Supreme Court dissent rate of under 15 percent for the period from 1900 to 1941.[14] The Indian Supreme Court has uniformly had few dissents. However, Australia, Canada, and the UK showed more variation. They all started the period with very similar dissent rates, but justices on the Supreme Court of Canada and the UK House of Lord dissented less often beginning in the mid-1970s whereas the Australian High Court judges began dissenting more often. Dissent rates in the UK and Canada began to creep up again in the early 1980s, though ending up slightly less than they started the period. The Australian High Court, on the other hand, ended the period with similar dissent rates to those in the United States.

14. Sunstein, "Unanimity", *supra* note 3 at 776–778.

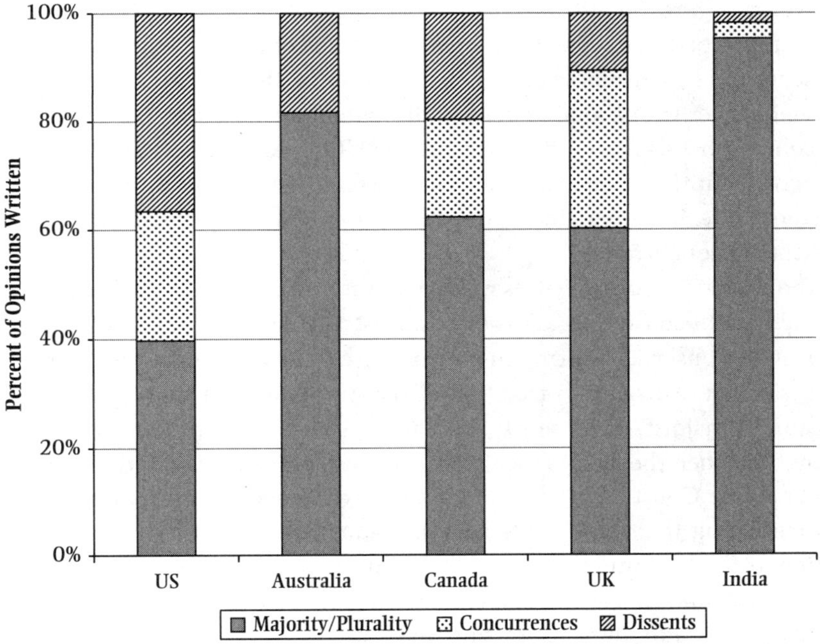


**Figure 8-3** Proportion of Written Judgments That Are Plurality/Majority Opinions, Concurrences and Dissents. The time periods covered are India and South Africa 1970–2000, UK, and Australia 1970–2002 and Canada and the United States 1954–2012. SOURCE: HCJD, Supreme Court of Canada Database and the US Supreme Court Database.

The dissent rate does not completely capture the level of disagreement on a court.[15] Three variables that are often studied are dissenting opinions, concurring opinions, and dissenting votes.[16] Figure 8-3 shows the percentage of written judgments on each court that was a majority or plurality judgment, a concurrence, or a dissent. The countries are ranked left to right from the highest levels of dissent to the lowest as in Figure 8-1. At the two ends of the spectrum are India with an extremely low rate of dissent (much lower than 10 percent) and the United States with a very high rate of dissent (almost 40 percent).

15. Andrew Lynch, "Dissent: Towards a Methodology for Measuring Judicial Disagreement in the High Court of Australia" (2002) 24 *Sydney Law Review* 470 at 476 [Lynch, "Dissent"]. Lynch notes that using dissent rates alone is overly simplistic as it neglects concurrences as it is counting concurrences as the same as dissents. He argues it is better to distinguish between dissents and concurrences.

16. Stacia L. Haynie, "Leadership and Consensus on the U.S. Supreme Court" (1992) 54:4 *Journal of Politics* 1158 at 1160 [Haynie, "Leadership"].

However, Figure 8-3 also shows that focusing on the dissent rate alone masks other forms of disagreements expressed through concurring judgments. If both dissents and concurrences are taken into account, the United States is an even greater outlier with about 60 percent of written decisions being either dissents or concurrences. Also on this measure the UK has a greater combined level of disagreement than Canada, as its lower dissent rate is offset by its higher concurrence rate. India remains at the extreme low end of disagreements, with few dissents or concurrences.

The absence of concurrences written in Australia points to a difficulty in analyzing rates of consensus across courts. Australia has been described as having "no single consensual norm," in part because of its tradition of seriatim judgments.[17] In a court with a tradition of seriatim judgment writing, there is no organized majority or minority, thus making it difficult to identify disagreement.[18] Further, the factors that affect consensus may vary over time. Both the US Supreme Court and the Supreme Court of Canada, for instance, began by disseminating their judgments seriatim, adopting a majority style only later (prior to the beginning of our study).[19] In order to allow comparison across courts and analyze core disagreement, we will focus on dissents rather than concurrences, although recognizing that it is only one form of disagreement.[20]

In this chapter we examine how norms of consensus relate to these patterns of agreement and disagreement. Before we get to the factors that affect consensus, it is important to note the underlying normative question of whether consensus is particularly desirable at all. Opinions are divided on this point. On the one hand, a united bench boosts the legitimacy of the court as a whole. In the United States, this was the view of Chief Justice Taft, who desired certainty in the law, and Chief Justice Marshall, who diverted the US Supreme Court from its previous seriatim tradition toward a practice of writing a single "opinion of

17. Smyth, "Historical Consensual," *supra* note 8 at 255, 264.

18. Lynch, "Dissent," *supra* note 15 at 490. Moreover, many civil law courts, such as the French Court of Cassation or the Constitutional Council, release only a single unanimous decision, prohibiting written dissents. Peter McCormick, "'With Respect . . .'— Levels of Disagreement on the Lamer Court 1990–2000" (2003) 48:1 *McGill Law Journal* 89 at 94 [McCormick, "With Respect"].

19. On the US Supreme Court, see Rebecca Gill, "Consensus or Ambivalence? Why Court Traditions Matter" (8 July 2011) [unpublished] online: http://ssrn.com/abstract=1881961. For the Canadian Supreme Court, see Emmett Macfarlane, "Consensus and Unanimity at the Supreme Court of Canada" (2010) 52 *Supreme Court Law Review* 379 at 382 [Macfarlane, "Consensus"].

20. Lynch, "Dissent," *supra* note 15 also focuses on such disagreement due to the nature of concurrences in Australia (pp 483ff). Caldeira & Zorn, "Of Time," *supra* note 4 explicitly examine the connection between dissents and concurrences through cointegration to see if there is evidence that the same factors influence both modes of disagreement.

the Court."[21] The counterargument centers on the beneficial effects of a multiplicity of views. Forcing a unanimous judgment may lead to unwanted compromise (or extremely narrow "lowest common denominator" decisions), or may cause the omission of an important point that ought not to be overlooked.[22] We will not enter into this normative argument in this chapter but instead focus on what influences whatever level of consensus exists on a particular court.

As we noted earlier it is impossible to observe norms of consensus directly. We therefore need to try to separate these norms from the other factors we have discussed that may influence how judges make decisions. In particular, in Chapter 2 we focused on policy preferences, reputation, identity, compensation, and leisure. To get a better idea of how norms influence levels of consensus across courts, we need to unpack how these factors relate to agreement and disagreement on a court. Following Epstein, Landes, and Posner, we argue that a judge will not dissent, or write a concurrence, unless the benefits of the dissent or concurrence outweigh the costs.[23] We group the factors influencing these costs and benefits into three categories: policy preferences, workload, and norms.[24]

## DO DIFFERENCES IN POLICY PREFERENCES INFLUENCE DISSENTS?

Differences in policy preferences are perhaps the most obvious potential source of disagreement between judges. A judge may dissent simply because he disagrees with the policy implications of the decision of the other judges. There is

21. Smyth, "Historical Consensual," *supra* note 8 at 256–257.

22. Russell Smyth, "'Some Are More Equal than Others'—An Empirical Investigation into the Voting Behaviour of the Mason Court" (1999) 6:1–2 *Canberra Law* Review 193 at 201–202 [Smyth, "Some Are More Equal"]. See also Donald R. Songer, John Szmer & Susan W. Johnson, "Explaining Dissent on the Supreme Court of Canada" (2011) 44:2 *Canadian Journal of Political Science* 389 at 390–392 [Songer et al., "Explaining Dissent"] for a discussion of the benefits and costs of unanimity.

23. Lee Epstein, William M. Landes & Richard A. Posner, *Behavior of Federal Judges: A Theoretical and Empirical Study of Rational Choice* (Cambridge, MA: Harvard University Press, 2013) [Epstein, Landes & Posner, *Behavior*] at 256. See also Caldeira & Zorn, "Of Time," *supra* note 4 at 877.

24. See also Songer et al., "Explaining Dissent," *supra* note 22 at 393–394 examining the influence of four categories of factors on dissent: attitudinal diversity (including case salience), structural influences (panel size and workload), legal factors (whether the Court reverses and case complexity) and leadership by the chief justice. There are other factors that may impact consensus that we do not examine. For example, Walker, Epstein & Dixon, *supra* note 8 discuss the potential role of the rate of turnover of judges and inexperience in the rise of dissensus on the US Supreme Court in the 1940s.

a disagreement in the literature about how great a role ideology plays. Under the attitudinal model, judges agree when they have similar policy preferences about the result of the particular appeal.[25] The cost of agreeing for a judge is that she must compromise on her policy preference where it differs from that of the majority.[26] Dissent, on this view, then arises from differences in views about policy outcomes.

Even where the judge dissents, there are trade-offs. As Epstein, Landes, and Posner note:

> Since writing a dissenting opinion requires effort, a judge will not dissent unless he anticipates a benefit that offsets that cost. One benefit is to undermine the influence of the majority opinions, with which by assumption he disagrees, although possible offsets are that a dissent will draw attention to the majority opinion and may even magnify its significance by exaggerating its potential scope in order to emphasize the harm that it will do.[27]

Despite possibly drawing attention to the majority opinion, a judge may be more likely to dissent if she is an ideological outlier, as her opinion would not otherwise be heard. She may also view dissent as providing the basis for future decisions. For example, between 1991 and 1997, Justice L'Heureux-Dubé of the Supreme Court of Canada dissented 61 times, by far the highest level of dissent on the Court, and 80 percent were solo dissents.[28] She has been described as the classic outsider,[29] and has written that dissenting opinions can be very

25. Paul H. Edelman, David E. Klein & Stefanie A. Lindquist, "Consensus, Disorder and Ideology on the Supreme Court" (2012) 9:1 *J. Empirical Legal Studies* 129 [Edelman et al.] ("[p]ut simply, the attitudinal account of consensus is that most or all the justices happen to prefer the same option in a given case" at 131).

26. A court may be split not only on difference in policy but on personal differences. Smyth argues that the Australian High Court was badly split by personal strife during the Latham era. Russell Smyth, "Judicial Interaction on the Latham Court: A Quantitative Study of Voting Patterns on the High Court 1935–1950" (2001) 47:3 *Australian Journal of Politics and History* 330 at 344. More recently, Rice and Zorn examined the language used in opinions at the US Supreme Court and found an increasing use of emotional language over time and changes in the positive versus negative valence of this language over time: Douglas R. Rice & Christopher Zorn, "The Evolution of Consensus in the U.S. Supreme Court" (2014) [unpublished], online: http://papers.ssrn.com/sol3/papers.cfm?abstract_id=2470029 [Rice & Zorn].

27. Epstein, Landes & Posner, *Behavior, supra* note 23 at 256.

28. C.L. Ostberg, Matthew Wetstein & Craig R. Ducat, "Leaders, Followers, and Outsiders: Task and Social Leadership on the Canadian Supreme Court in the Early Nineties" (2004) 36:3 *Polity* 505 at 521, n. 24, 522 [Ostberg et al., "Leaders"].

29. Ostberg et al., "Leaders," *supra* note 28 at 523.

important for the development of new and alternative approaches to the law by laying the foundations for future appeals.[30] Chief Justice Charles Evan Hughes of the US Supreme Court famously referred to dissents as "appeals to the brooding spirit of the law, to the intelligence of another day."[31]

One hypothesis about the dissent rate that follows therefore is:

*H1: A greater differences in ideology will lead to a higher dissent rate.*

We could think of identifying differences in ideology in different ways. First, we could specify a measure of ideological divergence on a court to see if the level of dissent increased as divergence increased. A related issue arises where courts hear appeals in panels. If a high court hears its decisions in panels, the ideological split on particular panels may influence the rate of disagreement (as opposed to just the overall split if the court hears decisions *en banc*). However, as discussed in Chapter 5, not only bare differences in ideology may matter, but also the composition of the panel. Panel composition can lead to whistleblower and ideological amplification effects, which may influence the level of dissent merely because of the presence (or absence) of like-minded colleagues.[32]

The other way to examine this issue is to look for indirect measures. If ideological preferences influence voting, dissent will be more common in cases involving contentious issues such as race, gender, and religion—subjects about which individuals form strong ideological and personal convictions.[33] The benefit of dissenting on an issue with a strong social dimension will generally be greater than the benefit of dissenting on an issue of pure legal doctrine. Even when dissent is rare as in India, these controversial cases will not always be unanimous.[34] Likewise, on a court that typically does have a high dissent rate, some types of cases may be *less* contentious.[35]

30. Justice Claire L'Heureux-Dubé, "The Dissenting Opinion: Voice of the Future?" (2000) 38:3 *Osgoode Hall Law Journal* 495 at 508 [L'Heureux-Dubé].

31. L'Heureux-Dubé, *supra* note 30 at 495.

32. See e.g. Cass R. Sunstein et al., *Are Judges Political? An Empirical Analysis of the Federal Judiciary* (Washington, DC: Brookings Institution Press, 2006).

33. Songer et al., "Explaining Dissent," *supra* note 22 at 395.

34. George H. Gadbois, Jr., "Indian Judicial Behaviour" (1970) 5:3 *Economic and Political Weekly* 149 at 154.

35. One example may be tort cases before the House of Lords: Brice Dickson, *Judicial Activism in Common Law Supreme Courts* (New York: Oxford University Press, 2007) at 392 (noting that "dissents are not particularly common" in tort cases, although also stressing that the House of Lords has had difficulty finding a collective approach to tort).

Relatedly if the docket is discretionary, rather than mandatory, we would expect a higher rate of dissent.[36] At the Supreme Court (or equivalent) level, some if not most cases will be controversial. However, if the court's docket is partly discretionary, the mandatory appeals will tend on average to be easier and less controversial.[37] The Supreme Court of Canada, for instance, should have a higher rate of consensus in criminal appeals as of right than in (discretionary) *Charter* appeals.[38]

One further factor that is related to these differences in policy preferences is the number of judges. If there are more judges on the court, there are more opportunities for differences of opinion.[39] Similarly, if there are more judges on a particular panel, there is a greater likelihood of a judge disagreeing. In addition, if a judge is averse to dissenting out of fear of alienating her colleagues, she may be more likely to dissent if there are many judges, as her colleagues may take disagreement less personally. However, an opposing theory is also plausible: the more judges there are, the greater the number of colleagues who will potentially be alienated. A risk-averse judge may decide not to dissent, with the result that "small panels can reach agreements, mitigating the effect of ideologies more easily" than larger ones.[40]

Fear of alienating colleagues by dissenting may not influence the US Supreme Court, which is so politicized that justices would not be likely to take disagreement personally: dissents from other justices are entirely expected and are part of a normal working day. For instance, Justice Ginsburg and Justice Scalia, who rarely agreed on a case, were known to be good friends who shared New Year's dinners together, with their spouses, for decades.[41] Epstein et al. found

36. Melinda Gann Hall, "Docket Control as an Influence on Judicial Voting" (1985) 10:2 *The Justice System Journal* 243 [Gann Hall, "Docket Control"]; Walker, Epstein & Dixon, *supra* note 8 at 365; Edelman et al., *supra* note 25 at 140; Lee Epstein, Jeffrey A. Segal & Harold J. Spaeth, "The Norm of Consensus on the U.S. Supreme Court" (2001) 45:2 *American Journal of Political Science* 362 at 364 [Epstein et al., "Norm of Consensus"].

37. Smyth, "Some Are More Equal," *supra* note 22 at 201; Benjamin Alarie, Andrew Green & Edward Iacobucci, "Panel Selections on High Courts" (2015) 65:4 *University of Toronto Law Journal* 335 [Alarie et al., "Panel Selections"].

38. McCormick, "With Respect," *supra* note 18 at 109.

39. Meghan E. Leonard & Joseph V. Ross, "Consensus and Cooperation on State Supreme Courts" (2013) 14:1 State Politics & Policy Quarterly 3 at 17 [Leonard & Ross].

40. Keren Weinshall-Margel, "Attitudinal and Neo-Institutional Models of Supreme Court Decision Making: An Empirical and Comparative Perspective from Israel" (2011) 8:3 *Journal of Empirical Legal Studies* 556 [Weinshall-Margel, "Attitudinal"].

41. Lawrence Wrightman, *The Psychology of the Supreme Court* (New York: Oxford University Press, 2006) at 173.

that although the US Supreme Court had gone through periods of poor relations among the justices, those periods did not appear to correspond to greater frequency of dissents.[42] These divergent possibilities may be the reason some scholars argue panel size is not an effective predictor of dissent rates.[43] However, at the very least, a greater number of judges leads to a higher probability of a judge having a different policy preference to the majority, and we therefore have to control for this factor where we are able.

## Direct Measures of Ideological Difference

The effect of judges' ideology on consensus on a court is a contentious topic in empirical studies of judicial decision-making. We might reasonably expect some variation across high courts, with ideology mattering more in countries with a politicized judicial system than for courts set in a more apolitical context, but even this is not near the mark. There is no clear consensus on the connection between ideology and agreement even within a given country.

Studies of the US Supreme Court differ on how ideology interacts with norms of consensus. Wahlbeck, Spriggs, and Maltzman's study of the Burger Court found that the justices' ideology does indeed affect rates of consensus, as justices are "more likely to author or join a separate opinion the further they are ideologically from the majority opinion author."[44] However, ideology is generally seen as one factor acting in combination with other considerations. Consider the work of Walker, Epstein, and Dixon (1988), which documents a large jump in dissents on the US Supreme Court. Walker, Epstein, and Dixon find that ideology may at times result in coalitions on the court, but that ideology alone cannot account for the sudden increase in separate judgments during the Stone era. A more compelling story, to them, is that there was a "generalized decline in the norms of cohesion."[45] In contrast, Haynie hypothesizes

42. Epstein, Landes & Posner, *Behavior, supra* note 3 at 264.

43. McCormick, "With Respect," *supra* note 18 at 106–107.

44. Forrest Maltzman, James F. Spriggs II & Paul J. Wahlbeck, "The Politics of Dissent and Concurrences on the US Supreme Court" (1999) 27:4 *American Politics Research* 488 at 501. Jeffrey A. Segal & Harold J. Spaeth, *The Supreme Court and the Attitudinal Model Revisited* (Cambridge: Cambridge University Press, 2002) at 281 (Segal and Spaeth note that assigning the majority opinion to the most marginal judge (the judge at highest risk of switching over to the dissent) does not help keep a majority coalition together or increase the size of the majority). See also Forrest Maltzman, James F. Spriggs II & Paul J. Wahlbeck, *Crafting Law on the Supreme Court: The Collegial Game* (Cambridge, UK: Cambridge University Press, 2000) at 133. They call this the "opinion distance hypothesis."

45. Walker, Epstein & Dixon, *supra* note 8 at 375. See also Sunstein, "Unanimity," *supra* note 3.

that courts with greater divisions along party lines will produce more separate opinions, but ultimately finds no relationship between ideology and dissent or concurrence.[46]

More recently, Edelman, Klein, and Lindquist examined whether ideology lies behind both disagreement and agreement. They analyzed the relationship between the degree of disordered voting (that is, voting that is not in line with ideological expectations) and the level of disagreement.[47] They found that for cases where there was a greater predicted level of disorder (non-ideological voting), there were fewer dissents. Although ideology leads to ordered voting and more dissents, there is greater consensus in disordered cases, and so ideological voting is not a factor (or at least not the only factor) leading to agreement.[48]

Differences in attitudes may matter to the dissent rate at the Supreme Court of Canada. Songer, Szmer, and Johnson examined the role of ideology (among other factors) in the rate of dissents on the Court between 1976 and 2005. To measure attitudinal difference, they used the difference in career liberalism scores for the most liberal and the most conservative justices on a particular panel. After controlling for a range of factors including panel size, legal area, workload, and chief justice, they found a positive and statistically significant relationship between attitudinal difference and dissent rates such that a one standard deviation increase in the attitudinal difference increases the probability of a dissent by about 22 percent.[49]

Studies of the Australian High Court, on the other hand, tend not to find that ideology has had a significant effect on consensus. For example, in the Latham era (1935–1950) justices' ideological compatibility was not significantly related to their likelihood of agreement.[50] On the other hand, between 1904 and 2001,

46. Haynie, "Leadership," *supra* note 16 at 1166.

47. Edelman et al., *supra* note 25.

48. At the state supreme court level, Leonard and Ross find that ideological diversity does not have a significant effect on the likelihood of unanimity, although elected judges show higher rates of dissent: Leonard & Ross, *supra* note 39 at 14, 18.

49. Songer et al., "Explaining Dissent," *supra* note 22 at 401. As discussed further in the subsequent sections, they also find that the presence of interveners, certain case issues (constitutional, civil liberties, and statutory interpretation), panel size, reversal, and complexity, along with being heard during Lamer's tenure as chief justice (relative to Laskin) were positively and statistically significantly related to the dissent rate. Neither the fact that the issue related to criminal law, or workload, or having Dickson or McLachlin as chief justice were statistically significant. See also Donald R. Songer, *The Transformation of the Supreme Court of Canada: An Empirical Examination* (Toronto: University of Toronto Press, 2008) at 86.

50. Russell Smyth, "Explaining Voting Patterns on the Latham High Court" (2002) 26:1 *Melbourne University Law Review* 88 at 106. See also Schubert's early study of agreement on the High Court concludes that differences in opinion agreement cannot be accounted for based on

when a conservative government was in power, conservative appointees dissented less often than Labor appointees, and judges who had a political career in the Labor party dissented more often overall.[51]

One measure of disagreement we can use to examine this issue of ideology and dissent across different courts is the number of opinions with at least one dissent. If we look at our data for 1970 to the early 2000s and measure the size of the ideological differences on a court by looking at the spread of the lifetime liberal voting scores of judges on that court in a given year, Figure 8-4 shows the predicted dissent rate across a range of such differences.[52] The horizontal axis shows the potential spread of liberal voting rates of judges on a court with the spread measured by the standard deviation of the lifetime liberal voting scores for the judges on the court in a given year. It encompasses the range of spreads on these courts in the period 1970 to the early 2000s. The Supreme Court of Canada in fact tended to have a lower spread of ideology (with a mean over the period of 0.051) and the United States a higher spread (with a mean of .148). The vertical axis is what we would predict the percent of opinions with at least one dissent would be at each of the possible differences in liberal voting rates.

The change in the differences in the ideological spread as measured by lifetime liberal voting rates does appear related to the dissent rate, but the impact varies considerably across courts. The US and Australian predicted rate of dissents is high across the spread of liberal votes rates, though the Australian High Court dissent rate is much more responsive to increases in differences in liberal voting rates on the Court. The dissent rate on the Supreme Court of Canada is also highly responsive to changes in the composition of the Court. The UK dissent rate is low and not as responsive to changes on the Court as the Court in Australia and Canada.

the relative conservatism of the judges. Glendon Schubert, "Opinion Agreement among High Court Justices in Australia" (1968) 4:1 *Australian and New Zealand Journal of Sociology* 2 at 15. In a broader study covering 1903 to 1975 Smyth finds that the commonly held hypothesis that Labor party judges dissent more often is only very weakly borne out in some tests and not in others. Russell Smyth, "Explaining Historical Dissent Rates in the High Court of Australia" (2003) 41:2 *Journal of Commonwealth and Comparative Politics* 83 at 107 [Smyth, "Explaining Historical Dissent"]. Smyth notes that by stopping in 1975, the paper misses several Labor appointees known to be above average dissenters (at 109).

51. Russell Smyth, "The Role of Attitudinal, Institutional and Environmental Factors in Explaining Variations in Dissent Rates on the High Court of Australia" (2005) 40:4 Australian Journal of Political Science) 519 at 535 [Smyth, "Role of Attitudinal"].

52. See Appendix 3 for a discussion of the variables used and the results of the related regressions. Note that the marginal values for idsd was significant at the .05 level for each country.

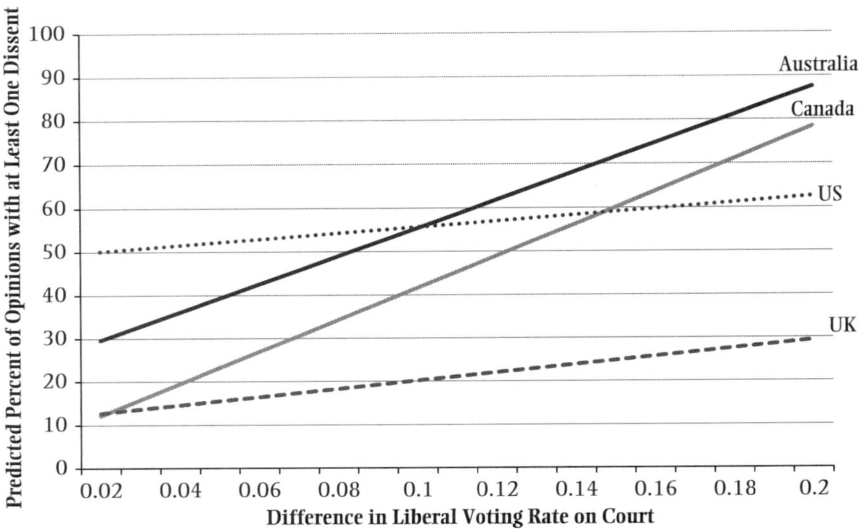


**Figure 8-4** Predicted percentage of opinions with at least one dissent based on the difference in the liberal voting rate on each court, 1970s to early 2000s. The difference in the liberal voting rate is the mean of the annual standard deviations of the lifetime liberal voting rates of judges on the court over the period. The predictions were found controlling for time and workload (total cases heard in the year). Canada and Australia were the most responsive to alterations in the composition of the court; the United States and the UK were much less so.

We can also measure how likely judges are to dissent by looking at the number of dissenting opinions per year—that is, not the number of cases per year that have dissents, but the number of times in a year that judges decide to dissent. To take account of differences in the caseload per year, we need to look at the fraction of dissenting opinions, which we find by dividing the number of dissenting opinions in a year by the number of decisions that year.[53] We saw in Chapter 1 (Figure 1-3) that there was a large difference across countries in terms of the fraction dissenting, from a high in the United States of almost 1.5 dissenting opinions for every decision down to almost zero for India. Our question now is—does the size of the difference in ideology on a court in a given year correlate with the differences in the fraction of dissenting opinions? It turns out it does in Canada, the UK, and the United States but does not in India and Australia. Assume again that we can measure the size of the ideological differences across courts by looking at the spread of the lifetime liberal voting scores

53. We follow Epstein, Landes & Posner, *Behavior, supra* note 3, who use fraction dissenting to explore the determinants of dissenting.

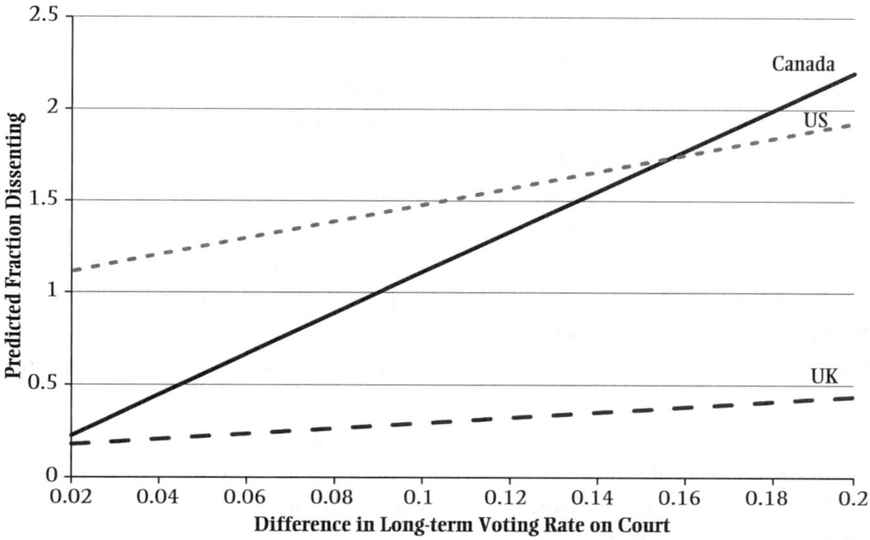


**Figure 8-5** Predicted percentage of fraction of opinions that are dissenting based on the difference in the liberal voting rate on each court, 1970s to early 2000s.[54] The difference in the liberal voting rate is the mean of the annual standard deviations of the lifetime liberal voting rates of judges on the court over the period. The predictions were found controlling for time and workload (total cases heard in the year). Justices on the Supreme Court of Canada appear most sensitive to changes in the composition of the Court.

of judges on the court in that year.[55] Figure 8-5 shows the connection between this spread of liberal voting rates and the fraction of dissenting opinions on a court. We did not include India and Australia as the relationship was not statistically significant in these countries.

As in Figure 8-4, the horizontal axis shows the potential spread of liberal voting rates of judges on a court (with the spread measured by the standard deviation of the lifetime liberal voting scores for the judges on the court in a given year). The vertical axis is what we would predict the fraction of dissenting opinions would be at each of the possible differences in liberal voting rates. The figure shows that the US Supreme Court has a fairly high baseline dissenting rate. Even if the justices were fairly similar on the Court (to the left end of the

54. See Appendix 3 for the regressions underlying this Figure. For this Figure, we used the estimates from regressions fraction dissenting on TotalCases, time, and idsd. We held TotalCases at its mean for each country and time at the median. The marginal values for idsd was significant at the .05 level for each country.

55. See Appendix 3 for a discussion of the variables used and the results of the related regressions.

horizontal axis), the justices would be relatively likely to dissent. However, this high dissenting rate is not particularly sensitive to increases in how diverse the justices on the Court are given the fraction dissenting rises relatively slowly as the voting tendencies on the Court become more spread out. The UK House of Lords, on the other hand, has a low base rate level of dissent, with justices relatively infrequently writing dissenting opinions. Interestingly, the UK House of Lords is also relatively insensitive to changes in the range of voting of its members. It has a low rate of dissenting even on a highly diverse court. The fraction dissenting on each of these courts could potentially be understood through norms. The US Supreme Court has a norm of dissenting and the UK House of Lords of not dissenting, both of which are fairly insensitive to the membership of the Court.

The Supreme Court of Canada, on the other hand, appears very sensitive to the voting behavior of its members. Like the UK House of Lords, it has a fairly low baseline of dissenting behavior, with a low fraction of dissenting opinions when the Court is fairly similar. However, as the voting behavior of the justices on the Court diverges (we move to the right on the figure), the justices on the Court are much more likely to dissent. The difference from the UK and the United States cannot be explained solely through the use of panels, because although the United States hears all cases *en banc*, the Canadian and UK courts hear decisions in panels. So in Canada the story appears slightly more complex than a possible consistent norms story.

We could also look at how individual judges vote to try to find the effect of differences in policy preferences. Figure 8-6 examines whether differences of a judge from her fellow panelists influences her probability of dissenting.[56] Moving from left to right along the horizontal axis represents moving from the judge having a similar lifetime liberal voting rate to the average of the other panelists to the judge having a progressively higher or lower lifetime liberal voting than the other panelists (that is, it is absolute value of the difference). The vertical axis is the probability of the judge dissenting. There are two key facts to note about the Figure.[57] First, a judge in the United States has the highest

56. We also examined whether a judge's dissent rate appeared correlated with both whether the judge was on a homogeneous panel (that is, all judges appointed by appointers from the same party), and whether the judge was a minority on the panel in terms of ideology (such as, for example, the sole liberal appointee on a panel where all the other judges were appointed by a conservative appointer). Overall, these results showed no significant difference in the probability of the judge dissenting.

57. These results were found using data on individual judge votes for each country. The dependent variable in each case was whether the judge dissented or was with the majority. The independent variables included the party appointing the judge, the lower court direction (liberal or conservative), the area of law, the panel size, and a time trend, as well as the difference between

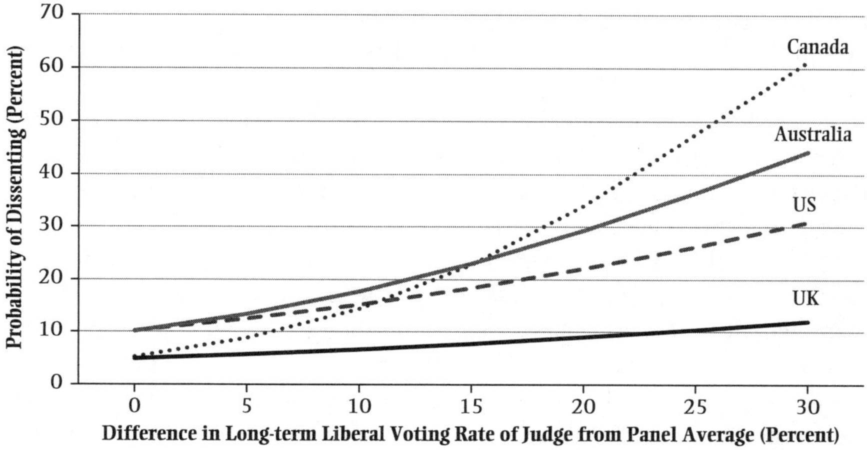


**Figure 8-6** Influence on the probability of a judge dissenting of the difference of the judge's lifetime liberal voting rate from the average lifetime liberal voting rate of the other panelists (percent). At the left hand side the judge's lifetime liberal voting rate is the same as the average of the other panelists. At the right hand side, the judge's lifetime liberal voting rate is 30 percent higher or lower than the average of the other panelists. The United States and Australia have the highest base rate of dissenting (the probability of a justice dissenting even if he is at the average of the other panelists), and Canada and the UK have the lowest. Justices in Canada and Australia are the most responsive to differences from their fellow panelists, and UK justices are the least.

dissent rate even if her lifetime liberal voting rate is the equal to the average of all the other panelists. We could think of this dissent rate as the baseline dissent rate as the judge's voting tendencies are similar to the average of others. Australian justices have comparably high dissent rates. The UK and Canada have similar and much lower base dissent rates.

Second, justices on the US Supreme Court and the UK House of Lords are both relatively unresponsive to being different to the average of the other panelists. As the justice's voting tendencies become increasingly different from the average of the other panelists (we move to the right in the Figure), the probability of dissent only slowly increases. For Canada and Australia, on the other hand, differences from the panel average are correlated with a much greater increase in the dissent rate. The United States and the UK may have stronger norms—for the United States a strong norm of disagreement may allow justices to overcome at least some of the negative consequences of dissenting (such as reputational effects with her fellow justices), and for the House of Lords a strong norm of agreement may mean that it is difficult to dissent even in the face of a large difference in voting tendencies of the justice and the other panelists. The Supreme Court of Canada and the Australian High Court may have weaker norms, leading to differences in dissent rates being more closely related to differences of the justice from the rest of the panel.

As we discussed, the ideology hypothesis may interact with an important institutional factor: panel size. The larger the panel (and, by extension, the larger the court), the greater the opportunity for ideological differences among judges. This difference is noticeable in India, where panel size has changed over time. When the Supreme Court used to sit in plenary sessions, there was at least one dissent in every freedom of speech case. Once smaller panels were instituted, dissent occurred less frequently.[58] Songer, Szmer, and Johnson find that the likelihood of a dissent increases on the Supreme Court of Canada as the panel size increases, with a one standard deviation increase in panel size increasing the odds of a dissent by over 42 percent.[59] However, it cannot be assumed that panel size alone is responsible for more pronounced ideological division. Larger panels may be used *because* a case is particularly divisive.[60] Likewise, smaller panels may have fewer dissents not only because there are fewer judges who could potentially disagree, but also because the cases heard by small panels tend to be more routine.[61] In any event, these results control for differences in panel size on a particular high court.[62]

the judge's lifetime liberal voting rate and the average of the other panelists. These results were all significant at the .01 level except for the UK, which was significant at the .1 level. We also ran the same regressions using the judge's lifetime liberal voting rate in criminal matters and examining non-criminal dissent rates. The results were similar, except that the Canadian dissent rate did not increase quite as quickly for when the party of the appointer was used, and that the UK did not have a significant change in the dissent rate as the judge became increasing different from the panel average.

58. Abhinav Chandrachud, "Speech, Structure and Behaviour on the Supreme Court of India" (2012) 25:2 *Columbia Journal of Asian Law* 222 at 252. Smyth has remarked that one reason that the Australian High Court produces more separate opinions than either the US or Canadian supreme courts is the panel size: the High Court's typical panel consists of only five judges. There is therefore less opportunity for large coalitions in Australia; coupled with the seriatim tradition, this makes for fragmented opinions. Smyth, "Some Are More Equal," *supra* note 22 at 200.

59. Songer et al., "Explaining Dissent," *supra* note 22 at 404.

60. Songer et al., "Explaining Dissent," *supra* note 22 at 404.

61. McCormick, "With Respect," *supra* note 18 at 107.

62. In our dissent regressions on individual judge votes, the panel size was positive and significant at the .01 level for Canada and the UK and insignificant for the other countries. See also Edelman et al., *supra* note 25, who suggest in passing that there will be more dissent as the panel size increases due to simple probability, and they control for number of judges. See also Alarie et al., "Panel Selections," *supra* note 37 for a discussion of panel size.

## Does Complexity or Controversy Matter?

A more indirect measure of whether differences in policy preferences influence dissents relates to the complexity or controversial nature of the case. The evidence is mixed on whether a change in the types of cases a court hears is associated with changes in the level of consensus. The large increase in disagreement on the US Supreme Court in the 1940s does not appear to have been caused by a change in case mix as there was no increase in the dissent-prone areas of law over this period.[63] Similarly, the earlier Waite Court (1874–1887 terms) had considerably higher rates of dissent in conference than in final opinions (across all areas of law) than later courts, which points more to a change in the norm of consensus rather than in the difficulty of the case mix.[64]

Conversely some studies have found a connection between dissents and certain areas of law for both the US and Canadian Supreme Courts. Hurwitz and Lanier describe a tripartite relationship among consensus, ideology, and the court's agenda. Ideological disparity on the US Court had a measurable effect on rates of consensus in certain contentious areas of law between 1888 and 1999. Civil rights and liberties cases had more non-consensual opinions as compared to economic decisions and a greater number of concurrences relative to dissents.[65] Similarly, constitutional, civil liberties, and statutory interpretation cases before the Supreme Court of Canada had higher levels of dissents than other cases as did cases with interveners.[66] Criminal cases, however, did not have a statistically significant higher rate of dissents than general cases.[67]

Overall, then, the existing findings concerning case mix and dissents are inconclusive. When we look at our data set covering the period 1970 to the early 2000s, the fraction of dissenting opinions on a court was not related to the fraction of cases raising civil liberties issues for any of the courts, even though civil liberties cases are arguably the most controversial types of cases.[68] Similarly, the fraction of cases raising constitutional issues had no or only a very weak effect

63. Walker, Epstein & Dixon, *supra* note 8 at 370 (examining the number and dissent rates of different areas of law but not undertaking a formal empirical analysis).

64. Epstein et al., "Norm of Consensus," *supra* note 36 at 376.

65. Mark S. Hurwitz & Drew Noble Lanier, "I Respectfully Dissent: Consensus, Agendas, and Policymaking on the U.S. Supreme Court 1888–1999" (2004) 21:3 *Review of Policy* 429 at 443.

66. Songer et al., "Explaining Dissent," *supra* note 22 at 403.

67. Songer et al., "Explaining Dissent," *supra* note 22 at 403.

68. See Appendix 3 for regression results relating to fraction of dissenting opinions.

in all the countries except the United States. For the US Supreme Court, as the fraction of the caseload that raised constitutional issues increased, the level of dissent in the form of the fraction of dissenting opinions rose considerably—the increase in the fraction of constitutional cases from 30 percent to 40 percent is related to a predicted fraction of dissenting opinions of about 13 percent.[69]

However, if we look not at the fraction of opinions in a year that are dissents but rather at the individual justice level, we do find some evidence of differences in dissents across areas of law for the US Supreme Court and the Supreme Court of Canada, although not for the other courts. For the US Supreme Court, a justice was no more likely to dissent in civil rights cases than criminal cases but was less likely to dissent in public law cases.[70] For the Supreme Court of Canada, on the other hand, justices were about 2 percent more likely to dissent in civil rights cases than criminal cases (significant at the .01 level) and there was no statistical difference for public law, private economic law, and criminal cases.[71]

One reason for the difference in the influence of criminal cases on dissents between the US and Canadian Supreme Courts stems from an alternate method of analyzing whether the caseload is complex or controversial. A court with a discretionary docket should exhibit a higher rate of dissent than a court with a mandatory docket, as there will be fewer routine or "easy" cases, and the cases that are granted leave are more likely to be controversial. Such a hypothesis is consistent with the higher relative dissent rate in the United States than in Canada (which has in part a mandatory criminal docket). Although, again, empirical findings are mixed.

In the United States, again looking at the rise of dissensus at the beginning of the 1940s, one hypothesis was that the rising level of disagreement was due to the granting of docket control to the Court under the *Judiciary Act of 1925* (the "Judges'

69. The positive connection for the US Supreme Court was significant at the .05 level, with the fraction dissenting for constitutional cases being 1.6 higher than for other cases. Moving from a fraction of the docket being constitutional cases of 30 percent to 40 percent leads to an increased fraction dissenting from 1.5 to 1.7, or about a 13 percent increase. There was actually a slightly lower fraction dissenting for constitutional cases than other cases in the UK (about 0.5 lower, significant at the .05 level).

70. See Appendix 3 for a description of the regressions on judge dissents using party of appointing president as the control for judge ideology. In controlling for area of law, criminal cases were the baseline (omitted) area, with the coefficient on civil rights case was statistically insignificant in all specifications. The difference in dissent rates was also not significant for private economic cases. On the other hand, public law cases had a 6 percent lower dissent rate, significant at the .05 level in all specifications. Public law cases also had a lower dissent rate (significant at the .01 level) when we ran similar regressions on non-criminal cases using the long-term liberal voting rate in criminal cases as the measure of the judge's ideology.

71. See Appendix 3 for a description of the regressions on judge dissents using party of the appointing prime minister as the control for judge ideology.

Bill").[72] However, the actual increase in dissensus did not occur until more than a decade later and "little support exists . . . for the position that the Judges' Bill alone initiated the significant elevation in individual judicial expression."[73] Although there is some limited, indirect evidence that the change in the case mix following the grant of docket control to the US Supreme Court led to a decline in consensus, the effect was minor compared to the influence of the characteristics of the confirming Senate.[74] Case selection discretion also appears to have had no statistically significant effect on dissent rates on the Australian High Court.[75] However, it is possible that the effect of case selection is being captured by the increased caseload, which was found to reduce dissent rates on the High Court.[76]

However, one possible partial explanation for the fact that criminal cases were as likely to lead to dissents as civil rights cases in the United States but not Canada is that in recent years approximately 30 percent of cases reach the Supreme Court of Canada as of right (that is, the Court had to hear them), all of which were criminal cases. Criminal cases in Canada should lead to some disagreement, as there are few truly "easy" cases due to both the discretionary docket and the high cost of pursuing an appeal at the highest level.[77] However, there may be a lower proportion of controversial cases on average than for civil rights cases.

In summary, although it seems reasonable to hypothesize that more controversial cases and greater docket control should lead to greater disagreement, there is as yet no clear empirical evidence of this influence other than some suggestive evidence from the United States and Canada.

72. Stephen C. Halpern & Kenneth N. Vines, "Institutional Disunity, the Judges' Bill and the Role of the U.S. Supreme Court" (1977) 30:4 *Western Political Quarterly* 471. Similarly, at the US state supreme court level, Hall found that "discretionary dockets produce substantially higher proportions of cases which are decided with dissent," and that a mandatory docket minimizes, but does not completely eliminate, judges' reliance on attitudinal considerations: Gann Hall, "Docket Control," *supra* note 36 at 251–252.

73. Walker, Epstein & Dixon, *supra* note 8 at 366. See also Sunstein, "Unanimity," *supra* note 3.

74. Brian Goff, "Supreme Court Consensus and Dissent: Estimating the Role of the Selection Screen" (2006) 127:3 *Public Choice* 375 at 388.

75. Russell Smyth, "What Explains Variations in Dissent Rates?: Time Series Evidence from the High Court" (2004) 26 *Sydney Law Review* 221 at 238 [Smyth, "Variations in Dissent"]; Paresh Kumar Narayan & Russell Smyth, "What Explains Dissent on the High Court of Australia? An Empirical Assessment Using a Cointegration and Error Correction Approach" (2007) 4:2 *Journal of Empirical Legal Studies* 401 at 418 [Narayan & Smyth, "What Explains Dissent"].

76. Narayan & Smyth, "What Explains Dissent," *supra* note 75 at 421.

77. McCormick, "With Respect," *supra* note 18 at 110.

## HOW IMPORTANT IS WORKLOAD TO DISSENT?

Whether a judge dissents may be influenced not only by his policy views but by how busy he is in deciding other appeals. A number of factors affect a judge's workload. There is of course the total number of cases heard by the court, although this is not an exogenous factor for many high courts given they can select both the number and type of cases they hear. At the most basic level, as the number of cases before the court increases, there is a greater probability that some will be easier and less divisive.

However, a judge's workload will not only depend on the total number of cases heard by the court but on the number of cases he has to hear. It takes time for a judge to write a dissenting judgment or a concurrence, and a busy judge may be less inclined to do so.[78] Although a judge with a lower caseload may have (and use) the extra time to forge compromises and reach consensus,[79] his opportunity cost of dissenting will clearly increase as the number of cases he hears increases. The number of cases per judge will depend on the total number of judges that sit on the court, as well as whether the court hears cases *en banc* or in panels, and on the size of those panels.[80]

An additional factor that may impact the cost of disagreement for a judge is whether a court employs law clerks. Law clerks will decrease the judges' workload, allowing for more time to author dissents. Of course, an opposing theory applies here as well: law clerks may give judges more time to reach a compromise and build consensus. The use of law clerks varies widely across high courts. In the United States and Canada, law clerks are given extensive responsibilities for analyzing material and helping draft opinions.[81] Justice Scalia wrote in *Conroy v. Aniskoff*: "I confess that I have not personally investigated the entire legislative history—or even that portion of it which relates to the four statutes listed above. The excerpts I have examined and quoted were unearthed by a hapless law clerk to whom I assigned the task."[82] In Australia, on

78. Smyth, "Variations in Dissent," *supra* note 75 at 224.

79. McCormick, "With Respect," *supra* note 18 at 108.

80. Further, the workload will vary with vacancies on the court. The workload per judge increases when the court is below complement, leading to less time and fewer resources to author dissents (to the extent the vacancies are not offset by a court accepting fewer cases on appeal).

81. For the United States, see Todd C. Peppers & Christopher Zorn, "Law Clerk Influence on Supreme Court Decision Making: An Empirical Assessment" (2008) 58 *DePaul Law Review* 51 at 56. For Canada, see Lorne Sossin, "The Sounds of Silence: Law Clerks, Policy Making and the Supreme Court of Canada" (1996) 30 *University of British Columbia Law Review* 279 at 287–298.

82. Jonathan Horton, "Justices' Associates: Some Observations" (2002) 22:1 *University of Queensland Law Journal* 114 at 119 [Horton].

the other hand, "associates" are given less responsibility, particularly in drafting opinions.[83] Justice Kirby of the High Court of Australia commented "I'm far too egocentric and idiosyncratic to allow anybody to write my peerless prose."[84] For the Indian Supreme Court, clerkships are less prestigious, and the use of clerks by judges varies significantly across judges.[85] Although we will not analyze the impact of clerks on judicial decision-making, they clearly have the potential to play a significant role.[86]

Leaving aside the issue of clerks, we will examine the following hypothesis:

> *H4: The consensus rate will increase as the workload increases, with workload depending on the total number of cases heard by a court and on the cases heard per judge.*

As with other hypotheses, empirical findings have been far from unanimous. Epstein, Landes, and Posner found that a 10 percent increase in workload was associated with a 3.3 percent decline in the dissent rate on the US Supreme Court. Similarly, for the High Court of Australia, Smyth found an increase in caseload had a negative effect on dissent rate, with a 1 percent increase in caseload per judge correlating with a 0.33 percent decrease in dissent rate.[87] Further, Narayan and Smyth conclude that increases in GDP per capita also have a negative effect on dissent rate, as this leads to more litigation and therefore a higher caseload.[88]

83. Horton, *supra* note 82 at 119. South Africa has in the past essentially not used law clerks, which may have contributed to a high judicial workload and reliance by judges on oral argument and legal briefs. Stacia L. Haynie & Kaitlyn L. Sill, "Experienced Advocates and Litigation Outcomes: Repeat Players in the South African Supreme Court of Appeal" (2007) 60:3 *Political Research Quarterly* 443 at 451.

84. Horton, *supra* note 82 at 121.

85. Abhinav Chandrachud, "From Hyderbad to Harvard: How U.S. Law Schools Make Clerking on India's Supreme Court Worthwhile" (2014) HLS Program on the Legal Profession Research Paper at 24, online: http://ssrn.com/abstract=2413576 [Chandrachud, "Hyderbad"].

86. The effect of law clerks on the connection between legal regimes is also an important area for further research. See e.g. Marie Gren, "An Empirical Study of Judicial Fertilization: The Use of Foreign Clerks by the Israeli Supreme Court" (paper delivered at the 9th World Congress Conference, "Constitutional Challenges: Global and Local," Oslo, June 16–20, 2014); Chandrachud, "Hyderbad," *supra* note 85.

87. Smyth, "Variations in Dissent," *supra* note 75 at 238; Smyth, "Role of Attitudinal," *supra* note 51 at 535.

88. Narayan & Smyth, "What Explains Dissent," *supra* note 75 at 420.

However, Walker, Epstein, and Dixon find no causal association between increased caseloads in the form of court filings and rates of individual expression on the US Supreme Court, and in fact found the increase in disagreement preceded the increase in filings.[89] However, they also note that the number of decided cases declined over time, which, although they do not analyze it, may provide evidence of a decreased workload leading to greater disagreement.[90] Similarly, neither McCormick nor Songer, Szmer, and Johnson find a correlation on the Supreme Court of Canada between workload and dissents.[91]

When we look at our annual data for the period 1970 to the early 2000s, there is only limited evidence of a correlation between the caseload of a court and measures of dissent.[92] The total caseload of the court is negatively correlated with the percent of cases with at least one dissent in the UK, but the effect is very small. There is no correlation with the probability of a dissent in a case in Canada, the United States, Australia, or India. Similarly, when we look at the relationship between the total caseload for a court and the fraction of opinions that are dissents (as opposed to whether a decision has at least one dissent), there is no statistically significant relationship in Canada, the United States, or India. In India at least, the caseload may be so high that there is only very limited appetite for dissenting at any of the levels seen in this period. There is only weak evidence that judges in Australia or the UK respond to the total caseload; in both cases the effect was as expected, with a higher total number of cases correlating with a lower fraction of dissenting opinions. In both cases, however, the effects disappeared when we control for who is the chief justice.

A judge may not care about the total number of cases heard by the court so much as the average (how many cases she on average hears in a given year).

89. Walker, Epstein & Dixon, *supra* note 8 at 367–368. In contrast, on courts of appeals, it has been found that an increased caseload makes authoring a dissent "quite unattractive," which is consistent with our hypothesis (see, for an early example, Burton M. Atkins & Justin J. Green, "Consensus on the United States Courts of Appeals: Illusion or Reality?" (1976) 20:4 *American Journal of Political* 735 at 746).

90. Walker, Epstein & Dixon, *supra* note 8 at 368, n. 4.

91. McCormick, "With Respect," *supra* note 18 at 108; Songer et al., "Explaining Dissent," *supra* note 22 at 404 (examining influences on dissents between 1976 and 2005 including workload defined as the number of cases heard by the Court in that term and finding no statistically significant relationship between workload and dissents, which they attribute to a relatively stable caseload over the period and docket control by the Court). As for Israel, Weinshall-Margel has hypothesized that a higher caseload will diminish the impact of justices' attitudes on their decisions, thereby reducing the frequency of dissent, but has not tested this hypothesis fully (Weinshall-Margel, "Attitudinal," *supra* note 40).

92. See Appendix 3 for regression results relating to fraction of dissenting opinions and to cases with at least one dissent.

However the results using average caseload (number of cases in a year divided by the number of judges hearing cases) are largely consistent with the story, looking at the total number of cases. The principal exception is the UK. For the UK House of Lords, there is a stronger negative relationship between the fraction of dissenting opinions and the caseload per judge, and this relationship does not go away when we account for differences across chief justices.

As with policy preferences, the story of the relationship between workload and dissenting is not clear-cut. Although there is some evidence of a negative relationship, that evidence is not strong, and even when there is a relationship, the effect does not appear to be large.

## NORMS AND THE CHIEF JUSTICE

The last category of factors that we will consider as affecting rates of disagreement is norms. As we saw in Chapter 2, a judge may follow a norm because of an internal or personal sense of guilt or shame at not meeting the norms of the court. Alternatively, he may face external penalties for not following a norm, such as esteem or disesteem of colleagues or, more directly, "sanctioning" by the chief justice, such as being left off important panels. Norms themselves may be hard to identify directly. Part of our analysis will rely on the notion of norms as the residual once the other factors are taken into account—that is, the level of consensus on the court, controlling for differences in policy preferences and workload.

A norm of consensus may overcome or mitigate differences in policy preferences judges may have in a particular outcome. The Israeli Supreme Court presents a good example of how a strong norm of consensus can overcome ideological division. Despite the ideological split on many contentious issues before the court, the ISC boasts a 95 percent unanimity rate.[93] Similarly, in the UK, the House of Lords appears to have had an overriding consensual norm such that the law lords went "to great lengths to attempt to ensure that they speak with a single voice"[94] and are also "less likely to reverse colleagues with whom they will have to work in the near future."[95]

In addition, however, it may be possible to analyze other factors directly related to norms. In particular, the identity of the chief justice is one of the

93. Weinshall-Margel, "Attitudinal," *supra* note 40.

94. T.T. Arvind & Lindsay Stirton, "Lawyers and the Legal Model: Judicial Ideology, Judicial Professionalism and Institutional Strategy among the Law Lords" (2012) at 39, online: https://extranet.sioe.org/uploads/isnie2012/arvind_stirton.pdf.

95. Chris Hanretty, "The Decisions and Ideal Points of British Law Lords" (2012) 43 *British Journal of Political Science* 703 at 715.

most important factors when considering norms of consensus. A chief justice can affect the cohesion of the court in a number of different ways.[96] Chief justices may have varying skills in social leadership (leading through force of personality) and task leadership (such as requiring formal meetings and debates and encouraging collaboration).[97] She may also have different mechanisms for enforcing a norm of consensus.[98] A chief justice's previous political experience may be helpful in becoming an effective leader, and it may be that "the ideal Chief Justice is a persuasive, esteemed, able, and well-liked judge who perceives, fulfills, and even expands his role as head of the Court."[99] Alternatively, a chief justice may use sanctions, such as leaving an individual who continually dissents off important panels or assigning him to difficult or uninteresting appeals.

In terms of task leadership, the chief justice may establish or encourage formal decision-making processes. There may be differences in procedures not only between courts but on the same court under different chief justices. For example, post-hearing conferences can be an important part of building consensus. In Canada, the justices attend a post-hearing conference during which they announce, in reverse order of seniority, how they would decide the case. The length of the conferences varies depending on the chief justice. Some chief justices allow for a substantive discussion of issues, whereas others prefer a brief statement of opinion.[100] Chief Justice McLachlin has even reconvened additional conferences, with the express goal of building consensus and reducing the number of written judgments.[101] The system in the United States is much the same, although the justices state their views in order of seniority.[102] The

96. These theories about the role of the chief justices are summarized in Jason Pierce, "Institutional Cohesion in the High Court of Australia: Do American Theories Travel Well Down Under?" (2008) 46:3 *Commonwealth & Comparative Politics* 318 at 324–325 [Pierce].

97. Rice & Zorn, *supra* note 26; Ostberg et al., "Leaders," *supra* note 28.

98. Caldeira & Zorn, "Of Time," *supra* note 4 at 878 (discussing the use of sanctions and rewards by chief justices to enforce norms); Walker, Epstein & Dixon, *supra* note 8 at 381.

99. David J. Danelski, "The Influence of the Chief Justice in the Decisional Process of the Supreme Court" in Sheldon Goldman & Austin Sarat, eds, *American Court Systems: Readings in Judicial Process and Behavior* (San Francisco: W.H. Freeman, 1978) at 507.

100. Macfarlane, "Consensus," *supra* note 19 at 388.

101. Macfarlane, "Consensus," *supra* note 19 at 409.

102. Bertha Wilson, "Decision-Making in the Supreme Court" (1986) 36 *University of Toronto Law Journal* 227 at 236. As in Canada, the length of the conference in the UK varied under different chief justices. Alan Paterson, *Final Judgment: The Last Law Lords and the Supreme Court* (Oxford: Hart, 2013) at 86 [Paterson] (noting that the presiding law lord directed the process of the conference).

Supreme Court of Israel, which tends to sit in panels of three, convenes two conferences, one before the hearing and one after.[103] At the other end of the spectrum is Australia, where there is no conference procedure and judges are markedly individualistic in their judgment writing.[104] Certain chief justices have tried to introduce a judicial conference procedure in Australia, but none has succeeded.[105]

There is an aspect of norms that may relate to workload. We had noted that a judge may be more likely to dissent on larger panels as there is a greater likelihood that she will differ from the majority in terms of policy preferences and the other judges may be less likely to take any disagreement personally.[106] Relatedly, if judges on larger courts are less frequently assigned to the same panels with other judges, the result may be weaker collegial norms. Examining this effect requires controlling for panel size because larger supreme courts, such as the Supreme Court of India, also happen to hear cases in smaller panels, and smaller panels may result in greater unanimity. It is therefore the interaction between the number of judges and likelihood of being placed on a panel with another judge repeatedly that may be important.

Although the impact of the chief justice will vary across courts, we hypothesize:

> *H5: The dissent rate will vary under the leadership of different chief justices, once we control for differences such as in panel size.*

There is a wide variance in the tenure of chief justices across the high courts. Since 1970, the US Supreme Court has had 3 chief justices, and Australia and Canada 6 each. India, on the other hand, has had 32 chief justices and the UK has had 11. Figure 8-7 shows the tenure of chief justices for each high court from 1970 to the present (it includes the chief justice of the court in 1970 (and their time even if before 1970) and the current chief justice for each country whose tenure is therefore truncated). Related to the number of chief justices in each country, chief justices spent very different times leading the courts. US Supreme Court chief justices held the position for on average 12 years, whereas in India chief justices averaged less than 2 years in the role. Chief justices

103. Yoram Shachar, "Inside the Supreme Court of Israel—Decision-Making in Small Panels" (Paper delivered at the IDC Law Review conference, March 19, 2014) [unpublished].

104. Smyth, "Some Are More Equal," *supra* note 22 at 201.

105. Dixon had limited success in the 1960s, but ultimately fared no better than Latham, Barwick, Mason, and Gleeson: Narayan & Smyth, "What Explains Dissent," *supra* note 75 at 405–406.

106. Edelman et al., *supra* note 25 at 142.

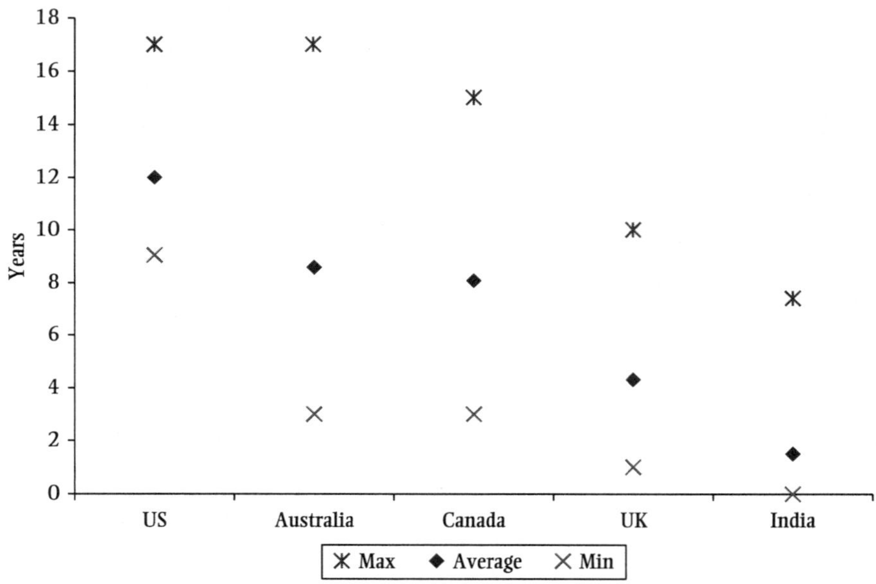


**Figure 8-7** Tenure of chief justices over the period from 1970 to the early 2000s, average tenure and range (years). Chief justices on the US Supreme Court on average stay in office longest whereas those on the Indian Supreme Court by far stay the shortest.

would likely have much greater ability to influence norms the longer they lead the court.

In the United States, the chief justice's leadership has figured prominently among the factors affecting consensual norms.[107] For example, the drastic rise in dissensus in the 1940s, seen in a rapid rise in both dissents and concurrences, occurred during the Stone Court. Marshall (1801–1835), Taft (1921–1930), and Hughes (1930–1941) were seen as actively seeking to minimize dissent whereas conversely, Stone (1941–1946), generally characterized as an ineffective leader, presided over an increasingly fragmented court.[108] A norm of consensus existed in the earlier time period (Waite Court in the 1880s) as evidenced by a high level of disagreements in conference that did not manifest in dissents in

107. Caldeira & Zorn, "Of Time," *supra* note 4 at 900 (arguing that there is a consensual norm on the US Supreme Court that changed over time influencing both dissents and concurrences and partly though not wholly related to changes in the chief justice).

108. Caldeira & Zorn, "Of Time," *supra* note 4 at 878. See also Sunstein, "Unanimity," *supra* note 3.

the final dispositions.[109] Stone was responsible for "changing the operational norms of the Court from institutional unity to permitting free expression of individual views."[110] Further, Chief Justice Hughes (Stone's predecessor) may have played a role in the demise of consensus, as the rate of concurrence rose under Hughes, paving the way for more open disagreement in the form of dissent under Stone.[111] More recently, the Rehnquist Court displayed high rates of dissent and concurrence—higher, in fact, than the lower appellate courts at the time.[112]

Similarly, dissent rates have varied under Canadian chief justices. As can be seen in Figure 8-8, dissents rates dropped to their lowest levels toward the end of Laskin's chief justiceship in 1984, but rose thereafter. This drop in unanimity (and along with a rise in the total number of dissenting votes) may be due more to the introduction of the Charter of Rights and Freedoms in the early 1980s than less successful leadership or a change in norms.[113] Looking across chief justices (and controlling for a range of factors including whether the cases were constitutional) we see the dissent rates were similar for the Court under chief justices Laskin (1973–1984), Dickson (1984–1990), and McLachlin (2000 to the end of the study in 2005). Only during the leadership of Chief Justice Lamer (1990–2000) was there a statistically higher rate of dissent, which may in part be due to the presence of Justice L'Heureux-Dubé.[114] However, Lamer has been argued to be an effective task leader, in the sense that his dissent rate was relatively low and he was frequently able to convince his colleagues to join him.[115]

109. Epstein et al., "Norm of Consensus," *supra* note 36 at 376.

110. Walker, Epstein & Dixon, *supra* note 8 at 384–385 (although they note that other factors were also influential such as a change in the court's docket control, the high turnover rate, and experience of the judges on the Court at the time).

111. Haynie, "Leadership," *supra* note 16 at 1164.

112. Scott D. Gerber & Keeok Park, "The Quixotic Search for Consensus on the U.S. Supreme Court: A Cross-Judicial Empirical Analysis of the Rehnquist Court Justices" (1997) 91:2 *American Political Science Review* 390 at 405.

113. Ostberg et al., "Leaders," *supra* note 28 at 523–524.

114. Songer et al., "Explaining Dissent," *supra* note 22 at 404–405.

115. Ostberg et al., "Leaders," *supra* note 28 at 526. Peter McCormick, "Follow the Leader: Judicial Power and Judicial Leadership on the Laskin Court, 1973–1984" (1998) 24 *Queen's LJ* 237 at 276 (using Laskin's own dissenting votes as a measure and finding that Laskin became less of a dissenter as time went on—an indication of a "strong and decisive leadership").

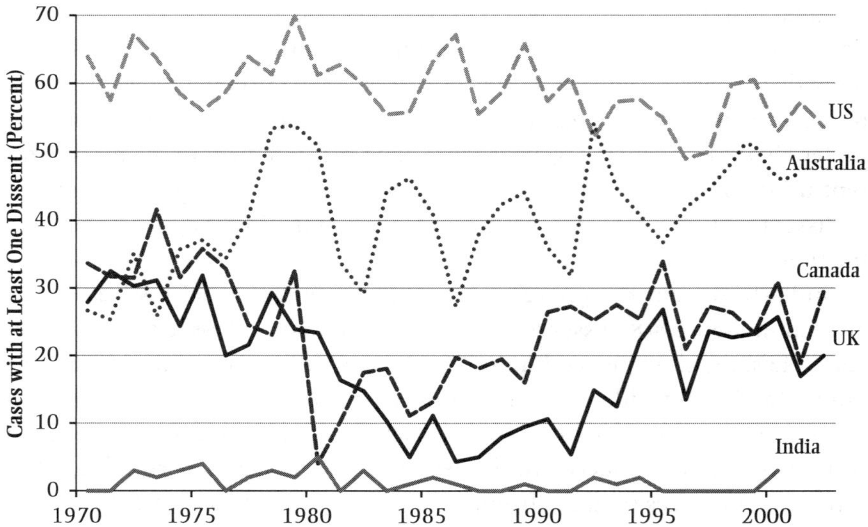


**Figure 8-8** Percent of cases with at least one dissent, 1970 to early 2000s. The dissent rate on the US Supreme Court was fairly uniformly high and on the Indian Supreme Court uniformly low over the whole period. In Canada, the dissent rate peaked in 1984, at the end of Chief Justice Laskin's tenure and right before the influx of cases under the new Canadian Charter of Rights and Freedoms. The Australian dissent rate rose over the period while the UK House of Lords saw a decline in dissents followed by an increase to prior levels.

Leadership may provide at least a partial explanation for dissent rates on the Australian High Court, as is evidenced by the changes in dissent patterns that coincide with the appointment of new chief justices.[116] Chief justices vary in their ability to build consensus, just as on the US Supreme Court.[117] For instance, chief justices Knox, Gavan-Duffy, Isaacs, Dixon, and Barwick did not have a statistically significant effect on dissent rates.[118] On the other hand, Latham had a negative effect, which is consistent with his characterization as a consensus-building judge.[119] Contrary to the norm at the US Supreme Court, the justices

116. Russell Smyth & Paresh Kumar Narayan, "Hail to the Chief! Leadership and Structural Change in the Level of Consensus on the High Court of Australia" (2004) 1:2 *Journal of Empirical Legal Studies* 399 at 423.

117. Smyth, "Historical Consensual," *supra* note 8 at 259.

118. Smyth, "Explaining Historical Dissent," *supra* note 50 at 102; Smyth, "Variations in Dissent," *supra* note 75 at 239; Smyth, "Role of Attitudinal," *supra* note 51.

119. Smyth, "Explaining Historical Dissent," *supra* note 50 at 102. But see Smyth, "Role of Attitudinal," *supra* note 51.

of the Australian High Court adhere to a deep-seated seriatim tradition, and it is not felt that formal conferences boost cohesion.[120] One interesting finding, which shows the power of the chief justice, is that the Australian High Court, under certain chief justices, saw a rise in *both* unanimity and dissent in constitutional cases. It was the middle ground of concurrence that became less common. In other words, constitutional cases had a polarizing effect.[121]

As we can see in Figure 8-8, dissent rates on the Indian Supreme Court were uniformly low over the period 1970 to 2000. Indian judicial leadership has not often been studied, though there is reason to believe that chief justices provide at least a partial explanation for dissent rates. Between 1950 and 2010, individualistic behavior was relatively rare on the Supreme Court but rates dropped as time went on. Chandrachud argues that the early disagreement was attributable to the Court's atmosphere under Chief Justice Kania, whereas the more recent positive consensual norm grew under S.R. Das's leadership.[122] The chief justice may have an impact when he sits on a constitutional bench, as in such cases unanimity is marginally more likely given their larger size and more controversial nature. Of course, the chief justice may merely select constitutional benches that are more likely to be unanimous from the start.[123]

In order to determine whether the dissent rates over the period from 1970 to the early 2000s are correlated with changes in the leadership of the court, we need to control for the caseload, the ideological makeup of the court at any given time, and the mix of cases. Once we do so, the level of dissent, as measured by the fraction of opinions with at least one dissent, was not consistently correlated across courts with the identity of the chief justice.[124]

120. Pierce, *supra* note 96 at 333.

121. Andrew Lynch, "Does the High Court Disagree More Often in Constitutional Cases? A Statistical Study of Judgment Delivery 1981–2003" (2005) 33 *Federal Law Review* 485 at 519.

122. Abhinav Chandrachud, "Speech, Structure and Behaviour on the Supreme Court of India" (2012) 25:2 *Columbia Journal of Asian Law* 222 at 252.

123. Nick Robinson et al., "Interpreting the Constitution: Supreme Court Constitution Benches since Independence" (2011) 41 *Economic & Political Weekly* 27 at 31. Similarly, in the UK Hanretty found that the presence of the president or deputy president of the Supreme Court increases the likelihood of agreement: Chris Hanretty, "Lumpers and Splitters on the United Kingdom Supreme Court" (2013) American Political Science Association 2013 Annual Meeting Paper, at 19.

124. See Appendix 3 for regression results relating to the fraction of dissenting opinions. These results used annual data for an OLS regression with the fraction of opinions in the year with at least one dissent as the dependent variable. The independent variables were the total cases in the year, the standard deviation of the lifetime liberal voting rates of the judges on the court in that year, the fraction of cases that involved civil liberties issues that year, and a series of dummy

Perhaps not surprisingly given the high caseload and the high rate of turnover of chief justices in India, the identity of the chief justice was not related to the fraction of opinions with at least one dissent over the period of the 1970s through 2000s. Interestingly at the other end of the spectrum, in the United States there were only two chief justice during this period, and they also did not appear to be correlated with differences in the fraction of opinions with at least one dissent.

For the other countries, the results were more mixed. Figure 8-9 shows the change in the fraction of cases with at least one dissent across chief justices relative to some baseline chief justice (for Australia, Chief Justice Gibbs, for Canada Chief Justice Laskin, and for the UK, Lord Reid). For Australia, the two most recent chief justices (Gleeson and Brennan) led courts with greater dissension than Chief Justice Gibbs, with a rate that was higher by 15 percent. In Canada, only the Lamer Court had a statistically different fraction dissenting than the Laskin Court. A higher dissent rate for the Laskin Court has been attributed at least in part to the presence of Justice L'Heureux-Dubé, who had a very high dissent rate. Finally in the UK, the fraction of dissenting opinions varies considerably across leaders of the House of Lords, with Lord Reid appearing to preside over a high point in agreement in the early 1970s, not seen again until Lord Goff and Lord Browne-Wilkinson in the late 1990s.

Interestingly, the results are slightly different when we look in Figure 8-10 at what makes individual judges dissent when we can control for a different set of factors. When we examine the probability that a judge will dissent and control for the party appointing the judge, the lower court direction, the area of law, and the panel size, there is still no statistically significant difference at the US Supreme Court or the Indian Supreme Court across chief justices. However, the patterns are different than when looking at the annual data in Figure 8-8 (note the different scales in the two figures). The probability that an individual judge dissents is no longer statistically different across chief justices in Australia. In Canada, the Lamer Court no longer has a statistically significant higher dissent rate. Instead once we control for the characteristics of the individual judge, the case mix, and the panel size, judges under the earlier chief justices are slightly more likely to dissent than later judges. Finally, the pattern in the UK becomes much more varied when we look at individual judges. Dissenting rates under Lords Goff and Browne-Wilkinson remain similar to those under Lord Reid but when looking at individual judges, we see they are slightly higher under Lords Diplock, Scarman, and Keith.

variables for chief justices. We also ran these regressions with fraction of dissenting opinions as the dependent variable and the results were similar, though the results for Australia were less significant, and the size of the impact amplified in Canada and the UK. See Appendix 3.

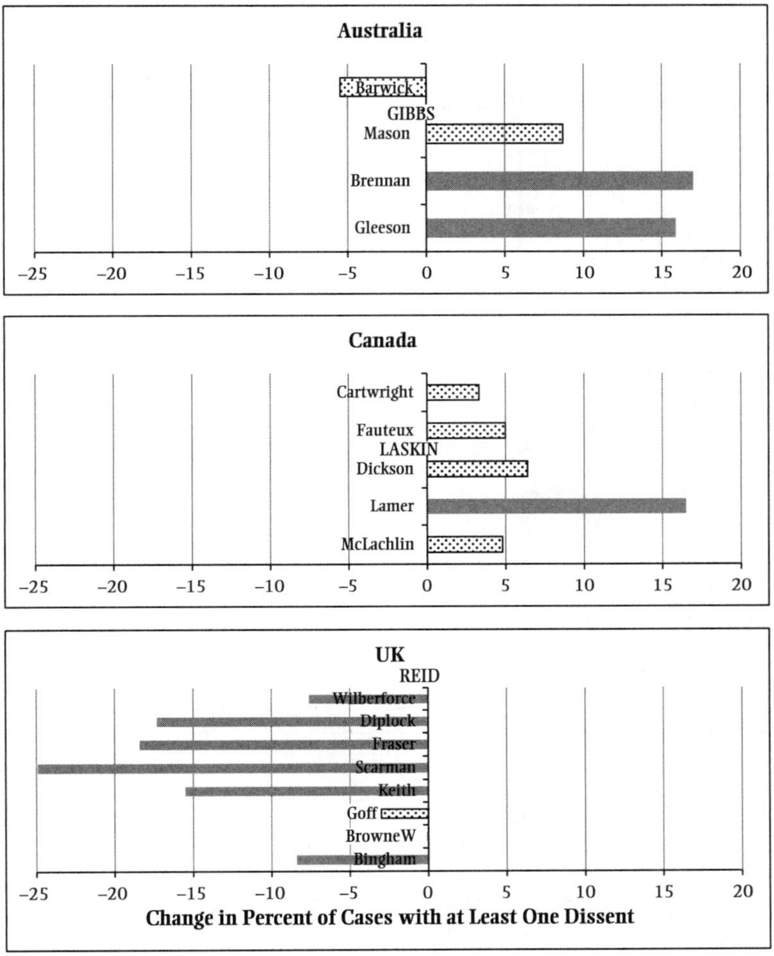


**Figure 8-9** The change in the percentage of cases with at least one dissent for each chief justice, 1970 to early 2000s. For Australia the change is relative to the percentage of cases with at least one dissent during Chief Justice Gibbs's tenure (1981–1987), for Canada relative to Chief Justice Laskin (1973–1984), and for the UK relative to Lord Reid (1969–1975). The chief justices for each country are ordered from furthest in the past at the top to most recent at the bottom. These differences were found using annual data, controlling for total cases per year, the ideological split on the court (measured by the standard deviation in the liberal voting rate on the court in the year), and the fraction of cases in the year that involved civil liberties issues. The solid bars are significant at at least the 0.5 level and the non-solid bars are not statistically significant at the 0.5 level. Each court has at least one chief justice with a statistically different rate of disagreement from the baseline chief justice, with the greatest differences for the earlier periods for the UK House of Lords.

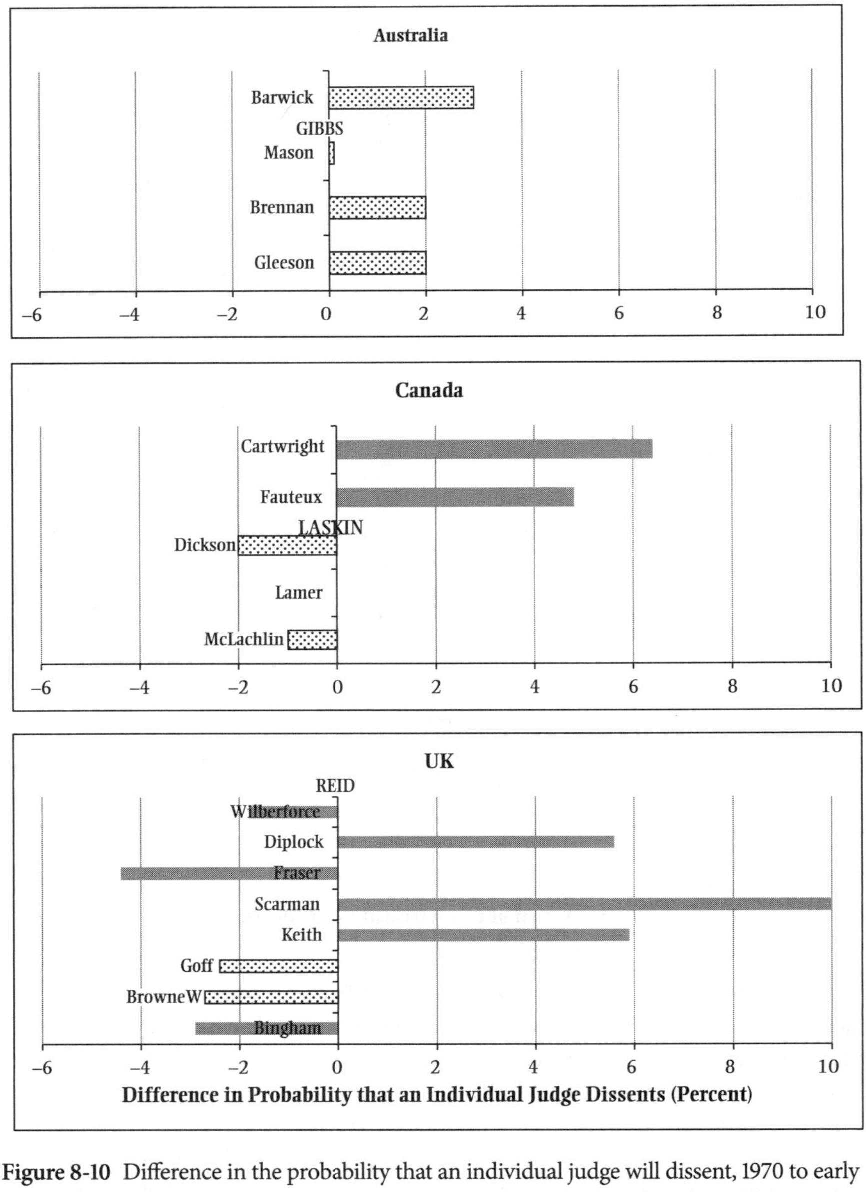


**Figure 8-10** Difference in the probability that an individual judge will dissent, 1970 to early 2000s. For Australia the change is relative to dissenting during Chief Justice Gibbs's tenure (1981–1987), for Canada relative to Chief Justice Laskin (1973–1984), and for the UK relative to Lord Reid (1969–1975). The chief justices for each country are ordered from furthest in the past at the top to most recent at the bottom. These differences were found using judge-specific data, controlling for the party appointing the judge, the lower court direction (liberal or conservative), the area of law, and the panel size. The solid bars are significant at at least the 0.05 level, and the non-solid bars are not statistically significant at the 0.05 level. The differences across chief justices on an individual judge level are not statistically significant for the Australian High Court. The probability of dissenting seems to have dropped under more recent chief justices in Canada, whereas the rates vary in the UK.

## NORMS AND IDEOLOGY

The size and causes of disagreement vary across countries.[125] Take the two extremes—the United States and India. The US Supreme Court had a high base rate of disagreement in the period we looked at, and this rate does not appear to be influenced by alterations in ideology on the Court, workload, or the identity of the chief justice. This high base rate may have been set by the chief justices or the context in the 1930s and 1940s but the norm of voicing disagreement seems incredibly sticky.[126] India, on the other hand, has an almost vanishingly low disagreement rate in this period. The rate seems not only due to a norm of agreement but also because of an outwardly crushingly high workload and a self-selection of new judges by those on the Court.

In between these extremes, the causes appear to differ. The UK House of Lords' relatively low disagreement rate does not seem influenced by changes in ideology on the Court but leadership on the Court does seem to matter. Changes in the dissent rate are correlated with chief justices. Both Canada and, particularly, Australia have higher dissent rates than the UK. Changes in the rates are correlated with changing membership on the Court but do not appear related to the identity of the chief justice.

Edelman, Klein, and Lindquist find that where ideology matters, there are higher levels of disagreement.[127] According to the attitudinal model, ideology should also matter for unanimous decisions but the ideology of the judges on the court or panel would in that case all be pointing in the same direction. Edelman, Klein, and Lindquist find that the less the judges are predicted to be "ordered" in their decisions (that is, predictably ideological in their voting), the greater the degree of unanimity. They conclude that there must be something other than ideology that is driving agreement. Given the data, we cannot clearly identify these other factors—ideology, workload, norms, and leadership seem

125. There are, of course, a range of other factors that influence the level of agreement. For example, how the writing of the opinion is assigned varies across courts and could be used to foster agreement or particular outcomes. In Canada, for example, the chief justice is formally responsible for assigning opinions, though the actual process has been described as a collegial one. Emmett MacFarlane, "The Supreme Court of Canada and the Judicial Role: An Historical Institutionalist Account" (PhD Dissertation, Queen's University, 2009) [unpublished] at 161–163; Peter McCormick, "Was It Something I Said? Losing the Majority on the Modern Supreme Court of Canada, 1984–2011" (2012) 50:1 *Osgoode Hall Law Journal* 93 at 95. At the House of Lords, opinion assignment was often determined by collective agreement. Paterson, *supra* note 102 at 93. In India, the most senior judge on the panel may choose to write the opinion himself or assign it to another panel member. Chandrachud, "Hyderbad," *supra* note 85 at 22.

126. See Sunstein, "Unanimity," *supra* note 3 discussing the path dependency of the norms on the US Supreme Court.

127. Edelman et al., *supra* note 25.

to play different roles in different contexts. Overall, judicial leadership may offer at best a partial explanation for the changing dissent rates in the countries considered here. This seems logical, as the chief justice sets the collegial climate of the court, influencing both institutional procedures and the interpersonal relations between the judges, but are embedded within a broader institutional structures and history.

# 9

# Conclusion

When we think about how judges decide disputes in front of them, we may be drawn to the notion that the rule of law should prevail—that somehow a judge does, or should, base his decision on the law applied to the facts in front of him. In law school, students are introduced to a linear form of legal reasoning: IRAC. When confronted with a legal problem, identify the Issue (I) between the parties, find the applicable Rule (R), Apply the rule to facts underlying the issue (A), and Conclude (C). Even if we have some sense that judges are individuals with their own interests and preferences, this view of judges finding and applying the law has substantial force. Considerable effort has been expended in recent years attempting to discover how much of a role the judge plays in the decision-making process as opposed to the positive application of the law.

In this book, we take as given that both the law and the judge himself contribute to the outcomes of high courts, and we have attempted to address the further question—does the design of the court influence how much of role each plays? Our answer is that it does and, in some circumstances, to what looks to be a very significant extent. At the most basic level, returning to the CC Space from Chapter 1 that we replicate in Figure 9-1, it seems unlikely such significant differences in the types of voting and agreement across high courts are solely due to differences in the law. We argue that there is a common structure to how judges decide—they make decisions like other individuals, taking into account their own preferences (including for following precedent) and the law—but that institutional design acts as a wedge, splitting high courts in different directions. It changes the incentives facing the judges and therefore how judges and courts as a whole decide.

At the most fundamental level, institutional design determines which judges will hear appeals. The appointment process obviously determines who is on the court at any given time, but there is an interesting interaction with whether or not the court hears appeals in panels. The US appointment system is clearly highly political, and on all our measures, the judges on the Court are the most overtly

Commitment and Cooperation on High Courts. Benjamin Alarie and Andrew J. Green.

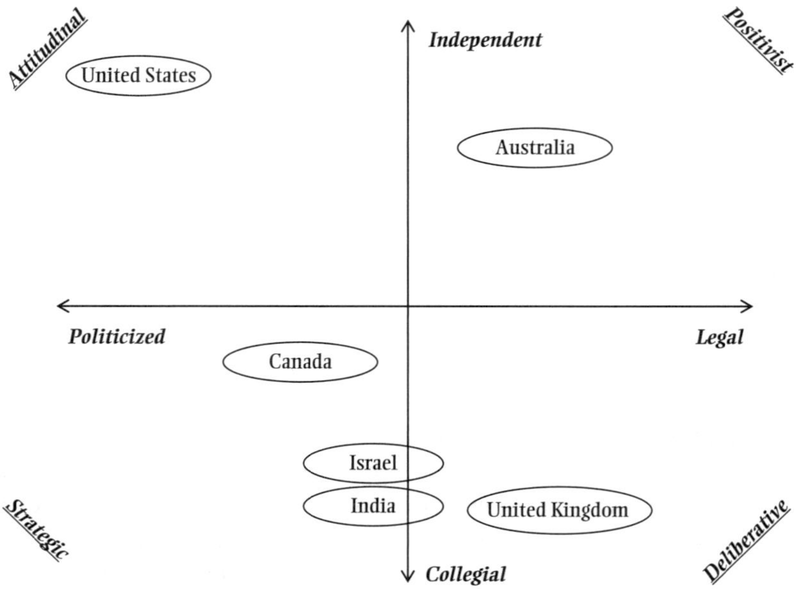


**Figure 9-1** Relative commitment and cooperation of various high courts—the CC Space. High courts of different countries may be provisionally arrayed on the quadrants from Figure 1-1 based on the existing literature and data relating to both how political and how cooperative are the judges on the courts. The US Supreme Court appears to be an outlier in terms of both its politicization and level of disagreement. However, there is also differentiation amongst the other high courts. This Figure is the same as Figure 1-5.

political—they are the most consistent across areas of law, form into disparate blocs, tend to vote consistently with the politics of who appointed them, and disagree with each other openly and often. As we discussed in Chapter 3, political selection may have some benefits such as potentially providing a balanced check on government,[1] although it may also raise rule-of-law concerns if the outcome depends on the panel selected to hear a particular appeal. The US Supreme Court offsets the political appointment process in part by not hearing appeals in panels—if there is a benefit to the shifting composition of the Court, it accrues to all appeals.

India, on the other hand, has taken the direct connection to politics (in the form of political appointers) out of the appointments process by allowing the judges themselves to choose appointees to the Court. Our results show judges who tend, not surprisingly given the self-selection, to agree with each other but are surprisingly varied in their voting patterns. They are not, however, political in the sense

1. Eric A. Posner, "Does Political Bias in the Judiciary Matter? Implications of Judicial Bias Studies for Legal and Constitutional Reform" (2008) 75 *University of Chicago Law Review* 853.

of being consistent across areas of the law. Despite the less political appointment process, the large number of judges and very small panel size provides ample opportunity for manipulation of the political views of who hears a particular appeal. As we saw in Chapter 4, the chief justice has tremendous opportunity to game the panel selection, and there is some evidence the chief justices may have done so by setting panels that lean toward their own voting behavior.

Canada, the UK, and Australia had a mix of both types of design issues in the period we studied. They had less overtly and publicly political appointment processes than the United States but retained a connection to politics through having the executive (such as in Canada the prime minister) appoint judges. They also, however, hear appeals in panels. Interestingly, none had as direct a tie between judicial voting and the party who appointed the judge as in the United States, even though we could imagine discretion in the executive could as readily lead to such a connection as the US model. However, other than this commonality, the outcomes from these courts differed significantly. The Australian High Court was more like the US Supreme Court in the sense that the justices were fairly consistent in the voting across areas and were relatively non-cooperative, yet at the same time the judges were not nearly as dispersed in their voting as in the United States. There is some evidence that the chief justice was important, possibly using the power to set panels to achieve outcomes in line with his preferences in some instances.

The UK House of Lords, on the other hand, had judges who were much less consistent and much more cooperative. As we have noted, the UK switched institutional forms in 2005 in ways that potentially impact who hears appeals. Most obviously, it has changed the method of appointment from complete executive control to greater use of a committee structure. At the same time it has potentially changed the panel structure. In the House of Lords days, panels were mostly panels of 5 of the 12 judges although it would occasionally hear appeals in larger panels. The UK Supreme Court also has 12 justices and may hear appeals in panels of as few as three justices. However, the Court has tended not to go with the smallest size of panels and has continued to hear most appeals in panels of five with some larger panels. The president has in the past appeared to have a significant ability to control outcomes, and there is some evidence that he may have done so. He has then been left with some discretion to set panels in line with his preferences on the new Court. but has at least in part refrained from making the move that would give him the greatest control—setting very small panels to hear appeals.

Canada is in the middle as it so often finds itself. Its justices tended not to be overly dispersed, nor entirely consistent or cooperative. There is a connection to the party appointing the justices but it is not as strong as in the United States. The chief justice has the ability to game the panel selection process, but appears in most cases to resist this temptation. Instead there is some indication that in the past the chief justice has used the panel selection powers (at least in terms of size) more than other courts on efficiency grounds—to tie larger panels to cases that appear on average more important and smaller panels to cases that the Court has to hear that are on average likely systematically less important.

How one decides who sits on the court or on a particular appeal therefore may push courts toward different quadrants in the CC Space. The type of case may also play an important role in the nature of the decision-making on a court. For example, a judge may be more willing or able to follow her own views of appropriate policy where the law is less clear. However, high court judges have, to differing degrees, the ability to choose the cases the court hears. Some courts have to hear a range of cases. These cases may not only be less important on average than cases the court chooses to hear, but also systematically easier. A court with a larger share of its docket being mandatory cases may appear both less political and more cooperative. Further, as we saw in Chapter 6, although workload and the area of law the case raises may make a difference to whether a court will agree to hear a case, some institutional structures make it easier or less risky for judges to choose the court's docket strategically. The US Supreme Court, for example, with its consistent voting and lack of panels faces a significant risk of justices strategically choosing some of their caseload such that they can pick up or avoid cases depending on how they want to shape the law. In Canada, on the other hand, the less consistent voting and the use of panels makes such prediction much more difficult.

Courts may then split off into different combinations of ideology and commitment given their set of judges (which depends on the design of the appointment process) and cases. In deciding these cases, these judges may face different incentives across courts depending on other institutional design choices. Different panel structures may, for example, affect outcomes more than just because different judges sit on the appeal. In Chapter 5 we saw that sitting with more liberal colleagues on a panel increased the probability of a judge voting in a liberal direction in Canada, Australia, and particularly the UK. Further in Chapter 8 we saw that larger panels may lead to a higher dissent rate both because of the greater likelihood of disagreement and because the social effects of disagreement may be lower. It may be more costly for a judge to follow her preferences if she has to incur reputational costs from disagreeing. As Epstein, Landes, and Posner note, a judge will dissent if the costs (such as from reputation or labor) are less than the benefits in the sense that she disagrees with the policy outcomes relative to others on the court. We saw in Chapters 5 and 8 that larger policy disagreements between judges on a panel are more likely connected with higher dissent rates. Judges on some courts are more sensitive to these differences in opinion than others. Justices in Canada and Australia, for example, were much more likely to dissent as the differences on the court or on the panel increased. For the US Supreme Court and the UK House of Lords, on the other hand, even relatively large divergence in preferences was not associated with a large jump in a judge's probability of dissenting.

A judge may also be influenced by other features of court design, though the evidence is mixed and causation is difficult to pin down. We saw in Chapter 7 that allowing interveners seemed associated with increases in dissent rates in Canada, the UK, and Australia, though not in the United States, possibly because of the overwhelming presence of interveners in most cases. Judges were not as influenced by other parties. Governments do appear to win at a high rate before most courts, but this success rate appears to disappear in most countries when other factors such as the area of law are taken into account. The Supreme Court of Canada is a principal exception, with the government appearing to have a high win rate relative to other parties, whether as appellant or respondent. Interestingly, as we saw in Chapters 5 and 7, the political alignment (or lack of alignment) of the judge and the government appears to have little influence on how the judge decides. For example, only in Canada and the UK was there (weak) evidence of a correlation between judges' decisions and simple measures of the politics of the government in power.

The thickest part of the wedge, however, may not be particular rules but the norms of the particular court. As we discussed in Chapter 8, these norms are difficult to directly identify, but indications are that they are strong and persistent. The United States, for example, has had a high baseline dissent rate, essentially since the 1940s, which does not seem to be significantly influenced by workload, changes in the chief justice, or even to a large extent by swings in the ideological composition of the bench. Both India and the UK, on the other hand, have low baseline dissent rates also seemingly uninfluenced by ideological or workload shifts, though leadership on the UK House of Lords may have made some difference to the degree of cooperation. However, unlike the other countries, Canada and Australia appeared to have less sticky dissent rates, as dissent rates fluctuated with changes in the composition of the court.

Of course all these design elements are interrelated. The choice of judges impacts which cases litigants are willing to bring forward.[2] The types of litigants or issues that are brought may influence whether the docket is discretionary or mandatory—such as where certain groups or issues get mandatory access to the court if they are felt to be either under-represented or particularly disadvantaged in the appeals process. The leadership or lack of leadership on the court may influence how new judges acclimatize to their jobs and the norms on the court. Any of these design elements may feed back into the choice of individuals to seek or accept nominations to the court and the extent to which the appointment

2. See Jeff Yates & Elizabeth Coggins, "The Intersection of Judicial Attitudes and Litigant Selection Theories: Explaining U.S. Supreme Court Decision-Making" (2009) 29 *Wash. U. J. L. & Pol'y* 263 (discussing how litigants may respond to alterations in the composition of the court).

process becomes politicized. More political courts with greater opportunity for gaming of outcomes may attract more political candidates for the court and deter less political individuals, and may create a more political process for the choice of the actual nominee. It is difficult to tease out these interrelated effects but the counteracting forces need to be considered in any reform proposals.

Our conclusions about the actual size of these institutional wedges are tentative. Haynie et al. have done a tremendous public service in creating the High Courts Judicial Database (HCJD), bringing data from a range of countries to researchers. Obviously we could always imagine more variables that we would like to have to permit a deeper or broader analysis of courts, though the database provides a nice array of variables that allows the creation of additional factors of analysis. However, the data has some limitations. One set of concerns arises not from errors in the data but from the difficulty in creating a common framework across different political and social contexts. The HCJD attempts to find the common framework through assigning directions to outcomes—either pro or con certain positions. We have attempted to use this directionality to tie to underlying political directions, similar to what has been done in the studies of the US Supreme Court and Supreme Court of Canada. However, its application across the different countries in this study is not straightforward, nor does it comfortably fit with how the law and politics are viewed in each country.

Further, in order to provide a manageable basis for our study, we have compared only a limited range of countries. We have left out one of the potentially largest wedges—that between common law and civil law courts. We have also only analyzed a small set of common law countries. Although we chose countries that had some common ties and at the same time provided an outlier with the Indian Supreme Court, our conclusions are limited both by the small number of countries we have looked at and by the limited time period of study as the HCJD starts in 1970 and ends in the early 2000s.

Future comparative work would benefit from better cross-country measures that allow more accurate comparison across diverse political and social backgrounds. Some work is being done on such measures, but more is needed given the varied contexts in which high courts operate.[3] Much of the work will be difficult as there is a trade-off of generalizable, efficient measures and more nuanced, accurate indicators of influences on judges. Measures of liberal or conservative voting are simple to devise and code but may not provide a good measure for assessing the role of law or other factors in judicial

3. For some examples of attempts to develop cross-country comparisons, see David Weiden, "Judicial Politicization, Ideology, and Activism at the High Courts of the United States, Canada, and Australia" 2011 64:2 *Political Research Quarterly* (2) 335 at 336; Keren Weinshall, Udi Sommer & Ya'acov Ritov, "Ideological Influences on Governance and Regulation: The Comparative Case of Supreme Courts," *Regulation & Governance* [forthcoming in 2017].

decision-making.[4] To get more sophisticated measures of influences on judges may require a greater attention to the facts in particular areas, an exercise that may be difficult across countries.[5] Moreover, the simple ideological measures likely do not capture important aspects of how judges see cases. For example, Fischman and Jacobi argue that even on the US Supreme Court, a left-right ideological focus ignores a second important split between legalistic and pragmatic judges.[6] Accounting for such other dimensions and their relationship to institutional design will be a challenge for future comparative work.

We cannot improve our high courts without understanding the effect of the incentives that different designs create. It is not a question of creating an "optimal" court for all countries. The diversity of political, social, and economic situations across countries makes the search for such a court futile. However, we can use the examples of our current high courts to draw lessons to allow countries to improve. Analysis of a single court without taking into account institutional design is bound to be partial and potentially misleading. Too much has been made of the US example without recognition of the alternatives offered in other countries.

And the pursuit of a better understanding of the design of high courts is important. The limitations in our data, range of courts, and time periods means we can only point to possible influences of institutional design on judicial decision-making. Yet the differences across courts we do find are informative. The failure to take such differences into account has real-world consequences. It may mean that we fail to fulfill the promise of the rule of law, such as where panels can be selected to foster particular outcomes or certain litigants are better able to have high courts hear their appeals. The design of the high court may undermine the development of the law—for example, is it more difficult for a consistent, principled common law to develop where a high court hears thousands of cases per year in small panels?[7] To move forward, we need a better grasp of these outcomes of differences in high court design.

The effects do not only arise from differences in individual design elements. Our study has signaled the importance of the trade-offs across different design choices—one can hear more cases, for example, through smaller panels, but

4. Charles M. Cameron & Lewis A. Kornhauser, "Rational Choice Attitudinalism? A Review of Epstein, Landes and Posner's 'The Behavior of Federal Judges: A Theoretical and Empirical Study of Rational Choice'" (2015) *European Journal of Law & Economics* [Cameron & Kornhauser].

5. Cameron & Kornhauser, *supra* note 4.

6. Joshua Fischman & Tonja Jacobi, "The Second Dimension of the Supreme Court" (2016) 57 *Wm. & Mary Law Review* 1671.

7. Andrew Green & Albert Yoon, "Triaging the Law: Developing the Common Law on the Supreme Court of India" (November 2016) [unpublished].

this choice may have knock-on effects on gaming of outcomes. Smaller panels yields a potential increase in gaming in a particular appeal depending on how the panel is chosen, but equally a potential reduction in gaming to the extent that smaller panels makes strategic choice of which appeals to hear more difficult. Any reforms to the design of a court need to take account of these interrelated effects.

We cannot point to an optimal design, yet we can look for predictable influences, both positive and negative, of certain design choices. We may be able to point to some choices or combinations that push us outside the range of what we would want to accept of a high court in a country controlled by the rule of law. If one were designing a high court from scratch, for example, one may not want to combine a highly politicized appointments process as in the United States with a broad latitude for the chief justice to choose the size and composition of the panel hearing a particular appeal and a wide discretion to limit the cases that come before the court. Although we cannot pinpoint the perfect combination of cooperation and commitment for all courts, we can say something about how such design elements may push us to extremes of one or the other or both. Yet there are interesting innovations in high court design in different countries, such as various committee approaches to appointments, which may be adapted to overcome concerns in particular countries. We cannot understand which way to go by myopically examining the courts of single countries in isolation. The way forward is comparative.

# Appendix 1

## The Data

### HIGH COURTS JUDICIAL DATABASE

The High Courts Judicial Database (HCJD) is a public access database assembled by Haynie, Sheehan, Songer, and Tate.[1] The HCJD provides coded data for a number of high courts. For our purposes, the HCJD covers all cases from:

- High Court of Australia: 1969–2003
- Supreme Court of Canada: 1969–2003
- United Kingdom, Judicial Committee of the House of Lords: 1970–2002
- Supreme Court of the United States: 1953–2005

It also provides coded information for a random sample of 100 decisions per year of the Indian Supreme Court over the period 1970–2000.

Below we have set out some general information about the coding used in the database. For more information, see the HCJD codebook available at http://artsandsciences.sc.edu/poli/juri/highcts.htm.

For the US data, we use the Supreme Court Database (the Spaeth Database) for most of the analysis as there seemed to be discrepancies in the number of cases for the US Court in the HCJD. For a description of the Spaeth database and the variable coding, see supremecourtdatabase.org.

1. Stacia L. Haynie et al. (2007) High Courts Judicial Database. Accessed at the University of South Carolina Judicial Research Initiative, online: www.cas.sc.edu/poli/juri.

Commitment and Cooperation on High Courts. Benjamin Alarie and Andrew J. Green.

## Areas of Law

The HCJD separates decisions into seven groups as follows:

- *Criminal*: Criminal includes murder, theft, and other crimes, along with business regulation and license violation.
- *Civil Rights and Liberties*: This group includes civil rights claims by prisoners, equal treatment under the law claims, and claims concerning voting rights, speech, press, religion, privacy, access to information, and aboriginal rights.
- *Public Law*: Public Law includes government regulation of health and safety, the environment, and labor; as well as taxation, government benefits, dispute over public office, disputes between levels of government, and certain aboriginal issues.
- *Private Economic Relations*: This group includes disputes involving creditor-debtor relations, insurance, contract, and land; along with intellectual property, corporate law, and private labor disputes.
- *Torts*: Torts include motor vehicle accidents, injured workers, medical malpractice, and other civil actions involving injury or harm to persons or property.
- *Family and Estates*: This includes the law of divorce, child custody, marital agreements, and wills and estates.
- *Other*: The other group includes regulation of the bar and judiciary, other issues, and issues that could not be classified.

In addition, we created a variable grouping of the cases into the following three categories:

- Criminal: as above
- Civil rights and liberties: as above
- Economic: all of the private economic relations cases plus public law cases that relate to government regulation of business activity (health and safety, environment, business, agriculture, land use, unions and business/labor issues, and other government regulation).

For the US Supreme Court database, we created similar groupings based on "issue" and "issueArea." For Civil Rights, we used First Amendment, Due Process, Privacy, and most of civil rights (other than immigration and indigent categories) from issueArea. For Economic, we used issues relating to labor-management disputes, and regulation of patents and copyright, as well as private law categories such as property, contracts, and commercial transactions.

## Directionality

The HCJD codes the "direction" of the outcomes of decisions. For those decisions for which the direction could be ascertained and that did not in part support both sides (that is, a split decision), the HCJD codes the decisions as follows:

- Criminal issues: for or against the position of the defendant;
- Civil rights and liberties: for or against the persons alleging that their civil rights were violated (except in "reverse discrimination" cases);
- Freedom of expression: for or against the expansion or the protection of assertions of rights of expression and religion;
- Private economic relations: for or against the economic underdog if one of the parties is clearly an economic underdog compared to the other;
- Torts: for or against the injured party;
- Copyrights, patents, trademarks: for or against the person alleging infringement of that person's copyright, patent, or trademark;
- Public law: for or against the government;
- Public employment and benefits: for or against the employee or recipient of benefits; and
- Disputes between levels of government: for the national government or for the subnational government.

For the United States, we used the code "direction," which has similar classification to the HCJD.

## Judge-Specific Data

The HCJD contains variables for the votes for each judge on each decision. The variables are for how the judge voted on the first issue and the second issue in each decision, identifying whether the judge

- Was on the court but did not participate;
- Voted with the majority;
- Dissented in part;
- Dissented; or
- Was not on the court at the time of the decision.

Similarly, the US Supreme Court Database has data for judges participating in a particular decision in its judge-centered data.

## HAND-COLLECTED DATA

In order to supplement the HCJD, we hand-collected the following data for Australia, Canada, India, the UK, and the United States for the relevant periods of the data in the HCJD:

- Chief Justice: The names and time in office of the chief justices of the court and, where relevant, the party in power when they were appointed;
- All Justices: The names, appointment dates, and time on the bench of all justices on the court during the relevant period along with, where relevant, the party in power when they were appointed.
- The Government: The parties that held power in the relevant periods, along with an assessment of their politics on a Left-Right scale (See below).

### Parties in Power and Assigned Political Leanings

#### Australia

| **1969–1972** | **Liberal/Country Coalition under Liberal PM "The Coalition"** |
|---|---|
| *1972–1974* | *Labor majority* |
| *1974–1975* | *Labor majority but overturned by Senate, results in ...* |
| **1975** | **Coalition led by Liberal PM** |
| **1975–1977** | **Coalition led by Liberal PM** |
| **1977–1980** | **Coalition led by Liberal PM** |
| **1980–1983** | **Coalition led by Liberal PM** |
| *1983–1984* | *Labor majority* |
| *1984–1987* | *Labor majority* |
| *1987–1990* | *Labor majority* |
| *1990–1993* | *Labor majority* |
| *1993–1996* | *Labor majority* |
| **1996–1998** | **Coalition led by Liberal PM** |
| **1998–2001** | **Coalition led by Liberal PM** |
| **2001–2004** | **Coalition led by Liberal PM** |
| **2004–2007** | **Coalition led by Liberal PM** |
| *2007–2010* | *Labor majority* |

| | |
|---|---|
| *2010–2013* | *Labor/independent members/Green Party coalition led by Labor PM* |
| **2013–present** | **Coalition led by Liberal PM** |

*Labor* is center-left (liberal).

**Liberal party, National Party (formerly National Country Party) and Coalition (mainly composed of Liberals and Nationals)** is taken as conservative.

SOURCE: http://www.aph.gov.au/About_Parliament/Parliamentary_Departments/Parliamentary_Library/pubs/rp/rp1112/12rp06

## CANADA

| | |
|---|---|
| *1968–1979* | *Liberal* |
| **1979–1980** | **Progressive Conservative** |
| *1980–1984* | *Liberal* |
| **1984–1993** | **Progressive Conservative** |
| *1993–2006* | *Liberal* |
| **2006–2015** | **Conservative** |

*Liberal* is center-left (liberal).

**Progressive Conservative** is center-right with the more recent Conservative party being further right (conservative).

SOURCE: http://www.parl.gc.ca/parlinfo/Compilations/ElectionsAndRidings/ResultsParty.aspx?Season=0&Parliament=1924d334-6bd0-4cb3-8793-cee640025ff6

## INDIA

| | |
|---|---|
| *1967–1971* | *Indian National Congress: left-wing (socialism/secularism)* |
| *1971–1977* | *Indian National Congress* |
| *1977–1980* | *Janata Party (appears left-wing)* |
| *1980–1984* | *Indian National Congress* |
| *1984–1985* | *Indian National Congress* |
| *1985–1989* | *Indian National Congress* |
| *1989–1991* | *National Front (coalition led by Janata Dal, appears left-wing)* |
| *1991–1996* | *Indian National Congress* |
| 1996–1998 | **Minority government: BJP lasted 13 days but could not establish a coalition** |
| | United Front: Janata Dal, INC, many parties with conflicting ideologies, no dominant ideology, lasted 18 months |

| | |
|---|---|
| 1998–1999 | **National Democratic Alliance coalition (center-right)** |
| 1999–2004 | **National Democratic Alliance** |
| 2004–2014 | *United Progressive Alliance, led by Indian National Congress and containing the center-left* |

*Indian National Congress, the Janata Party, National Front and the United Progressive Alliance* are taken as left-wing (liberal).

The 1990s **Minority government** as well as the **National Democratic Alliance** are taken as center-right (conservative).

SOURCE: http://www.smetimes.in/smetimes/general-elections-2009/miscellaneous/2009/Mar/23/history-of-lok-sabha-elections5584.html

## United Kingdom

| | |
|---|---|
| **2015** | **Conservative** |
| **2010–2015** | **Conservative** |
| *2005–2010* | *Labour* |
| *2001–2005* | *Labour* |
| *1997–2001* | *Labour* |
| **1992–1997** | **Conservative** |
| **1987–1992** | **Conservative** |
| **1983–1987** | **Conservative** |
| **1979–1983** | **Conservative** |
| *October 1974–1979* | *Labour minority* |
| *February 1974–October 1974* | *Labour minority* |
| **June 1970–1974** | **Conservative** |
| *1966–June 1970* | *Labour* |

*Labour* is taken as left-wing (liberal).

**Conservative** is taken as right-wing (conservative).

SOURCE: http://news.bbc.co.uk/2/hi/uk_news/politics/election_2010/8654338.stm

## United States

| Presidential elections | President | Senate elections | Senate Majority |
|---|---|---|---|
| 1969–1974 | **Nixon** | 1968–1970 | *Democrat* |
| | | 1970–1972 | *Democrat* |
| | | 1972–1974 | *Democrat* |

| Presidential elections | President | Senate elections | Senate Majority |
|---|---|---|---|
| 1974–1977 | **Ford** | 1974–1976 | *Democrat* |
| 1977–1981 | *Carter* | 1976–1978 | *Democrat* |
| | | 1978–1980 | *Democrat* |
| 1981–1989 | **Reagan** | 1980–1982 | **Republican** |
| | | 1982–1984 | **Republican** |
| | | 1984–1986 | **Republican** |
| | | 1986–1988 | *Democrat* |
| 1989–1993 | **George H.W. Bush** | 1988–1990 | *Democrat* |
| | | 1990–1992 | *Democrat* |
| 1993–2001 | *Clinton* | 1992–1994 | *Democrat* |
| | | 1994–1996 | **Republican** |
| | | 1996–1998 | **Republican** |
| | | 1998–2000 | **Republican** |
| 2001–2009 | **George W. Bush** | 2000–2002 | No majority. While Al Gore was VP until 2001, he held the tiebreaking vote for Democrats. When Cheney became VP in 2001 he held the tiebreaking vote for Republicans. |
| | | 2002–2004 | **Republican** |
| | | 2004–2006 | **Republican** |
| | | 2006–2008 | *Democrat* |
| 2009–2016 | *Obama* | 2008–2010 | *Democrat* |
| | | 2010–2012 | *Democrat* |
| | | 2012–2014 | *Democrat* |
| | | 2014–present | **Republican** |

*Democrat* is coded as liberal.

**Republican** is coded as conservative.

SOURCE:
Presidential elections: http://www.archives.gov/federal-register/electoral-college/votes/index.html (1789–2012)

For Senate elections: http://www.senate.gov/history/partydiv.htm

# Appendix 2

## Influences on Judges' Votes

### INDIVIDUAL JUDGES' VOTES

In order to analyze the relationship between a judge's votes and factors such as the judge's policy preferences or workload, we ran a series of regressions based on the following relationship:[1]

$V_i$ = f(Ideology, Lower Court Direction, Area of Law, Ideology of Other Panelists, Position on Court, Government in Power, year)

Where the variables are defined as follows:

| Dependent Variable | | |
|---|---|---|
| $V_i$ | | Whether the judge i votes in a liberal direction in the particular decision, where:<br>Conservative = 0<br>Liberal = 1<br>Note: where ideology is measured by the judge's lifetime liberal voting rate, the regression is limited to non-criminal cases |

1. Lee Epstein, William M. Landes & Richard A. Posner, *Behavior of Federal Judges: A Theoretical and Empirical Study of Rational Choice* (Cambridge, MA: Harvard University Press, 2013), analyzed whether US Supreme Court justices voted conservatively based on some of the same factors, including ideology, the justice's first term on the Court, the direction of the lower court decision, time, area of law, and the fraction of the Court that is conservative. They also use other variables for which we do not have information across high courts, including whether the judge was an appellate judge before appointment to the Court and the composition of the US Senate, and they ran a two-stage regression examining whether there were any ideological impacts independent of other ideological measures.

| Independent Variables | | |
|---|---|---|
| | **Variable Name** | **Description** |
| IDEOLOGY | | |
| Party of Appointing Government | Party Appointing | The politics of the party appointing the particular judge, where<br>Conservative = 0<br>Liberal = 1<br>See Appendix 1 for a categorization of parties in each country. |
| Lifetime Liberal Voting Rate in Criminal Cases | Criminal Liberal Voting | Average of the judge's liberal voting rate over the judge's whole career in criminal cases |
| LOWER COURT DIRECTION | | |
| Lower Court Direction | Lower Court Direction | Direction of the lower court decision being considered where:<br>Conservative = 0<br>Liberal = 1<br>See Appendix 1 for a description of directionality of decisions |
| AREA OF LAW | | |
| Area of Law | [Name of Area of Law] | See Appendix 1 for a description of the different areas of law |
| IDEOLOGY OF OTHER PANELISTS | | |
| Panel Liberal Voting Rate | Average LV of Others on Panel | Mean of panel members' liberal voting rates [Note: other than judge i] |
| Fraction Liberal | Fraction Liberal Appointees | Fraction of the other panel members who were appointed by a Liberal government |
| POSITION ON COURT | | |
| Judge voting is new to the court | Freshman | Whether the decision was made by the judge in his or her first three years on the court where<br>After first three years = 0<br>In first three years = 1 |
| The judge is the chief justice | CJ Voting | If the judge deciding is the chief justice, where<br>Judge is not chief justice = 0<br>Judge is the chief justice = 1 |

*(Continued)*

| Independent Variables | | |
|---|---|---|
| | **Variable Name** | **Description** |
| | GOVERNMENT IN POWER | |
| Government in power at time of decision | Liberal Gov. in Power | The politics of the government in power at the time of the decision where<br>Conservative government = 0<br>Liberal government = 1<br>See Appendix 1 for a description of governments in different countries |
| | INTERVENERS | |
| Presence of intervener | | As a measure of whether the case is controversial, whether an intervener participated in the appeal where<br>No intervener = 0<br>At least one intervener = 1 |
| | NORMS | |
| Chief justices | | To identify any effects of norms relating to chief justices, we use dummy variables for the chief justice at the time of the decision. |

*Table A2-1.* Summary Statistics

Australia (1970–2003)

| | Mean | Standard Deviation | Minimum | Maximum |
|---|---|---|---|---|
| Liberal Vote | .542 | .498 | 0 | 1 |
| Party of Appointing Government | .438 | .496 | 0 | 1 |
| Lower Court Direction | .419 | .494 | 0 | 1 |
| Average Panel Lifetime Liberal Voting Rate | .543 | .026 | .455 | .567 |
| Fraction Liberal | .438 | .161 | .143 | .8 |
| Panel Size | 6.92 | .273 | 5 | 8 |
| Government in Power | .465 | .499 | 0 | 1 |

*Table A2-1.* Continued

Canada (1969–2003)

| | Mean | Standard Deviation | Minimum | Maximum |
|---|---|---|---|---|
| Liberal Vote | .444 | .497 | 0 | 1 |
| Party of Appointing Government | .468 | .499 | 0 | 1 |
| Lower Court Direction | .384 | .486 | 0 | 1 |
| Average Panel Lifetime Liberal Voting Rate | .444 | .027 | .378 | .52 |
| Fraction Liberal | .472 | .290 | 0 | 1.4 |
| Panel Size | 7.14 | 1.58 | 1 | 9 |
| Government in Power | .708 | .455 | 0 | 1 |

India (1970–2000)

| | Mean | Standard Deviation | Minimum | Maximum |
|---|---|---|---|---|
| Liberal Vote | .535 | .499 | 0 | 1 |
| Party of Appointing Government | N/A | | | |
| Lower Court Direction | .451 | .498 | 0 | 1 |
| Average Panel Lifetime Liberal Voting Rate | .535 | .042 | .459 | .599 |
| Fraction Liberal | N/A | | | |
| Panel Size | 2.63 | .944 | 1 | 7 |
| Government in Power | .899 | .302 | 0 | 1 |

UK (1969–2002)

| | Mean | Standard Deviation | Minimum | Maximum |
|---|---|---|---|---|
| Liberal Vote | .459 | .498 | 0 | 1 |
| Party of Appointing Government | .316 | .465 | 0 | 1 |
| Lower Court Direction | .449 | .498 | 0 | 1 |
| Average Panel Lifetime Liberal Voting Rate | .459 | .032 | .342 | .603 |
| Fraction Liberal | .314 | .263 | 0 | 1 |
| Panel Size | 4.98 | .333 | 3 | 7 |
| Government in Power | .345 | .475 | 0 | 1 |

*(Continued)*

*Table A2-1.* Continued

United States (1970–2002)

| | Mean | Standard Deviation | Minimum | Maximum |
|---|---|---|---|---|
| Liberal Vote | .459 | .498 | 0 | 1 |
| Party of Appointing Government | .306 | .461 | 0 | 1 |
| Lower Court Direction | .52 | .5 | | 1 |
| Average Panel Lifetime Liberal Voting Rate | .460 | .031 | .385 | .569 |
| Fraction Liberal | .31 | .064 | 0 | .8 |
| Panel Size | 8.74 | .582 | 5 | 9 |
| Government in Power | .300 | .458 | 0 | 1 |

*Table A2-2.* Basic Regressions, Party Appointing the Judge (Marginal Effects)

The dependent variable is liberal vote by a judge.

| | Australia | | Canada | | UK | | US | |
|---|---|---|---|---|---|---|---|---|
| Party Appointing | .063* (.025) | .063* (.025) | .056** (.017) | .045** (.017) | .029* (.014) | .034* (.015) | .092 (.09) | .093 (.091) |
| Lower Court Direction | .007 (.027) | −.006 (.028) | .125** (.0155) | .08** (.015) | .098** (.012) | .068** (.012) | −.186** (.019) | −.195** (.019) |
| Civil Rights | | −.013 (.038) | | .112** (.022) | | .081** (.023) | | 0.106** (.019) |
| Public Law | | .035 (.03) | | .192** (.022) | | .228** (.021) | | 0.111* (.046) |
| Private Economic | | −.039 (.029) | | .149** (.022) | | .06* (.025) | | .125** (.039) |
| Tort | | .064** (.02) | | .192** (.023) | | .117** (.028) | | – |
| Family | | – | | – | | – | | – |
| Other | | −.018 (.091) | | −.151** (.045) | | −.025 (.056) | | −.058 (.045) |

Standard errors in parenthesis.

**p<0.01

*p<0.05

Note: The results are the same when we control for chief justice. The excluded area of law is criminal.

*Table A2-3.* Basic Regressions, Criminal Liberal Voting Rate (Marginal Effects)

The dependent variable is liberal vote by judge (on non-criminal decisions)

| | **Australia** | | **Canada** | | **India** | | **UK** | | **US** | |
|---|---|---|---|---|---|---|---|---|---|---|
| Criminal Liberal Voting | .183<br>(.126) | .184<br>(.127) | .13*<br>(.06) | .13*<br>(.06) | −.042<br>(.036) | −.045<br>(.036) | −.135<br>(.092) | −.128<br>(.097) | .483**<br>(.05) | .492**<br>(.05) |
| Lower Court Direction | .013<br>(.03) | .006<br>(.031) | .085**<br>(.018) | .075**<br>(.017) | .015<br>(.025) | .016<br>(.025) | .087**<br>(.015) | .075**<br>(.016) | −.179**<br>(.014) | −.183**<br>(.015) |
| Public Law | | .045<br>(.033) | | .087**<br>(.022) | | −.016<br>(.039) | | .148**<br>(.029) | | .019<br>(.024) |
| Private Economic | | −.027<br>(.033) | | .043*<br>(.018) | | .012<br>(.047) | | −.019<br>(.027) | | .012<br>(.026) |
| Torts | | .077**<br>(.037) | | .086**<br>(.022) | | .227**<br>(.079) | | .035<br>(.033) | | – |
| Family | | – | | – | | – | | – | | – |
| Other | | −.013<br>(.084) | | −.257**<br>(.047) | | – | | −.106<br>(.066) | | −.168**<br>(.026) |

Standard errors in parenthesis.

**p<0.01

*p<0.05

NOTE: The results are similar if we control for chief justice. The omitted area of law is civil rights (as these are all non-criminal cases).

*Table A2-4.* Panel Effects Regressions, Party Appointing the Judge (Marginal Effects)

The dependent variable is liberal vote by a judge.

| | **Australia** | | **Canada** | | **UK** | | **US** | |
|---|---|---|---|---|---|---|---|---|
| Party Appointing | .057* (.027) | .06* (.028) | .037* (.018) | .045* (.018) | .003 (.019) | .011 (.019) | .093 (.089) | .091 (.088) |
| Lower Court Direction | –.002 (.029) | –.004 (.03) | .080** (.015) | .081** (.015) | .066** (.012) | .066** (.012) | –.195** (.019) | –.195** (.019) |
| Civil Rights | –.016 (.037) | –.012 (.037) | .111** (.022) | .111** (.022) | .089** (.024) | .085** (.024) | .104** (.019) | .103** (.019) |
| Public Law | .039 (.029) | .040 (.03) | .193** (.023) | .193** (.023) | .230** (.021) | .232** (.021) | .111* (.045) | .111* (.045) |
| Private Economic | –.036 (.03) | –.035 (.03) | .152** (.022) | .15** (.022) | .06* (.025) | .056* (.026) | .123** (.041) | .121** (.040) |
| Tort | .065** (.021) | .066** (.021) | .197** (.022) | .196** (.022) | .122** (.029) | .126** (.029) | – | – |
| Family | – | – | – | – | – | – | – | – |
| Other | –.013 (.090) | –.021 (–.020) | –.158** (.045) | –.155** (.046) | –.025 (.057) | –.016 (.06) | –.058 (.045) | –.058 (.045) |
| Year | .002* (.001) | .0001 (.001) | .001 (.001) | .002 (.001) | –.002 (.001) | .005** (.001) | –.003 (.004) | .0003 (.023) |
| Fraction Liberal Appointees | –.035 (.057) | | .045* (.022) | | .071* (.028) | | –.001 (.1) | |
| Average LV of Others on Panel | | .916** (.292) | | .637* (.261) | | 3.05** (.235) | | –4.61** (.651) |

Standard errors in parenthesis.

$^{**}p<0.01$

$^{*}p<0.05$

Note: The results are the same when we control for chief justice. The excluded area of law is criminal.

*Table A2-5.* Position on Court Regressions, Party Appointing (Marginal Effects)

The dependent variable is liberal vote by a judge

| | Austr. | | | Can. | | | UK | | | US | | |
|---|---|---|---|---|---|---|---|---|---|---|---|---|
| Party Appointing | .055* (.026) | .049* (.024) | .055* (.026) | .048** (.016) | .044** (.016) | .048** (.016) | .02 (.017) | .026 (.016) | .015 (.016) | .088 (.88) | .069 (.088) | .093 (.089) |
| Lower Court Direction | –.002 (.03) | –.002 (.029) | –.002 (.03) | .080** (.015) | .079** (.015) | .080** (.015) | .066** (.012) | .065** (.012) | .064** (.012) | –.198** (.019) | –.195** (.019) | –.195** (.019) |
| Civil Rights | –.015 (.038) | –.015 (.038) | –.015 (.038) | .111** (.022) | .110** (.022) | .111** (.022) | .088** (.024) | .088** (.024) | .087 (.024) | .103** (.019) | .104** (.019) | .104** (.019) |
| Public Law | .039 (.029) | .039 (.029) | .039 (.029) | .194** (.023) | .194** (.023) | .194** (.024) | .228** (.021) | .228** (.021) | .228** (.021) | .112* (.045) | .111* (.045) | .111* (.045) |
| Private Economic | –.035 (.03) | –.035 (.03) | –.036 (.029) | .152** (.022) | .152** (.022) | .152** (.023) | .060* (.025) | .06* (.025) | .059* (.025) | .123** (.040) | .123** (.041) | .123** (.040) |
| Tort | .065** (.021) | .065** (.021) | .065** (.021) | .195** (.022) | .196** (.022) | .195** (.023) | .121** (.029) | .120** (.028) | .120** (.029) | – | – | – |
| Family | – | – | – | – | – | – | – | – | – | – | – | – |
| Other | –.011 (.091) | –.013 (.091) | –.010 (.091) | –.153** (.045) | –.146** (.042) | –.153** (.046) | –.024 (.056) | –.028 (.056) | –.029 (.056) | –.059 (.045) | –.057 (.045) | –.059 (.045) |
| Year | 0.002 (.001) | .002 (.001) | .002 (.001) | .001 (.001) | .001 (.001) | .001 (.001) | –.002** (.001) | –.002** (.001) | –.003** (.001) | –.002 (.002) | –.002 (.003) | –.002 (.003) |
| Freshman | .007 (.016) | | | –.003 (.012) | | | –.017 (.012) | | | –.095* (.041) | | |

*(Continued)*

*Table A2-5.* Continued

| | Austr. | | | Can. | | | UK | | | US | | |
|---|---|---|---|---|---|---|---|---|---|---|---|---|
| CJ Voting | | –.05* (.024) | | | .026 (.026) | . | | –.032 (.025) | | | –.159** (.053) | |
| Liberal Gov. in Power | | | –.005 (.017) | | | –.001 (.013) | | | .036** (.013) | | | –.014 (.017) |

Standard errors in parenthesis.

**p<0.01

*p<0.05

Note: The results are the same when we control for chief justice. The excluded area of law is criminal.

# Appendix 3

## Dissent Analysis

In order to analyze when judges dissent, we analyzed both aggregate annual data and how individual judges decided cases. In Part A below, we set out our results relating to the annual data both in terms of whether there was at least one dissent in a decision and the fraction of dissenting opinions that were dissents. In Part B we set out our results relating to the probability of an individual judge dissenting.

### A. ANNUAL DATA RESULTS

### A.1 Is there a dissent?

Chapter 8 identified the three broad factors that may influence the probability of a dissent as ideology, workload, and norms. We therefore first estimated the following regression for the probability that there will be at least one dissenting opinion in a decision (Pd):[1]

Pd = f(Ideological Split, Workload, Norms, Area of Law)

1. Lee Epstein, William M. Landes & Richard A. Posner, *Behavior of Federal Judges: A Theoretical and Empirical Study of Rational Choice* (Cambridge, MA: Harvard University Press, 2013) at 127 estimate the probability of a unanimous decision as a function of whether the lower court decision was reversed; the chief justice; the subject matter, along with whether there was a dissent in the court below; whether there was a court of appeal or other conflict; whether the issue could not be identified in an ideological direction; and whether it was from the Ninth Circuit. Donald R. Songer, John Szmer & Susan W. Johnson, "Explaining Dissent on the Supreme Court of Canada" (2011) 44:2 *Canadian Journal of Political Science* 389 at 401 examined whether the existence of a dissent was related to political factors (attitudinal difference, interveners, constitutional issue, statutory interpretation, civil liberties issue, criminal issue, legal access issue), institutional factors (panel size, workload), legal factors (reversal, complexity), and leadership factors (identity of the chief justice).

Where the variables are defined as follows:

| Dependent Variable | | |
|---|---|---|
| Dissenting Opinion | | Whether there is at least one dissenting opinion in the decision, where:<br>Unanimous = 0<br>At least one dissent = 1 |
| **Independent Variables** | | |
| | **Variable Name** | **Description** |
| IDEOLOGICAL SPLIT | | |
| Spread in Conservative Voting | Idsd | Standard deviation in lifetime conservative voting scores for the judges participating in the decision |
| WORKLOAD | | |
| Total Cases per year | TotalCases | The total number of decisions rendered by the high court in the year |
| Average Caseload per year | | The total number of decisions rendered by the high court in the year divided by the number of judges on the court |
| NORMS | | |
| Chief Justice | [Name of Chief Justice] | To identify any effects of norms relating to chief justices, we use dummy variables for the chief justice at the time of the decision. |
| Time | time | To identify if there is a change in the probability of a dissent over time. |
| AREA OF LAW | | |
| Fraction of Civil Liberties Cases | FracCivilLib | Fraction of cases in a year that relate to civil liberties issues |
| Fraction of Constitutional Cases | FracConst | Fraction of cases in a year that relate to constitutional issues |

*Table A3-1.* Description of Independent Variables for Annual Dissent Regressions

| | Mean (Standard Deviation) | Minimum | Maximum |
|---|---|---|---|
| AUSTRALIA (1970–2002) | | | |
| Total Cases per year | 57.3<br>(10.78) | 34 | 79 |
| Average Caseload per year | 7.78<br>(1.32) | 4.86 | 10.71 |

*Table A3-1.* Continued

| | Mean (Standard Deviation) | Minimum | Maximum |
|---|---|---|---|
| Spread in Conservative Voting | .054 (.019) | .032 | .085 |
| Fraction Civil Liberties | .041 (.029) | 0 | .093 |
| Fraction Constitutional | .181 (.062) | .08 | .347 |
| **CANADA (1970–2002)** | | | |
| Total Cases per year | 91.7 (16.26) | 52 | 119 |
| Average Caseload per year | 9.67 (1.71) | 5.78 | 13.22 |
| Spread in Conservative Voting | .051 (.017) | .030 | .08 |
| Fraction Civil Liberties | .054 (.041) | 0 | .143 |
| Fraction Constitutional | .18 (.123) | .018 | .431 |
| **INDIA (1970–2000)** | | | |
| Total Cases per year | 5986 (4461) | 1681 | 16790 |
| Average Caseload per year | 298.2 (197.3) | 112.07 | 837.45 |
| Spread in Conservative Voting | .092 (.045) | .034 | .252 |
| Fraction Civil Liberties | .002 (.002) | 0 | .007 |
| Fraction Constitutional | .003 (.002) | .001 | .008 |
| **UK (1970–2002)** | | | |
| Total Cases per year | 47.30 (9.17) | 35 | 70 |
| Average Caseload per year | 3.02 (.628) | 1.95 | 4.62 |
| Spread in Conservative Voting | .073 (.035) | .036 | .153 |

*(Continued)*

*Table A3-1.* CONTINUED

| | Mean (Standard Deviation) | Minimum | Maximum |
|---|---|---|---|
| Fraction Civil Liberties | .056 (.04) | 0 | .142 |
| Fraction Constitutional | .124 (.121) | 0 | .543 |
| **US (1970–2004)** | | | |
| Total Cases per year | 183.1 (64.9) | 85 | 287 |
| Average Caseload per year | 20.07 (7.24) | 9.44 | 31.89 |
| Spread in Conservative Voting | .166 (.027) | .110 | .209 |
| Fraction Civil Liberties | .505 (.063) | .393 | .623 |
| Fraction Constitutional | .295 (.055) | .222 | .401 |

*Table A3-2.* ONE DISSENT REGRESSIONS, BY COUNTRY

Australia

| | (1) | (2) | (3) | (4) | (5) | (6) |
|---|---|---|---|---|---|---|
| **VARIABLES** | **FractOneDissent** | **FractOneDissent** | **FractOneDissent** | **FractOneDissent** | **FractOneDissent** | **FractOneDissent** |
| TotalCases | −0.00193 | −0.00237 | −0.00180 | −0.00192 | −0.00281 | −0.00168 |
| | (0.00145) | (0.00156) | (0.00149) | (0.00169) | (0.00194) | (0.00173) |
| Idsd | 3.217*** | 3.118*** | 2.985** | 4.275** | 3.978** | 3.721* |
| | (1.086) | (1.100) | (1.183) | (1.775) | (1.808) | (1.936) |
| Barwick | | | | −0.0552 | −0.0595 | −0.0399 |
| | | | | (0.0445) | (0.0449) | (0.0493) |
| Mason | | | | 0.110* | 0.0873 | 0.106 |
| | | | | (0.0628) | (0.0673) | (0.0636) |
| Brennan | | | | 0.166** | 0.170** | 0.159* |
| | | | | (0.0763) | (0.0766) | (0.0774) |
| Gleeson | | | | 0.180** | 0.159** | 0.169** |
| | | | | (0.0724) | (0.0759) | (0.0744) |
| Time | 0.00809*** | 0.00798*** | 0.00765*** | | | |
| | (0.00233) | (0.00235) | (0.00250) | | | |
| FracCivilLib | | −0.361 | | | −0.573 | |
| | | (0.458) | | | (0.612) | |
| FracConst | | | 0.113 | | | 0.184 |
| | | | (0.212) | | | (0.245) |

(Continued)

*Table A3-2.* Continued

| VARIABLES | (1) FractOneDissent | (2) FractOneDissent | (3) FractOneDissent | (4) FractOneDissent | (5) FractOneDissent | (6) FractOneDissent |
|---|---|---|---|---|---|---|
| Constant | 0.202 | 0.249* | 0.195 | 0.238 | 0.338* | 0.218 |
| | (0.130) | (0.144) | (0.133) | (0.164) | (0.196) | (0.168) |
| | | | | | | |
| Observations | 33 | 33 | 33 | 33 | 33 | 33 |
| R-squared | 0.431 | 0.443 | 0.436 | 0.377 | 0.398 | 0.391 |

Standard errors in parentheses.

***p<0.01, **p<0.05, *p<0.1

Canada

| VARIABLES | (1) FractOneDissent | (2) FractOneDissent | (3) FractOneDissent | (4) FractOneDissent | (5) FractOneDissent | (6) FractOneDissent |
|---|---|---|---|---|---|---|
| TotalCases | 0.00107* | 0.00110* | 0.000808 | 0.000348 | 0.000286 | 0.000225 |
| | (0.000588) | (0.000596) | (0.000595) | (0.000528) | (0.000544) | (0.000545) |
| idsd | 3.679*** | 3.767*** | 4.393*** | 4.781*** | 4.780*** | 4.985*** |
| | (1.062) | (1.087) | (1.122) | (1.087) | (1.100) | (1.112) |
| Cartwright | | | | 0.0346 | 0.0326 | 0.0348 |
| | | | | (0.0489) | (0.0496) | (0.0490) |
| Fauteux | | | | 0.0501 | 0.0500 | 0.0539 |
| | | | | (0.0406) | (0.0411) | (0.0409) |

| | (1) | (2) | (3) | (4) | (5) | (6) |
|---|---|---|---|---|---|---|
| VARIABLES | FractOneDissent | FractOneDissent | FractOneDissent | FractOneDissent | FractOneDissent | FractOneDissent |
| Dickson | | | | 0.0522 | 0.0640 | 0.0226 |
| | | | | (0.0344) | (0.0399) | (0.0468) |
| Lamer | | | | 0.152*** | 0.165*** | 0.123** |
| | | | | (0.0358) | (0.0426) | (0.0475) |
| McLachlin | | | | 0.0380 | 0.0476 | 0.00974 |
| | | | | (0.0376) | (0.0412) | (0.0483) |
| time | 0.00216 | 0.00166 | 0.000459 | | | |
| | (0.00168) | (0.00193) | (0.00193) | | | |
| FracCivilLib | | 0.226 | | | −0.216 | |
| | | (0.417) | | | (0.357) | |
| FracConst | | | 0.278 | | | 0.166 |
| | | | (0.169) | | | (0.177) |
| Constant | −0.0764 | −0.0863 | −0.109 | −0.0919 | −0.0811 | −0.106 |
| | (0.102) | (0.105) | (0.101) | (0.0773) | (0.0803) | (0.0789) |
| | | | | | | |
| Observations | 35 | 35 | 35 | 35 | 35 | 35 |
| R-squared | 0.340 | 0.346 | 0.395 | 0.631 | 0.636 | 0.643 |

Standard errors in parentheses.

***p<0.01, **p<0.05, *p<0.1

*(Continued)*

*Table A3-2.* CONTINUED

India

| | (1) | (2) | (3) | (4) | (5) | (6) |
|---|---|---|---|---|---|---|
| VARIABLES | FractOneDissent | FractOneDissent | FractOneDissent | FractOneDissent | FractOneDissent | FractOneDissent |
| TotalCases | –4.64e-08* | –2.94e-08 | –7.85e-09 | –6.91e-08* | –4.26e-08 | –1.78e-08 |
| | (2.50e-08) | (2.52e-08) | (2.93e-08) | (3.88e-08) | (3.89e-08) | (4.50e-08) |
| idsd | –0.00294 | –0.00324 | –0.00312 | –0.0127* | –0.0155** | –0.0104 |
| | (0.00245) | (0.00233) | (0.00230) | (0.00672) | (0.00642) | (0.00627) |
| Hidayathullah | | | | –0.000340 | –0.000199 | –0.000382 |
| | | | | (0.000662) | (0.000617) | (0.000605) |
| Shah | | | | 0.000604 | 0.000959 | 0.000115 |
| | | | | (0.00100) | (0.000949) | (0.000953) |
| Sikri | | | | 0.000803 | 0.000605 | 0.000577 |
| | | | | (0.000507) | (0.000482) | (0.000479) |
| Beg | | | | –0.000120 | 3.39e-06 | –1.89e-05 |
| | | | | (0.000616) | (0.000574) | (0.000566) |
| Chandrchud | | | | 0.000295 | 0.000271 | –6.85e-05 |
| | | | | (0.000411) | (0.000380) | (0.000424) |
| Bhagwati | | | | 0.000207 | 0.000212 | –0.000254 |
| | | | | (0.000741) | (0.000685) | (0.000721) |
| Pathak | | | | –0.000443 | –0.000405 | –0.000722 |
| | | | | (0.000494) | (0.000458) | (0.000476) |

| | (1) | (2) | (3) | (4) | (5) | (6) |
|---|---|---|---|---|---|---|
| VARIABLES | FractOneDissent | FractOneDissent | FractOneDissent | FractOneDissent | FractOneDissent | FractOneDissent |
| Venkataramiah | | | | −0.000175 | −5.21e-05 | −0.000480 |
| | | | | (0.000630) | (0.000587) | (0.000599) |
| Mukherjee | | | | −0.000408 | −0.000311 | −0.000792 |
| | | | | (0.000631) | (0.000586) | (0.000612) |
| MisraSingh | | | | −0.000185 | −4.05e-05 | −0.000376 |
| | | | | (0.000659) | (0.000615) | (0.000611) |
| Kania | | | | 0.000581 | 0.000561 | 9.81e-05 |
| | | | | (0.000825) | (0.000763) | (0.000798) |
| Sharma | | | | −0.000103 | 0.000209 | −0.000154 |
| | | | | (0.000642) | (0.000620) | (0.000587) |
| Venkatachaliah | | | | 0.000443 | 0.000519 | 2.97e-05 |
| | | | | (0.000760) | (0.000704) | (0.000729) |
| Ahmadi | | | | 0.000445 | 0.000617 | 0.000112 |
| | | | | (0.000668) | (0.000625) | (0.000636) |
| VermaPucchi | | | | 0.000306 | 0.000527 | −0.000193 |
| | | | | (0.000830) | (0.000777) | (0.000805) |
| Anand | | | | 0.00178 | 0.00241* | 0.00111 |
| | | | | (0.00126) | (0.00122) | (0.00120) |
| time | −1.12e-05 | −3.00e-06 | −1.52e-05 | | | |
| | (1.38e-05) | (1.38e-05) | (1.31e-05) | | | |

*(Continued)*

*Table A3-2.* CONTINUED

| | (1) | (2) | (3) | (4) | (5) | (6) |
|---|---|---|---|---|---|---|
| VARIABLES | FractOneDissent | FractOneDissent | FractOneDissent | FractOneDissent | FractOneDissent | FractOneDissent |
| FracCivilLib | | 0.127* | | | 0.134 | |
| | | (0.0637) | | | (0.0770) | |
| FracConst | | | 0.146** | | | 0.159* |
| | | | (0.0666) | | | (0.0862) |
| Constant | 0.00112*** | 0.000713** | 0.000558 | 0.00171*** | 0.00150*** | 0.00103* |
| | (0.000248) | (0.000312) | (0.000347) | (0.000455) | (0.000438) | (0.000557) |
| | | | | | | |
| Observations | 31 | 31 | 31 | 31 | 31 | 31 |
| R-squared | 0.305 | 0.398 | 0.413 | 0.654 | 0.729 | 0.736 |

Standard errors in parentheses.

***p<0.01, **p<0.05, *p<0.1

United Kingdom

| | (1) | (2) | (3) | (4) | (5) | (6) |
|---|---|---|---|---|---|---|
| VARIABLES | FractOneDissent | FractOneDissent | FractOneDissent | FractOneDissent | FractOneDissent | FractOneDissent |
| TotalCases | −0.00357** | −0.00393** | −0.00359** | −0.00272** | −0.00227* | −0.00274** |
| | (0.00143) | (0.00169) | (0.00145) | (0.00107) | (0.00120) | (0.00102) |
| idsd | 0.925** | 0.955** | 0.870** | −0.0733 | −0.142 | −0.0322 |
| | (0.366) | (0.378) | (0.385) | (0.290) | (0.304) | (0.277) |

| | (1) | (2) | (3) | (4) | (5) | (6) |
|---|---|---|---|---|---|---|
| VARIABLES | FractOneDissent | FractOneDissent | FractOneDissent | FractOneDissent | FractOneDissent | FractOneDissent |
| Wilberforce | | | | −0.0758** | −0.0761** | −0.0678** |
| | | | | (0.0275) | (0.0277) | (0.0265) |
| Diplock | | | | −0.179*** | −0.173*** | −0.168*** |
| | | | | (0.0461) | (0.0470) | (0.0443) |
| Fraser | | | | −0.183*** | −0.184*** | −0.161*** |
| | | | | (0.0540) | (0.0545) | (0.0530) |
| Keith | | | | −0.159*** | −0.155*** | −0.146*** |
| | | | | (0.0271) | (0.0277) | (0.0268) |
| Scarman | | | | −0.248*** | −0.249*** | −0.242*** |
| | | | | (0.0535) | (0.0540) | (0.0511) |
| Goff | | | | −0.0461 | −0.0317 | −0.0218 |
| | | | | (0.0394) | (0.0434) | (0.0398) |
| BrowneW | | | | −0.0137 | −0.00178 | 0.0581 |
| | | | | (0.0413) | (0.0441) | (0.0560) |
| Bingham | | | | −0.1000** | −0.0842* | −0.00471 |
| | | | | (0.0390) | (0.0437) | (0.0645) |
| Time | −0.00234* | −0.00269 | −0.00289 | | | |
| | (0.00135) | (0.00160) | (0.00173) | | | |
| FracCivilLib | | 0.190 | | | −0.257 | |
| | | (0.453) | | | (0.313) | |

*(Continued)*

*Table A3-2.* Continued

| | (1) | (2) | (3) | (4) | (5) | (6) |
|---|---|---|---|---|---|---|
| VARIABLES | FractOneDissent | FractOneDissent | FractOneDissent | FractOneDissent | FractOneDissent | FractOneDissent |
| FracConst | | | 0.0728 | | | −0.244* |
| | | | (0.139) | | | (0.135) |
| Constant | 0.329*** | 0.339*** | 0.334*** | 0.419*** | 0.414*** | 0.429*** |
| | (0.0705) | (0.0754) | (0.0721) | (0.0511) | (0.0519) | (0.0489) |
| | | | | | | |
| Observations | 33 | 33 | 33 | 33 | 33 | 33 |
| R-squared | 0.363 | 0.367 | 0.369 | 0.793 | 0.799 | 0.821 |

Standard errors in parentheses.

***p<0.01, **p<0.05, *p<0.1

United States

| | (1) | (2) | (3) | (4) | (5) | (6) |
|---|---|---|---|---|---|---|
| VARIABLES | FractOneDissent | FractOneDissent | FractOneDissent | FractOneDissent | FractOneDissent | FractOneDissent |
| TotalCases | −0.000405** | −0.000530*** | −0.000257 | −0.000357* | −0.000441** | −0.000172 |
| | (0.000192) | (0.000191) | (0.000210) | (0.000204) | (0.000210) | (0.000222) |
| idsd | 0.730 | 0.293 | 0.489 | 1.265** | 1.030* | 0.966* |
| | (0.565) | (0.571) | (0.572) | (0.549) | (0.567) | (0.555) |
| time | −0.00254* | −0.00350** | −0.00212 | | | |
| | (0.00130) | (0.00131) | (0.00130) | | | |

| | (1) | (2) | (3) | (4) | (5) | (6) |
|---|---|---|---|---|---|---|
| **VARIABLES** | **FractOneDissent** | **FractOneDissent** | **FractOneDissent** | **FractOneDissent** | **FractOneDissent** | **FractOneDissent** |
| FracCivilLib | | 0.299** | | | 0.207 | |
| | | (0.139) | | | (0.149) | |
| FracConst | | | 0.226 | | | 0.273* |
| | | | (0.143) | | | (0.151) |
| Burger | | | | 0.0118 | 0.0213 | 0.000535 |
| | | | | (0.0242) | (0.0249) | (0.0242) |
| Constant | 0.569*** | 0.531*** | 0.508*** | 0.420*** | 0.365*** | 0.361*** |
| | (0.100) | (0.0966) | (0.105) | (0.0677) | (0.0775) | (0.0732) |
| | | | | | | |
| Observations | 35 | 35 | 35 | 35 | 35 | 35 |
| R-squared | 0.331 | 0.421 | 0.382 | 0.254 | 0.299 | 0.327 |

Standard errors in parentheses.

***p<0.01, **p<0.05, *p<0.1

## A.2 How many dissenting opinions?

We are not only interested in whether there is a dissent as a measure of cooperation but also the fraction of opinions that are dissenting. Epstein, Landes, and Posner examine whether the fraction of dissenting opinions at the US Supreme Court in a term is related to the caseload, the difference in ideology across the Court, and time (along with taking account of an anomalous period).[2] Similarly, we estimate the following regression to account for the fraction of dissenting opinions (Fd), taking into other factors such as the case mix in a term:

Fd = f(Ideological Split, Workload, Norms, Area of Law)

Where the variables are defined as follows:

| Dependent Variable | |
|---|---|
| Fraction dissenting | The number of dissenting opinions divided by the total number of decisions |
| **Independent Variables** | |
| *Defined the same as in A.1 above* | |

2. Epstein, Landes & Posner, *Behavior, supra* note 1 at 281–222 (for differences in ideology across the Court they used the standard deviation of the Segal-Cover scores for the Court).

*Table A3-3.* Fraction Dissenting Regressions, by Country

Australia

| | (1) | (2) | (3) | (4) | (5) | (6) |
|---|---|---|---|---|---|---|
| VARIABLES | **FracDissent** | **FracDissent** | **FracDissent** | **FracDissent** | **FracDissent** | **FracDissent** |
| TotalCases | −0.00518* | −0.00574* | −0.00438 | −0.00416 | −0.00464 | −0.00302 |
| | (0.00291) | (0.00315) | (0.00286) | (0.00319) | (0.00373) | (0.00308) |
| idsd | 3.692 | 3.563 | 2.278 | 6.768* | 6.606* | 4.185 |
| | (2.183) | (2.226) | (2.278) | (3.358) | (3.473) | (3.446) |
| Barwick | | | | −0.0761 | −0.0785 | −0.00470 |
| | | | | (0.0842) | (0.0862) | (0.0877) |
| Mason | | | | 0.252** | 0.240* | 0.233** |
| | | | | (0.119) | (0.129) | (0.113) |
| Brennan | | | | 0.289* | 0.292* | 0.258* |
| | | | | (0.144) | (0.147) | (0.138) |
| Gleeson | | | | 0.271* | 0.260* | 0.221 |
| | | | | (0.137) | (0.146) | (0.132) |
| time | 0.0104** | 0.0102** | 0.00771 | | | |
| | (0.00468) | (0.00475) | (0.00481) | | | |
| FracCivilLib | | −0.473 | | | −0.313 | |
| | | (0.927) | | | (1.175) | |
| FracConst | | | 0.688 | | | 0.860* |
| | | | (0.409) | | | (0.437) |

*(Continued)*

*Table A3-3.* Continued

| | (1) | (2) | (3) | (4) | (5) | (6) |
|---|---|---|---|---|---|---|
| **VARIABLES** | **FracDissent** | **FracDissent** | **FracDissent** | **FracDissent** | **FracDissent** | **FracDissent** |
| Constant | 0.584** | 0.646** | 0.537** | 0.442 | 0.497 | 0.350 |
| | (0.262) | (0.291) | (0.256) | (0.311) | (0.377) | (0.299) |
| | | | | | | |
| Observations | 33 | 33 | 33 | 33 | 33 | 33 |
| R-squared | 0.364 | 0.369 | 0.422 | 0.383 | 0.385 | 0.466 |

Standard errors in parentheses.

***p<0.01, **p<0.05, *p<0.1

Canada

| | (1) | (2) | (3) | (4) | (5) | (6) | (7) |
|---|---|---|---|---|---|---|---|
| **VARIABLES** | **FracDissent** | **FracDissent** | **FracDissent** | **FracDissent** | **FracDissent** | **FracDissent** | **FracDissent** |
| TotalCases | 0.00279 | 0.00278 | 0.00268 | 0.00103 | 0.000891 | 0.00106 | 0.00106 |
| | (0.00198) | (0.00202) | (0.00208) | (0.00201) | (0.00206) | (0.00208) | (0.00208) |
| idsd | 10.96*** | 10.92*** | 11.19*** | 14.19*** | 14.19*** | 14.13*** | 14.13*** |
| | (2.812) | (2.885) | (3.055) | (3.238) | (3.287) | (3.373) | (3.373) |
| Cartwright | | | | −0.151 | −0.157 | −0.152 | −0.152 |
| | | | | (0.189) | (0.192) | (0.193) | (0.193) |
| Fauteux | | | | −0.0952 | −0.0959 | −0.0963 | −0.0963 |
| | | | | (0.122) | (0.124) | (0.125) | (0.125) |

| | (1) | (2) | (3) | (4) | (5) | (6) | (7) |
|---|---|---|---|---|---|---|---|
| VARIABLES | FracDissent | FracDissent | FracDissent | FracDissent | FracDissent | FracDissent | FracDissent |
| Dickson | | | | 0.0907 | 0.121 | 0.0995 | 0.0995 |
| | | | | (0.102) | (0.119) | (0.143) | (0.143) |
| Lamer | | | | 0.348*** | 0.382*** | 0.357** | 0.357** |
| | | | | (0.108) | (0.128) | (0.147) | (0.147) |
| McLachlin | | | | 0.113 | 0.137 | 0.122 | 0.122 |
| | | | | (0.129) | (0.139) | (0.169) | (0.169) |
| t | 0.00988** | 0.0102* | 0.00918 | | | | |
| | (0.00476) | (0.00552) | (0.00590) | | | | |
| FracCivilLib | | −0.132 | | | −0.549 | | |
| | | (1.083) | | | (1.066) | | |
| FracConst | | | 0.0969 | | | −0.0495 | −0.0495 |
| | | | (0.467) | | | (0.548) | (0.548) |
| Constant | −0.449 | −0.445 | −0.456 | −0.390 | −0.364 | −0.385 | −0.385 |
| | (0.282) | (0.289) | (0.288) | (0.257) | (0.265) | (0.267) | (0.267) |
| | | | | | | | |
| Observations | 33 | 33 | 33 | 33 | 33 | 33 | 33 |
| R-squared | 0.381 | 0.382 | 0.382 | 0.536 | 0.541 | 0.536 | 0.536 |

Standard errors in parentheses.

***p<0.01, **p<0.05, *p<0.1

*(Continued)*

*Table A3-3.* Continued

India

| | (1) | (2) | (3) | (4) | (5) | (6) |
|---|---|---|---|---|---|---|
| **VARIABLES** | **FracDissent** | **FracDissent** | **FracDissent** | **FracDissent** | **FracDissent** | **FracDissent** |
| TotalCases | −5.36e-08 | −4.18e-08 | −8.58e-09 | −7.48e-08 | −6.06e-08 | −8.19e-09 |
| | (3.33e-08) | (3.54e-08) | (3.98e-08) | (5.27e-08) | (5.87e-08) | (6.20e-08) |
| idsd | −0.00290 | −0.00311 | −0.00311 | −0.0141 | −0.0156 | −0.0111 |
| | (0.00327) | (0.00328) | (0.00313) | (0.00913) | (0.00968) | (0.00863) |
| Hidayathullah | | | | −0.000533 | −0.000457 | −0.000587 |
| | | | | (0.000899) | (0.000931) | (0.000832) |
| Shah | | | | 0.000519 | 0.000709 | −0.000116 |
| | | | | (0.00136) | (0.00143) | (0.00131) |
| Sikri | | | | 0.00108 | 0.000969 | 0.000781 |
| | | | | (0.000689) | (0.000728) | (0.000659) |
| Beg | | | | −3.89e-05 | 2.75e-05 | 9.30e-05 |
| | | | | (0.000837) | (0.000866) | (0.000778) |
| Chandrchud | | | | 0.000161 | 0.000148 | −0.000312 |
| | | | | (0.000558) | (0.000573) | (0.000584) |
| Bhagwati | | | | 0.000125 | 0.000127 | −0.000475 |
| | | | | (0.00101) | (0.00103) | (0.000993) |
| Pathak | | | | −0.000652 | −0.000632 | −0.00102 |
| | | | | (0.000671) | (0.000690) | (0.000655) |

| | (1) | (2) | (3) | (4) | (5) | (6) |
|---|---|---|---|---|---|---|
| VARIABLES | FracDissent | FracDissent | FracDissent | FracDissent | FracDissent | FracDissent |
| Venkataramiah | | | | −0.000130 | −6.45e-05 | −0.000526 |
| | | | | (0.000856) | (0.000885) | (0.000824) |
| Mukherjee | | | | −0.000611 | −0.000559 | −0.00111 |
| | | | | (0.000856) | (0.000883) | (0.000843) |
| MisraSingh | | | | −0.000369 | −0.000291 | −0.000617 |
| | | | | (0.000895) | (0.000928) | (0.000840) |
| Kania | | | | 0.000450 | 0.000440 | −0.000177 |
| | | | | (0.00112) | (0.00115) | (0.00110) |
| Sharma | | | | −0.000301 | −0.000134 | −0.000367 |
| | | | | (0.000872) | (0.000934) | (0.000807) |
| Venkatachaliah | | | | 0.000633 | 0.000674 | 9.57e-05 |
| | | | | (0.00103) | (0.00106) | (0.00100) |
| Ahmadi | | | | 0.000321 | 0.000414 | −0.000110 |
| | | | | (0.000907) | (0.000943) | (0.000875) |
| VermaPucchi | | | | 0.000183 | 0.000301 | −0.000465 |
| | | | | (0.00113) | (0.00117) | (0.00111) |
| Anand | | | | 0.00201 | 0.00235 | 0.00115 |
| | | | | (0.00171) | (0.00184) | (0.00166) |
| time | −1.57e-05 | −9.97e-06 | −2.03e-05 | | | |
| | (1.84e-05) | (1.93e-05) | (1.78e-05) | | | |

*(Continued)*

*Table A3-3.* Continued

| | (1) | (2) | (3) | (4) | (5) | (6) |
|---|---|---|---|---|---|---|
| VARIABLES | FracDissent | FracDissent | FracDissent | FracDissent | FracDissent | FracDissent |
| FracCivilLib | | 0.0882 | | | 0.0720 | |
| | | (0.0895) | | | (0.116) | |
| FracConst | | | 0.171* | | | 0.206 |
| | | | (0.0906) | | | (0.119) |
| Constant | 0.00136*** | 0.00107** | 0.000697 | 0.00205*** | 0.00193** | 0.00116 |
| | (0.000330) | (0.000439) | (0.000472) | (0.000618) | (0.000660) | (0.000766) |
| | | | | | | |
| Observations | 31 | 31 | 31 | 31 | 31 | 31 |
| R-squared | 0.257 | 0.284 | 0.346 | 0.616 | 0.629 | 0.699 |

Standard errors in parentheses.

***p<0.01, **p<0.05, *p<0.1

UK

| | (1) | (2) | (3) | (4) | (5) | (6) |
|---|---|---|---|---|---|---|
| VARIABLES | FracDissent | FracDissent | FracDissent | FracDissent | FracDissent | FracDissent |
| TotalCases | −0.00461* | −0.00483* | −0.00460* | −0.00306 | −0.00239 | −0.00311* |
| | (0.00231) | (0.00273) | (0.00235) | (0.00181) | (0.00205) | (0.00158) |
| idsd | 1.427** | 1.445** | 1.452** | −0.0872 | −0.191 | 0.0115 |
| | (0.590) | (0.611) | (0.624) | (0.491) | (0.517) | (0.431) |

|  | (1) | (2) | (3) | (4) | (5) | (6) |
|---|---|---|---|---|---|---|
| VARIABLES | **FracDissent** | **FracDissent** | **FracDissent** | **FracDissent** | **FracDissent** | **FracDissent** |
| Wilberforce |  |  |  | −0.122** | −0.123** | −0.103** |
|  |  |  |  | (0.0466) | (0.0471) | (0.0413) |
| Diplock |  |  |  | −0.310*** | −0.301*** | −0.284*** |
|  |  |  |  | (0.0782) | (0.0800) | (0.0691) |
| Fraser |  |  |  | −0.291*** | −0.292*** | −0.237*** |
|  |  |  |  | (0.0917) | (0.0927) | (0.0826) |
| Keith |  |  |  | −0.245*** | −0.240*** | −0.213*** |
|  |  |  |  | (0.0459) | (0.0471) | (0.0418) |
| Scarman |  |  |  | −0.400*** | −0.401*** | −0.386*** |
|  |  |  |  | (0.0908) | (0.0919) | (0.0796) |
| Goff |  |  |  | −0.117* | −0.0950 | −0.0582 |
|  |  |  |  | (0.0668) | (0.0739) | (0.0621) |
| BrowneW |  |  |  | −0.0221 | −0.00411 | 0.151* |
|  |  |  |  | (0.0701) | (0.0750) | (0.0872) |
| Bingham |  |  |  | −0.203*** | −0.179** | 0.0261 |
|  |  |  |  | (0.0661) | (0.0744) | (0.101) |
| Time | −0.00403* | −0.00424 | −0.00378 |  |  |  |
|  | (0.00218) | (0.00259) | (0.00280) |  |  |  |
| FracCivilLib |  | 0.115 |  |  | −0.387 |  |
|  |  | (0.733) |  |  | (0.532) |  |

*(Continued)*

*Table A3-3.* CONTINUED

| | (1) | (2) | (3) | (4) | (5) | (6) |
|---|---|---|---|---|---|---|
| VARIABLES | **FracDissent** | **FracDissent** | **FracDissent** | **FracDissent** | **FracDissent** | **FracDissent** |
| FracConst | | | −0.0332 | | | −0.586** |
| | | | (0.226) | | | (0.211) |
| Constant | 0.458*** | 0.464*** | 0.456*** | 0.588*** | 0.580*** | 0.610*** |
| | (0.114) | (0.122) | (0.117) | (0.0867) | (0.0884) | (0.0762) |
| | | | | | | |
| Observations | 33 | 33 | 33 | 33 | 33 | 33 |
| R-squared | 0.328 | 0.328 | 0.328 | 0.758 | 0.764 | 0.823 |

Standard errors in parentheses.

***p<0.01, **p<0.05, *p<0.1

US

| | (1) | (2) | (3) | (4) | (5) | (6) |
|---|---|---|---|---|---|---|
| VARIABLES | **FracDissent** | **FracDissent** | **FracDissent** | **FracDissent** | **FracDissent** | **FracDissent** |
| TotalCases | −0.000701 | −0.000958 | 0.000118 | −0.000644 | −0.000877 | 0.000268 |
| | (0.000618) | (0.000640) | (0.000619) | (0.000609) | (0.000630) | (0.000598) |
| idsd | 3.927** | 3.027 | 2.601 | 3.963** | 3.311* | 2.488 |
| | (1.812) | (1.915) | (1.684) | (1.642) | (1.703) | (1.498) |
| time | 0.00461 | 0.00263 | 0.00695* | | | |
| | (0.00417) | (0.00438) | (0.00381) | | | |

| | (1) | (2) | (3) | (4) | (5) | (6) |
|---|---|---|---|---|---|---|
| VARIABLES | FracDissent | FracDissent | FracDissent | FracDissent | FracDissent | FracDissent |
| FracCivilLib | | 0.616 | | | 0.573 | |
| | | (0.465) | | | (0.448) | |
| FracConst | | | 1.242*** | | | 1.348*** |
| | | | (0.422) | | | (0.409) |
| Burger | | | | −0.110 | −0.0835 | −0.165** |
| | | | | (0.0725) | (0.0747) | (0.0653) |
| Constant | 0.868** | 0.789** | 0.530* | 0.988*** | 0.836*** | 0.696*** |
| | (0.322) | (0.324) | (0.310) | (0.203) | (0.233) | (0.197) |
| | | | | | | |
| Observations | 35 | 35 | 35 | 35 | 35 | 35 |
| R-squared | 0.136 | 0.183 | 0.329 | 0.163 | 0.207 | 0.386 |

Standard errors in parentheses.

***p<0.01, **p<0.05, *p<0.1

## B. INDIVIDUAL JUDGE DATA RESULTS

In addition to annual data on decisions of each court, we also had data on the voting of individual judges (see Appendix 1 for a description of the data). We therefore were also able to analyze the factors that were correlated with the probability of an individual judge dissenting. We estimated the following regression concerning the probability that an individual judge will dissent, taking into other factors such as the case mix in a term:

Di = f(Ideology, Area of Law, Norms, Panel Size, Other)

Table A3-4 provides the basic results by country, and Table A3-5 provides the results for the regressions examining panel effects, where the variables are defined as follows:

| **Dependent Variable** | | |
|---|---|---|
| Dissenting Vote | | Whether the judge dissented in a particular case, which takes the following values:<br>In majority = 0<br>In dissent = 1 |
| **Independent Variables** | | |
| *Defined the same as for the regression in Appendix 2, except:* | | |
| | **Variable Name** | **Description** |
| Ideological Difference from the rest of the Panel | LLV Diff from Others on Panel | The difference between the lifetime liberal voting rate of the particular judge and the average lifetime liberal voting rate of the rest of the panel |
| Panel Size | Panel Size | The number of judges who participated in the particular decision |

*Table A3-4.* Basic Judge Vote Regressions, by Country

The dependent variable for these regressions is Dissenting Vote. For each country the first set of regressions uses the party appointing the judge as the measure of ideology, and the second uses the judge's liberal voting rate in criminal cases (and omits dissents in criminal cases), except for India where only the regressions using a judge's long-term liberal voting rate in criminal cases are included as there is no party appointing variable.

Australia

| | (2) | (3) | (4) | (5) | (6) | (7) |
|---|---|---|---|---|---|---|
| VARIABLES | Marginal Effects | Marginal Effects | Marginal Effects | Marginal Effects | Marginal Effects | Marginal Effects |
| Party_Appointing_Judge | 0.0132 | 0.0139 | 0.0129 | 0.0130 | 0.0139 | 0.00835 |
| | (0.0304) | (0.0319) | (0.0319) | (0.0309) | (0.0321) | (0.0301) |
| lower_ct_direction_lib_is_1 | −0.00739 | −0.0104 | −0.00798 | −0.00764 | −0.00768 | −0.00723 |
| | (0.00919) | (0.00852) | (0.00842) | (0.00876) | (0.00878) | (0.00845) |
| civilrights | −0.00919 | −0.0226 | −0.00740 | −0.00972 | −0.00915 | −0.00905 |
| | (0.0259) | (0.0254) | (0.0262) | (0.0254) | (0.0256) | (0.0255) |
| publiclaw | −0.00781 | −0.00980 | −0.0108 | −0.0102 | −0.00816 | −0.00807 |
| | (0.0125) | (0.0129) | (0.0118) | (0.0119) | (0.0127) | (0.0123) |
| privateecon | −0.0443** | −0.0423** | −0.0457** | −0.0455** | −0.0446** | −0.0439** |
| | (0.0202) | (0.0212) | (0.0205) | (0.0208) | (0.0211) | (0.0202) |
| torts | −0.00505 | −0.00186 | −0.00573 | −0.00549 | −0.00525 | −0.00486 |
| | (0.0127) | (0.0133) | (0.0127) | (0.0129) | (0.0129) | (0.0128) |

*(Continued)*

*Table A3-4.* Continued

| | (2) | (3) | (4) | (5) | (6) | (7) |
|---|---|---|---|---|---|---|
| **VARIABLES** | **Marginal Effects** | **Marginal Effects** | **Marginal Effects** | **Marginal Effects** | **Marginal Effects** | **Marginal Effects** |
| panel_size | 0.0136 | 0.0141 | 0.00913 | 0.00804 | 0.0145 | 0.0147 |
| | (0.0185) | (0.0179) | (0.0145) | (0.0166) | (0.0172) | (0.0172) |
| CJGleeson | | | 0.0236 | | | |
| | | | (0.0415) | | | |
| CJBrennan | | | 0.0218 | | | |
| | | | (0.0367) | | | |
| CJMason | | | 0.00645 | | | |
| | | | (0.0233) | | | |
| CJBarwick | | | 0.0322* | | | |
| | | | (0.0195) | | | |
| year | | −0.000437 | | −3.22e-05 | −0.000140 | −0.000108 |
| | | (0.00128) | | (0.00122) | (0.00128) | (0.00128) |
| intervenor | | 0.0386*** | | | | |
| | | (0.0108) | | | | |
| government_in_power | | | | −0.0241 | | |
| | | | | (0.0194) | | |
| freshman | | | | | −0.00587 | |
| | | | | | (0.0149) | |

| VARIABLES | (2)<br>Marginal Effects | (3)<br>Marginal Effects | (4)<br>Marginal Effects | (5)<br>Marginal Effects | (6)<br>Marginal Effects | (7)<br>Marginal Effects |
|---|---|---|---|---|---|---|
| CJ_Vote | | | | | | −0.0502 |
| | | | | | | (0.0326) |
| | | | | | | |
| Observations | 6,819 | 6,819 | 6,819 | 6,819 | 6,819 | 6,819 |

Standard errors in parentheses.

*** p<0.01, ** p<0.05, * p<0.1

| VARIABLES | (2)<br>Marginal Effects | (3)<br>Marginal Effects | (4)<br>Marginal Effects | (5)<br>Marginal Effects | (6)<br>Marginal Effects | (7)<br>Marginal Effects |
|---|---|---|---|---|---|---|
| CrimLV | 0.128 | 0.135 | 0.156 | 0.133 | 0.142 | 0.111 |
| | (0.142) | (0.139) | (0.129) | (0.127) | (0.138) | (0.128) |
| lower_ct_direction_lib_is_1 | −0.0143 | −0.0168* | −0.0156* | −0.0154* | −0.0151* | −0.0148* |
| | (0.00921) | (0.00869) | (0.00851) | (0.00887) | (0.00894) | (0.00876) |
| publiclaw | 0.00383 | 0.0129 | −0.00287 | 0.00101 | 0.00278 | 0.00309 |
| | (0.0256) | (0.0244) | (0.0259) | (0.0253) | (0.0255) | (0.0257) |
| privateecon | −0.0332 | −0.0204 | −0.0377* | −0.0344 | −0.0342 | −0.0333 |
| | (0.0218) | (0.0216) | (0.0225) | (0.0226) | (0.0224) | (0.0220) |

*(Continued)*

*Table A3-4.* Continued

| | (2) | (3) | (4) | (5) | (6) | (7) |
|---|---|---|---|---|---|---|
| VARIABLES | **Marginal Effects** | **Marginal Effects** | **Marginal Effects** | **Marginal Effects** | **Marginal Effects** | **Marginal Effects** |
| torts | 0.00489 | 0.0190 | 0.00144 | 0.00496 | 0.00437 | 0.00500 |
| | (0.0241) | (0.0238) | (0.0244) | (0.0240) | (0.0241) | (0.0244) |
| panel_size | 0.0256 | 0.0275 | 0.0167 | 0.0185 | 0.0270 | 0.0270 |
| | (0.0192) | (0.0190) | (0.0165) | (0.0175) | (0.0181) | (0.0181) |
| CJGleeson | | | 0.0364 | | | |
| | | | (0.0366) | | | |
| CJBrennan | | | 0.0359 | | | |
| | | | (0.0283) | | | |
| CJMason | | | 0.0109 | | | |
| | | | (0.0193) | | | |
| CJBarwick | | | 0.0488*** | | | |
| | | | (0.0160) | | | |
| year | | −0.000645 | | −0.000224 | −0.000402 | −0.000299 |
| | | (0.00129) | | (0.00117) | (0.00128) | (0.00125) |
| intervenor | | 0.0334** | | | | |
| | | (0.0159) | | | | |
| government_in_power | | | | −0.0316* | | |
| | | | | (0.0175) | | |

| VARIABLES | (2)<br>Marginal Effects | (3)<br>Marginal Effects | (4)<br>Marginal Effects | (5)<br>Marginal Effects | (6)<br>Marginal Effects | (7)<br>Marginal Effects |
|---|---|---|---|---|---|---|
| freshman | | | | | −0.00729 | |
| | | | | | (0.0118) | |
| CJ_Vote | | | | | | −0.0318 |
| | | | | | | (0.0253) |
| | | | | | | |
| Observations | 4,808 | 4,808 | 4,808 | 4,808 | 4,808 | 4,808 |

Standard errors in parentheses.

*** p<0.01, ** p<0.05, * p<0.1

Canada

| VARIABLES | (2)<br>Marginal Effects | (3)<br>Marginal Effects | (4)<br>Marginal Effects | (5)<br>Marginal Effects | (6)<br>Marginal Effects | (7)<br>Marginal Effects |
|---|---|---|---|---|---|---|
| Party_Appointing_Judge | 0.00809 | −0.000955 | 0.0125 | −0.000597 | 0.000295 | −0.00300 |
| | (0.0156) | (0.0128) | (0.0123) | (0.0129) | (0.0130) | (0.0131) |
| lower_court_direction_lib_is_1 | −0.00357 | −0.00282 | −0.00345 | −0.00326 | −0.00285 | −0.00316 |
| | (0.00273) | (0.00275) | (0.00279) | (0.00273) | (0.00274) | (0.00275) |
| civilrights | 0.0249*** | 0.0181*** | 0.0233*** | 0.0279*** | 0.0276*** | 0.0291*** |
| | (0.00726) | (0.00694) | (0.00691) | (0.00701) | (0.00703) | (0.00753) |

*(Continued)*

*Table A3-4.* Continued

| | (2) | (3) | (4) | (5) | (6) | (7) |
|---|---|---|---|---|---|---|
| VARIABLES | **Marginal Effects** | **Marginal Effects** | **Marginal Effects** | **Marginal Effects** | **Marginal Effects** | **Marginal Effects** |
| publiclaw | −0.00729 | −0.0161** | −0.0125 | −0.0131* | −0.0112 | −0.0108 |
| | (0.00702) | (0.00784) | (0.00781) | (0.00792) | (0.00746) | (0.00755) |
| privateecon | 0.00688 | 0.000554 | 0.000972 | −0.00152 | 0.00165 | 0.00109 |
| | (0.00803) | (0.00870) | (0.00892) | (0.00913) | (0.00872) | (0.00887) |
| torts | 0.0252** | 0.0190** | 0.0171* | 0.0164* | 0.0198** | 0.0194** |
| | (0.00993) | (0.00889) | (0.00969) | (0.00914) | (0.00890) | (0.00936) |
| otherlaw | −0.0114 | −0.0130 | −0.00182 | −0.0106 | −0.00627 | −0.00738 |
| | (0.0382) | (0.0375) | (0.0367) | (0.0372) | (0.0372) | (0.0384) |
| panelsize | 0.0165*** | 0.0162*** | 0.0174*** | 0.0157*** | 0.0170*** | 0.0172*** |
| | (0.00213) | (0.00215) | (0.00217) | (0.00185) | (0.00210) | (0.00229) |
| CJCartwright | | | 0.0637*** | | | |
| | | | (0.0170) | | | |
| CJFauteux | | | 0.0476*** | | | |
| | | | (0.0155) | | | |
| CJDickson | | | −0.0237* | | | |
| | | | (0.0141) | | | |
| CJLamer | | | 0.00886 | | | |
| | | | (0.0108) | | | |

| | (2) | (3) | (4) | (5) | (6) | (7) |
|---|---|---|---|---|---|---|
| **VARIABLES** | **Marginal Effects** | **Marginal Effects** | **Marginal Effects** | **Marginal Effects** | **Marginal Effects** | **Marginal Effects** |
| CJMcLachlin | | | −0.0119 | | | |
| | | | (0.0134) | | | |
| year | | −0.00175** | | −0.00135* | −0.00144* | −0.00152** |
| | | (0.000754) | | (0.000687) | (0.000740) | (0.000762) |
| intervenor | | 0.0217*** | | | | |
| | | (0.00478) | | | | |
| government_in_power | | | | 0.0195** | | |
| | | | | (0.00916) | | |
| freshman | | | | | −0.0156* | |
| | | | | | (0.00893) | |
| CJ_Vote | | | | | | 0.00971 |
| | | | | | | (0.0159) |
| | | | | | | |
| Observations | 17,652 | 17,652 | 17,652 | 17,652 | 17,652 | 17,652 |

Standard errors in parentheses.

*** $p<0.01$, ** $p<0.05$, * $p<0.1$

*(Continued)*

*Table A3-4.* Continued

| VARIABLES | (2) Marginal Effects | (3) Marginal Effects | (4) Marginal Effects | (5) Marginal Effects | (6) Marginal Effects | (7) Marginal Effects |
|---|---|---|---|---|---|---|
| CrimLV | 0.0668 | 0.0610 | 0.0832 | 0.0629 | 0.0663 | 0.0628 |
| | (0.0839) | (0.0614) | (0.0556) | (0.0593) | (0.0592) | (0.0672) |
| lower_court_direction_lib_is_1 | −0.0106** | −0.00996** | −0.00791* | −0.00950** | −0.00940** | −0.0106** |
| | (0.00419) | (0.00430) | (0.00451) | (0.00433) | (0.00429) | (0.00448) |
| publiclaw | −0.0298*** | −0.0347*** | −0.0321*** | −0.0386*** | −0.0373*** | −0.0384*** |
| | (0.00929) | (0.00942) | (0.00934) | (0.00986) | (0.00972) | (0.0102) |
| privateecon | −0.0177 | −0.0220** | −0.0190* | −0.0282** | −0.0260** | −0.0282** |
| | (0.0111) | (0.0106) | (0.0110) | (0.0113) | (0.0113) | (0.0119) |
| torts | 6.14e−05 | −0.00335 | −0.00219 | −0.00982 | −0.00755 | −0.00994 |
| | (0.0136) | (0.0112) | (0.0123) | (0.0124) | (0.0125) | (0.0134) |
| otherlaw | −0.0322 | −0.0290 | −0.0187 | −0.0337 | −0.0302 | −0.0333 |
| | (0.0419) | (0.0410) | (0.0412) | (0.0414) | (0.0412) | (0.0424) |
| panelsize | 0.0152*** | 0.0172*** | 0.0190*** | 0.0168*** | 0.0175*** | 0.0180*** |
| | (0.00219) | (0.00189) | (0.00227) | (0.00180) | (0.00187) | (0.00215) |
| CJCartwright | | | 0.0674*** | | | |
| | | | (0.0142) | | | |
| CJFauteux | | | 0.0458*** | | | |
| | | | (0.0133) | | | |

| | (2) | (3) | (4) | (5) | (6) | (7) |
|---|---|---|---|---|---|---|
| **VARIABLES** | **Marginal Effects** | **Marginal Effects** | **Marginal Effects** | **Marginal Effects** | **Marginal Effects** | **Marginal Effects** |
| CJDickson | | | –0.0193 | | | |
| | | | (0.0159) | | | |
| CJLamer | | | 0.00648 | | | |
| | | | (0.0102) | | | |
| CJMcLachlin | | | –0.0199 | | | |
| | | | (0.0170) | | | |
| year | | –0.00179*** | | –0.00156*** | –0.00165*** | –0.00167*** |
| | | (0.000540) | | (0.000516) | (0.000531) | (0.000563) |
| intervenor | | 0.0106 | | | | |
| | | (0.00660) | | | | |
| government_in_power | | | | 0.0129 | | |
| | | | | (0.00940) | | |
| freshman | | | | | –0.0180* | |
| | | | | | (0.00975) | |
| CJ_Vote | | | | | | –0.00625 |
| | | | | | | (0.0103) |
| | | | | | | |
| Observations | 9,131 | 9,131 | 9,131 | 9,131 | 9,131 | 9,131 |

Standard errors in parentheses.

*** p<0.01, ** p<0.05, * p<0.1

*(Continued)*

*Table A3-4.* Continued

India

| | (1) | (2) | (3) |
|---|---|---|---|
| **VARIABLES** | **Marginal Effects** | **Marginal Effects** | **Marginal Effects** |
| CrimLV | 0.000533 | 0.000571 | 0.000339 |
| | (0.00632) | (0.00616) | (0.00404) |
| lower_court_direction_lib_is_1 | 0.00262 | 0.00289 | 0.00140 |
| | (0.00218) | (0.00221) | (0.00167) |
| Publiclaw | | −0.00514 | −0.00202 |
| | | (0.00374) | (0.00239) |
| privateecon | | −0.00854 | −0.00492* |
| | | (0.00537) | (0.00287) |
| year | | | −0.000269** |
| | | | (0.000137) |
| intervenor | | | 0.00684*** |
| | | | (0.00255) |
| Observations | 3,220 | 3,143 | 3,143 |

Standard errors in parentheses.

*** $p<0.01$, ** $p<0.05$, * $p<0.1$

UK

| VARIABLES | (2) Marginal Effects | (3) Marginal Effects | (4) Marginal Effects | (5) Marginal Effects | (6) Marginal Effects | (7) Marginal Effects |
|---|---|---|---|---|---|---|
| Party_Appointing_Judge | 0.0104 | 0.00289 | 4.78e-05 | −0.000266 | 0.00227 | 0.00333 |
| | (0.0104) | (0.0112) | (0.00837) | (0.00990) | (0.0116) | (0.0119) |
| lower_court_direction_lib_is_1 | 0.00788 | 0.00614 | 0.00582 | 0.00528 | 0.00627 | 0.00685 |
| | (0.00664) | (0.00654) | (0.00615) | (0.00670) | (0.00664) | (0.00686) |
| civilrights | −0.00963 | −0.00453 | −0.00318 | −0.00617 | −0.00510 | −0.00539 |
| | (0.0116) | (0.0113) | (0.0108) | (0.0113) | (0.0112) | (0.0110) |
| publiclaw | 0.0114 | 0.0116 | 0.0122* | 0.0109 | 0.0109 | 0.0106 |
| | (0.00804) | (0.00771) | (0.00739) | (0.00762) | (0.00771) | (0.00791) |
| privateecon | 0.00923 | 0.00986 | 0.00782 | 0.00803 | 0.00918 | 0.00898 |
| | (0.0110) | (0.0107) | (0.0104) | (0.0105) | (0.0107) | (0.0108) |
| torts | −0.000522 | 0.00204 | 0.000521 | 0.00137 | 0.00131 | 0.00138 |
| | (0.00914) | (0.00871) | (0.00850) | (0.00874) | (0.00887) | (0.00900) |
| otherlaw | 0.00410 | −0.00388 | 0.00999 | 0.00586 | 0.00699 | 0.00754 |
| | (0.0278) | (0.0272) | (0.0262) | (0.0268) | (0.0272) | (0.0275) |
| panelsize | 0.0326*** | 0.0333*** | 0.0291*** | 0.0332*** | 0.0342*** | 0.0373*** |
| | (0.00741) | (0.00698) | (0.00622) | (0.00701) | (0.00711) | (0.00795) |
| CJWilber | | | −0.0183** | | | |
| | | | (0.00804) | | | |

*(Continued)*

*Table A3-4.* CONTINUED

| VARIABLES | (2) Marginal Effects | (3) Marginal Effects | (4) Marginal Effects | (5) Marginal Effects | (6) Marginal Effects | (7) Marginal Effects |
|---|---|---|---|---|---|---|
| CJDiplock | | | −0.0557*** | | | |
| | | | (0.0146) | | | |
| CJFraser | | | −0.0439** | | | |
| | | | (0.0206) | | | |
| CJScarman | | | −0.0995*** | | | |
| | | | (0.0325) | | | |
| CJKeith | | | −0.0587*** | | | |
| | | | (0.0127) | | | |
| CJGoff | | | −0.0239 | | | |
| | | | (0.0155) | | | |
| CJBrowne | | | −0.0271* | | | |
| | | | (0.0161) | | | |
| CJBingham | | | −0.0286** | | | |
| | | | (0.0125) | | | |
| year | | −0.00134** | | −0.00127** | −0.00124* | −0.00119* |
| | | (0.000650) | | (0.000554) | (0.000649) | (0.000643) |
| intervenor | | 0.0294** | | | | |
| | | (0.0123) | | | | |

| | (2) | (3) | (4) | (5) | (6) | (7) |
|---|---|---|---|---|---|---|
| VARIABLES | **Marginal Effects** | **Marginal Effects** | **Marginal Effects** | **Marginal Effects** | **Marginal Effects** | **Marginal Effects** |
| government_in_power | | | | 0.0211*** | | |
| | | | | (0.00675) | | |
| freshman | | | | | −0.00700 | |
| | | | | | (0.00877) | |
| CJ_Vote | | | | | | 0.00264 |
| | | | | | | (0.0121) |
| | | | | | | |
| Observations | 6,013 | 6,013 | 6,013 | 6,013 | 6,013 | 6,013 |

Standard errors in parentheses.

*** p<0.01, ** p<0.05, * p<0.1

| | (2) | (3) | (4) | (5) | (6) | (7) |
|---|---|---|---|---|---|---|
| VARIABLES | **Marginal Effects** | **Marginal Effects** | **Marginal Effects** | **Marginal Effects** | **Marginal Effects** | **Marginal Effects** |
| CrimLV | −0.0763 | −0.0868 | −0.0238 | −0.0736 | −0.0907 | −0.103* |
| | (0.0499) | (0.0549) | (0.0552) | (0.0524) | (0.0555) | (0.0575) |
| lower_court_direction_lib_is_1 | 0.00920 | 0.00705 | 0.00632 | 0.00552 | 0.00688 | 0.00778 |
| | (0.00783) | (0.00769) | (0.00728) | (0.00793) | (0.00769) | (0.00795) |

*(Continued)*

*Table A3-4.* CONTINUED

| VARIABLES | (2) Marginal Effects | (3) Marginal Effects | (4) Marginal Effects | (5) Marginal Effects | (6) Marginal Effects | (7) Marginal Effects |
|---|---|---|---|---|---|---|
| publiclaw | 0.0219* | 0.0159 | 0.0163 | 0.0171 | 0.0158 | 0.0151 |
| | (0.0115) | (0.0107) | (0.0103) | (0.0109) | (0.0108) | (0.0104) |
| privateecon | 0.0211 | 0.0154 | 0.0125 | 0.0153 | 0.0152 | 0.0148 |
| | (0.0138) | (0.0127) | (0.0121) | (0.0127) | (0.0128) | (0.0127) |
| torts | 0.00895 | 0.00564 | 0.00432 | 0.00684 | 0.00565 | 0.00544 |
| | (0.0154) | (0.0154) | (0.0149) | (0.0154) | (0.0154) | (0.0149) |
| otherlaw | 0.0168 | 0.00920 | 0.0175 | 0.0153 | 0.0152 | 0.0158 |
| | (0.0286) | (0.0268) | (0.0272) | (0.0281) | (0.0281) | (0.0280) |
| panelsize | 0.0393*** | 0.0402*** | 0.0353*** | 0.0411*** | 0.0407*** | 0.0449*** |
| | (0.00844) | (0.00778) | (0.00719) | (0.00778) | (0.00781) | (0.00888) |
| CJWilber | | | −0.0220** | | | |
| | | | (0.0105) | | | |
| CJDiplock | | | −0.0466*** | | | |
| | | | (0.0162) | | | |
| CJFraser | | | −0.0580** | | | |
| | | | (0.0228) | | | |
| CJScarman | | | −0.0873*** | | | |
| | | | (0.0335) | | | |
| CJKeith | | | −0.0634*** | | | |
| | | | (0.0126) | | | |

| | (2) | (3) | (4) | (5) | (6) | (7) |
|---|---|---|---|---|---|---|
| VARIABLES | Marginal Effects | Marginal Effects | Marginal Effects | Marginal Effects | Marginal Effects | Marginal Effects |
| CJGoff | | | −0.0258* | | | |
| | | | (0.0148) | | | |
| CJBrowne | | | −0.0362** | | | |
| | | | (0.0177) | | | |
| CJBingham | | | −0.0321** | | | |
| | | | (0.0129) | | | |
| year | | −0.00143** | | −0.00139*** | −0.00136** | −0.00141** |
| | | (0.000604) | | (0.000536) | (0.000576) | (0.000594) |
| intervenor | | 0.0152 | | | | |
| | | (0.0140) | | | | |
| government_in_power | | | | 0.0170** | | |
| | | | | (0.00732) | | |
| freshman | | | | | −0.0119 | |
| | | | | | (0.00860) | |
| CJ_Vote | | | | | | 0.0128 |
| | | | | | | (0.00969) |
| | | | | | | |
| Observations | 4,311 | 4,311 | 4,311 | 4,311 | 4,311 | 4,311 |

Standard errors in parentheses.

*** $p<0.01$, ** $p<0.05$, * $p<0.1$

*(Continued)*

*Table A3-4.* Continued

US

[Note: T-statistics in parenthesis for this table]

| | **Marginal Effects** | **m3** | **m4** | **m5** | **m6** |
|---|---|---|---|---|---|
| Party_Appointing_Judge | 0.0193 | 0.0194 | 0.0191 | 0.0163 | 0.0115 |
| | (0.45) | (0.45) | (0.45) | (0.37) | (0.27) |
| lower_court_direction_lib_is_1 | 0.0166 | 0.0160 | 0.0168 | 0.0166 | 0.0167 |
| | (0.91) | (0.88) | (0.91) | (0.85) | (0.91) |
| civilrights | −0.0127 | −0.0137 | −0.0139 | −0.0143 | −0.0143 |
| | (−0.93) | (−1.02) | (−1.02) | (−0.99) | (−1.01) |
| publiclaw | −0.0615** | −0.0609** | −0.0609** | −0.0632** | −0.0615** |
| | (−2.47) | (−2.49) | (−2.50) | (−2.48) | (−2.50) |
| privateecon | −0.0321 | −0.0334 | −0.0336 | −0.0337 | −0.0342 |
| | (−1.46) | (−1.48) | (−1.48) | (−1.42) | (−1.48) |
| torts | 0 | 0 | 0 | 0 | 0 |
| | (.) | (.) | (.) | (.) | (.) |
| family | 0 | 0 | 0 | 0 | 0 |
| | (.) | (.) | (.) | (.) | (.) |
| otherlaw | −0.102*** | −0.102*** | −0.102*** | −0.106*** | −0.101*** |
| | (−4.57) | (−4.60) | (−4.59) | (−4.64) | (−4.54) |
| panelsize | 0.0699*** | 0.0729*** | 0.0733*** | 0.0537*** | 0.0702*** |
| | (7.76) | (8.68) | (8.77) | (8.23) | (8.86) |

| | Marginal Effects | m3 | m4 | m5 | m6 |
|---|---|---|---|---|---|
| CJRehnquist | | −0.0157 | | | |
| | | (−0.63) | | | |
| term | | | −0.000809 | −0.00115 | −0.000933 |
| | | | (−0.59) | (−0.80) | (−0.67) |
| government_in_power | | | −0.00593 | | |
| | | | (−0.80) | | |
| freshman | | | | −0.0545** | |
| | | | | (−2.47) | |
| CJ_Vote | | | | | −0.0567** |
| | | | | | (−2.26) |
| | | | | | |
| Observations | 39914 | 39914 | 39914 | 38598 | 39914 |

*t* statistics in parentheses.

** $p < 0.05$, *** $p < 0.01$

| | Marginal Effects | n3 | n4 | n5 | n6 |
|---|---|---|---|---|---|
| CrimLV | 0.200*** | 0.200*** | 0.200*** | 0.204*** | 0.203*** |
| | (5.66) | (5.17) | (5.28) | (5.09) | (4.29) |
| lower_court_direction_lib_is_1 | 0.0225 | 0.0225 | 0.0225 | 0.0233 | 0.0225 |
| | (1.94) | (1.93) | (1.95) | (1.90) | (1.95) |
| publiclaw | −0.0441*** | −0.0441*** | −0.0441*** | −0.0463*** | −0.0442*** |
| | (−3.18) | (−3.33) | (−3.34) | (−3.35) | (−3.35) |

*(Continued)*

*Table A3-4.* Continued

| | Marginal Effects | n3 | n4 | n5 | n6 |
|---|---|---|---|---|---|
| privateecon | −0.0178 | −0.0178 | −0.0178 | −0.0178 | −0.0178 |
| | (−1.43) | (−1.42) | (−1.43) | (−1.36) | (−1.43) |
| torts | 0 | 0 | 0 | 0 | 0 |
| | (.) | (.) | (.) | (.) | (.) |
| family | 0 | 0 | 0 | 0 | 0 |
| | (.) | (.) | (.) | (.) | (.) |
| otherlaw | −0.0819*** | −0.0819*** | −0.0819*** | −0.0856*** | −0.0819*** |
| | (−7.64) | (−8.20) | (−8.13) | (−8.08) | (−8.17) |
| panelsize | 0.0625*** | 0.0626*** | 0.0625*** | 0.0432*** | 0.0625*** |
| | (8.68) | (8.73) | (9.13) | (6.42) | (9.03) |
| CJRehnquist | | −0.000446 | | | |
| | | (−0.02) | | | |
| term | | | 0.0000284 | −0.0000671 | 0.0000247 |
| | | | (0.03) | (−0.07) | (0.03) |
| government_in_power | | | −0.00115 | | |
| | | | (−0.19) | | |
| freshman | | | | −0.0194** | |
| | | | | (−2.07) | |
| CJ_Vote | | | | | 0.00589 |
| | | | | | (0.27) |
| | | | | | |
| Observations | 30473 | 30473 | 30473 | 29409 | 30473 |

*t* statistics in parentheses.

$^{**}p < 0.05$, $^{***}p < 0.01$

*Table A3-5.* Dissent Regressions, panel effects

The dependent variable is whether the judge dissented.

| | Australia | | Canada | | India | UK | | US |
|---|---|---|---|---|---|---|---|---|
| Party Appointing | –.0001<br>(.022) | | –.007<br>(.01) | | | .004<br>.011) | | .017<br>(.022) |
| Criminal Liberal Voting | | –.009<br>(.076) | | .008<br>(.039) | –.009<br>(.076) | | –.079<br>(.063) | |
| Lower Court Direction | –.001<br>(.008) | –.015<br>(.008) | –.003<br>(.003) | –.009*<br>(.004) | –.015<br>(.008) | .006<br>(.007) | .007<br>(–.008) | .016<br>(.017) |
| Civil Rights | –.008<br>(.025) | –.005<br>(.024) | .026**<br>(.007) | .037<br>(.040) | –.005<br>(.024) | –.004<br>(.011) | –.014<br>(.029) | –.014<br>(.013) |
| Public Law | –.008<br>(.013) | –.002<br>(.014) | –.012<br>(.007) | – | –.002<br>(.014) | .011<br>(.011) | .002<br>(.026) | –.060**<br>(.022) |
| Private Economic | –.044*<br>(.021) | –.039*<br>(.016) | –.004<br>(.009) | .008<br>(.035) | –.039*<br>(.016) | .009<br>(.011) | .001<br>(.029) | –.034<br>(.021) |
| Tort | –.004<br>(.013) | – | .014<br>(.01) | .027<br>(.035) | – | .002<br>(.009) | –.009<br>(.028) | – |
| Family | – | – | – | – | – | – | – | – |
| Other | – | – | –.016<br>(.036) | – | – | .007<br>(.027) | – | –.101**<br>(.019) |
| Panel Size | .009<br>(.016) | .022<br>(.018) | .015**<br>(.002) | .017**<br>(.002) | .022<br>(.018) | .034**<br>(.007) | .041**<br>(.008) | .075**<br>(.007) |

*(Continued)*

*Table A3-5.* Continued

| | Australia | | Canada | | India | UK | | US |
|---|---|---|---|---|---|---|---|---|
| Year | .002<br>(.001) | .002<br>(.001) | –.001<br>(.001) | –.001<br>(.001) | .002<br>(.001) | –.001<br>(.001) | –.001*<br>(.0005) | .0001<br>(.001) |
| LLV Diff from Others on Panel | .872**<br>(.160) | .892**<br>(.129) | .746**<br>(.127) | .532**<br>(.105) | .892**<br>(.129) | .160<br>(.095) | .097<br>(.144) | .644**<br>(.138) |

Standard errors in parenthesis.

** $p<0.01$

* $p<0.05$

# Index



Commitment and Cooperation on High Courts. Benjamin Alarie and Andrew J. Green.